F R A M E W O R K S

Landlord and Tenant

Fourth Edition

J M Male
Barrister

with contributions by
J Cotter
LLB, F Inst L Ex

Harlow
Toronto
Taipei

ris • Milan

Pearson Education Limited
Edinburgh Gate
Harlow
Essex CM20 2JE
England

and Associated Companies throughout the world

Visit us on the World Wide Web at:
http://www.pearsoneduc.com

First edition published in Great Britain 1982
Fourth edition 1995

© Pearson Pofessional Limited 1995

ISBN 0 273 63437 2

British Library Cataloguing in Publication Data
A CIP catalogue record for this book can be obtained from the British Library.

Produced by Pearson Education Asia Pte Ltd.
Transferred to digital print on demand, 2006
Printed and bound by CPI Antony Rowe, Eastbourne

Contents

accommodation; Discretionary cases; Schedule 15, Part II; Miscellaneous provisions concerning security of tenure

Part four: Long leases

Part five: Agricultural tenancies

Preface

When I first thought of writing this book there seemed to me to be a lack of a very basic book on landlord and tenant setting out the main general principles without the detailed analysis of the more learned textbooks. I think that there still is, to a certain extent, such a lack in what is a very complicated field of the law and I hope that the fourth edition of this book goes a small way towards filling the gap.

The book should be suitable for those studying for law degrees, for the Bar, Solicitors' and Legal Executives' professional examinations and also for courses in estate management and surveying.

I am very fortunate to have been assisted in the preparation of this edition by Mr Jim Cotter of Nabarro Nathanson, who has great practical experience in the fields of business tenancies and private sector residential tenancies. Mr Cotter has updated the sections dealing with business tenancies, the Landlord and Tenant Act 1987 and the Housing Act 1988. He has also written the new sections on the Leasehold Reform, Housing and Urban Development Act 1993.

With the increasing complexity of landlord and tenant legislation I cannot stress sufficiently that all the chapters on statutory protection give only the most basic outline. Accordingly, if any question of detail arises, rather than one of general principle, on one of the statutory codes, reference must be made to some more learned text.

JMM
December 1994

Table of cases

Part one
Landlord and tenant at common law

1

Introduction

The law

1. The relationship of landlord and tenant. This book is concerned with the legal effect of the relationship between landlord and tenant. The law on the subject falls conveniently into two parts. They are:

(a) the general principles governing the relationship of landlord and tenant; and
(b) the statutory control of the relationship.

The purpose of this chapter is to provide a brief, general introduction and to define basic terms.

2. History. The relationship of landlord and tenant confers on the tenant an estate in land. This has not always been so, for in medieval land law the relationship was regarded as a matter of contract only. It gave rise to a purely personal right and not to any right of property. This meant that it bound only the two parties to the agreement and did not, as is the case today, create rights and obligations binding upon third parties. It was not until the end of the fifteenth century that the law treated the relationship as conferring on the tenant a right in property which was binding on other people.

The more recent history of the law of landlord and tenant is concerned with the various statutes enacted to regulate and control the relationship. Such statutes started to appear in the mid-nineteenth century and there has since been a steady flow of them. They first dealt with agricultural lettings in the nineteenth century. Since the 1914–18 War, however, there have been Acts dealing with residential lettings, business lettings and, more recently, leasehold enfranchisement as well as others dealing with agricultural lettings. In 1980 there was statutory regulation of local authority lettings. With the Housing Act 1988, there was phasing out of the Rent Acts and the introduction of assured tenancies under which a tenant can have security of tenure but the landlord may charge an open market rent, and assured shorthold tenancies with minimal security of tenure and control only of excessive rents. Most recently, the Leasehold Reform, Housing and Urban Development Act 1993 provides for the enfranchisements of, or the grant of lease extensions of, flats and extends the scope of the Leasehold Reform Act 1967.

Tenancy

3. The essential attributes of a tenancy. In the following chapter there is a detailed consideration of what constitutes a tenancy. At this stage it will be convenient to outline the two essential attributes of a tenancy. They are:

(a) that the tenant has exclusive possession of land;
(b) that the possession is for a period subject to a definite time limit or which can be made subject to a definite limit by either party.

Unless these two elements are present, there will be no tenancy.

4. The creation of a tenancy. A tenancy may arise in one of two ways. First, it may be created by an express or implied agreement between the two parties. This may be either the simplest of oral agreements with the most elementary terms – parties, property, rent and period – or it may be a formal document running to many pages and dealing with every possible eventuality from responsibility for cleaning the windows to liability in the event of destruction by fire or other similar disaster. Second, it may be created by statute. This is a method of recent origin but which is now a fundamental and well-established part of English law.

5. The subject matter of a tenancy. The relationship of landlord and tenant may arise in relation to an infinite variety of property. The central factor is that there must always be a letting of *land*. Consequently a tenancy may be created in relation to a farm, a funeral parlour, a department store, a mews house, a stately home, a mine, a lake, a road or simply a hole in the ground. The possible situations in which it may arise are limitless and the reported cases on landlord and tenant bear witness to this fact as will be seen throughout this book.

Approach to problems

6. The proper approach to a landlord and tenant problem. It has already been stated that the law falls into two broad parts (see 1). In any problem which arises in this field, whether it is an examination question or a point which arises in everyday practice, the best approach is first to apply the general principles and then to consider the statutory controls. Whilst this may appear an obvious approach, it is one which will bear rewards when considering the later parts of this book which concern statutory controls.

Other matters

7. Terminology. The following is a selection of some of the basic terms which are used in this book.

(a) *Assignment*: the transfer of an interest; it may be the landlord's interest or the tenant's interest which is assigned.

(b) *Concurrent lease*: a lease granted for a term to commence before the end of a previous lease of the same premises to another person.

(c) *Covenants*: the terms contained in a lease which cast obligations on the landlord and tenant.

(d) *Deed*: a formal document which normally has to be signed, sealed and delivered to be effective.

(e) *Demise*: another term for to let or to lease (also sometimes means a lease).

(f) *Demised premises*: the land or building which is the subject of the lease.

(g) *Distress*: the lawful taking of goods to enforce the payment of rent.

(h) *Fine/premium*: a sum of money or other consideration paid normally by the tenant to the landlord on the grant or assignment of a lease.

(i) *Head lease*: a lease out of which lesser interests (called sub-leases) have been granted.

(j) *Holding over*: where a tenant continues to occupy the demised premises after the end of his lease.

(k) *Lease/tenancy*: (*i*) a tenant's interest in the land; and (*ii*) a document creating the interest and recording the terms.

(l) *Lessee/tenant*: the person to whom the lease is granted.

(m) *Lessor/landlord*: the person who grants the lease.

(n) *Licence*: (*i*) a permission to do an act; and (*ii*) a contractual right to use or occupy land not creating a tenancy.

(o) *Parol*: oral, not in writing.

(p) *Rent*: a certain profit issuing yearly out of land.

(q) *Rent review clause*: a provision in a lease, the purpose of which is to ensure that the rent payable over the term of the lease keeps pace with inflation or increases in the value of the premises.

(r) *Reversion*: the interest retained by the lessor on the grant of a lease.

(s) *Reversionary lease*: a lease granted to take effect at a future date.

(t) *Right of re-entry/forfeiture*: a right for the landlord to determine the lease and re-enter the land in the event of a breach of covenant by the tenant.

(u) *Sub-lease*: a lease granted by a person who is himself a lessee and which is necessarily for a period shorter than the lease out of which it is derived.

8. Specimen lease.   At the end of this book (see Appendix 1) there is a form of lease containing some typical terms encountered in practice. It is not intended as a precedent but as an illustration of typical terms. Reference should be made to the lease when mention is made in the text of terms contained in a lease.

Progress test 1

1. What are the two essential attributes of a tenancy?   **(3)**

2. In what ways may a tenancy be created?   **(4)**

3. When were the first statutory restrictions on the relationship of landlord and tenant? What form of letting did they concern?   **(2)**

4. What do the following terms mean:
   (a) covenant;
   (b) premium;
   (c) sub-lease;
   (d) lessor?   **(7)**

2

Creation of leases

Introduction

1. Creation. There are normally two stages to the creation of a lease. They are:

(a) an agreement for a lease;
(b) the grant of a lease

By an agreement for a lease the parties agree that one will grant and the other will take a lease. By the lease that agreement is carried out and the lease is actually granted. It is not necessary that there be both an agreement for a lease and then a lease: sometimes the parties will proceed straight to the second stage and a lease will be granted without a prior agreement for it. Sometimes the parties may not proceed beyond the first stage. As appears later (*see* **30**), the legal effects at each stage are different. Short lettings of residential premises are sometimes entitled 'tenancy agreements'; despite the words used these are usually leases not agreements for a lease.

The agreement

2. Agreement for a lease. Whether there is a binding agreement for a lease must be decided by reference to the ordinary rules of the law of contract. These rules require that there be an offer by one party and an acceptance of that offer by the other party. In the case of an agreement for a lease, the offer will be to let land at a certain rent for a certain period from a certain date. Whether there has been an offer and an acceptance will depend on the circumstances of each case. So far as the form of the agreement is concerned, it is necessary to consider the position under:

(a) Law of Property Act 1925, s. 40;
(b) Law of Property (Miscellaneous Provisions) Act 1989, s. 2.

The 1925 Act deals with agreements made on or before 27th September 1989, and the 1989 Act with agreements made after that date.

Agreements made on or before 27th September 1989

3. Law of Property Act 1925, s. 40 Formerly, there was no requirement that an agreement for a lease be in writing or any specific form. A requirement of form, however, might be introduced in an indirect way by the Law of Property Act 1925, s. 40, which provided that:

'40 (1) No action may be brought upon any contract for the sale or other disposition of land or any interest in land, unless the agreement upon which such action is brought, or some memorandum or note thereof, is in writing, and signed by the party to be charged or by some other person thereunto by him lawfully authorised.

(2) This section . . . does not affect the law relating to part performance. . . .'

An agreement for a lease is, of course, within this provision because it is a contract for the disposition of an interest in land. The origin of the provision is the Statute of Frauds 1677, whose object was to prevent fraudulent practices in relation to various sales including the sale of land. The difficulty facing the courts was that, in the absence of evidence such as a document, parties might perjure themselves in order to establish, or get out of, an agreement. The solution was to require the party seeking to enforce the agreement to produce some evidence in writing of the agreement signed by the other party; this removed the necessity to rely upon oral evidence. At first the requirement of a memorandum under the Statute of Frauds 1677 was strictly enforced by the courts of law. The courts of equity, however, developed an exception to the statutory requirement of writing in favour of a party who could show that he had carried out acts in performance of the contract. In such a case equity considered it unfair to allow one party to rely on the lack of writing if the other party had by his conduct committed himself to the contract. This is known as the doctrine of part performance. The exception is specifically preserved by the Law of Property Act 1925, s. 40(2).

In summary, the effect of s. 40 is that while an agreement for a lease may be made orally, unless there is an act of part performance or a sufficient memorandum in writing, it will be unenforceable. In the absence of part performance there will, in effect, be a requirement of form.

NOTE: The effect of s. 40(1) is not to render an agreement void but simply to make it unenforceable by action. The distinction is of importance. If the agreement were void because of an absence of writing there could be no question of it being enforced where there was part performance.

4. Sufficient memorandum in writing. The essentials of a sufficient memorandum are:

(a) it must be in writing;
(b) it must contain the material terms of the agreement, which are:
  (*i*) the parties;
  (*ii*) the price, i.e. the rent, and the premium if there is to be one;
  (*iii*) the property;
  (*iv*) the period of the tenancy;
(c) it must be signed by the party 'to be charged', i.e. by the person against whom it is desired to enforce the agreement.

In practice, a memorandum may be derived from a letter setting out the terms, or perhaps a receipt, or a note of a conversation. It is possible to derive a memorandum from several documents provided there is some reference linking one document to another: *Timmins* v. *Moreland Street Property Co. Ltd* (1958). Where an agreement for a lease is derived from correspondence, as may often occur, the various letters have to be linked to form the memorandum.

5. Doctrine of part performance. Where there is an oral agreement for a lease but there is no memorandum, the agreement may still be enforceable if there is part performance of the agreement. In order to establish this, the party seeking to enforce the agreement must show that:

(a) there is a binding agreement; and
(b) there have been sufficient acts of part performance by him; and
(c) those acts point to the existence of an agreement and are consistent with the agreement alleged.

If the party can show these matters the court will normally give effect to the agreement by means of the equitable remedy of specific performance.

The principle underlying the doctrine of part performance is that, where one party to the agreement has carried out the contract (whether in part or to completion), it would be inequitable to allow the other party to rely on the Law of Property Act 1925, s. 40(1): *see Maddison* v. *Alderson* (1883) *per* Selbourne LC.

6. What are sufficient acts of part performance? The following have been held to be sufficient acts of part performance:

(a) the taking of possession of land by one party with the consent of the other (*Caton* v. *Caton* (1867));

(b) the carrying out of repairs and alterations to the premises to be let (*Rawlinson* v. *Ames* (1925));
(c) the erection of new buildings on the land to be let;
(d) the giving up by a housekeeper of her former home and moving into her employer's home (*Wakeham* v. *Mackenzie* (1968)).

In contrast, the following have been held not to be sufficient acts of part performance:

(a) the continuing in possession by a former tenant (*Wills* v. *Stradling* (1797));
(b) the viewing and visiting of the land (*Clerk* v. *Wright* (1737)).

7. Payment of money. At one time it was thought that the payment of money, normally the purchase price or rent in advance, could not be a sufficient act of part performance. However, the House of Lords has said that there is no general rule that the payment of money cannot constitute an act of part performance: *Steadman* v. *Steadman* (1974).

Agreements made after 27th September 1989

8. Law of Property (Miscellaneous Provisions) Act 1989. By this Act, passed on 27th July 1989, s. 40 of the 1925 Act is repealed. Section 2(1) of the 1989 Act provides that a contract for the sale or other disposition of an interest in land can only be made in writing and only by incorporating all the terms which the parties have expressly agreed in one document or, where contracts are exchanged, in each. The terms may be incorporated in a document either by being set out in it or by reference to some other document: s. 2(2). The document incorporating the terms or, where contracts are exchanged, one of the documents incorporating them, must be signed by or on behalf of each party to the contract.

These are important new provisions. However, they do not apply to contracts made before the section came into force: s. 2(7). To that extent the old law set out above is still relevant. Further, they do not apply to a contract to grant such a lease as is mentioned in s. 54(2) of the 1925 Act: *see* 22. Section 2 came into force on 27th September 1989.

9. Operation of the 1989 Act. A number of cases has now been decided on the 1989 Act from which the following propositions appear. First, section 2 is of relevance only to executory contracts and has no application to contracts which have been completed: *Tootal Clothing Ltd* v. *Guinea Properties Ltd* (1992). Secondly, section 2 does not apply to a collateral contract which is independent of the contract of sale or disposition: *Record* v. *Bell* (1991). Thirdly, in the case of an option it is the original grant which must satisfy the requirements of section 2; the exercise of the option need not satisfy those requirements: *Spiro* v. *Glencrown Properties Ltd* (1991). In the latter case it was stated that 'the plain purpose of section 2 was to prescribe the formalities for recording the consent of the parties'.

10. Check list under the 1989 Act. Unless the case comes within one of the exceptions a contract must satisfy the following:

(a) It must be in writing.
(b) All the express terms must be incorporated in one document.
(c) Where contracts are exchanged all the express terms must be incorporated in each part.
(d) The one document, or in the case of exchange one of the documents, must be signed by each party to the contract.

An oral agreement, even with part performance, or an agreement arising out of a series of letters, will not suffice unless relating to a lease within s. 54(2) of the 1925 Act.

Enforcement

11. Enforcement of an agreement for a lease If either party refuses to go ahead with the agreement and grant a lease the other party has two remedies:

(a) specific performance;
(b) damages.

Specific performance is an equitable remedy by which the court orders that the party in breach shall perform his side of the bargain. As an equitable remedy, it is a matter for the discretion of the court to decide if it should be decreed. In exercising its discretion the court has regard to matters which include the conduct of the parties, the effect of the order and whether it would cause hardship. If, for instance, the party seeking specific performance is guilty of bad conduct or has delayed unreasonably in enforcing his rights he may not obtain the decree. The right to specific performance will also, of course, depend upon satisfying the Law of Property Act 1925, s. 40 or the Law of Property (Miscellaneous Provisions) Act 1989, s. 2 as the case may be. Thus in order to obtain specific performance of an agreement there must be either a sufficient memorandum or sufficient acts of part performance (*see* **3, 5**), or in cases after 27th September 1989 compliance with s. 2 of the 1989 Act.

Damages are the ordinary common law remedy for breach of contract. In addition there are what are sometimes called 'equitable damages', that is damages awarded by a court in pursuance of its equitable jurisdiction in addition to or in lieu of specific performance. The power to award equitable damages was first given to the Chancery courts by the Chancery Amendment Act 1858.

Granting a lease

12. The lease. Having considered an agreement for a lease, it is now possible to consider the second stage – the lease itself. As already indicated, the parties may go straight to this second stage without a prior agreement for a lease. Whether they do so will depend upon the speed with which they choose to act, the value of the property and the length and proposed terms of the tenancy. The more valuable the property and the more complicated the proposed terms, the more likely it is that the parties will first set matters out in an agreement and then proceed to the actual lease.

13 Creation of a lease. A lease is created when one of the parties grants to the other the right of exclusive possession of land or buildings for a definite period or for a period which can be made definite by either party. In the case of leases for more than three years, various formalities must be complied with. In summary, then, there must be:

(a) exclusive possession;
(b) a definite period (this is considered separately in 3:3); and
(c) (in the case of leases over three years) compliance with formalities.

It should be noted that the reservation of a rent is not a necessary pre-condition to the creation of a lease.

14. Exclusive possession. The right of exclusive possession of land means the right to control of the land and to exclude all other persons from it. Where a person is granted the right to use the premises without the right to exclusive possession, the grant is a licence and not a lease.

15. Lease or licence? The distinction between a lease and a licence is of considerable importance nowadays. This is because of the effect of the Rent Act 1977 and Housing Act 1988, which protect residential tenancies, and the Landlord and Tenant Act 1954, Part II, which protects business tenancies. These Acts apply only to tenancies and do not apply to licences.

16. Street *v*. Mountford. In a series of cases decided up to 1985, the significance of exclusive possession in distinguishing a lease from a licence was much reduced. However in *Street* v. *Mountford* (1985), the House of Lords reviewed these cases and reaffirmed the traditional view that an occupier of land for a term at a rent is a tenant provided the occupier is granted exclusive possession. The case is of prime importance and requires careful study. For present purposes its effect may be summarised as follows. It is necessary to consider whether exclusive possession of the subject premises has been granted to the occupier. If exclusive possession has not been granted, then the occupier is not a tenant but a licensee. If exclusive possession has been granted, it is necessary to consider whether there are circumstances which negative the creation of a tenancy. One example of such circumstances is where there is no intention to create legal relations, e.g. a family arrangement, or one of kindness or generosity. Another example is where the right to exclusive possession is referable to a legal relationship other than a lease, e.g. occupation under a contract for the sale of land, occupation pursuant to a contract of employment or occupation referable to holding an office. These are examples and may not be exhaustive of all the circumstances where the creation of a tenancy is negatived.

In the case of joint occupiers, the occupancy of four occupiers of a flat under separate agreements made at different times on different terms with the occupants paying different monthly amounts and enjoying exclusive possession of one bedroom each but sharing the rest of the accommodation was held to amount to a *licence* and not a collective joint tenancy: *A.G. Securities* v. *Vaughan* (1990). In contrast the occupancy of a small flat granted to an unmarried couple by two contemporaneous agreements which were interdependent on one another was held to be a joint tenancy and the purported retention by the owner of the right to share the flat was rejected as a pretence to deprive the occupiers of Rent Act protection: *Antoniades* v. *Villiers* (1990).

An agreement between a local authority and a homeless person having priority need to occupy temporary accommodation at a local authority hostel for homeless single men was held to be a licence in *Westminster City Council* v. *Clarke* (1992).

17. General applicability. Whilst *Street* v. *Mountford* was concerned with a letting of residential accommodation, it would appear that the principles enunciated are of general application to business and other premises.

18. Illustrations. The following cases illustrate the principles in **16** above.

> *Cobb* v. *Lane* (1952). A house was bought by a woman who allowed her brother to occupy it free of charge. The brother lived there for more than 13 years and the woman paid the rates throughout the period. The Court of Appeal HELD that the brother was only a licensee as this was a family arrangement which negatived any intention to create a lease.

> *Heslop* v. *Burns* (1974). The owner of a cottage allowed a family to live there rent free. It was HELD that no tenancy had been created because the parties did not intend any legal relationship.

19. Employees. Where an employee, such as a caretaker or shop manager, is required to occupy premises for the better performance of his duties, he is considered to be what is called a service licensee or service occupier. The requirement may be contained in his contract of employment or implied from the circumstances of his employment. If the requirement is not present the employee will be a service tenant, provided the other requirements of a tenancy are satisfied. Whether or not that service tenant then enjoys the protection of the Rent Act 1977 or the Housing Act 1988 as the case may be will depend upon whether the other conditions for protection under those Acts are met.

20. Definite period. This is the second requirement to create a valid lease; it is dealt with in 3:3.

Formalities

21. Introduction. At common law a lease could be validly created by a purely oral transaction. This was subsequently altered by statute and formalities were required in certain cases. The relevant provisions are now contained in the Law of Property Act 1925, ss. 52 and 54.

22. Law of Property Act 1925, ss. 52 and 54. So far as relevant these provide:

> '52(1) All conveyances of land or of any interest therein are void

for the purposes of conveying a legal estate unless made by deed.

(2) This section does not apply to:

(*d*) leases or tenancies or other assurances not required by law to be made in writing.'

'54(1) All interests in land created by parol and not put in writing and signed by the persons so creating the same or by their agents thereunto lawfully authorised in writing have, notwithstanding any consideration having been given for the same, the force and effect of interests at will only.

(2) Nothing in the foregoing provisions of this Part of this Act shall affect the creation by parol of leases taking effect in possession for a term not exceeding three years (whether or not the lessee is given power to extend the term) at the best rent which can be reasonably obtained without taking a fine.'

23. Effect of 1925 provisions. The combined effect of these two provisions is that:

(a) a lease may be made orally, or in writing, if it satisfies the conditions in s. 54(2);

(b) a lease for a term of more than three years must be made by deed, i.e. under seal.

NOTES: (1) Once a lease has been validly created, it must be assigned by deed in order for there to be a valid legal assignment: Law of Property Act 1925, s. 52(1). Thus even if a tenancy was created orally, it may be assigned only by deed *Crago* v. *Julian* (1992)

(2) There is nothing to stop a term of less than three years being made by deed if the parties require it to be so made.

24. Parol leases. The leases which fall within the Law of Property Act 1925, s. 54(2), are those which:

(a) take effect in possession (i.e. start) from the date of grant;

(b) are for a term not exceeding three years; and

(c) are at a full rent.

This will include periodic tenancies although their ultimate duration may exceed three years.

Absence of formalities

25. Introduction. In order to consider the effect of failure to comply with the formalities described above, it is necessary to examine the position at common law and in equity, and then to consider the position after the Judicature Act 1873.

26. Position at common law. A lease which failed to comply with the requirement of formality was void at law. Despite this, if the tenant entered into possession with the landlord's consent, he would become what is called a tenant at will. If he paid rent to the landlord a periodic tenancy was created. The period of the tenancy would depend upon the basis on which rent was paid.

Example

T purports to take a seven-year lease of Blackacre from L. The transaction is oral. T enters into possession and pays rent on a monthly basis. The oral transaction would be ineffective to create a seven-year lease but T would have a monthly tenancy by reason of the payment and acceptance of rent on a monthly basis.

27. Position in equity. If the informal lease was either sufficiently evidenced in writing or supported by acts of part performance, equity would treat it as an agreement for a lease. Specific performance of the agreement could then be granted, provided the conditions for granting it were satisfied (*see* **11**). Where the tenant had the right to apply for specific performance, in equity the lease would be deemed to be granted whether or not the tenant actually sought it. The tenant's position would then be the same as if the lease had been validly granted to him. Such a lease was called an 'equitable lease'.

28. The Judicature Act 1873. As appears from the above paragraphs, before 1873 a tenant under an informal lease might have different rights depending on whether the matter was before the courts of law or the courts of equity. At law the tenant would have a periodic tenancy; in equity he might have a specifically enforceable agreement for a lease. There was, therefore, a conflict between the rules of law and equity and this was eventually resolved by the Judicature Act 1873, which provided that where there was a conflict between law and equity, the equitable rules should prevail. In *Walsh* v. *Lonsdale* (1882) it was confirmed that the effect of the Judicature Act was that the equitable lease should prevail over the periodic tenancy.

29. Walsh v. Lonsdale. L agreed to grant to W a lease of a mill for seven years. Under the terms of the lease it was agreed that L might at any time demand payment of one year's rent in advance. No deed was executed but W went into possession and paid rent; subsequently

L demanded one year's rent in advance, which W refused to pay. L then distrained for the rent. W brought this action for damages for illegal distress and argued that he had only a yearly tenancy and that there could be no obligation to pay rent in advance implied into his yearly tenancy. HELD: That since the Judicature Act it was no longer the rule that a tenant held under a periodic tenancy but that he held under the terms of the agreement. Accordingly, the distress was lawful as it was permitted by the agreement.

30. The effect of Walsh *v.* Lonsdale. As a result of this case it is sometimes said that an agreement for a lease is as good as a lease. In broad terms such a proposition is correct. There are, however, certain ways in which an agreement for a lease (or equitable lease) is not as satisfactory as an actual lease. The more important are:

(a) An equitable lease is dependent upon the agreement being specifically enforceable. Specific performance is a discretionary remedy and is not granted in all cases: e.g. if a tenant were guilty of breaches of covenant, he might not be granted specific performance.

Coatsworth v. *Johnson* (1886). L agreed to grant T a 21-year lease of a farm. T entered into possession under the agreement without a lease being executed. Before any rent was due L gave T notice to quit and took possession because T had failed to cultivate the farm properly. This would have been a breach of the covenants intended to be inserted in the lease. T sued L for trespass claiming that he could have obtained specific performance and was, therefore, entitled to an equitable lease. HELD: Specific performance would not have been granted because of T's breach of covenant. Therefore, T did not enjoy an equitable lease and, as he had paid no rent, was at most a tenant at will and L was entitled to take possession.

(b) An equitable lease is not always enforceable against third parties. An agreement for a lease made after 1925 can be protected by registration under the Land Charges Act 1972, and is registrable as an estate contract. Failure to register it will render it void against a purchaser for money or money's worth of a legal estate in the land.

Example
L grants T a lease of Blackacre for a term of seven years. There is no deed and, therefore, no valid lease. T fails to register the agreement for a lease as a land charge. L sells his reversion to X. X is not bound by T's interest.

31. Significance of doctrine. The doctrine in *Walsh* v. *Lonsdale* is of practical importance in two categories of case. The first is when there is a true agreement for a lease which is specifically enforceable. It is for most purposes as good as an actual lease. The second category is where the parties have purported to create a lease but there is some formal deficiency. The courts will treat the defective lease as an agreement to create the lease, and the doctrine in *Walsh* v. *Lonsdale* will then apply to the 'deemed' agreement as to a true agreement for a lease, i.e. it will for most purposes be as good as an actual lease.

32. Summary. A lease may be validly created in the following ways:

(a) if it is for under three years it may generally be made orally, or in writing or by deed;

(b) if it is for more than three years it must be by deed;

(c) if it is for more than three years and is made orally and there is part performance, by virtue of the doctrine in *Walsh* v. *Lonsdale*, an equitable lease will arise;

(d) if it is for more than three years and there is a sufficient written memorandum, by virtue of the doctrine in *Walsh* v. *Lonsdale* an equitable lease will arise;

(e) if it comes within **(c)** or **(d)** but the tenant has been guilty of bad conduct or for some other reason specific performance would not be granted, the doctrine in *Walsh* v. *Lonsdale* will not apply and there will be no equitable lease; but if the tenant enters and pays rent, a periodic tenancy will arise;

(f) if it is for more than three years and there is neither a sufficient memorandum nor part performance it will be unenforceable by specific performance and the doctrine in *Walsh* v. *Lonsdale* will not apply. On the other hand, if the tenant enters into possession with the consent of the landlord and pays rent a periodic tenancy will arise.

NOTE: These matters now have to be considered in the light of the Law of Property (Miscellaneous Provisions) Act 1989, s. 2(1) which is noted at **8** to **10** above.

Progress test 2

1. How is a lease created? **(1)**

2. What formalities are needed to create
   (a) a weekly tenancy;
   (b) a tenancy for 99 years;
   (c) a tenancy for two years at no rent? **(23, 24)**

3. What is an agreement for a lease? **(2)**

4. What is a licence? **(14)**

5. How can a lease be distinguished from a licence? **(15)**

6. L permits J to occupy a flat as a favour in circumstances where J's house has just been destroyed by fire and on terms whereby J pays no rent. L now wishes to recover possession of the flat. Advise L. **(16)**

7. What is the rule in *Walsh* v. *Lonsdale*? **(29)**

8. 'An agreement for a lease is as good as a lease'. Comment. **(30)**

9. What leases must be under seal? **(23)**

10. L agrees orally to let Blackacre to T for 99 years. L now refuses to go ahead with the agreement. Advise T. Would the position be different if T had gone into possession and carried out works to Blackacre? **(8)**

11. What is part performance? Can the payment of money constitute part performance? **(6)**

12. What is exclusive possession? **(14)**

13. C has a game-keeper, M, who has to live in a cottage on C's estate so that he can carry out his duties. M is dismissed but refuses to leave. Advise C. **(19)**

14. What is the effect of the Law of Property Act 1925, s. 40? **(3)**

15. What are the requirements of a valid lease? **(32)**

3

Tenancies

Types of tenancy

1. Introduction. This chapter deals with three important matters:

(a) the different types of tenancy (*see* **3–21**);
(b) certain statutory modifications to particular classes of tenancy (*see* **22–27**);
(c) concurrent and future leases (*see* **28, 29**).

2. The different types. A tenancy may be:

(a) a tenancy for a fixed term (*see* **3–7**);
(b) a periodic tenancy (*see* **8–15**);
(c) a tenancy at will (*see* **16–18**);
(d) a tenancy at sufferance (*see* **19**);
(e) a tenancy by estoppel (*see* **20, 21**).

Fixed term tenancies

3. Tenancies for a fixed term. This is a tenancy for a fixed period of any length, be it one month, 100 years, 1000 years or any other term of years, months, weeks or days. The commencement and the duration of the period must be certain before the tenancy takes effect, otherwise the tenancy will be void.

> *Lace* v. *Chantler* (1944). A lease 'for the duration of the war' was HELD to be void at common law for uncertainty because there was no way to ascertain the duration of the period when the agreement took effect.

> *Prudential Assurance Co. Ltd* v. *London Residuary Body* (1992). A tenancy which was to continue until the land was required by the London County Council for road widening was HELD to grant a term of uncertain duration and as a result did not create a lease. However as the tenant had entered the land and paid a yearly rent he became a tenant from year to year, each party having the power to determine the tenancy by six months notice to quit.

NOTE: To avoid the effect of *Lace* v. *Chantler*, legislation was passed which converted such tenancies and agreements made during the Second World War into terms of ten years: Validation of War-Time Leases Act 1944. This Act was repealed by the Statute Law (Repeals) Act 1976, but may still be relevant where there has at some stage been a tenancy of this type.

The test of certainty will be satisfied if the period is capable of being rendered certain before the agreement takes effect.

Example

A tenancy is granted to commence on 25th December 1988 'for as many years as A shall name'. If A names the period before the commencement date, the tenancy is valid. If A fails to name the period before that date then it will be void because it is not a certain term.

4. Commencement. A tenancy for a fixed term may take effect from the date of the grant, or from some past or future date. Where it takes effect from the date of the grant, e.g. a lease granted on 1st January 1989 for three years from 1st January 1989, it is said to take effect in possession. Where it takes effect in the future, e.g. a lease granted on 1st January 1989 for three years from 1st January 1990, it is sometimes called a reversionary lease but this may cause confusion and it is best to call it simply a future lease. *See also* **29,** below.

5. Law of Property Act 1925, s. 149(3). There is a limitation in law upon how far in the future a tenancy may take effect. By s. 149(3) it is provided that a term, at a rent or for a fine, to take effect more than 21 years from the date of the instrument purporting to create it, will be void, and any agreement to create such a lease will also be void. (The purpose of the above rule with its comparatively short time limit is obscure, especially when it is remembered that leases may be granted for any length of time and that options to renew leases may have effect during a much longer period.) The effect of this provision is illustrated by the following examples.

Examples

(1) By a lease dated 1st January 1989 L grants to T a lease to take effect from 1st January 1999. The lease is valid because it takes effect less than 21 years from the date of the lease.

(2) By a lease dated 1st January 1989 L grants to T a lease to take effect from 1st January 2019. The lease is void because it will take effect more than 21 years from the date of the lease.

6. Effect of s. 149(3). The conclusion in the examples above would be the same whether there was a lease or an agreement for a lease. The words 'any contract to create such a term shall also be void', however only invalidate a contract to grant a lease which, *when granted*, will take effect more than 21 years after its date. They do not invalidate a *contract* to grant, at a date more than 21 years after the date of the *contract*, a lease which when granted will not infringe the rule in s. 149(3): *Re Strand and Savoy Properties Ltd* (1960). This principle is best illustrated by examples.

Examples _____

(1) On 1st January 1989 L agrees that he will grant to T a lease on 1st January 2019 which will take effect from 1st January 2029. Although the contract will operate more than 21 years in the future, the lease when actually granted will take effect within ten years of its grant and the contract is therefore valid.

(2) On 1st January 1989 L agrees that he will grant to T a lease on 1st January 2019 which will take effect from 1st January 2069. In this case the lease when actually granted will take effect more than 21 years from the date of its grant and the contract is therefore void. If in due course the lease were actually granted as contemplated it would also be void.

7. Termination. At common law a tenancy for a fixed term automatically comes to an end at the expiration of the term without the necessity for notice to quit (*see* 7:**2**).

Periodic tenancies

8. Introduction. A periodic tenancy is one which continues automatically from period to period until it is determined by a valid notice to quit given by one party to the other. The periods are normally either a year, a quarter, a month or a week, but any period may be chosen. In one case the period was 364 days.

9. Yearly tenancy. This continues from year to year. It may be created by:

(a) express agreement; or
(b) implication; or
(c) statute.

Creation by statute is dealt with in relation to agricultural holdings (*see* Chapter 28).

10. Creation by express agreement. A yearly tenancy may be created by the parties agreeing to a tenancy 'from year to year' or that the tenant shall be a 'yearly tenant' or by the use of any words showing a similar intent. If, however, the parties agree to a tenancy 'for one year and so on from year to year' there is created a tenancy for a fixed term of one year which is followed by a yearly tenancy. It follows that such a tenancy cannot be determined during the first year.

11. Creation by implication. This is sometimes called creation by operation of law. A yearly tenancy will arise by implication whenever the following conditions are satisfied:

(a) a person occupies land with the owner's permission but not as a licensee and not for an agreed period; and
(b) rent is paid and accepted and is expressed to be, or calculated as, a yearly sum.

The requirement that there be a yearly rent is satisfied if the rent reserved is expressed as an annual sum. It does not matter by what instalments the annual sum is payable. So, for instance, where the rent is £52 per year payable weekly, that will give rise to a yearly tenancy. In contrast, where the rent is £1 per week, that will give rise to only a weekly tenancy.

The satisfaction of the two conditions just mentioned gives rise to a presumption of a yearly tenancy. The presumption can always be rebutted by any evidence that the parties did not in fact intend that a yearly tenancy should be created.

12. Examples. The following are examples of creation of a yearly tenancy by operation of law:

(a) L grants to T a lease of land for ten years. At the end of that lease T holds over with L's consent and pays rent on a yearly basis. In the absence of evidence to the contrary T becomes a yearly tenant.
(b) L allows T to occupy land; subsequently rent is paid and accepted on a yearly basis. T thereby becomes a yearly tenant.
(c) L agrees to grant a lease; before the agreement is completed T enters into possession and pays rent to L on a yearly basis. T thereby becomes a yearly tenant.

13. Effect of statute. As appears from the previous two paragraphs, at common law a yearly tenancy might arise from the mere acceptance of rent. In modern times statutes have given certain tenants the right to remain in occupation of premises after the termination of their lease. As a result the courts are less likely to infer a tenancy simply because rent is accepted from a person who is holding over and who may have some statutory right to occupy. The position was explained by Denning LJ in *Marcroft Wagons Ltd* v. *Smith* (1951):

> 'If the acceptance of rent can be explained on some other footing than a contractual tenancy, as, for instance, by reason of an existing or possible statutory right to remain, then a new tenancy should not be inferred.'

Marcroft Wagons Ltd v. *Smith* (1951). A Rent Act protected tenant died in 1936. His widow was entitled to continue to live in the house as a statutory tenant, and did so with her daughter. In March 1950 the widow died. The landlord allowed the daughter to reside in the premises until September 1950 and accepted the same sum as the widow had paid as rent. The landlord brought proceedings for possession. The daughter claimed that by his conduct the landlord had granted her a periodic tenancy. The Court of Appeal HELD that a tenancy should not be inferred as the acceptance of periodical payments could be explained on a footing other than that a contractual tenancy was being created, i.e. by reference to the statutory rights. In effect the existence of a statutory right to remain is a fact which rebuts the presumption of an annual tenancy.

More recently, in *Longrigg, Burrough & Trounson* v. *Smith* (1979) CA, Lord Scarman explained the position in the following way: 'Indeed, one would have thought that today, where tenants have in one respect or another the protection of the law for possession of premises to which they would have at common law no contractual entitlement, the courts would not be as quick to infer a new tenancy as in the old days they would have been where there was nothing to explain the presence of a defendant upon the premises or upon the land other than a trespass or a contract.' The same point appears from *Javad* v. *Aqil* (1991): see **18** below.

14. Determination. A yearly tenancy can be determined in such manner as the parties agree. In the absence of agreement, it can be determined by the giving of at least a half-year's notice to expire at the end of a complete year of the tenancy. This is considered more fully in 7:**13**.

15. Other periodic tenancies. What has been said above in relation to yearly tenancies applies with appropriate modifications to other periodic tenancies. Quarterly, monthly and weekly tenancies can be created in the same way as a yearly tenancy. They can be created by express agreement or by implication where rent is paid and accepted on a quarterly, monthly or weekly basis. They are determinable on giving notice of at least one full period to expire at the end of a period of the tenancy, e.g. one month's notice to expire at the end of a complete month of the tenancy is required to end a monthly tenancy.

Tenancy at will

16. Introduction. A tenancy at will arises when a tenant occupies land with the consent of the owner on terms that the tenancy may be determined by either party at any time. A demand for possession by the landlord will suffice to determine such a tenancy. A tenancy at will comes to an end if either party dies or parts with his interest in the land. It may be created:

(a) by express agreement; or
(b) by implication.

17. Creation by express agreement. A tenancy at will may be created by express agreement. Whilst a tenancy at will of residential premises is protected by the Rent Acts, such a tenancy of business premises is outside the scope of the Landlord and Tenant Act 1954, Part II. An express tenancy at will therefore provides a means of avoiding the effect of Part II of the 1954 Act. The creation of an express tenancy at will is a comparatively rare phenomenon. The reservation of a rent in the agreement is not necessarily inconsistent with the nature of a tenancy at will.

> *Hagee Ltd* v. *Erikson* (1976). L let premises to T for use as a showroom with exclusive occupation but as 'tenants at will only'. L purported to determine the tenancy but T refused to leave the premises and claimed the protection of Part II of the 1954 Act. HELD: A tenancy at will created by an express agreement was not within the scope of Part II of the 1954 Act.

18. Creation by implication. A tenancy at will is created by implication where a person is in possession of land with the consent of the owner, but does not possess it by virtue of any freehold estate or any tenancy for a fixed term or a periodic tenancy or any licence. The following are examples:

(a) occupation by permission of the landlord without payment of rent;

(b) where a purchaser of land has been let into possession pending completion of the sale;

(c) where a prospective tenant is allowed into possession while negotiations proceed on the terms of the lease to be granted to him.

In example (c) there will normally be a tenancy at will even if rent is paid. This is because in the absence of any other material factors it is to be inferred that the parties intended to create a tenancy at will rather than a periodic tenancy pending the outcome of the negotiations since the parties could not be taken to have intended that the periodic payments of rent would create a periodic tenancy when they were not agreed as to the terms on which the prospective tenant would occupy: *Javad* v. *Aqil* (1991).

Other tenancies

19. Tenancy at sufferance. A tenancy at sufferance arises when a tenant holds over on the expiry of his lease without the consent or dissent of the landlord. Such a tenancy can only be created by implication and not by express agreement; it will become a tenancy at will if the landlord should give his consent to the tenant's occupation. The tenancies are of little practical importance today.

20. Tenancy by estoppel. Estoppel is often said to be a principle of the law of evidence. It operates to prevent one party from denying the existence of certain facts which he has previously represented to be true. The application of the principle to the law of landlord and tenant is as follows. If a person purports to grant a lease of land but has no legal estate in the land entitling him to grant the lease, both parties will be bound by that purported lease and they will be estopped as against each other from denying that the grant was effective. The tenancy is called a tenancy by estoppel and it binds both parties and their successors in title although no estate in land has, in fact, been granted. The tenancy and the reversion expectant on it are capable of being transferred to a successor in title.

Example _____

L is under the mistaken impression that he owns certain land and lets this land to T. There arises a tenancy by estoppel.

_____

21. The consequences of a tenancy by estoppel. The main consequences are as follows:

(a) the tenant is estopped from denying the title of his landlord, and the landlord cannot deny the validity of the lease on the grounds of his lack of title;

(b) the estoppel does not bind a third party who is not a party to the transaction;

(c) a tenant by estoppel may claim the protection of the Rent Act 1977;

(d) if the landlord later acquires the legal estate this ends the estoppel, but the tenant then acquires a legal estate himself. This is called feeding the estoppel.

Example

Taking the facts in the example above (*see* **20**), suppose that later L acquires title to the land. When he acquires it, T's tenancy becomes a true legal tenancy, just as if L had had proper title at the date of the grant.

Statutory modifications

22. Introduction. There are certain statutory provisions which deal with special kinds of leases. Of particular importance to students are:

(a) perpetually renewable leases (*see* **23, 24**); and

(b) leases for lives or until marriage (*see* **25, 26**).

23. Perpetually renewable leases. Perpetually renewable leases are rare, and the courts tend to lean against them in construing a lease. They may arise where a lease contains an option to renew the lease on the same terms and the same terms then include the option clause. The effect is that there will always be a further option and the lease could go on for ever.

> *Caerphilly Concrete Products Ltd* v. *Owen* (1972). A lease contained an option clause which provided: 'the landlord will on the written request of the tenant made six months before the expiration of the term . . . grant to him a lease . . . for a further term of five years . . . at the same rent and including the like covenants and provisos (including an option to renew such lease) for a further term of five years at the expiration thereof.' It was HELD that this clause entitled the tenant to an option to renew at the end of each succeeding term of five years and that there was, therefore, a perpetually renewable lease.

24. The statutory provisions. Perpetually renewable leases may be both unfair and inconvenient. There are now special provisions dealing with them in the Law of Property Act 1922, s. 145, Sch. 15. Students should note the following:

(a) all perpetually renewable leases are converted into terms of 2,000 years;

(b) a perpetually renewable sub-lease is converted into a term of 2,000 years less one day;

(c) the 2,000 year term will be held on the same terms and conditions as the original lease with the following modifications:

(*i*) the tenant, but not the landlord, may determine the lease by giving at least ten days' written notice before any day upon which, but for the conversion by the Act, the lease would have expired if it had not been renewed;

(*ii*) the tenant must register with the landlord every assignment or devolution of the lease within six months of it taking place;

(*iii*) an original tenant who assigns the lease is not liable for breaches of covenant after the assignment. (This is an exception to the general rule (*see* 6: **21**) that despite an assignment an original tenant remains liable for all breaches occurring during the term.)

25. Leases for lives or until marriage.   The leases involved here are:

(a) leases for a life or lives, e.g. a lease to T for his own life or for the life of A;

(b) leases for a term of years determinable with life or lives, e.g. a lease to T for 21 years if A shall so long live;

(c) leases for a term of years determinable on the marriage of the lessee, e.g. a lease to T for 21 years until T marries.

26. The statutory provisions.   By virtue of s. 149(6) of the Law of Property Act 1925, a lease at a rent or a fine 'for life or lives or for any term of years determinable with life or lives or on the marriage of the lessee' is converted into a term of 90 years. This 90 year term may be determined by written notice given by either party upon the death or marriage of the named person as the case may be. Such notice must be in writing and must give at least one month's notice to expire on one of the quarter days applicable to the tenancy.

> NOTE: It is important to note that this provision only applies to cases where the lease is at a rent or for a fine. If a person is given a life interest in land without any monetary consideration, a settlement of land within the ambit of the Settled Land Act 1925 will come into existence.

27. Concurrent and future leases.   The previous paragraphs have been concerned with the different types of tenancies. It is now necessary to consider two particular situations, one of which has already been touched upon. They are:

(a) where a landlord grants a lease to run at the same time as a pre-existing lease: this is called a concurrent lease (*see* **28**);
(b) where a landlord grants a lease to take effect in the future: this is called a future (or reversionary) lease (*see* **29**).

28. Concurrent leases. This is best illustrated by an example: suppose that L grants to T a lease of Blackacre for 21 years from 1st January 1989. In 2000 L grants a further lease of Blackacre to S for a term of ten years from 1st January 2000.

The lease to S operates as a lease of the reversion on T's lease. S is therefore entitled to receive the rent from T for the ten years of his term. If S's lease were for more than T's lease, at the end of T's lease S would be entitled to possession of the land. The effect of a concurrent lease is therefore that the concurrent lessee is interposed in the chain of interests between the original lessor and lessee and becomes the landlord to the original lessee. The position of the original lessee becomes in most respects that of a sub-lessee. Concurrent leases are, confusingly, sometimes called reversionary leases because they are a lease of the landlord's reversion. It is best if the expression reversionary lease is either not used at all or is confined to use as a synonym for future leases as described in the next paragraph.

29. Future leases. This is where the landlord grants to the tenant a lease which will take effect at a future date. The detailed rules regarding these leases have already been considered in 4–6 above.

Progress test 3

1. What different types of tenancy are there? **(2)**

2. In 1940 L grants to T a lease of a dwelling-house until the end of the War. What is the effect of the lease? **(3)**

3. What is a tenancy by estoppel? **(20)**

4. How would you differentiate between a tenancy for a fixed term and a periodic tenancy? **(3, 8)**

5. What are concurrent leases? **(28)**

6. What are the normal periods of a periodic tenancy? **(8)**

7. How far in the future can
   (a) a lease and
   (b) an agreement for a lease take effect? **(5)**

8. How can a periodic tenancy be created? **(9)**

9. L allows T to occupy his land in return for a payment of £100 per year payable in monthly instalments. What sort of tenancy is created? **(11)**

10. What are the common law rules concerning the creation of periodic tenancies by operation of law? How has statute affected these rules? **(13)**

11. Is a tenancy at will protected by
   (a) the Rent Act;
   (b) Part II of the Landlord and Tenant Act of 1954? **(17)**

12. What are the differences between a tenancy at will and a tenancy at sufferance? **(19)**

13. How can a tenancy at will be created? **(16)**

14. What is the effect of the following arrangements:
   (a) L agrees to sell his freehold farm to T. Before completion L lets T into possession:
   (b) L mistakenly thinks he owns Blackacre and agrees to let it to T;
   (c) L lets land to T with an option 'to renew on the same terms including this option'. **(18, 20, 23)**

15. What is feeding the estoppel? **(21)**

16. What special statutory provisions apply to:
   (a) perpetually renewable leases;
   (b) leases for lives;
   (c) lease until marriage? **(24, 26)**

17. What is the effect of the decision in *Re Strand and Savoy Properties*? **(6)**

4

Implied covenants

Implied covenants in a lease

1. Generally. A landlord and tenant will generally agree expressly the terms upon which the land is to be held by the tenant. If, however, there are no express terms, the common law implies certain basic terms or covenants into the lease in order to give effect to it.

2. Implied covenants. If there is no express covenant dealing with these matters, the common law will imply the following covenants into a lease:

(a) by the landlord:
  (*i*) for quiet enjoyment;
  (*ii*) not to derogate from his grant;
  (*iii*) in limited circumstances, an implied condition of fitness;
(b) by the tenant;
  (*i*) to pay rent;
  (*ii*) to pay rates and taxes;
  (*iii*) an obligation not to commit waste;
  (*iv*) an obligation to use the premises in a tenant-like manner.

3. Limitations to implied covenants. It should be noted that no other covenants than these are implied. In particular, the law does not imply a proviso for re-entry. If a lease is silent about a matter which does not fall within the above categories, at common law there is simply no covenant or obligation with respect to that matter. Also, if a lease deals expressly with any of these matters, the express covenant will, naturally, prevail over the implied covenants.

Landlord's implied covenants

4. The covenant for quiet enjoyment. This covenant protects the tenant's possession and enjoyment of the demised premises. It entitles the tenant:

(a) to be put into possession and enjoyment of the demised premises; and

(b) to enjoy possession of the demised premises without physical interruption by any person to whom the covenant extends.

If there is a breach of the covenant, the tenant will have remedies against his landlord for damages or, in certain cases, an injunction. However, it would seem that damages for breach of the covenant for quiet enjoyment cannot be awarded for any distress, frustration, anxiety, displeasure, vexation, tension or aggravation: *Branchett* v. *Beaney* (1992).

5. Extent of the covenant. The implied covenant for quiet enjoyment is a 'qualified' covenant. This means that it only applies to the acts of the landlord and those people who derive title from him, e.g. other tenants of property owned by the same landlord. It does not extend to the acts of other people or people with a title superior to that of the landlord, e.g. a freehold owner of land which has been let on a sub-lease. Where there is disturbance of the tenant's enjoyment of the demised premises by a person with a superior title to that of the landlord it is called 'disturbance by title paramount'. Where this occurs the tenant has no remedy against his landlord under this covenant.

> NOTE: In contrast to a qualified covenant, there is an absolute covenant which extends to disturbance by people with a title superior to that of the landlord. Express covenants for quiet enjoyment may be in the qualified or the absolute form.

6. What amounts to a breach of the covenant? There is a breach of covenant if the tenant's ordinary enjoyment of the demised premises is substantially interfered with by either the landlord or by those claiming under him (*see* 5 above). It was at one time thought that there was only a breach of covenant if there was some physical interruption of the tenant's enjoyment but today mere nuisance such as excessive noise is probably enough (*see Kenny* v. *Preen* (1962), and *McCall* v. *Abelesz* (1976)). The implied covenant protects the tenant's enjoyment of the premises against any such interruption by his landlord. It also gives the tenant a remedy against his landlord in respect of lawful acts by other people claiming through the landlord and which disturb the tenant's enjoyment of the demised premises. The reason why the covenant only extends to lawful acts is that if the act is unlawful the tenant will have a remedy, normally in the law of tort, against the person who disturbs him. The following cases illustrate these principles.

Owen v. *Gadd* (1956). L erected scaffolding in front of T's shop and blocked the entrance. HELD: There was a breach of the covenant for quiet enjoyment entitling T to damages.

Sanderson v. *Berwick-upon-Tweed Corporation* (1884). L let three farms to T1, T2, T3. T1's farm suffered damage from flooding of drains on the other two farms. T2 had defective drains but he had used them properly. T3's drains were in good order but he had used them improperly. T1 sued L for breach of the covenant for quiet enjoyment. HELD: L was liable for T2's drains but not for T3's drains because T3 had acted unlawfully and therefore his acts were outside the scope of the covenant for quiet enjoyment.

7. Covenant not to derogate from grant. A landlord must not derogate from his grant. What this means is that if he lets land, he must not subsequently do anything which is inconsistent with the purpose of the letting. The remedy is an action for an injunction or damages.

Aldin v. *Latimer Clark, Muirhead & Co.* (1894). L let land to T, a timber merchant, for use as drying sheds for timber. L then let certain neighbouring buildings which impeded the flow of air to the drying sheds and interfered with the drying process. HELD: There was a breach by L of his covenant not to derogate from his grant.

8. Implied condition of fitness. Generally there is no implied warranty or condition by the landlord that the premises are fit for any particular purpose. The rule is *caveat emptor* – let the buyer beware. It is for the tenant to ensure that the condition of the premises is suitable for his purposes. There is one exception to this rule: in the case of furnished premises there is an implied condition that the premises are fit for habitation at the start of the tenancy.

Smith v. *Marrable* (1843). L let a furnished house to T. It was infested with bugs. HELD: There was an implied condition that the house should be reasonably fit for habitation. T could repudiate the tenancy and recover damages.

There is also a condition as to fitness of small dwellings implied by the Landlord and Tenant Act 1985, s. 8 (*see* **16**).

9. Repairing obligations. In a limited number of cases the courts have been prepared to imply an obligation on the landlord to repair. The cases are best regarded as exceptional. The following are examples.

Liverpool City Council v. *Irwin* (1976). A tower block was divided into flats let on terms containing no express repairing covenants. The House of Lords HELD the landlord to be subject to an implied obligation to take reasonable care to repair and maintain the common parts of the block.

Barrett v. *Lounavon (1982) Ltd* (1988). The tenant of residential premises was liable under the terms of an express tenancy for all internal repairs. The Court of Appeal HELD that the landlord was under an implied obligation to repair the outside because the covenant imposed on the tenant could not be complied with unless the outside was kept in repair.

Tenant's implied covenants

10. Covenant to pay rent. If there is no express covenant to pay rent, there will be an implied covenant to pay rent from the time of entry by the tenant onto the demised premises.

11. Covenant to pay rates and taxes. There is an implied covenant that the tenant will pay all rates and taxes except those for which the landlord is liable. The landlord's liability will be determined by reference to the statute which imposes the rates or tax.

12. Obligation not to commit waste. If a tenant does anything to alter the premises he is said to commit waste. There are four kinds of waste:

(a) *voluntary waste*, namely any act causing damage to the land e.g. cutting trees, demolishing buildings;
(b) *ameliorating waste*, namely alterations which improve the land;
(c) *permissive waste*, namely waste which is due to a failure to maintain, e.g. allowing a house to fall into disrepair;
(d) *equitable waste*, this is an aggravated form of voluntary waste and includes extreme and serious acts of waste, e.g. cutting trees intentionally planted to shelter a house.

The landlord's remedy if the tenant commits waste is an action for damages, or an injunction to prevent apprehended waste.

13. Extent of obligation. The obligation not to commit waste varies with the nature of the tenancy:

(a) a tenant for a fixed term is liable for voluntary and permissive waste;

(b) a tenant under a yearly tenancy is liable for voluntary waste; he is not liable for permissive waste save that he must keep the premises wind- and water-tight, fair wear and tear excepted: *Warren* v. *Keen* (1954);

(c) a tenant under a lesser periodic tenancy is liable for voluntary waste only.

14. Tenant-like user. A tenant is under an implied obligation to use the demised premises in a tenant-like manner. In *Warren* v. *Keen* (1954), Denning LJ said of this obligation 'The tenant must take proper care of the place. He must, if he is going away for the winter, turn off the water and empty the boiler. He must clean the chimneys, when necessary, and also the windows. He must unstop the sink when it is blocked by his waste. In short, he must do the little jobs about the place which a reasonable tenant would do. But apart from such things, if the house falls into disrepair through fair wear and tear or lapse of time, or for any reason not caused by him, then the tenant is not liable to repair it'.

> NOTE: The tenant's duties under the law of waste and the implied obligations as to tenant-like user are very much narrower than the onerous duties created by express tenant's covenants to repair.

15. Covenants implied by statute. The above covenants are implied at common law, and will apply to all tenancies unless there is an express provision dealing with the matter. In relation to certain residential tenancies, statute has intervened and imposed obligations on the parties. The main provisions are:

(a) Landlord and Tenant Act 1985, s. 8 (*see* **16**).
(b) Landlord and Tenant Act 1985, s. 11 (*see* **17**).
(c) Housing Act 1980, s. 81 (*see* **18**).

16. Landlord and Tenant Act 1985, s. 8. Where a house is let on a tenancy at a rent not exceeding £80 per year in London, or £52 per year elsewhere, there is implied upon the part of the landlord:

(a) a condition that at the start of the tenancy the house is fit for human habitation; and
(b) an undertaking that he will keep the house fit for human habitation.

This does not apply to a tenancy of a house for a term of not less than three years on terms that the tenant is liable to put it into a condition reasonably fit for human habitation. Nor does it apply to a tenancy determinable at the option of either party before the expiration of three years.

NOTE: a landlord's liability under the undertaking is dependent upon him being given notice of the defect: *McCarrick* v. *Liverpool Corporation* (1947).

17. Landlord and Tenant Act 1985, s. 11. Where on or after 24th October 1961 a dwelling-housing is let for a term of less than seven years, there are implied covenants by the landlord:

(a) to keep in repair the structure and exterior of the house, including drains, gutters and external pipes.

(b) to keep in repair and proper working order the installations in the house:

(*i*) for the supply of water, gas and electricity and for sanitation (including basins, sinks, baths and sanitary conveniences but not other fixtures, fittings and appliances for making use of water, gas and electricity); and

(*ii*) for space heating or heating water;

(c) where the lease is of a dwelling-house which forms part only of a building, then the implied covenant extends to any part of the building in which the landlord has an estate or interest and to any installation serving the dwelling-house and forming part of the building in which the landlord has an estate or interest, provided that the landlord has a defence if he does not have a sufficient right of access to that part or that installation and makes reasonable endeavours to obtain such access.

NOTES: (1) A landlord cannot contract out of these obligations except with the consent of the tenant and the approval of the court.

(2) A landlord is only liable under this Act for defects of which he has notice: *O'Brien* v. *Robinson* (1973). However, the notice may be acquired by the landlord from a third party: *McGreal* v. *Wake* (1984).

(3) The provisions of the Act of 1985, s. 11 do not apply to leases granted after 3rd October 1980 in favour of the Crown, local authorities and certain other public bodies.

(4) If a landlord receives a registered rent (*see* Chapter 19) assessed on the basis that he is liable for s. 11 repairs, he may be estopped from claiming that the tenant is liable to do such repairs: *Brikom Investments Ltd* v. *Seaford* (1981).

(5) Section 11 does not apply to a new lease granted to an existing tenant, or to a former tenant still in possession, if the previous lease was not a lease to which s. 11 applied.

18. Housing Act 1980, s. 81. By virtue of s. 81 it is a term of every protected tenancy and statutory tenancy (*see* 16: **3**) that the tenant will not make any improvement without the written consent of the land-lord. In other words such tenants are given a qualified right to carry out improvements. The consent required is not to be unreasonably withheld and, if unreasonably withheld, will be treated as given: s. 81(3). The term 'improvement' means:

> 'Any alteration in, or addition to, a dwelling-housing and includes:
> **(a)** any addition to, or alteration in, landlord's fixtures and fittings and any addition or alteration connected with the provision of any services to a dwelling-house;
> **(b)** the erection of any wireless or television aerial; and
> **(c)** the carrying out of external decoration.'
> Item **(c)** does not apply to a protected or statutory tenancy if the landlord is under an obligation to carry out external decorations or to keep the exterior of the dwelling-house in repair (*ibid.*).

Section 81 applies to tenancies granted before as well as after the coming into operation of the provision. In the case of some protected tenancies the provisions are modified: *see* s. 81(4).

There is a similar term implied into every secure tenancy by s. 97 of the Housing Act 1985.

Implied covenants in agreements for a lease

19. General note. So far this chapter has been concerned with the implication of covenants in a lease. Where there is an agreement for a lease and the agreement says nothing about what terms are to be included in the lease, there is implied into the agreement a term that the lease shall contain the 'usual covenants'. These are:

(a) by the landlord:
  (*i*) a qualified covenant for quiet enjoyment;
(b) by the tenant:
  (*i*) to pay rent;
  (*ii*) to pay rates and taxes not payable by the landlord;
  (*iii*) to keep the premises in repair;
  (*iv*) to permit the landlord to enter and view the state of repair.

In addition to the above covenants there will be inserted whatever other covenants are usual having regard to the nature of the premises, their situation, the purposes for which they are being let, the length of the term, the evidence of conveyancers and the books of precedents: *see* for example, *Chester* v. *Buckingham Travel Ltd* (1981).

These 'usual' covenants are only implied into an agreement for a lease which is open, i.e. where the agreement is silent as to the terms of the lease agreed to be granted. They will become express terms in the lease when it is actually executed. They do not concern or affect the implied covenants in a lease.

Progress test 4

1. What is the covenant for quiet enjoyment? **(4)**

2. What is the difference between an absolute and a qualified covenant for quiet enjoyment? **(5)**

3. What are the 'usual covenants'? In what situation are they relevant? **(19)**

4. L grants a tenancy of a factory to T. L then obstructs the access to the factory. What remedies does T have against L? **(6, 7)**

5. What are the covenants implied into a lease by
   (a) the landlord, and
   (b) the tenant? **(2)**

6. Can a landlord forfeit a lease if there is no express forfeiture clause? **(3)**

7. What is the scope of the covenant not to derogate from grant? **(7)**

8. T rents a building from L for use as a shop. In fact the shop is not fit for such use. Does T have any remedy against L? **(8)**

9. What is waste? **(12)**

10. What are the different types of waste? **(12)**

11. How does liability for waste vary with the type of tenancy? **(13)**

12. What is the effect on the terms of a tenancy of:
   (a) the Landlord and Tenant Act 1985, ss 8 and 11,
   (b) the Housing Act 1980,
   (c) the Housing Act 1985? **(16, 17, 18)**

5

Express covenants

Introduction

1. Generally. The covenants in a lease govern and regulate the relationship between landlord and tenant. They are the terms of the contract between the two parties and they allocate the responsibility for matters arising out of the lease, e.g. the amount of rent payable, the liability for repairs, the responsibility for insurance. If a lease is silent about some matter it means that, unless a term is implied by law (see Chapter 4), neither party is responsible for it. So, if a lease says nothing about the question of repairs and there is no implied term neither party will be responsible.

2. Types of covenant. The covenants considered in this chapter are those relating to:

(a) rent (see **3–15**);
(b) repairs (see **16–33.**);
(c) alterations and improvements (see **34–37**);
(d) user (see **38–40**);
(e) insurance (see **41–42**);
(f) options (see **43–49**);
(g) service charges (see **50–51**).

These are the covenants most frequently encountered in leases. It needs hardly be said that there is no limit to the variety of other covenants which may be found.

Rent

3. Introduction. Rent is the compensation or consideration which the tenant pays to the landlord for the exclusive possession of land under a lease. The following points should be noted:

(a) rent does not have to be money, it may be the performance of services or payment in kind;

(b) rent must be certain or capable of being ascertained with certainty; if it is not certain the tenancy will be of no effect;
(c) rent is payable by the tenant to the landlord or to his authorised agent; it must be paid in the manner specified in the lease;
(d) if the lease is silent about the manner of payment, rent is payable at the end of each period of a periodic tenancy, or at the end of each year of a term of years;
(e) rent is payable without deduction unless the lease authorises the making of deductions or the tenant has paid sums which the landlord has a duty to pay.

4. The obligation to pay rent. In the absence of an express provision, the tenant's obligation to pay rent will normally continue unaffected by any changes in the nature of the demised premises. The doctrine of frustration, however, applies in principle to leases and the obligation to pay rent may therefore be ended by a frustrating event, although such events are likely to be rare: *National Carriers Ltd* v. *Panalpina (Northern) Ltd* (1981) HL.

It is sometimes the practice to insert in a lease a term suspending the obligation to pay rent in the event of an occurrence such as destruction of the demised premises by fire or some other similar serious event.

Where a tenant is evicted from the demised premises by his landlord or by a person with title paramount, the obligation to pay rent ceases.

5. Rent books. Where residential property is let and the rent is payable weekly, the landlord is obliged to provide a rent book: Landlord and Tenant Act 1985, s. 4. The book must contain the name and address of the landlord and various detailed matters which are contained in s. 5 or prescribed by regulation. The current regulations are the Rent Books (Forms of Notices) Regulations 1982 as amended by the Rent Book (Forms of Notices) Regulations 1990. The matters prescribed include:

(a) a statement of the tenant's rights in relation to:
  (*i*) security of tenure, and
  (*ii*) rent regulation;
(b) the amount of rent,
(c) an explanation of any rent allowance schemes.

6. Rent demands in case of dwellings. Where a demand for rent or other sums payable to the landlord under the terms of the tenancy of a dwelling (not being a tenancy to which Part II of the Landlord and Tenant Act 1954 applies) is given to the tenant, the demand must contain the name and address of the landlord and, if that address is not in England and Wales, an address there at which notice may be served on the landlord: Landlord and Tenant Act 1987, s. 47(1). If such a demand is given which does not contain the required information, then any rent or other amount demanded which consists of a service charge shall be treated as not being due until the information is provided by notice given by the landlord to the tenant: s. 47(2).

7. Rent review clauses. In recent years it has become common to include in leases, and particularly in leases of commercial property, a rent review clause to counter the effect of inflation. Such a clause usually provides for the rent to be reviewed at fixed intervals during the term. At each review date the market rent then current for the demised premises will be assessed and substituted for the rent previously payable. The form of these clauses varies from lease to lease. A properly drafted clause should make clear:

(a) the review period;
(b) the time for taking steps in having the rent reviewed;
(c) whether time is, or is not, of the essence;
(d) the procedure for determining the reviewed rent by agreement or, in default of agreement, by an independent expert or by arbitration;
(e) the basis of valuation, i.e. what is and what is not to be taken into account in fixing the rent;
(f) the effect of a late review, i.e. from when rent is payable and whether interest is payable thereon;
(g) whether the rent can go down.

8. Time limits in rent review clauses. A rent review clause will normally contain a timetable for taking the steps which lead to the rent being reviewed. In recent years the courts have had to consider the effect of a failure to comply with such a timetable. For instance, if the landlord should fail to serve a notice requiring the rent to be reviewed at the specified time, does this deprive him of the right to have the rent reviewed and of the right to receive a reviewed rent during the period until the next review date? In legal terms the question is whether 'time is of the essence'. Prior to 1977 there were several conflicting cases on this question. In *United Scientific Holdings* v. *Burnley Borough Council* (1977), the House of Lords considered this problem and overruled certain earlier cases.

The principle of law now applied is that in time stipulations in rent review clauses there is a presumption that time is not of the essence. Time will only be of the essence

(a) if it is expressly so provided by the terms of the lease; or
(b) if there is some indication in the lease that time is to be of the essence, e.g. where the rent review is linked to an option to determine the lease and time is of the essence as regards that option; or
(c) if there is some indication in the surrounding circumstances that time is to be of the essence.

9. Decisions on time limits since *United Scientific.* Since 1977 cases on time limits in rent review clauses have continued unabated. In some it has been held that time was of the essence notwithstanding the general rule in **8** above.

> *Drebbond* v. *Horsham District Council* (1979). A clause requiring the landlord to give notice requiring arbitration within a certain time limit 'but not otherwise' was HELD to make time of the essence because of those quoted words.

> *Al Saloom* v. *Shirley James Travel Services Ltd* (1981). Where the time limits of a rent review clause (in particular the time for service of the landlord's notice initiating the review) were closely linked to those of a break clause, time was held to be of the essence. This was because time was clearly of the essence of the break clause and that clause was linked to the rent review time limits to give the tenant a way out if the reviewed rent was too high. Therefore, if the landlord had been allowed to give a late rent review notice, the tenant would have lost his way out. However, this case must be compared with *Metrolands Investments Ltd* v. *J.H. Dewhurst Ltd* (1986), where the interrelation between a break clause and a review clause was held not to make time of the essence because the event as to which it was alleged time was of the essence (the decision of the arbitrator) was outside the control of the landlord, and because the tenant could set the arbitration machinery in motion.

> *Lewis* v. *Barnett* (1982). The review clause provided that the landlord's rent review notice would be void if served late. HELD: time was of the essence in view of this clear provision.

> *Trustees of Henry Smith's Charity* v. *A.W.A.D.A. Trading and Promotion Services* (1984). Complicated provisions in a review clause which meant that failure to give notice in time gave rise to a deemed reviewed rent were HELD to make time of the essence.

It will be appreciated from the above that a rent review clause must be carefully scrutinised because, notwithstanding the general principle above, time may still be of the essence in complying with the time limits in the machinery. However, where time is not of the essence a lengthy delay will not deprive the landlord of his right to a review unless there is such a combination of delay by the landlord and such hardship to the tenant as will cause an estoppel to arise: *Amherst* v. *James Walker Goldsmith and Silversmith* (1983).

10. Other cases on rent review clauses. Rent review clauses have continued to prove a fruitful source of litigation. There is now a mass of rent review cases which cannot be treated properly in this book. For proper consideration of a rent review problem, reference should be made to one of the specialist works on rent review. Many of the later cases concern the basis of valuation. The following is a very limited selection of some of the more important cases.

Ponsford v. *HMS Aerosols Ltd* (1978). A rent review clause provided that the reviewed rent was to be 'assessed as a reasonable rent for the demised premises'. The premises were burnt down and rebuilt by the landlords with substantial improvements which were paid for by the tenants. On review, the question arose whether in assessing a 'reasonable rent' account should be taken of the improvements paid for by the tenants. The landlords argued that as the improvements were incorporated in the premises they must be taken into account. The tenants argued that a 'reasonable rent' meant a rent which was reasonable between the parties. It was HELD (by the House of Lords (3:2)): On a true construction of the lease the rent was payable for the demised premises and this meant the premises as improved. An independent surveyor would have to assess a reasonable rent for the premises and not a reasonable rent between the parties.

Plinth Property Investments v. *Mott, Hay & Anderson* (1981). Where there was a very strict user clause the Court of Appeal HELD that no account should be taken of the possibility that the landlords might relax the covenant; the valuer had to look at the legal position of the parties only.

Pivot Properties Ltd v. *Secretary of State for the Environment* (1979). The Court of Appeal HELD that in assessing the rent under a rent review clause rights under the Landlord and Tenant Act 1954 are to be taken into account.

Beer v. *Bowden* (1981). Where a review clause failed to provide machinery for assessing the rent if the parties failed to agree, it was HELD by the Court of Appeal that the rent must be a fair rent representing what the premises were reasonably worth at the review date.

British Gas Corporation v. *Universities Superannuation Scheme Ltd* (1986). Where the review clause provided for the hypothetical letting to contain 'the same provisions (other than as to the yearly rent) as are herein contained', it was HELD that these words were not apt to exclude from the hypothetical letting the fact that the actual lease contained provision for future rent review. This case is illustrative of a general tendency of the courts to hold that the hypothetical letting should be on the same terms as the actual letting unless there are clear indications to the contrary.

Basingstoke BC v. *Host Group Ltd* (1986). The Court of Appeal HELD that the principles applicable to rent review of premises comprising land and buildings were equally applicable to the review of a ground rent. Thus in the absence of an indication to the contrary, the hypothetical letting was to be on the same terms (other than as to the amount of rent) as those contained in the actual, existing lease.

11. Judicial review of rent review clause. A review by the courts of a rent review clause may generally arise in one of two ways. First, one of the parties to the lease may seek a decision of the court (usually by way of an originating summons for declaratory relief in the Chancery Division of the High Court) on the true construction of the review clause. Secondly, a decision of an arbitrator in a rent review arbitration may be challenged in the High Court by way of an appeal under s. 1 of the Arbitration Act 1979. Such an appeal lies on a question of law, and only if all other parties to the arbitration consent or if the court grants leave, which it will not do unless the determination of the question of law could substantially affect the rights of one or more of the parties. The circumstances in which leave may be granted in a rent review case were considered in *Ipswich B.C.* v. *Fisons plc* (1990). The test is the same as in other arbitrations in that there must be a strong prima facie case of error of law.

In the case of a decision of an expert in order to set the decision aside, it is necessary to show that the expert answered the wrong question; if the expert answers the right question in the wrong way that will not suffice: see *Nikko Hotels (UK) Ltd* v. *MEPC plc* (1991). This is a hard test to satisfy in practice. The only other possible remedy in the case of an unsatisfactory decision by an expert is an action for negligence against the expert.

12. Non-payment of rent. If a tenant fails to pay rent, the landlord may seek to recover it by,

(a) levying distress; or
(b) an action on the covenant to pay rent; or
(c) if there is a forfeiture clause, an action for forfeiture of the lease.

13. Distress. Distress is the taking of goods by one person from another, without legal process, in order to hold the goods as a pledge for the satisfaction of a debt or the performance of a duty. A landlord may secure the payment of rent by seizing goods found on the premises in respect of which rent is due. The right to distrain arises as soon as any rent is due and unpaid. The landlord may then enter and take goods to the value of the rent owed. In general the landlord may distrain on all goods on the demised premises, but certain articles are privileged against distress, e.g. property of the Crown. After the goods are seized, the tenant then has time within which he can pay the arrears and recover the goods. If the tenant fails to pay, the landlord may sell the goods and keep so much of the proceeds as covers the arrears.

NOTE: The subject of distress for rent is very complicated. In *Abingdon R.D.C.* v. *O'Gorman* (1968), Lord Denning MR described it as 'an archaic remedy which has largely fallen into disuse'. The Law Commission has recommended its abolition. It is a subject replete with ancient technicalities. Accordingly in this book it is dealt with in this single paragraph. Where a tenancy is protected by the Rent Act 1977 the leave of the court is needed before the landlord may levy distress.

14. An action for rent. This action is based on the express or implied covenant in the lease by the tenant to pay rent. The action must be brought within six years from when the rent fell due, otherwise it will be barred by the Limitation Act 1980, s. 19.

15. Forfeiture for non-payment of rent. This topic is dealt with in Chapter 8.

Repairs

16. Generally. If there is no express covenant to repair by either party, subject to the law of waste (*see* 4: **12**) to the Landlord and Tenant Act 1985 (*see* 4: **16, 17**) and to certain exceptional circumstances (*see* 4: **9**), neither party is obliged to repair the demised premises and neither party can require the other to carry out repairs. It is, however, normal to make express provision for one party to repair, or for one party to repair part of the demised premises and for the other party to repair the rest. In short leases the landlord will often be responsible, while in long leases the tenant will be responsible. In leases of flats or offices which form part of a larger building it is frequently the practice to require the tenant to keep the interior in repair while the landlord is responsible for the exterior. The landlord will often seek to recover the cost of fulfilling his obligations from the tenant by way of a service charge.

17. The meaning of 'repair'. The word 'repair' in this context means 'making good damage so as to leave the subject as far as possible as though it had not been damaged. It involves renewal of subsisting parts': *Calthorpe* v. *McOscar* (1924). It does not mean the replacement or renewal of the whole or substantially the whole of the demised premises: *see Lurcott* v. *Wakely* (1911). The modern tendency is to see whether on a common sense approach the work required is within the ambit of the word repair: *see Brew Brothers* v. *Snax Ltd*.(1970).

It is important to bear in mind that there must be 'damage' or 'disrepair' before liability under a repairing covenant may arise. Thus where the structure of a basement was defective so as to allow water to enter, but no damage had been caused to any part of the building by the defect, which was in the same state as when the building was built, it was held by the Court of Appeal that there was no disrepair and that therefore the tenant was under no liability to the landlord under the tenant's repairing covenant to carry out any work to remedy the defect: *Post Office* v. *Aquarius Properties Ltd* (1987).

It was sometimes considered that work to remedy an inherent defect could not be a repair although there was never any real support for such a proposition. In *Ravenseft Properties Ltd* v. *Davstone (Holdings) Ltd* (1979), Forbes J expressly rejected the submission that there was any rule of law to that effect. The judge adopted a test that it was always a question of degree whether what the tenant was being asked to do could properly be described as repair, or whether it would involve giving back to the landlord a wholly different thing from that which he demised.

18. Illustrations. The following cases illustrate the scope of repairs.

Lister v. *Lane* (1893). A house was built on poor ground. In order to put the house in good condition it was necessary to underpin it to a great depth. The Court of Appeal HELD: The tenant was not liable to do these works as they would produce a new house and not a repaired house. The works were not repairs and they were outside the scope of his covenant to repair.

Lurcott v. *Wakely* (1911). The front wall of an old house had to be rebuilt because it had become dangerous. The Court of Appeal HELD: This was a repair and the tenant was liable to do it. The works were the renewal of a defective part rather than the replacement of the whole.

Collins v. *Flynn* (1963). L let a house to T. A structure supporting part of the back and side wall of the house collapsed and it was necessary to rebuild the structure and the walls with new foundations. HELD: This was an improvement which would require the tenant to give up the premises in a different condition from that which they were let in and therefore it was not a repair.

Brew Brothers v. *Snax Ltd* (1970). The putting in of entirely different foundations was HELD not to be a repair within the tenant's repairing covenant.

Quick v. *Taff Ely BC* (1985). L let a house to T. L was subject to the implied repairing covenant under s. 11 of the Landlord and Tenant Act 1985 to repair the 'structure and exterior' of the house. The house suffered from severe condensation due to design defects in the windows. However the windows were in no different state from what they had been in when the tenant first became tenant and there was no evidence of damage or disrepair. L was therefore not liable to rectify the defects in the windows.

19. The standard of repair. The standard of repair required under a repairing covenant will vary from property to property. The general rule as described by Lord Esher MR in *Proudfoot* v. *Hart* (1890), requires: 'such repair as having regard to the age, character, and locality of the house would make it reasonably fit for the occupation of a reasonably-minded tenant of the class who would be likely to take it'.

In determining the standard required by a particular covenant these matters must be considered as at the beginning of the lease and not as at the end of it, as in the following case.

Calthorpe v. *McOscar* (1924). A house was let on a 95-year lease in 1825 in what was then a fashionable area of London but which by 1920 had deteriorated. HELD: The standard of repair must be determined by reference to the character of the premises at the beginning of the lease rather than at the end.

20. Particular covenants. The following are some typical repairing covenants and their effect:

(a) *to keep in repair*; this requires the landlord or tenant to repair the premises up to the standard described in it and carries with it an implied obligation to put and to leave in repair: *Payne* v. *Haine* (1847); *Proudfoot* v. *Hart* (1890). It is obvious that where a tenant takes a lease of run-down premises and enters into an ordinary covenant to repair he may assume a very onerous burden since he will not be required merely to keep the premises in the poor state in which he takes them but to put them into a proper state of repair;
(b) *to leave, deliver or yield up in repair*; the liability under this covenant only arises at the end of the lease;
(c) *to repair and renew*; this is in fact the same as in **(a)** above; the word 'renew' adds nothing to an ordinary covenant: *Collins* v. *Flynn* (1963);
(d) *to carry out structural repairs*; this requires repairs to the main structure of the building i.e. wall, floors, roofs.

21. The landlord's remedies for tenant's breach of covenant.
Where a tenant is in breach of a repairing covenant, the landlord may

(a) sue for damages for breach of covenant; or
(b) if there is a forfeiture clause, forfeit the lease (*see* Chapter 8).

In the case of certain leases, the landlord cannot start proceedings for either damages or forfeiture without the leave of the court under the Leasehold Property (Repairs) Act 1938.

22. The Leasehold Property (Repairs) Act 1938, s. 1. This Act applies where the lease was granted for a term of seven or more years and there are at least three years of the term unexpired. Where the Act applies, the landlord cannot proceed to forfeit the lease or to sue for damages for breach of repairing covenant without first giving a notice under the Law of Property Act 1925, s. 146 (*see* 8: **21**) informing the tenant of his right to serve a counter-notice claiming the benefit of the Act. If the tenant serves such a counter-notice within 28 days no further proceedings (by action or otherwise) may be taken unless the court gives leave. The court may give leave if the landlord establishes that one of the grounds specified in s. 1(5) is satisfied. These grounds are that:

(a) the value of the reversion has been substantially diminished;

(b) immediate repair is necessary to comply with any Act;

(c) immediate repair is necessary to protect another occupier;

(d) the cost of immediate repair would be small compared to the cost of future repair;

(e) special circumstances render it just and equitable to grant leave.

On an application for leave under the 1938 Act, the landlord must make out his case on the balance of probabilities and not merely make out a prima facie case: *see Associated British Ports plc v. C.H. Bailey plc* (1990). This means that the battle takes place at the stage of the application for leave and not at the trial of the forfeiture proceedings.

Where a term in a lease enables a landlord to enter and do repairs in default of the tenant doing them under his obligations and provides for the recovery by the landlord of the cost of those repairs, an action for the cost is not subject to the 1938 Act: *Hamilton v. Martell Securities Ltd* (1984), not following *Swallow Securities Ltd v. Brand* (1983). *See also Colchester Estates (Cardiff) Ltd v. Carlton Industries* (1984) following *Hamilton*.

23. An action for damages. The procedure is that the landlord will start proceedings in the High Court or the county court claiming damages from the tenant for his failure to perform his repairing covenants. The damages which a landlord may recover for breach of a repairing covenant are subject to special statutory rules. In order to understand these rules it is first necessary to consider the position at common law (*see* **24**) and then to consider the changes effected by statute (*see* **25, 26**).

24. The measure of damages at common law. Where the action is brought during the term, the landlord is entitled to damages representing the diminution in the value of the reversion which has resulted from the breach. This means the amount by which the market value of the landlord's interest is reduced by the disrepair. Accordingly the longer the residue of the term, the less this diminution should be.

Where the action is brought after the lease has ended, it is based on the tenant's covenant to yield up the premises in repair. At common law the measure of damages was the actual cost of carrying out the repair necessary to put the premises into the state of repair required by the covenant: *Joyner v. Weeks* (1891). This was the measure even if the premises were to be demolished so that the repairs were useless. A landlord could also recover for the loss of rent during the period the repairs were being carried out: *Woods v. Pope* (1835).

25. Landlord and Tenant Act 1927, s. 18(1). It is provided by this section that damages for breach of a covenant to keep or put premises in repair during the currency of a lease or to put premises in repair at the end of a lease may in no case exceed the amount, if any, by which the value of the reversion in the premises is diminished owing to the breach, and in particular no damages will be recoverable for any such breach of a covenant to leave or put in repair if it is shown that the premises would at or shortly after the end of the lease have been or be pulled down, or such structural alterations would have been made as would render valueless the repairs covered by the covenant.

26. The effect of s. 18(1). The provision has the following effects:

(a) the tenant is no longer liable for damages on his covenant to yield up in repair where the premises have been or are to be demolished or structurally altered;
(b) there is now an upper limit on the amount of damages recoverable whether the action is brought during the term or at its end: the limit is the diminution in value of the reversion caused by the breach;
(c) the proper approach to assessing damages is to ascertain the amount recoverable at common law (*see* **24**) and to ascertain the diminution in value of the reversion. The lesser of the two sums will be the recoverable damages.

27. Tenant's remedies for landlord's breach of repairing covenant. The extent of a landlord's liability to repair will, like a tenant's covenant, depend upon the exact wording of the covenant. Also, the landlord's liability to repair will not arise until he is given notice of the defect or he has knowledge of it: *McCarrick* v. *Liverpool Corpn.* (1947). Where the landlord is in breach of his repairing covenant and the tenant has given notice of the disrepair, the tenant has the following remedies:

(a) an action for damages for breach of covenant (*see* **28**);
(b) an action for specific performance of the landlord's covenant (*see* **29**);
(c) self-help, i.e. do the work himself and then recoup the expenditure from his landlord (*see* **30**);
(d) the appointment of a receiver (*see* **31**).

28. Action for damages. The measure of damages in an action by the tenant is such pecuniary compensation as will restore the tenant to the position he would have been in if there had been no breach; this may include

(a) the cost of alternative accommodation,

(b) the cost of any repairs paid for by the tenant, and

(c) compensation for living in unpleasant premises: *Calabar Properties Ltd* v. *Stitcher* (1983).

The tenant may start proceedings for recovering such damages. Alternatively, he may withhold his rent and then if he is sued by the landlord for arrears of rent, may set off against the landlord's claim for arrears of rent the damages to which he is entitled: *see British Anzani (Felixstowe) Ltd* v. *International Marine Management (UK) Ltd* (1979).

29. Action for specific performance. In a suitable case, the court will compel a landlord to perform his repairing covenants if he is clearly in breach and if there is no doubt about what is required to remedy the breach.

> *Jeune* v. *Queens Cross Properties Ltd* (1973). L let a flat to T and covenanted to repair. L failed to repair a balcony so that it collapsed. T sought an order compelling L to do the necessary repairs. HELD: In an appropriate case where there was a clear breach and it was clear what had to be done, the court would compel a landlord to perform his repairing obligations. This was an appropriate case.

It is provided by the Landlord and Tenant Act 1985, s. 17 that in any proceedings in which a tenant of a dwelling-house alleges a breach on the part of the landlord of a repairing covenant relating to any part of the premises in which the dwelling is comprised, the court may in its discretion order specific performance of that covenant. This power is in addition to the power of the court to order specific performance in accordance with ordinary equitable principles as was done in *Jeune* v. *Queens Cross Properties Ltd.*

> NOTE: There is old authority that a landlord cannot get specific performance of a tenant's repairing covenant against the tenant: *Hill* v. *Barclay* (1810).

30. Self-help. Where a landlord is in breach of his repairing covenant and he has notice of the defect, at common law a tenant who carries out the repairs may recoup himself out of future rents for the money expended on the repairs: *Lee-Parker* v. *Izzet* (1971). This means that a tenant can do the repairs himself and then deduct the cost from future rents to be paid to the landlord. If the landlord should sue the tenant for such rents, the tenant will have a good defence to the claim. It must be remembered that this can only be done where the repairs fall within the scope of the landlord's repairing covenant and he has notice of the breach.

31. Appointment of a receiver. Where the landlord refuses or neglects to perform the covenants in the lease to repair and to insure, the court may appoint a receiver to manage the property in accordance with the rights and obligations of the reversioner: *Hart* v. *Emelkirk* (1983). However, after the commencement of Part II of the Landlord and Tenant Act 1987 (*see* Chapter 24) such an application may not be made by a tenant in any circumstances in which an application could be made by him for an order under s. 24 appointing a manager to act in relation to those premises: s. 21(6) of the 1987 Act.

32. Landlord's right to enter and execute repairs. Where a landlord has covenanted to repair, in the absence of an express provision relating to entry on the premises, the law implies a licence by the tenant so that the landlord may enter and carry out repairs within his covenant: *Saner* v. *Bilton* (1878). In practice a lease will usually contain an express provision to enter to view the state of repair and, if necessary, carry out repairs. Where the express provision enables the landlord to recover costs incurred on repairs for which the tenant is liable, the sum recoverable is a debt, not damages, and is not therefore subject to the 1938 Act (*see* **22**).

33. Defective Premises Act 1972, s. 4. Where a landlord is under an obligation to repair or maintain the premises, or he has the right to enter the premises to maintain or repair them, s. 4 of the 1972 Act provides that the landlord owes a duty of care to all who might reasonably be expected to be affected by defects in the premises, e.g. the tenant, his family, his visitors. The duty is to take reasonable care to see that the people to whom the duty is owed are reasonably safe. The duty is only owed if the defects fall within the landlord's repairing obligation and he knows or ought reasonably to have known of the defect. If the landlord is in breach of his duty, a person to whom the duty is owed and who is injured by reason of the breach may recover damages from the landlord.

Alterations and improvements

34. Generally. We now turn from the liability to repair to the question of altering or improving the premises. A lease usually contains a covenant by the tenant not to make any alterations to the demised premises. In this context an alteration occurs when the actual fabric of the demised premises is altered. Such a covenant may be qualified by words such as 'not without the consent of the landlord'; alternatively, it may be an absolute prohibition on the making of alterations. The former covenant is referred to as a 'qualified covenant' and the latter as an 'absolute covenant'.

A lease does not usually contain a covenant against the making of improvements. The reason is that the making of improvements will normally be an alteration which will fall within the covenant against alterations. The word 'improvement', however, is used in the Landlord and Tenant Act 1927, and it is therefore important to consider its meaning.

35. What is an improvement? This can be a difficult question to answer. In considering the question, the following points must be borne in mind:

(a) the question has to be considered from the tenant's point of view, not from the landlord's;

(b) an improvement need not necessarily increase the value of the demised premises.

The above points are derived from *Woolworth & Co. Ltd* v. *Lambert* (1937). In that case the tenant wished to convert two shops held under separate leases into one shop. The Court of Appeal HELD that the proposed alterations were improvements even though the letting value would be reduced.

36. Landlord and Tenant Act 1927 s. 19(2). This provides that a covenant against the making of improvements without the consent of the landlord (i.e. a qualified covenant) is deemed to be subject to a proviso that consent will not be unreasonably withheld. It also provides that the landlord is not precluded from requiring, as a condition of his licence or consent:

(a) the payment of a reasonable sum in respect of any damage to or diminution in the value of the premises or of any neighbouring premises belonging to the landlord;

(b) the payment of any legal or other expenses properly incurred in connection with such licence or consent;

(c) in the case of an improvement which does not add to the letting value, an undertaking by the tenant to re-instate the premises to the condition in which they were before the improvement was executed.

NOTE: Section 19(2) does not apply to tenancies of dwelling-houses which are either secure tenancies or protected tenancies or statutory tenancies; instead there are special provisions in the Housing Act 1980, s. 81 and the Housing Act 1985, s. 97. (*see* 4:**18**).

37. Effect of s. 19(2).   In summary therefore, the effect of s. 19(2) on a covenant against making alterations is as follows:

(a) if the covenant is absolute, s. 19(2) does not apply and no alterations or improvements can be made unless the landlord, in his absolute discretion, permits it;

(b) if the covenant is qualified *but* the alteration is not an improvement, s. 19(2) does not apply and so the tenant can only carry out the alteration if the landlord gives his consent;

(c) if the covenant is qualified and the alteration is an improvement, the landlord cannot unreasonably withhold his consent, but he can require as a condition of his consent certain payments and an undertaking (*see* **36(a)**–**(c)**).

The use of premises

38. Introduction.   Unless the lease contains an express restriction on the use of the demised premises, subject to compliance with planning and similar restrictions, the tenant may use the premises for any purpose provided it is not illegal or immoral. Most leases contain a covenant by the tenant restricting the use of the premises to one particular use, or prohibiting the use of the premises for certain specific uses. Such covenants will vary from lease to lease and their effect will depend upon their precise terms.

39. Landlord and Tenant Act 1927, s. 19(3).   It is provided that a covenant against the alteration of the use of the demised premises without licence or consent (i.e. a qualified covenant) is, if the alteration does not involve any structural alteration, deemed to be subject to a proviso that no fine or sum of money in the nature of a fine will be payable for or in respect of such licence or consent. This provision, however, does not stop a landlord requiring the payment of a reasonable sum in respect of any damage to or diminution in the value of the premises or in any neighbouring premises belonging to him and of any legal or other expenses incurred in connection with such licence or consent. It is further provided that where a dispute as to the reasonableness of any sum has been determined by a court, the landlord is bound to grant the licence on payment of the sum determined to be reasonable.

40. Effect of s. 19(3). In summary, therefore, the effect of s. 19(3) on a user covenant is as follows:

(a) if the covenant is absolute, s. 19(3) does not apply and the use cannot be altered unless the landlord in his absolute discretion consents;

(b) if the covenant is qualified *but* the change of use involves structural alterations to the demised premises, s. 19(3) does not apply;

(c) if the covenant is qualified and the change of use does not involve structural alteration, s. 19(3) applies and the landlord cannot take a fine for his consent to a change of use;

(d) s. 19(3) does not, *however*, make the covenant subject to the proviso that the landlord may not unreasonably withhold his consent.

Insurance

41. Introduction. In leases other than short leases it is the normal practice to place the liability for insurance on one party. If the covenant to insure is by the tenant, he must arrange the insurance and pay the premium. There will be a breach of covenant if the property is uninsured at any time, even though the property is not damaged. If the covenant to insure is by the landlord, normally there will be a further term which will enable him to recover the premium from the tenant by way of additional rent. The following points should be noted:

(a) if the covenant is to insure with a specified company or other company approved by the landlord, the landlord can refuse to approve any company other than that specified without giving his reasons: *Viscount Tredegar* v. *Harwood* (1929);

(b) if the covenant is to insure with a specific company and the tenant takes from that company their usual policy which excepts certain risks, the tenant is not liable under this covenant if the house is destroyed in one of the excepted ways: *Upjohn* v. *Hitchins* (1918);

(c) if the landlord covenants to insure the premises, the court will not normally imply a term that he should place the insurance so as not to put an unnecessarily high burden on the tenant who is obliged to pay the premium by way of additional rent: *Bandar Holdings Ltd* v. *Darwen* (1968).

42. Insurance money. When insurance money is received following the destruction of the premises, the position is as follows:

(a) if the landlord or tenant takes out a policy without being obliged to do so, he is not liable to spend the insurance money on re-instatement of the premises;

(b) where there is an express term providing for re-instatement, as is normally the case, the insurance money must be applied in accordance with that term;

(c) where a landlord covenanted to insure at the tenant's expense, but there was no covenant to re-instate, the landlord was held liable to apply the policy money on re-instatement because the insurance covenant was intended to benefit both landlord and tenant: *Mumford Hotels Ltd* v. *Wheeler* (1964);

(d) where a tenant covenanted to insure in joint names of landlord and tenant and when the money was paid re-instatement was impossible because of legislation, it was held that the money belonged to the tenant alone because it was he who had paid the premiums: *Re King* (1963);

(e) where a landlord covenanted to insure and to apply insurance moneys received in reinstating the premises, the tenant covenanting to pay additional rent to cover premiums, when the premises were destroyed and by implied agreement the insurance moneys were not used in rebuilding, it was HELD that the insurance moneys belonged to the landlord and the tenant in shares proportionate to their respective interests in the premises because each party had an interest in the moneys through their respective covenants: *Beacon Carpets Ltd* v. *Kirby* (1984).

Options

43. Introduction. A lease may give to the tenant three kinds of option:

(a) an option to purchase (*see* **44–46.**);
(b) an option to renew (*see* **47–48**);
(c) an option to determine (*see* **49**).

44. Option to purchase. An option to purchase is a term which gives the tenant the opportunity to buy the landlord's interest in the demised premises. The normal form of such an option is a covenant by the landlord that, if the tenant at a specified time gives notice to the landlord of his desire to exercise the option, the landlord will sell his interest to the tenant for a specified sum. An option to purchase is not a contract because until it is exercised neither party is obliged to purchase or to sell. An option to purchase is in the nature of an offer to sell which cannot be revoked. Upon exercise of the option a binding contract for sale arises. Contracts which create options are sometimes called unilateral contracts (in the sense that they impose obligations on one party only) as distinct from ordinary contracts (which impose mutual obligations).

45. Effect of assignment of the lease on an option to purchase. If the lease is assigned the benefit of an option to purchase will normally pass with the lease to the assignee, unless the option is limited in its terms to the original lessee.

46. Effect of assignment of the reversion on an option to purchase. Whether an assignee of the reversion will be bound by an option to purchase will vary depending on whether the land has registered title.

(a) If the land has unregistered title, the validity of the option depends on whether it (the option) was registered under the Land Charges Act 1972. Under s. 2(4) of that Act, an option to purchase is registrable as a Class C land charge as an estate contract. The Act provides that failure to register the option will make it void against a purchaser of the legal estate for money or money's worth.
(b) If the land has registered title, an option exercisable by a tenant in occupation has been held to be an 'overriding interest' under the Land Registration Act 1925, s 70(1), which is binding on an assignee of the reversion without the need for any sort of registration under the Act: *Webb* v. *Pollmount* (1966). Where the tenant is not in occupation the option must be protected by an entry on the register.

47. Option to renew. This gives the tenant the option to take a lease for a further term. Such an option will normally be worded so that the new lease excludes the option itself. If the option is in fact worded so as to include all the clauses of the original lease including the option itself, the lease may be perpetually renewable (*see* 3: **23**). An option to renew is usually made expressly dependent upon the tenant complying with all the covenants in the lease. Thus if the tenant is in breach of any of his obligations at the time of exercise of the option or any other time specified in the clause, then however trivial the breach, the tenant will be unable to exercise the option. However, under such a clause, a tenant will not be prevented from exercising the option by past breaches of covenant which have become spent prior to exercising the option.

West Country Cleaners (Falmouth) Ltd v. *Saly* (1966). T was entitled to an option to renew. He failed to observe a covenant to repaint at fixed intervals. HELD by the Court of Appeal: the breach disentitled T from exercising the option.

Bass Holdings Ltd v. *Morton Music Ltd* (1987). In 1984 the tenant committed breaches of covenant to pay rent and rates and not to apply for planning permission without the landlord's consent. Relief from forfeiture was granted in 1985 and the conditions of relief complied with. Later in 1985 the tenant sought to exercise an option to renew which the landlord refused to accept due to the past breaches of covenant. HELD that as the breaches were spent prior to exercising the option, they did not prevent the valid exercising of the option; further, it was irrelevant whether the past breaches were of positive or negative covenants.

48. Effect of assignment on the option to renew. The rules set out at **45** and **46** above apply to an option to renew.

49. Option to determine. A lease for a term of years may give either party the right to determine the lease at a specified time or when a specified event occurs. For instance the landlord may wish to redevelop the premises when economic conditions permit or the tenant may wish to re-locate his business at a specific time in the future.

An option to determine is often called a 'break-clause'. The exercise of such a clause will depend on its precise terms. Frequently it is made a pre-condition of its exercise by the tenant that the tenant must have performed all his obligations under the lease.

If the lease is assigned, the clause becomes exercisable by the assignee. If the reversion is assigned, the new lessor is bound by the clause. The validity of an option to determine is not dependent on any form of registration.

Service charges

50. Service charges. It is common in leases of flats to provide for the recovery by the landlord from the tenant of service charges in respect of heating, lighting, porterage and other services provided by the landlord. The recovery of such sums is subject to regulation by the Landlord and Tenant Act 1985, ss. 18 to 30 (as amended by the Landlord and Tenant Act 1987) the effect of those provisions being:

(a) to limit the landlord's right to recover a service charge to reasonable sums reasonably incurred or to be incurred; and

(b) to require the landlord to obtain estimates for work costing more than a specified sum; and

(c) to require the landlord on request by the tenant to supply a written summary of costs and to permit the tenant to inspect supporting accounts;

(d) to require the landlord in certain cases to consult the tenant;

(e) to provide that sums paid by the tenant are held on trust to defray costs incurred in connection with the matters for which the service charges were payable and subject to that on trust for the persons who are the contributing tenants for the time being.

NOTE: 1. These provisions do not apply to short leases granted by certain public authorities: s. 26(1).

2. These provision now apply to leases of 'dwellings': Landlord and Tenant Act 1987, s. 41(1).

51. Rights of tenants of dwellings with respect to insurance.
Where a tenant of a dwelling pays a service charge which includes an amount directly or indirectly for insurance, the tenant has certain rights under s. 30A of, and the Schedule to, the Landlord and Tenant Act 1985. In summary, these are:

(a) to require the landlord to provide a written summary of the insurance;

(b) to require the landlord to permit the tenant to inspect and copy the policy or any documents evidencing payment of the premium;

(c) to notify the insurers of possible claims in respect of damage to the dwelling;

(d) to challenge the landlord's choice of insurer.

NOTE: These provisions do not apply to short leases granted by certain public authorities.

Progress test 5

1. What are the essential attributes of rent? **(3)**

2. When is rent payable under
   (a) a periodic tenancy; and
   (b) a term of years? **(3)**

3. What is the effect of frustration on the obligation to pay rent? **(4)**

4. In what circumstances must a landlord give a tenant a rent book? What information must it contain?   **(5)**

5. L lets land to T on a 21-year lease with rent reviews every seven years. There is a procedure for carrying out the review with time limits at various stages. Time is expressed to be of the essence. L fails to initiate the rent review by the first time limit. Advise L.   **(8)**

6. What is a rent review clause?   **(7)**

7. What is the effect of the decision in *Ponsford* v. *HMS Aerosols Ltd?* **(10)**

8. Outline the steps available to a landlord to recover unpaid rent. **(12)**

9. In the absence of an express covenant to repair who is liable to repair property let under a lease?   **(16)**

10. What standard of repair is required under a repairing covenant? **(19)**

11. What remedies does a landlord have against a tenant who is in breach of his repairing obligations? How do these remedies differ from those available to a tenant for breach of landlord's repairing obligations?   **(21)**

12. What is the measure of damages at common law for breach of a tenant's repairing covenant? How has statute affected the measure?   **(24)**

13. When is leave needed under the Leasehold Property (Repairs) Act 1938? To what actions does the Act apply? On what grounds may leave be granted?   **(22)**

14. What is the difference in the measure of damages (1) before 1927 and (2) today, in an action brought during the term and at the end of the term for breach of repairing covenants?   **(23–26)**

15. What does s. 4 of the Defective Premises Act 1972 provide?   **(33)**

16. L is obliged to repair T's roof under the terms of the lease to T. T refuses to permit L to enter. Advise L.   **(32)**

17. What constitutes an improvement for the purposes of the Landlord and Tenant Act 1927?   **(35)**

18. What is the effect of s. 19(2) of the 1927 Act on
   (a) an absolute covenant against making improvements;
   (b) a qualified covenant against making improvements? **(37)**

19. L lets a house to T with no user clause. To which of the following uses may T put the premises:
   (a) residential use;
   (b) a brothel;
   (c) light industrial use? **(38)**

20. What is the effect of s. 19(3) of the 1927 Act on user covenants? **(40)**

21. Who is normally responsible for insuring premises let under a lease? What arrangements do the parties normally make regarding insurance? **(41)**

22. L lets property to T and covenants to insure, T being obliged to repay the premium to L. The premises are burnt down and L refuses to use the insurance money to rebuild the premises. Advise T. **(42)**

23. What are the three different kinds of option that may be given to a tenant? **(43)**

24. What is the effect of
   (a) an assignment of the lease, and
   (b) an assignment of the reversion on the three kinds of option mentioned in Question 23? **(45, 46)**

25. What is a 'break clause'? **(49)**

6
Assigning and sub-letting

Introduction

1. Generally. This chapter is concerned with the different ways in which a landlord and tenant may deal with their respective interests and the effect of such dealings. The major topics dealt with in the chapter are:

(a) assignments and sub-lettings generally (*see* **2–7**);
(b) the requisite formalities;
(c) covenants against assigning and sub-letting (*see* **8–19**);
(d) the enforceability of covenants upon assignment (*see* **20–32**);
(e) devolution of leases (*see* **33–35**).

Assignments and sub-lettings

2. Assignment of the lease. An assignment of the lease takes place when the tenant transfers to another person his entire interest in the property for the whole of the residue of the term of the lease.

3. Formalities of an assignment. In order to effect a valid assignment, the following formalities must be satisfied.

(a) An agreement to assign a lease will not be enforceable unless it satisfies the requirements of the Law of Property Act 1925, s. 40 or the Law of Property (Miscellaneous Provisions) Act 1989, s. 2(1): *see* 2: **3, 8.**
(b) The assignment must be by deed if the legal estate is to pass to the assignee: Law of Property Act 1925, s. 52(1). This rule applies to any tenancy. It produces the result that while a periodic tenancy or some other tenancy for a period less than three years can be created orally (*see* 2: **24**), an assignment of it must be by deed in order to be effective.
(c) If (b) is not complied with but there is an agreement to assign for value, this may be effective to pass an equitable interest to the assignee.

4. Sub-letting. A sub-letting takes place where a tenant of property lets it or part of it to another person for a period less than the residue of his own term. The period of the sub-lease must be at least one day less than the unexpired period of the lease. If a tenant tries to sub-let the property for a period equal to, or more than, the unexpired period of his own lease this operates as an assignment of the term, not as a sub-letting.

Example
L lets land to T for seven years from 1st January 1975. Later T purports to grant a sub-lease to S for three years from 1st January 1979. Three years equals the residue of the lease and the purported sub-lease therefore operates as an assignment, not as a sub-lease.

5. Sub-letting by a periodic tenant. A periodic tenancy, whether it be weekly, monthly or yearly, is regarded in law as continuing until it is actually determined. Accordingly a tenant under a periodic tenancy can validly grant a sub-lease for a term of years without infringing the rule described in **4** above. The sub-letting will not operate as an assignment. This can produce unusual results, as shown by an example.

Example
L lets land to T on a yearly tenancy. T sub-lets the land to S for a term of ten years. This operates as a valid sub-letting, not as an assignment. Thus in theory a weekly tenant can create a valid sub-lease of, e.g. 99 years or more. Of course, at common law, the sub-lease will end with the determination of the interest out of which it is carved. The 99-year sub-lease will, therefore, end if the weekly head-lease is validly ended by notice to quit.

6. Formalities of sub-letting. The same rules apply to the creation of a sub-lease as apply to the creation of a lease: *see* **2: 18.**

7. The right to assign and sub-let. In the absence of any provision to the contrary, the tenant has the right to deal with his interest as he wishes; he may assign or sub-let freely. In practice, however, many leases contain a covenant by the tenant not to assign or sub-let. A common form is that the tenant covenants not to assign, sub-let or part with possession of the demised premises or any part thereof. If the tenant assigns or sub-lets in breach of such a covenant the result is as follows: the assignment or sub-letting will be effective to vest a legal estate in the assignee or sub-lessee, but the landlord will have the right to forfeit the lease (provided there is a proviso for re-entry) and will in any event have a right to damages for breach of covenant.

NOTE: Where a tenant assigns his lease in breach of covenant the assignment is, as stated above, effective and any notice of forfeiture of the lease under the Law of Property Act 1925, s. 146 (*see* 8: **20** *et seq.*) must be served on the assignee, who is the person concerned to avoid forfeiture, not on the original tenant (who is no longer the tenant): *see Old Grovebury Manor Farm Ltd* v. *W. Seymour Plant Sales & Hire Ltd (No. 2)* (1979).

Covenants against assigning or sub-letting

8. Introduction. The operation of these covenants depends on their precise wording. There are many cases dealing with this topic. In each case it is necessary to look at the words of the covenant in the lease and consider if what the tenant wishes to do falls within the restriction imposed by the covenant. The courts tend to construe such covenants against the landlord in accordance with the general rule of construction of contracts that terms are construed *contra proferentem*, i.e. against the person who has inserted the term for his benefit. The following cases illustrate the approach that the courts have adopted in construing these covenants.

Cook v. *Shoesmith* (1951). L let land to T who agreed 'not to sub-let.' T sub-let a part of the premises. HELD: The sub-letting of part was no breach unless the covenant expressly extended to 'the demised premises or any part thereof'. This covenant did not so extend and therefore there was no breach.

Crusoe d. Blencowe v. *Bugby* (1771). A covenant against assigning was not broken by an underletting of the premises.

Lam Kee Ying v. *Lam Shes Tong* (1974). T covenanted not to assign, underlet or part with possession of the demised premises or any part thereof. The Privy Council said that a covenant against parting with possession was not broken by a tenant who, in law, retained possession even though he allowed another to use and occupy the premises. Accordingly, a tenant who grants a licence to another to use the demised premises does not commit a breach of covenant unless the agreement with the licensee ousts the tenant entirely from the legal possession.

Marks v. *Warren* (1979). T covenanted not to underlet or part with possession of the demised premises, without the landlord's consent. T assigned without getting the landlord's consent. In proceedings between the assignee and T, the question arose whether an assignment fell foul of the covenant. HELD: the assignment by T necessarily involved a parting with possession and was therefore a breach of the covenant.

Field v. *Barkworth* (1986). T covenanted 'not to assign or underlet any part of the premises'. The question arose whether this prohibited the tenant from assigning the whole of the premises or only part. HELD: the words 'any part' prohibited a tenant from assigning the whole or any part.

The effect of *Lam Kee Ying* v. *Lam Shes Tong* (1974) above is that the restrictive effect of a covenant against assigning, sub-letting or parting with possession may be evaded by the tenant granting a licence to the occupier provided the tenant is not entirely ousted from the legal possession. In consequence landlords are well advised to insist upon covenants not to allow any other person to *occupy* the demised premises.

9. Involuntary assignments. A covenant against assigning is not broken by an involuntary assignment, i.e. an assignment which takes place by operation of law rather than by the act of the parties. The following are examples of involuntary assignments:

(a) when the lease passes on the death of the tenant (*see* **34**);
(b) when the lease passes on the bankruptcy of the tenant to his trustee in bankruptcy (*see* **35**);
(c) when the lease is acquired by a public body exercising compulsory purchase powers.

10. Absolute and qualified covenants. There are two different types of covenant against assigning and sub-letting:

(a) an absolute covenant, i.e. the tenant covenants not to assign or sub-let;
(b) a qualified covenant, e.g. the tenant covenants not to assign or sub-let without the landlord's consent.

Under the first type the tenant is absolutely prohibited from assigning or sub-letting. If the tenant wishes to assign he will have to cast himself on the landlord's mercy and the landlord will be entitled either to refuse his consent or to impose onerous conditions on the grant of his consent. Under the second type, the tenant may assign or sub-let if the landlord gives his consent. There are statutory provisions which restrict the grounds upon which a landlord may withhold his consent and the conditions which he may attach to his consent (*see* Chapter 11). These provisions only apply to qualified covenants; they do not apply to absolute covenants.

11. Statutory provisions relating to qualified covenants. The provisions are contained in

(a) the Law of Property Act 1925, s. 144;
(b) the Landlord and Tenant Act 1927, s. 19(1);
(c) the Landlord and Tenant Act 1988.

12. Law of Property Act 1925, s. 144. This provides that where a lease contains a covenant against assigning or sub-letting without licence or consent (i.e. a qualified covenant), except where the lease contains an express provision to the contrary, the covenant is deemed to be subject to a proviso that no fine or sum of money in the nature of a fine will be payable for such licence or consent. The landlord is not, however, precluded from requiring payment in respect of any legal or other expenses in relation to the licence or consent.

13. Landlord and Tenant Act 1927, s. 19(1). Where a lease contains a covenant against assigning or sub-letting without licence or consent, notwithstanding any express provision to the contrary, the covenant is deemed to be subject to a proviso that the licence or consent is not to be unreasonably withheld. The effect of this is as follows.

(a) Before the tenant assigns, he must seek the landlord's consent even though consent could not reasonably be withheld. If the tenant fails to seek the landlord's consent, and proceeds with the assignment, the lease will be liable to forfeiture by the landlord: *Eastern Telegraph Co.* v. *Dent* (1899).
(b) If the tenant seeks the landlord's consent but the landlord unreasonably withholds his consent, the tenant is free to assign without the landlord's consent: *Treloar* v. *Bigge* (1874). Thereafter the landlord cannot rely on different grounds to justify his withholding: *Bromley Park Garden Estates Ltd* v. *Moss* (1982).
(c) Alternatively, and more prudently, if the landlord unreasonably withholds his consent, the tenant may apply to the court for a declaration that consent has been unreasonably withheld. Upon the granting of the declaration, the tenant can go ahead and assign the lease.

> NOTES: (1) Leases frequently provide in express terms that consent to an assignment or sub-letting will not be unreasonably withheld; if this is the case, there is no need to invoke the statutory proviso.

(2) Where a qualified covenant is subject to a proviso that the tenant should first offer a surrender of the lease to the landlord, the proviso is lawful and is *not* invalidated by s. 19(1): *see Bocardo S.A.* v. *S & M Hotels Ltd* (1979).

14. Unreasonable withholding of consent. The following are examples of an unreasonable withholding of consent to an assignment or sub-letting. They apply to both the statutory and express proviso.

Parker v. *Boggan* (1947). L withheld consent because the proposed assignee had diplomatic immunity against legal proceedings.

Bates v. *Donaldson* (1896). L withheld his consent because he wanted to gain possession for himself.

Houlder Bros. v. *Gibbs* (1925). L withheld consent because the proposed assignee already held premises from L and if the assignment went through, the assignee would give up those premises which would then prove difficult to re-let.

Bromley Park Garden Estates Ltd v. *Moss* (1982). L withheld consent so as to obtain a surrender of the lease and another lease in the same building.

International Drilling Fluids Ltd v. *Louisville Investments (Uxbridge) Ltd* (1986). L withheld consent on the ground that the proposed user (which was permitted under the lease) would diminish the value of the landlord's reversionary interest. L did not propose to realise the reversion during the term and had failed to consider the disproportionate detriment which T would suffer if consent was refused as opposed to the minimal loss which L would suffer through diminution in the paper value of his reversion.

NOTE: By virtue of the Race Relations Act 1965, s. 5(1), where consent is withheld on the ground of colour, race or ethnic or national origins, it is deemed to be unreasonably withheld. This does not apply to a tenancy of part of a dwelling-house of which the remainder, or part of the remainder is occupied by the person whose licence or consent is required and if the tenant is entitled in common with that person to the use of any accommodation other than the means of access.

15. Reasonable withholding of consent. The following are examples of a reasonable withholding of consent.

Pimms Ltd v. *Tallow Chandlers Company* (1964). L withheld his consent because the assignee wished to profit from redevelopment plans by means of the nuisance value of the remainder of the lease.

Bridewell Hospital (Governors) v. *Faulkner and Rogers* (1892). L withheld his consent because other property owned by him would be injured by the use to which the proposed assignee wished to put the demised premises.

16. Reasonableness and statutory protection. There are many cases which deal with the difficult question whether a landlord may reasonably refuse his consent to an assignment on the grounds that an assignee will gain a statutory protection that the assignor did not enjoy. The cases fall into two broad groups. First, there is a line of cases which concern the Rent Act. In these it was held that the landlord acted reasonably in refusing his consent to an 'abnormal' assignment. By this is meant an assignment, usually at or near the end of the lease, designed to gain for the assignee some protection under the Rent Act which the assignor did not have. The cases in this group include:

Lee v. *K. Carter Ltd* (1949). The assignor was a company which could not enjoy full Rent Act protection. The assignee was a director of the company who could enjoy that protection. HELD: The landlord could reasonably withhold his consent to the assignment where the term has only a short time to run.

Swanson v. *Forton* (1949). The assignor was not actually occupying the premises and sought to assign the lease to someone who would occupy them and thereby gain the protection of the Rent Act. HELD: The landlord could reasonably withhold his consent as the term only had a short time to run and the assignee would gain a protection the assignor did not enjoy.

It was thought as a result of these cases that there was a general principle that a landlord could reasonably refuse his consent to an abnormal assignment but not to one which was otherwise normal. Doubt has now been cast on there being such a general principle by the second line of cases. These are two recent decisions of the Court of Appeal.

Norfolk Capital Ltd v. *Kitway* and *Bickel* v. *Duke of Westminster* (1976). The landlords in these cases refused their consent to assignments by tenants who would not be entitled to the benefit of the Leasehold Reform Act 1967 to assignees who would be so entitled. The assignments were otherwise perfectly normal and were not devised in order to secure the statutory protection. HELD by the Court of Appeal: the landlords acted reasonably in refusing their consent because the assignments would adversely affect the value of the landlords' interest and it could not therefore be said that they were being unreasonable in refusing their consent.

Following the two above cases it is doubtful whether there is any doctrine of normal and abnormal assignments left even in Rent Act cases. This appears from:

West Layton Ltd v. *Ford* (1979). L let to T a butcher's shop with residential accommodation above. T covenanted not to let the living accommodation except as a furnished tenancy for which L's consent was not to be unreasonably withheld. At the time the lease was granted a furnished tenant had no security of tenure. In 1977 when a furnished tenant had Rent Act protection T wished to let the living accommodation separately to sub-tenants who would have full Rent Act protection. L refused to give his consent and T sought a declaration that this was unreasonable. HELD by the Court of Appeal: it was not unreasonable for L to refuse his consent as the effect of the sub-letting would be to alter the nature of the property from a commercial property to a property let on multiple occupancy of a shop and separate residential accommodation, and this was not the purpose of the covenant.

17. Applications to the court for a declaration that consent has been unreasonably withheld. As has already been noted (*see* **13**(*c*)) a tenant may apply to the court for a declaration that consent has been unreasonably withheld. If the court makes such a declaration the tenant may assign his lease. On such an application, the burden of proof is on the tenant to show that consent has been unreasonably withheld: *Shanly* v. *Ward* (1913).

By virtue of the Landlord and Tenant Act 1954, s. 53(1), the county court has jurisdiction to make a declaration that consent has been unreasonably withheld. The county court has jurisdiction irrespective of the rateable value of the demised premises. The High Court also has jurisdiction, but the county court will normally be a quicker and cheaper forum.

18. Building leases. Where a lease is granted for more than 40 years and is made in consideration of the erection of buildings (i.e. is a building lease), if it contains a qualified covenant against assigning etc., the following special provision applies. The Landlord and Tenant Act 1927, s. 19(1)(*b*) provides that in such a lease, there is implied a proviso that no consent is required to an assignment made more than seven years before the end of the term provided written notice is given to the landlord within six months after the assignment. This is therefore a special case where no consent is required. It does not apply, how-ever, where the landlord is a public or statutory authority. The value of s. 19(1)(*b*) as a statutory rule today is doubtful.

19. Landlord and Tenant Act 1988. A landlord who receives a writ-ten application for consent to an assignment or sub-letting under a qualified covenant is under a statutory duty to deal with the matter within a reasonable time. He must respond in writing and give rea-sons for his refusal; if a conditional consent is given the conditions must be given in writing. Failure to comply with the duty will give rise to an action for damages for breach of statutory duty. Further, under this Act if the landlord unreasonably withholds his consent, the tenant will be entitled to damages. This Act is therefore of great practical importance.

Effect of assignment on covenants and their enforceability

20. Introduction. It is now necessary to consider the extent to which an assignee of either the lease or the reversion is bound by the cove-nants contained in the lease. This subject is dealt with in the following way:

(a) enforceability generally (*see* **21**);
(b) between the original parties (*see* **22–23**);
(c) against and by an assignee of the lease (*see* **24–25**);
(d) against and by an assignee of the reversion (*see* **26–27**);
(e) liability between assignor and assignee of the lease (*see* **28**);
(f) underlessees (*see* **29–30**).

21. The enforceability of covenants generally. Between the origi-nal landlord and the original tenant, there is what is called 'privity of contract'; what is meant is simply that there is a contractual relation-ship between them. So long as the lease and the reversion upon it are vested in the original parties, there is also another relationship be-tween them, 'privity of estate'. This subsists so long as they own their respective interests. If the landlord sells his reversion or the tenant sells his lease there is no longer privity of estate between them. There is then privity of estate between the new landlord and the old tenant or between the old landlord and the new tenant. There is, however, no privity of contract between these parties for there is, of course, no contract between them. It can be seen therefore that the original landlord and tenant are in a special position, and the enforceability of covenants between them is therefore considered separately before considering the position of assignees.

22. Enforceability of covenants between the original parties. As has already been said, privity of estate lasts only as long as the reversion and the lease remain vested in the original parties. When the privity of estate ceases, either because the reversion or the lease has been assigned, there continues to be privity of contract between the original parties. Privity of contract continues between them until the lease ends. It means that the original tenant continues to be liable to the original landlord on the covenants in the lease even though he no longer holds the lease. In the absence of an express term to that effect, the liability of the original tenant will not continue beyond the contractual term during any period of statutory continuation under, for example, Part II of the Landlord and Tenant Act 1954: *see City of London Corpn* v. *Fell* (1993).

Example

L lets land to T who covenants to repair the property. T assigns his interest to A who fails to repair the property. L may sue both A and T: he may sue A because there is privity of estate between them; he may sue T because there is privity of contract between them because of the original contract whereby L let the land to T.

Consequently an original tenant must be wary about any person to whom he assigns his interest for if he assigns it to a person who proves to be an irresponsible tenant, the original tenant may find himself bearing the responsibility for the assignee's breaches of covenant. Normally the landlord will pursue his remedies against the assignee of the lease (with whom he has privity of estate) rather than suing the original tenant. If, however, the assignee has no assets the landlord may prefer to sue the original tenant.

23. Exceptions. There are only two exceptions to the rule concerning the liability of the original tenant. They are:

(a) where the original landlord and tenant agree that the tenant shall not be liable:
(b) where there is an assignment of a perpetually renewable lease (*see* 3: **24**).

24. The enforceability of covenants against and by an assignee. The problem to be considered here is as follows. Suppose a tenant assigns his lease to an assignee, can the landlord enforce the tenant's covenants against the assignee? Can the assignee enforce the landlord's covenants against the landlord? The rule is that if the relevant covenant 'touches and concerns' the land, it runs with the land and is enforceable by or against an assignee of the lease: *Spencer's Case* (1583).

Example
_____
L lets land to T who assigns his lease to A. Whether A can sue or be sued on the covenants in T's lease will depend on whether the relevant covenant touches and concerns the land.
_____

The assignee's liability depends upon there being privity of estate between him and the landlord. This means that if the assignee should assign his interest his liability will cease, unless he has entered into a separate agreement with the landlord.

It is often the practice on an assignment for the assignee to enter into a direct agreement with the landlord that he will observe the covenants, the object being that there should be privity of contract between the assignee and the landlord. On account of this privity the assignee will remain liable to the landlord on the covenants in the lease even if he should further assign the lease and thus cease to be in privity of estate with the landlord.

25. Covenants which touch and concern the land. The best way to understand what constitutes a covenant which touches and concerns the land is to consider some examples.

The following are covenants which touch and concern the land:

(a) by the landlord:
    (*i*) for quiet enjoyment (*Spencer's Case* (1583));
    (*ii*) to repair (*ibid.*);
    (*iii*) to renew the lease (*Muller* v. *Trafford* (1901));
(b) by the tenant:
    (*i*) to pay rent (*Parker* v. *Webb* (1693));
    (*ii*) to repair (*Martyn* v. *Clue* (1852));
    (*iii*) not to assign without consent (*Goldstein* v. *Sanders* (1915));
    (*iv*) to insure (*Vernon* v. *Smith* (1821));
    (*v*) to use the premises for a specific purpose (*Wilkinson* v. *Rogers* (1863));
(c) by a surety:

A covenant by a surety guaranteeing performance of the tenant's covenants does touch and concern the land (*Kumar* v. *Dunning* (1987); *P & A Swift Investment* v. *Combined English Stores Group Plc* (1988)). Also, a covenant by a surety to accept a lease replacing the lease granted to the tenant if the tenant became insolvent and his lease was disclaimed runs with the land: *Coronation Street Industrial Properties Ltd* v. *Ingall Industries plc* (1989).

The following are covenants which do not touch and concern the land:

(a) by the landlord:
    (*i*) a covenant that the tenant shall have an option to buy land other than the demised premises (*Collinson* v. *Lettsom* (1815));
    (*ii*) to keep in repair other land (*Dewar* v. *Goodman* (1908));
    (*iii*) permitting the tenant to display advertisements on other land (*Re No. 1 Albermarle Street* (1959));
    (*iv*) to repay a deposit which was paid by the tenant to the landlord and returnable at the end of the term if the tenant's covenants were observed (*Hua Chiao Commercial Bank Ltd* v. *Chiaphua Industries Ltd* (1987)).

(b) by the tenant:
    (*i*) to pay rates in respect of other land (*Gower* v. *Postmaster General* (1887));
    (*ii*) not to employ men from other parishes (*Congleton Corporation* v. *Pattison* (1808)).

26. The enforceability of covenants by and against an assignee of the reversion. The question here is, if the landlord assigns his reversion, can the new landlord enforce the tenant's covenants against the tenant? Similarly, can the tenant enforce the landlord's covenants against the new landlord? The rule is that an assignee of the reversion can sue or be sued upon the covenants in the lease which have 'reference to the subject-matter of the lease'. This rule is contained in the Law of Property Act 1925, ss. 141 (benefit of tenant's covenants) and 142 (burden of landlord's covenants). The words 'reference to. . . .' have the same meaning as the words 'touch and concern'. Accordingly, the cases in **25** above can be used to illustrate what this rule applies to. The rules which govern the situation described in this paragraph are entirely statutory and derive originally from the Grantees of Reversions Act 1540.

27. The position after an assignment of the reversion. Where the reversion is assigned, the Law of Property Act 1925, s. 141 provides that the assignee acquires all 'the benefit' of the tenant's covenants. The courts have held that the effect of this is that after an assignment the assignee alone is entitled to sue the tenant for breaches of a covenant in the lease, whether the breaches occurred before or after the assignment.

Re King (1963). In 1895 T let to B a factory for 80 years at £100 per year. B covenanted to keep the premises in repair. In 1908 the lease vested in K. In the 1950s the freehold interest of T was compulsorily acquired by the LCC and the sale was completed in 1960. After completion the question arose who was entitled to sue K for breaches of covenant occurring before the assignment, i.e. was it T or the LCC? HELD by the Court of Appeal: under s. 141, the rights of the assignor to sue the lessee for breaches occurring before the assignment passed on the assignment to the assignee as part of 'the benefit' of every covenant under s. 141. This meant that the LCC had the right to sue for breaches of the repairing covenants.

Arlesford Trading Co. Ltd v. *Servansingh* (1971). L let land to T who failed to pay rent. T assigned the lease to A. Later, L assigned the reversion to R. Accordingly there was never any privity of either contract or estate between R and T. R sued T for the rent which he had failed to pay. HELD: R could sue T for the rent by virtue of the Law of Property Act 1925, s. 141, even though there had never been privity between them. The right to sue for this rent was one of the 'benefits' which passed to R under s. 141. T was liable as original tenant (*see* **22**).

28. Liability between tenant and assignee. When the lease is assigned to an assignee, he becomes responsible for the performance of the covenants and for the payment of the rent. However the assignor remains liable to the landlord for breaches of covenant which he committed while a tenant. It has already been seen that the original tenant continues to be liable contractually for the performance of the covenants and the payment of the rent. As between the tenant and the assignee, it is the assignee who is primarily liable. In order to protect the original tenant, there is implied by statute in every conveyance after 1925 of the interest created by a lease, a covenant by the assignee that he will pay all the rent and perform the covenants in the lease and indemnify the assignor against any proceedings costs and claims arising from any omission to pay the rent or any breach of the covenants: Law of Property Act 1925, s. 77. Frequently the deed of assignment contains an express covenant of indemnity.

The original tenant is also entitled, at common law, to an indemnity from the assignee responsible for any breach. This indemnity arises from general principles of the law of restitution or quasi-contract. Thus in most cases where an assignee fails to observe a covenant and the original tenant is sued by the landlord, he can recover from the assignee what he had been compelled to pay (*a*) on any express covenant, or (*b*) on the statutorily implied covenant, or (*c*) under the rules of quasi-contract.

29. The enforceability of covenants against and by an underlessee. Until now this chapter has been concerned with the enforcement of covenants by or against assignees of the lease or the reversion. It is now necessary to consider this question in relation to an underlessee. The position is more straight forward. Suppose L grants a lease to T who grants a sub-lease to S. The position is as follows:

(a) between L and T there is privity of contract and of estate;
(b) between T and S there is privity of contract and of estate;
(c) between L and S there is neither relationship.

This means that the covenants in S's sub-lease are enforceable only between T and S. If therefore S should commit a breach of covenant, only T can sue S; L cannot sue S. L could in many cases sue T since S's breach of covenant would probably be a breach of the terms of T's lease.

30. Exceptions. There are only two exceptions to the above rule. First, where there is an express contract between the sub-tenant (S) and the head landlord (L), L can sue S. This may arise where L only allows the sub-letting on condition that S enters into a direct contract with him. The second exception is where the head lease contains a covenant restricting user. The covenant may then be enforceable against the sub-tenant by virtue of the general principles of restrictive covenants: *see Tulk* v. *Moxhay* (1848).

31. Effect of assignment of lease on landlord. By analogy with the rule that a tenant's liability for breach of covenant committed before an assignment survives the assignment (*see* **28**), a landlord's liability to the tenant for breach of covenant also survives the assignment of the lease: *see City and Metropolitan Properties Ltd* v. *Greycroft* (1987).

32. Example. The foregoing paragraphs deal with a number of difficult principles. The following example is intended to illustrate all the principles.

Example
_____
L lets land to T who assigns to A who then assigns to B who sub-lets to S. S commits a breach of covenant. The position is as follows:

(a) S is liable to B by privity of estate and of contract (*see* **29**);

(b) S is not liable to L unless there is a direct contract between them or the breach relates to a restrictive covenant and S is liable under the general principles of restrictive covenants:

(c) B is liable to L by privity of estate or by a direct contract if there is one;

(d) A is not liable to L unless there is a direct contract between them (*see* **24**);

(e) T is liable to L by privity of contract (*see* **22**);

(f) T is entitled to an indemnity from A by reason of the Law of Property Act 1925, s. 77 (*see* **28**);

(g) T is entitled to an indemnity from B at common law (*see* **28**);

(h) A is entitled to an indemnity from B by reason of the Law of Property Act 1925, s. 77 (*see* **28**);

(i) A remains liable to L for any breach of covenant committed by A before the assignment to B notwithstanding the assignment (*see* **28**);

(j) L remains liable to A for any breach of covenant committed by L while A was tenant notwithstanding the assignment (*see* **30**).

Devolution of leases

33. Introduction. It is now necessary to consider a matter associated with the question of assignment. It concerns the way in which a lease passes or 'devolves' upon the happening of the following events:

(a) the death of the tenant (*see* **34**);

(b) the bankruptcy of the tenant (*see* **35**).

34. Devolution on death of tenant. Where a tenant dies, the lease vests in his personal representatives: Administration of Estates Act 1925, s. 1. In the case of a tenant who dies leaving a will, the vesting takes place at the time of the testator's death by operation of law. In the case of a tenant who dies intestate, the administrator derives title only from the moment that the court grants letters of administration; until then the lease vests in the probate judge: Administration of Estates Act 1925, s. 9. The personal representatives then hold the lease and will be responsible for the payment of rent and the performance of the covenants. Their liability is limited, however, to the extent of their estate.

35. Bankruptcy of the tenant. The lease vests in the trustee on his appointment or, in the case of the official receiver, on his becoming trustee: Insolvency Act 1986, s. 306. The trustee may disclaim the lease if it is an onerous property: s. 315. This is done by giving the prescribed notice and serving a copy of the disclaimer on every person claiming under the bankrupt as undertenant or mortgagee; those persons may then apply, within a prescribed period, for a vesting order and the disclaimer does not take effect until either no application is made or, if an application is made, the court directs that the disclaimer is to take effect: ss. 317 and 320. In the case of a dwelling-house a copy of the disclaimer must be served on every person in occupation of, or claiming a right to occupy, the dwelling who may apply for a vesting order.

NOTE: By virtue of s. 283(3A) of the Insolvency Act 1986-(added by the Housing Act 1988) there is excluded from the bankrupt's estate (*i*) an assured tenancy the terms of which inhibit assignment, (*ii*) a protected tenancy for which no premium can be lawfully required on assignment, (*iii*) a tenancy protected by the Rent (Agriculture) Act 1976 whose terms inhibit assignment and (*iv*) a secure tenancy which is not capable of assignment. However, the trustee can give notice vesting such a tenancy in himself.

Progress test 6

1. How do you distinguish between an assignment and a sub-letting **(4)**

2. L lets property to T for seven years from 1st January 1980. T purports to sub-let the property to S for five years from 1st January 1984. What is the effect of the transaction? **(4)**

3. What formalities are required on the making of an assignment? **(3)**

4. What is the effect of a covenant by the tenant against:
   (a) sub-letting and assigning;
   (b) assigning;
   (c) parting with possession? **(12, 13)**

5. What is the difference between a qualified and an absolute covenant against alienation? **(10)**

6. What is the effect on a qualified covenant of
   (a) s. 144 of the Law of Property Act 1925, and
   (b) s. 19(1) of the Landlord and Tenant Act 1927? **(7)**

7. L grants to T a lease of premises on terms that T should not assign or sublet without the consent of L. T assigns the lease to A without seeking L's consent. Advise L. **(7)**

8. Give examples of the grounds on which a landlord may
(a) reasonably, and
(b) unreasonably, withhold his consent to an assignment. **(14, 15)**

9. L grants to T Ltd a lease of Rent Act protected property for ten years. The lease prohibits assigning or sub-letting without consent. At the end of the term T Ltd wishes to assign the lease to A who is a director of T Ltd. Advise L. **(16)**

10. Explain the difference between 'privity of estate' and 'privity of contract'. **(21)**

11. 'An original tenant is always liable on the covenants in a lease.' What are the exceptions to this rule? **(23)**

12. L lets land to T who assigns the lease to A. Advise L which of the following covenants he can enforce against A:
(a) repairing;
(b) insurance;
(c) option to buy other land. **(25)**

13. What is the effect of the Law of Property Act 1925, s. 141 on the assignment of the reversion of a lease? **(26)**

14. L lets land to T who assigns the lease to A. At the end of the lease, the property is in disrepair and L sues T for damages. Advise T. **(28)**

15. L lets land to T who sub-lets a part to S. What remedies does L have against S if he is in breach of covenant? **(29, 30)**

16. What happens to a lease on
(a) the death, and
(b) the bankruptcy of a tenant? **(33–35)**

7

Termination of tenancies

Introduction

1. The different methods of termination. The main ways in which a tenancy may be ended are as follows:

(a) effluxion of time (*see* **2**);
(b) under a power (*see* **3**);
(c) operation of a condition subsequent (*see* **4**);
(d) merger (*see* **5–7**);
(e) surrender (*see* **8–11**);
(f) notice to quit (*see* **12–20**);
(g) disclaimer (*see* **21–22**);
(h) forfeiture (*see* **23**);
(i) frustration (*see* **24**).

Effluxion of time

2. Generally. This only applies to a tenancy for a fixed term. At common law the tenancy will end on the expiry of the term and the landlord will then be entitled to possession. In practice the landlord's right to possession has been restricted by the modern legislation which operates to continue certain types of tenancy beyond the expiry of the term. For example, in the case of a tenancy of business premises the term is continued by statute until it is determined in accordance with any of the specified methods of termination (*see* the Landlord and Tenant Act 1954, Part II).

Under a power

3. Generally. A tenancy may contain a term enabling either party to end the tenancy at a particular time or on the happening of a particular event. This is often called a 'break clause' and is normally found in tenancies for a fixed term.

Examples

(1) L lets land to T for a term of 14 years with a term enabling T to end the tenancy by notice at the end of the seventh year.

(2) L lets land to T for a term of 14 years with a term enabling L to end the tenancy by six months' notice given at any time in the event of his intending to demolish the buildings on the land and to rebuild.

In order to exercise a break clause a party must comply strictly with the conditions attached to it. So, in the first example, the tenant can only end the tenancy at the end of the seventh year – no earlier and no later. In the second example, L must show that he actually intends to demolish and to rebuild. It is usual to provide that notice of determination should be given within a certain period. In such a case time will be of the essence. Of course, a power of determination may be vested in a tenant as well as a landlord.

Condition subsequent

4. Operation. The duration of a tenancy may be limited by a condition, in which case the tenancy will continue until the condition is satisfied. The following is a common example:

An employer provides his employee with accommodation subject to the condition that the employee's tenancy shall determine on the termination of his employment. When the employment ends the condition is fulfilled and the tenancy will determine.

Merger

5. Definition. When a tenancy and the reversion immediately expectant on it are held by the same person in the same capacity, the term is said to merge with the reversion. The effect of merger is that the term and the reversion become one. It is essential that the same person holds the two interests in the same capacity. If, for example, he held one as a trustee and the other in his own right, the two interests could not merge.

6. Effect of a merger on sub-tenancies. At common law the merger of a term of years and the reversion destroyed the covenants in any sub-tenancy. It is now provided by the Law of Property Act 1925, s. 139, that where a reversion expectant on a lease is merged, the reversioner becomes the immediate reversioner on any sub-tenancies and is entitled to the benefit of (and must bear the burden of) the sub-tenant's covenants.

Example

L grants a lease of land to T who sub-lets to S. X, a third party, buys the interests of both L and T. At common law the sub-lease to S would be of no effect because of the merger of L's and T's interests which amounts to the termination of T's lease. The effect of s. 139 is that X would become S's landlord and would be entitled to enforce S's covenants against S. Similarly S would be entitled to enforce T's covenants against X.

---

7. Retention of reversion. Where a merger occurs it is sometimes convenient to keep the reversion and the lease in being notwithstanding that they are vested in the same person in the same capacity. It is possible to achieve this in two ways. One is by including a declaration against merger in the appropriate instrument, e.g. in the example in the last paragraph the transfer to X might contain an express statement that no merger was intended. The other method is by the operation of the doctrine of equity that merger will not be taken to have occurred where it would be against the interests of the parties involved for there to be a merger.

At common law, merger was automatic; the equitable doctrine set out above now prevails by express statutory provision: Law of Property Act 1925, s. 185.

Surrender

8. Generally. Surrender takes place where the tenant gives up his interest to his landlord and is therefore akin to merger. A surrender may be either:

(a) an express surrender; or

(b) a surrender by operation of law.

9. Express surrender An express surrender takes place where the parties expressly agree to the making of a surrender. The following formalities must be complied with:

(a) if the lease is for a period not exceeding three years and is at the best rent which can reasonably be obtained without taking a fine, the surrender may be made in writing signed by the surrenderor: Law of Property Act 1925, ss. 53(1), 54(2).

(b) if the lease is for a period exceeding three years, the surrender must be by deed: Law of Property Act 1925, s. 52.

A formal deed of surrender is usual.

10 Surrender by operation of law. In certain cases the conduct of the parties is such that the law implies a surrender. This is called a surrender by operation of law, and is also sometimes called an implied surrender. It occurs where the conduct of the parties is inconsistent with the continued existence of the old lease. The following cases illustrate this form of surrender.

Lyon v. *Reed* (1844). L granted to T a new lease that was to begin before T's old lease expired. The old lease was therefore impliedly surrendered. T was bound by the terms of the new lease.

Wallis v. *Hands* (1893). L granted a lease to T. Later, during the currency of T's lease, L granted a new lease to X. T consented to this and gave up possession to X. T's old lease was impliedly surrendered.

Cannan v. *Hartley* (1850). L granted to T a lease. During the currency of the lease T gave up possession to L who unequivocally accepted it. T's lease was impliedly surrendered.

The last case illustrates one of the more common forms of surrender by operation of law. It may sometimes be a difficult question whether the tenant has actually given up possession to the landlord. There is a sufficient giving up if the tenant gives up the keys and the landlord accepts them with the intention of ending the tenancy. In contrast, if the landlord simply enters the premises to carry out essential repairs, or the tenant simply abandons the premises, there will be no surrender by operation of law until the landlord does some act whereby he treats the tenancy as at an end.

The essential components of a surrender by operation of law are

(a) the actual giving up of possession to the landlord; and
(b) an intention on the part of both parties that the tenancy shall be brought to an end.

Sometimes the parties prefer to end the lease by an implied surrender rather than by an express surrender, e.g. to save stamp duties.

11. The effect of surrender on sub-tenancies. The surrender of a tenancy does not affect any sub-tenancies created out of that tenancy. On surrender, by virtue of the Law of Property Act 1925, s. 139, the head-landlord becomes the reversioner to any sub-tenant as in the example in **6** above.

Notice to quit

12. Introduction. A periodic tenancy can be determined by the service of a notice to quit. The notice may be served by either the landlord or the tenant. In the absence of an express term in the lease, the period of notice required is determined by the rules at common law. If the parties make an express agreement as to the manner of giving notice, the notice is governed by that agreement. It is not, however, open to either party to deprive himself permanently of his right to serve a notice to quit.

> *Centaploy* v. *Matlodge Ltd* (1973). L granted to T a weekly tenancy which was 'to continue until determined by T'. The question arose whether this provision deprived L of the right to determine the tenancy. HELD: The tenancy could be determined by L serving notice to quit notwithstanding the words of the agreement because to hold that L had no such right was repugnant to the nature of the tenancy granted. *Per* Whitford J: 'It must be basic to a tenancy that at some stage the person granting the tenancy shall have the right to determine it and a tenancy in which the landlord is never going to have the right to determine at all . . . is a complete contradiction in terms.'

> *Prudential Assurance Co. Ltd* v. *London Residuary Body* (1992) where a tenant entered land under an agreement which was to continue until the land was required for road widening this was of uncertain duration and did not create a lease. As the tenant had entered the land and paid a yearly rent he became a yearly tenant. However the right to terminate was not fettered by the requirement for road-widening provision because a power for nobody to determine or for one party only to be able to determine is inconsistent with the concept of a term from year to year.

13. Period of notice. If the parties have not made any express agreement, the periods of notice required to determine a periodic tenancy are as follows:

(a) a yearly or greater tenancy – six months' notice;
(b) a quarterly tenancy – one quarter's notice;
(c) a monthly tenancy – one month's notice;

(d) a weekly tenancy – one week's notice.

It can be seen that, except in the case of yearly tenancies, the period of notice must equal the period of the tenancy.

14. Residential tenancies. The rule described above has been modified in the case of residential tenancies. The Protection from Eviction Act 1977, s. 5 (re-enacting part of the Rent Act 1957) requires a minimum of four weeks' notice to determine a periodic residential tenancy. This means that **13(d)** above is modified in the case of residential tenancies.

> NOTE: The operation of s. 5 of the Protection from Eviction Act 1977 has been extended to certain periodic licences to occupy premises as a dwelling; *see* s. 5(1A), added by s. 32 of the Housing Act 1988.

15. Agricultural holdings. The rules described above have also been modified in the case of tenancies of agricultural holdings. In summary, a year's notice expiring at the end of the current year of the tenancy is required to determine a tenancy of an agricultural holding: *see* Chapter 30.

16. Business tenancies. A notice determining a tenancy of business premises must be at least six months in duration: *see* Chapter 11.

17. Expiration of notice to quit. The notice to quit must not only satisfy the requirements relating to the period of the notice, but it must also expire at the end of a period of the tenancy. If this requirement is not satisfied the notice will be bad. If, for example, a yearly tenancy began on 1st January, its period ends each year on 31st December. Strictly speaking therefore, the notice to quit must take effect on 31st December. The courts have construed the end of the period of the tenancy to include the anniversary of the commencement of the tenancy: *see Sidebotham* v. *Holland* (1895). The result is that, in the example above, a notice to quit would be effective if it took effect on either 1st January or 31st December.

It is often difficult to ascertain when a tenancy began, and accordingly it is often difficult to know when the notice to quit should take effect. To avoid the danger of an error like this invalidating the notice to quit, it is the practice in drafting such a notice:

(a) to specify as the date on which the notice will expire the date on which it is believed the tenancy expires; and
(b) to add general words of the following sort 'or at the end of the

(year or other period) of the tenancy which will expire next after the end of (one half-year or other period required to determine the tenancy) from the date of the service of this notice'.

By doing this an error as to the specific date given under (a) should not invalidate the notice because the general words should provide a date which will be the anniversary of the tenancy: *Addis* v. *Burrows* (1948).

18. Form of the notice to quit. A notice to quit must satisfy the following requirements:

(a) it must be clear and unambiguous;

(b) it need not be in any specific form unless this is required by the terms of the tenancy or the provisions of a statute. In theory, a notice may be given orally, although this would be inadvisable because of the evidential problems it would cause;

(c) it must relate to the whole of the land let under the tenancy; notice to quit part only of the land is void unless there is a provision to that effect in the agreement.

NOTE: The Protection from Eviction Act 1977, s. 5, requires that a notice to quit in respect of any premises let as a dwelling must be in writing and contain certain prescribed information. This information is designed to tell the tenant what his rights are under the Rent Act. This is now extended to certain periodic licences: *see* the note to **14** above.

19. Service of notice to quit. The following points must be noted with regard to service:

(a) The notice to quit must be given by the landlord to his immediate tenant or by the tenant to his immediate landlord. In the case of a joint tenancy held by two or more joint tenants, it may be determined by a notice to quit given by one of the joint tenants without the concurrence of any of the other joint tenants unless the terms of the tenancy provide otherwise: *Hammersmith and Fulham London Borough Council* v. *Monk* (1992).

(b) The notice may be given in any of the following ways:

(*i*) by ordinary post;

(*ii*) by registered or recorded delivery post;

(*iii*) by or on an authorised agent;

(*iv*) by personal service; or

(*v*) by any other means prescribed by the lease.

NOTE: In the case of notices required to be served by any instrument affecting property, s. 196 of the Law of Property Act 1925 prescribes certain methods of service which if used in compliance with the section constitute sufficient service. These methods are (*i*) service at the tenant's last known place of abode or business in the UK, (*ii*) affixing or leaving the notice on the land or building in the lease and (*iii*) sending by post in a registered or recorded delivery letter addressed to the tenant at the last known place of abode or business.

20. Conduct subsequent to the notice to quit. It is often the case that something done (notably the acceptance of rent by the landlord) after the service of notice to quit amounts to the grant of a new tenancy. This gives rise to difficult questions and the following points should be noted.

(a) Whether a new tenancy has been granted will depend on whether there was an intention to create a new tenancy.

(b) The payment and acceptance of rent will only create a new tenancy if it is shown that there was a common intention to create a new tenancy: *Doe d. Cheney* v. *Batten* (1775): *Clarke* v. *Grant* (1949). So if the landlord accepts rent 'without prejudice' to his rights under a notice to quit there can be no intention to create a new tenancy.

(c) The court will not imply an intention to create a new tenancy simply because a tenant protected in his occupation by statute continues to occupy the demised premises and makes payment for his occupation; such a tenant's occupation is attributable to his statutory right and not to the creation of a new tenancy: *Marcroft Wagons Ltd* v. *Smith* (1951) (*see* 3: **13**).

The process just described is sometimes called 'waiver' of the notice to quit. This term is inaccurate since the notice to quit has full effect to end the tenancy; the acceptance of rent creates a new tenancy by implication.

Disclaimer

21. Introduction. In certain cases a lease may be disclaimed by the person in whom it is vested:

(a) where a lease is vested in a bankrupt, his trustee in bankruptcy may disclaim it under the Insolvency Act 1986, s. 315;

(b) where a lease is vested in a company which is being wound up, the liquidator may disclaim it under the Insolvency Act 1986, s. 178.

The trustee or liquidator will generally wish to disclaim the lease if he cannot assign it for value or put it to some beneficial use.

22. The effect of disclaimer. There are various cases on earlier provisions concerning the effect of disclaimer, which would appear still to be relevant to the new provisions in the 1986 Act. In order to consider the effect of disclaimer it is necessary to distinguish between two situations:

(a) where the disclaimed lease is still vested in the original tenant; and
(b) where the disclaimed lease is vested in an assignee and not in the original tenant.

In the first situation, the disclaimer operates to terminate the lease which ceases to exist: see *Stacey* v. *Hill* (1901). The rights and liabilities of the bankrupt or the company cease to exist. In the second situation, the disclaimer terminates only the rights and liabilities of the assignee, but the original lessee remains liable on the covenants in the lease.

> *Warnford Investments Ltd* v. *Duckworth* (1978). W granted a lease of business premises to D. With W's consent, D later assigned the lease to L Ltd, a company, which went into voluntary liquidation. The liquidator of L disclaimed the lease. W sued D for rent falling due after the date of the disclaimer. HELD: Where a lease has been assigned to a company which goes into liquidation and the liquidator disclaims the lease, leaving the lease without an owner until a vesting order is made in respect of the lease, the disclaimer does not destroy the lease. D remained directly and primarily liable to W for the rent throughout the remainder of the term.

23. Forfeiture. This is dealt with in Chapter 8.

Frustration

24. Introduction. The doctrine of frustration is a part of the general law of contract. Under the doctrine a contract will be discharged and both parties released from further contractual obligations where the circumstances surrounding the contract are radically altered by unforeseen events so that the whole basis of the contract changes, e.g. destruction of the subject-matter of the contract by war, fire, earthquake.

At one time, it was not clear whether the doctrine of frustration applied to leases because a lease created an estate in land which, it was said, endured irrespective of changes in the nature of land. Until 1981 the law was as stated in the following case.

Cricklewood Property and Investment Trust Ltd v. *Leightons Investment Trust Ltd* (1945). The question here was whether a building lease for 99 years was frustrated by war-time building restrictions. The House of Lords HELD: on these facts the lease was not frustrated for the restrictions were of a temporary nature. Lords Russell and Goddard took the view that the doctrine of frustration could not apply to a lease of land. Lords Simon and Wright, however, considered that the doctrine might apply if the alleged frustrating event was more permanent than on these facts and affected the land for the whole term. The fifth law lord expressed no view.

It has now, however, been held by the House of Lords that the doctrine of frustration does, in principle, apply to leases, though the cases in which it can properly be applied are limited.

National Carriers Ltd v. *Panalpina (Northern) Ltd* (1981). A warehouse was let to the tenants for ten years from January 1974. The only vehicular access to the warehouse was by a road which the local authority closed in May 1979 because of the dangerous condition of a nearby derelict building. The period of closure was likely to be 20 months. The landlord sued for arrears of rent and the tenant argued that the lease was frustrated. The House of Lords HELD: the doctrine of frustration was in principle applicable to a lease but on the facts here it did not apply.

Progress test 7

1. What are the various ways in which a lease may come to an end? **(1)**

2. Does the doctrine of frustration apply to leases? **(24)**

3. What is a 'break clause'? How does it operate? **(3)**

4. Why is no notice to quit necessary at the end of a tenancy for a fixed term **(2)**

5. What is the effect of a lease subject to a condition? **(4)**

6. How does the merger of a lease and the reversion expectant on the same affect a sub-tenancy created out of the term? **(6)**

7. What are the two kinds of surrender? What is the difference between them? **(8)**

8. What formalities are necessary for a surrender? **(9)**

9. How does a surrender affect sub-tenants? **(11)**

10. What period of notice is required to end
   (a) a weekly tenancy;
   (b) a yearly tenancy;
   (c) a tenancy for a fixed term? **(13)**

11. Can a landlord deprive himself of the right to serve notice to quit? **(12)**

12. What special requirements apply to notices to quit:
   (a) residential property;
   (b) business property;
   (c) agricultural land? **(14–16)**

13. L grants to T a yearly tenancy running from 1st January 1978. In September 1980 L decides that he wishes to end the tenancy. When is the earliest date on which he can do this? Would your answer be different if the tenancy was
   (a) a weekly tenancy;
   (b) a monthly tenancy; or
   (c) a quarterly tenancy? **(17)**

14. Can notice to quit be given orally? **(18)**

15. What is 'waiver of a notice to quit'? **(20)**

16. What is the effect of a disclaimer of a lease? Who may disclaim a lease? **(21)**

17. L lets property to T on a weekly tenancy. L wishes to end the tenancy. Consider the validity of a notice to quit by L served on:
   (a) T;
   (b) T's wife;
   (c) T's solicitor; and
   (d) T's next door neighbour. **(19)**

18. What is the effect of *Warnford* v. *Duckworth*? **(22)**

8
Forfeiture

Introduction

1. Generally. A lease will normally contain a clause which enables the landlord, in certain specified circumstances, to terminate the lease and to re-enter the demised premises. This is called a forfeiture clause or a proviso for re-entry. The specified circumstances will normally be where the tenant is in breach of any of his obligations under his tenancy. The clause may, however, be drafted so as to cover other matters, e.g. the bankruptcy of the tenant. If there is no express proviso for re-entry in a lease, the law will *not* imply one. Even if there is no express proviso the landlord may still be able to re-enter if the tenant is in breach of a condition of his tenancy. The law has developed various rules relating to forfeiture and this is therefore a complicated subject. In this chapter the subject is dealt with in the following sequence:

(a) breach of a condition (*see* **2**);
(b) construction of forfeiture clauses (*see* **3**);
(c) their operation (*see* **4**);
(d) re-entry (*see* **5–7**);
(e) the effect of forfeiture (*see* **8–9**);
(f) waiver (*see* **11–14**);
(g) restrictions on forfeiture (*see* **15** *et seq.*)

2. Breach of a condition. If a term of the tenancy is framed as a condition rather than as an ordinary covenant, the landlord is entitled to re-enter the premises if the tenant is in breach of that condition. Whether a clause is a condition is a question of construction of the words used. The distinction between a covenant and a condition is not always clear; the use, however, of words such as 'provided always' or 'upon condition that' will generally, though not always, give rise to a condition.

> *Doe d. Henniker* v. *Watt* (1828). L let land to T. By the lease it was 'stipulated and conditioned' that T should not assign, transfer or underlet any part of the land other than to his immediate family.

HELD: by this clause a condition was created, for the breach of which L might re-enter the land.

Operation of forfeiture clauses

3. Construction of forfeiture clauses. There is a general rule of construction that contractual terms are construed against the party for whose benefit they have been inserted (the *contra proferentem* rule). Applying this rule, the courts construe forfeiture clauses against the landlord and in favour of the tenant. The following cases illustrate this.

> *Doe d. Spencer* v. *Godwin* (1815). A forfeiture clause referred to the covenants 'thereinafter' contained. In fact the covenants were all contained *before* the forfeiture clause. HELD: the forfeiture clause was of no effect.

> *Doe d. Abdy* v. *Stevens* (1832). A forfeiture clause referred to the tenant doing 'any act matter or thing contrary to and in breach of the covenants' in the lease. HELD: this wording did not extend to a breach of a repairing covenant which was an omission and not an act.

4. Operation of a forfeiture clause. A typical clause may be in the following form:

> 'Provided that if the rent hereby reserved or any part thereof is at any time in arrear and unpaid for 21 days after it is due, whether legally demanded or not, or if there shall be any breach of any of the covenants on the part of the tenant contained herein then it shall be lawful for the landlord at any time thereafter to re-enter the demised premises and thereupon the term shall absolutely cease and determine.'

Such a clause operates in the following way. If the tenant commits an act of forfeiture (i.e. if the rent is unpaid and in arrears and unpaid for 21 days or if he is in breach of another covenant), the landlord may elect to do one of two things. He may treat the lease as continuing or he may forfeit it. The tenant's conduct does not therefore end the lease but makes it determinable by the landlord at his option. It is therefore only the landlord who can end the lease on forfeiture; the tenant cannot end it in this way.

5. The landlord's right to forfeit. If the landlord decides to forfeit the lease (rather than allowing the lease to continue) he may enforce his right either by:

(a) actually re-entering on the land (*see* **6**); or
(b) bringing proceedings for possession (*see* **7**).

6. Actual re-entry on the land. This will normally take the form of a re-occupation of the premises or a re-letting of them to another person. There are certain statutory restrictions on this method of enforcing a right of re-entry. As a result this method of re-entry is not often relied on by landlords. The restrictions are:

(a) the Criminal Law Act 1977 (*see* **9: 4**);
(b) the Protection from Eviction Act 1977. Section 2 of this Act provides that where premises are let as a dwelling on a lease containing a right of re-entry it is not lawful to enforce the right otherwise than by proceedings in court while any person is lawfully residing in the premises or any part of them.

7. Bringing proceedings for possession. Currently, the normal method of enforcing a right of re-entry is by issuing proceedings claiming possession of the premises. The writ must contain an unequivocal demand for possession in order to operate as an effective re-entry.

8. When the forfeiture takes effect. It used to be thought that it was the issue of the writ which operated as the landlord's final election to determine the lease. In fact it is the service of the writ upon the tenant which operates as the final election: *Canas Property Co. Ltd* v. *K.L. Television Services Ltd* (1970). This means that from the date of service of the writ the lease is at an end.

9. The effect of forfeiture. When a landlord actually forfeits his tenant's lease by taking either of the steps above, it has the following effect:

(a) the lease comes to an end;
(b) any underlease derived from the lease also ends;
(c) the landlord can only claim rent falling due before the forfeiture took place; thereafter his claim is for mesne profits;
(d) the right of re-entry is no longer capable of being waived (*see* **11**).

> NOTE: Although the lease is at an end, the tenant may enforce the landlord's covenants if he is pursuing an application for relief from forfeiture: *Peninsular Maritime Ltd* v. *Padseal Ltd* (1981).

Waiver of forfeiture

10. Introduction. If, before he has exercised his right of re-entry, the landlord with knowledge of the breach does some act which acknowledges the continuance of the tenancy, he will be taken to have elected not to forfeit the lease. The landlord is said to have waived the forfeiture.

11. Elements of waiver. The elements of waiver are:

(a) the landlord's knowledge of the breach;
(b) an act by the landlord which recognises the continuation of the tenancy prior to the exercise by the landlord of his right to re-enter.

12. Knowledge of the breach. It is a prequisite for waiver that the landlord knows of the breach. The expression 'knowledge' in this context has a wide meaning as is illustrated by the following cases.

Central Estates (Belgravia) Ltd v. *Woolgar* (1972). T committed a breach of covenant. L employed managing agents who instructed their staff to refuse rent from T. The instructions did not reach one of the clerks who sent out a demand for rent to T; he paid the rent and was then sent a receipt by the agents. HELD: there was a waiver of the forfeiture because L, through his agents, knew of the breach and still accepted rent.

David Blackstone Ltd v. *Burnetts (West End) Ltd* (1973). A lease contained a covenant against sub-letting without L's consent. L gave his consent to a proposed sub-letting by T to A and B. In fact T sub-let to a company owned by A and B, i.e. a different person in law to the proposed sub-lessee. T told L's solicitors of this change. Later, while the solicitors were still considering if this change amounted to a breach of covenant, an employee in an associated company of L sent out a rent demand. HELD: L had knowledge of the breach because he knew of it through his solicitors.

13. Examples. The following are examples of acts which, with the appropriate knowledge, amount to waiver:

(a) demanding or accepting rent due after the breach (*David Blackstone Ltd* v. *Burnetts (West End) Ltd* (1973));
(b) distraining for rent (*Green's Case* (1582));
(c) express consent to the breach;
(d) acceptance of rent 'without prejudice' (*Segal Securities Ltd* v. *Thoseby* (1963)).

The following are examples of acts not amounting to waiver:

(a) accepting rent due before the breach (*Green's Case* (1582));
(b) standing by and seeing a breach incurred;
(c) assigning the reversion 'subject to the lease' (*London & County (A. & D.) Ltd* v. *Wilfred Sportman Ltd* (1971)).

Cases where there has been an acceptance of rent, or a demand, have been said to fall into a special category; where no acceptance or demand is involved the court is free to look at all the circumstances of the case to consider whether the act relied upon as amounting to a waiver was so unequivocal that, when considered objectively, it could only be regarded as having been done consistently with the continued existence of the tenancy: *Expert Clothing Service & Sales Ltd* v. *Hillgate House Ltd* (1985).

14. Waiver and different types of breach. A breach may be either a 'continuing' breach or a 'once and for all' breach. A breach of a repairing covenant is an example of a continuing breach for it continues to exist until it is remedied by the execution of the necessary repairs. A breach of the covenant against sub-letting is a once and for all breach because it consists of a single, non-recurring act, i.e. the grant of the sub-lease. If there is a waiver of a once and for all breach, the right to forfeit for that breach is lost forever. In contrast, if there is a waiver of a continuing breach, a fresh right of forfeiture will arise on the day after the waiver because the breach continues from day to day.

Restrictions on forfeiture

15. Introduction. It is now necessary to consider certain rules which restrict the operation of forfeiture clauses. It is said that the law leans against forfeitures: this means simply that the law restricts the landlord's rights under the clause. This is apparent from the way in which the courts construe forfeiture clauses (*see* **3**) and the rules relating to waiver (*see* **11**). It also appears from the restrictions which, in summary, require:

(a) that the landlord satisfy certain pre-conditions;
(b) that the tenant be granted relief from forfeiture in certain cases.

There are different rules relating to forfeiture for non-payment of rent and forfeiture for other breaches of covenant and these matters are therefore considered separately in the following paragraphs.

Forfeiture for non-payment of rent

16. Forfeiture for non-payment of rent. At common law a landlord could only forfeit a lease for non-payment of rent if he had made a formal demand for the rent due. A formal demand must be:

(a) made by the landlord or his authorised agent;
(b) for the exact sum due;
(c) made on the day it falls due; and
(d) made at the demised premises.

If a landlord failed to make a formal demand then he could not forfeit the lease. There therefore grew up a practice of providing in a forfeiture clause a term that the lease could be forfeited for non-payment of rent in arrear for a certain number of days 'whether formally demanded or not'. The effect is that a formal demand is no longer necessary.

Even if a lease contains no words dispensing with the necessity for a formal demand, it may be unnecessary if the Common Law Procedure Act 1852, s. 210, is satisfied. The statute provides that a formal demand is unnecessary where at least six months' rent is in arrears and no sufficient distress is to be found on the demised premises.

17. Relief against forfeiture for non-payment of rent. Originally equity granted relief against forfeiture for non-payment of rent to a tenant who paid all the arrears and any costs. In the main, the position is now governed by statute but the position is somewhat different according to whether the proceedings are in the High Court or the county court.

18. Relief in the High Court. If the landlord brings an action in the High Court for forfeiture on the ground of non-payment of rent, the tenant has the following rights:

(a) In cases where there are at least six months' arrears of rent, the tenant is entitled to an automatic stay of the proceedings if he pays all the arrears of rent and any costs into court or to the landlord before judgment is given: Common Law Procedure Act 1852, s. 212.
(b) If judgment is given in a case to which **(a)** applies, under s. 212 the tenant has the right to apply to the court for relief within six months of the landlord's actual entry under the court order.
(c) In cases to which s. 212 does not apply (i.e. where there is less than six months' rent in arrears or where the landlord re-enters peaceably without proceedings) relief is available under what was formerly the

Judicature Act 1925 s. 46 and is now the Supreme Court Act 1981, s. 38. Relief is available in the same way as it was originally granted by the old courts of equity. This means that relief will normally be granted prior to re-entry by the landlord if the tenant pays all the rent and costs. After re-entry relief will only be granted if that would be just.

19. Relief in the county court. Here the position where the action is for arrears of rent only is governed by the County Courts Act 1984, s. 138, which provides that:

(a) if not less than five clear days before the date fixed for trial the tenant pays into court the arrears and the costs of the action the action will cease;

(b) if the action does not cease under **(a)**, at the trial the court, if satisfied that the landlord is entitled to enforce the right of re-entry, will make an order in the following terms. The form is that the landlord 'shall have possession unless the tenant pays into court all arrears and costs within (a specified time)'. The specified time cannot be less than four weeks from the date of the order. If the tenant then pays the arrears and costs within the specified time he will continue to hold the premises under the lease. Also at any time before the landlord recovers possession, the tenant may apply to court for the period to be extended;

(c) if the order is enforced and the landlord recovers possession then subject only to what is said in **(e)** below neither the county court nor the High Court has jurisdiction to grant relief because s. 138(7) provides that 'the lessee shall be barred from all relief';

(d) where the court extends the period for payment at a time when that period has expired and a warrant has been issued for possession, the court shall suspend the warrant for the extended period and if the tenant pays the arrears within the extended period, the court shall cancel the warrant: s. 138(9);

(e) when the landlord forfeits the lease by actually re-entering, the tenant may apply to the county court for such relief as the High Court could have given provided he applies within six months of re-entry: s. 138(9A), (9B) and (9C);

(f) where the tenancy is protected by the Rent Act 1977 an order for possession will also be required under that Act for an order under s. 138 only serves to end the contractual tenancy;

(g) where a mortgagee failed to apply for relief within the six months mentioned under **(e)** above, it was held that the High Court had no jurisdiction to grant relief: *see United Dominions Trust Ltd* v. *Shellpoint Trustees Ltd* (1993).

Forfeiture for breaches other than non-payment of rent

20. Introduction. Where a tenant commits a breach of covenant other than the non-payment of rent, the landlord's right to forfeit is subject to two restrictions contained in the Law of Property Act 1925, s. 146. They are:

(a) in order to enforce a right to forfeit, the landlord must first serve on the tenant a special form of notice (called a s. 146 notice);
(b) the tenant has the right to apply for relief from forfeiture.

21. Service of a s. 146 notice. The Law of Property Act 1925, s. 146 provides that:

'A right of re-entry or forfeiture under any proviso or stipulation in a lease shall not be enforceable by action or otherwise unless or until the lessor serves on the lessee a notice:

(a) specifying the particular breach complained of; and
(b) if the breach is capable of remedy, requiring the lessee to remedy the breach; and
(c) in any case requiring the lessee to make compensation in money for the breach;

and the lessee fails within a reasonable time thereafter to remedy the breach if it is capable of remedy, and to make reasonable compensation in money to the satisfaction of the lessor for the breach.'

22. Requirements of a valid s. 146 notice. Section 146(1) specifies three requirements. Requirement **(a)** is essential and cannot be omitted. It must make clear to the tenant what it is that the landlord is complaining of so that he will have an opportunity to remedy the breach before any proceedings are started: *Jolly* v. *Brown* (1916). Failure to comply with this requirement will invalidate the notice. Requirement **(b)** need not be included if the breach is incapable of remedy (*see* **24**). Requirement **(c)** need not be included if the landlord does not want compensation in money: *Lock* v. *Pearce* (1893).

23. Effect of service of s. 146 notice. When a valid s. 146 notice has been served the landlord may then start proceedings for forfeiture of the lease. If the tenant is required to remedy the breach then it is normal to require him to do so within a reasonable period, the duration of which will depend upon the circumstances of the case. It is only at the expiration of that period that the proceedings can be started if the tenant has failed to remedy the breach.

24. Breaches incapable of remedy. The following are examples of breaches incapable of remedy:

(a) once and for all breaches (*see* **14**) such as a breach of the covenant against sub-letting: *Scala House & District Property Co. Ltd* v. *Forbes* (1974);

(b) where the breach is of such a nature that it must cast a stigma on the premises, e.g. use for gambling or use as a brothel or for other immoral purposes: *see Rugby School Governors* v. *Tannahill* (1935).

In *Expert Clothing Service and Sales Ltd* v. *Hillgate House Ltd* (1985), it was held that the issue of remediability of breach turned on the question whether the harm that has been done to the landlord by the relevant breach is for practical purposes capable of being remedied; so the court has to consider whether full compliance with the relevant covenant plus payment of any appropriate compensation would have remedied the harm which the landlord has suffered from the breach. It will be appreciated that it may not always be clear if a breach is capable of remedy. In cases of doubt it is therefore safest for a landlord to serve a notice requiring his tenant to remedy the breach adding such words as 'if capable of remedy'.

25. Method of service. A s. 146 notice must be served on the tenant or his duly authorised agent. If there are joint tenants the notice must be served on all of them. Section 196 of the Law of Property Act 1925 applies to service of such a notice; *see* 7: **19**.

26. Relief against forfeiture for breaches of covenant other than non-payment of rent. The Law of Property Act 1925, s. 146(2) makes provision for relief in cases such as this in the following terms:

'Where a lessor is proceeding, by action or otherwise, to enforce such a right of re-entry or forfeiture, the lessee may in the lessor's action, if any, or in any action brought by himself, apply to the court for relief; and the court may grant or refuse relief, as the court, having regard to the proceedings and conduct of the parties under the foregoing provisions of this section, and to all the other circumstances, thinks fit; and in case of relief may grant it on such terms if any, as to costs, expenses, damages, compensation, penalty, or otherwise, including the granting of an injunction to restrain any like breach in the future, as the court, in the circumstances of each case, thinks fit.'

Once a s. 146 notice has been served, a landlord 'is proceeding' and an application for relief can then be made by the tenant: *Pakwood*

Transport Ltd v. *15 Beauchamp Place Ltd* (1978). When a landlord has forfeited by re-entry without first obtaining a court order, the tenant can apply for relief after the landlord has re-entered: see *Billson* v. *Residential Apartments Ltd* (1992).

27. The granting of relief. In granting relief the court considers various factors, including:

(a) the nature of the breach;
(b) whether the breach was serious or deliberate;
(c) whether the tenant is able and willing to remedy the breach.

These factors are not exhaustive. In *Hyman* v. *Rose* (1912), the House of Lords said that strict rules should not be laid down to guide the court in exercising its discretion because it was a matter for the court to consider in each case.

In appropriate circumstances the court may grant relief in respect of part only of the demised premises: *GMS Syndicate Ltd* v. *Gary Elliott Ltd* (1981).

28. The position of sub-tenants. Where a landlord forfeits a lease, the rule at common law is that any sub-tenancies end with the forfeited lease. This could be very unfair because the sub-tenant may not be at fault at all. The harshness of the rule has been mitigated by allowing a sub-tenant to apply for relief as against the person who has forfeited the lease. The relevant provisions are now contained in s. 146(4) of the 1925 Act which provides:

'Where a lessor is proceeding by action or otherwise to enforce a right of re-entry or forfeiture under any covenant, proviso or stipulation in a lease, or for non-payment of rent, the court may, on application by any person claiming as underlessee any estate or interest in the property comprised in the lease or any part thereof, either in the lessor's action (if any) or in any action brought by such person for that purpose, make an order vesting for the whole term of the lease or any less term the property comprised in the lease or any part thereof in any person entitled as underlessee to any estate in such property upon such conditions as to the execution of any deed or other document, payment of rent, costs, expenses, damages, compensation, giving security, or otherwise, as the court in the circumstances of each case may think fit, but in no case shall any such underlessee be entitled to require a lease to be granted to him for any longer term than he had under his original sub-lease.'

NOTE: (1) This provision applies both to forfeiture for non-payment of rent and to forfeiture for other breaches of covenant.

(2) A mortgagee by way of legal charge may apply for relief under s. 146(4) in the same way as if he were a sub-tenant, but see *United Dominions Trust* v. *Shellpoint Trustees Ltd* (1993) noted at **19** above.

29. Illustration. The following example is intended to illustrate the way in which the Law of Property Act 1925, s. 146(4) works.

Example

L lets land to T who sub-lets half to S. T falls behind with his rent and L starts proceedings against T for forfeiture on this ground. T is unable to pay the arrears and L gets judgment against T for possession of the land and the arrears of rent. After judgment is entered against T, S applies to court for relief under s. 146(4). The court will normally grant him relief by ordering that he hold the term of his old sub-lease direct from L and that he enter into a deed with L for this purpose. S may also be ordered, as a condition of relief, to pay a proportion of the arrears due from T to L.

This is the normal practice in cases such as in the example: *see Chatham Empire Theatre Ltd* v. *Ultrans Ltd* (1961), where a sub-tenant was granted relief on terms that he pay a proportion of the arrears due from the intermediate tenant.

30. Sexual Offences Act 1965. Section 35(2) of this Act gives to a landlord a statutory right to determine a lease where the tenant is convicted of knowingly permitting the premises to be used as a brothel. The statutory right only arises if, first, the landlord requests the tenant to assign the lease to some person approved by the landlord and, second, the tenant fails to assign it within three months. If the tenant fails to assign the lease within that period, the landlord can get a summary order from the court for the delivery of possession.

31. Other procedural requirements. Rules of Court now require a landlord bringing forfeiture proceedings to give notice of such proceedings to under-tenants and mortgagees of which he knows and to deal with such notification in his pleading; *see* RSC Ord. 6 r. 2(1)(c)(iii) and CCR Ord. 6 r. 3(1)(f).

Progress test 8

1. What is the effect of the *contra proferentem* rule on forfeiture clauses? **(3)**

2. How may a landlord enforce his right to forfeit the lease? **(5)**

3. What is the effect of the Criminal Law Act 1977 and the Protection from Eviction Act 1977 on forfeiture clauses? **(6)**

4. When does a forfeiture take effect? **(8)**

5. What is the effect of a forfeiture on sub-tenancies? **(9, 28)**

6. How may a breach of covenant be waived? **(11)**

7. What is a s. 146 notice? In what circumstances must it be served? **(20)**

8. How may a tenant apply for relief from forfeiture? **(18, 19, 26)**

9. How do the rules relating to relief from forfeiture for non-payment of rent differ from those relating to forfeiture for other breaches of covenant? **(26)**

10. L lets land to T at a rent of £2000 p.a. There is a forfeiture clause in the lease. T falls into arrears and L brings proceedings in the county court for forfeiture. Advise T. What would the position be if the proceedings were brought in the High Court? **(18, 19)**

11. What must a valid s. 146 notice contain? **(21)**

12. How does the court decide whether or not to grant relief from forfeiture for breaches other than non-payment of rent? **(27)**

9
The parties' rights on termination

Common law rights

1. Generally. This chapter is concerned with the parties' rights at common law at the end of a tenancy. The position has, of course, been changed considerably by statute and these changes are considered later. In summary the landlord's main right is to possession while the tenant's is to remove certain items.

Landlord's rights

2. The landlord's rights. At common law at the end of the tenancy a tenant is bound to give up possession of the demised premises to his landlord. A lease will normally contain an express covenant to that effect; in the absence of such a covenant the law implies a term to that effect. If the tenant failed to give up possession, at common law a landlord could sue for damages. He would be entitled to recover

(a) a sum for use and occupation of the land for the period the tenant withholds possession, and

(b) subject to any question of remoteness of damage, any damages and costs the landlord incurs as a result of the tenant's failure to give possession; e.g. if the landlord had agreed to relet the premises and the new tenant was unable to take possession and suffered loss which he claimed from the landlord.

Recovery of possession

3. Introduction. A landlord may enforce his right to possession by either

(a) actually re-entering the premises provided he can do so without infringing the Criminal Law Act 1977 and the Protection from Eviction Act 1977, or

(b) bringing proceedings for possession.

4. Actual re-entry. A landlord can only enforce his right to possession by re-entering if he does so peaceably. Until 1977 this rule was contained in old statutes – the Statutes of Forcible Entry 1381 to 1623 – which made it a criminal offence for a landlord to take forcible possession of premises. They have now been replaced by the Criminal Law Act 1977. Section 6 provides that any person who, without lawful authority, uses or threatens violence for the purpose of securing entry into any premises for himself or any other person is guilty of an offence if,

(a) there is someone on the premises who is opposed to the entry; and

(b) the person using the violence knows that is the case.

It is specifically provided by s. 6(2) that the fact that a person has any interest or right to possession of the premises (such as a landlord at the end of a tenancy) does not constitute lawful authority for the purpose of securing entry.

The effect of this provision is that a person seeking to recover possession of premises must use his civil remedies to recover possession rather than try to use or threaten violence. Section 6(4) provides that it is immaterial whether the violence is directed against person or property.

There is only one exception to the above rule. It is provided for in s. 6(3), which states that it is a defence to any proceedings to prove that the accused was a 'displaced residential occupier' of the premises in question. Such a person is defined by s. 12 as a person who was occupying the premises as a residence immediately before being excluded from occupation by anyone who entered the premises as a trespasser. This is intended to assist a person who lives in premises, goes away for a time and returns to find that trespassers have entered the premises. Such a person has a defence to any proceedings brought if he should use or threaten violence to secure entry to the premises.

NOTE: Where any premises have been let as a dwelling under a tenancy which is not a statutorily protected tenancy, and (*a*) the tenancy comes to an end but (*b*) the occupier continues to reside in the premises, it is unlawful for the owner to enforce his right to recover possession otherwise than by proceedings: Protection from Eviction Act 1977, s. 3(1). This provision has been extended by the Housing Act 1988, s. 30 to certain licences other than 'excluded licences'; *see* s. 3(2B) of the 1977 Act. Excluded licences are defined in s. 3A of the 1977 Act.

5. Recovery of possession by action. A landlord will normally enforce his right to possession by bringing an action for possession. He may combine this with any other claims that arise out of the tenant's occupation of the land, e.g. a claim for arrears of rent or mesne profits (*see* 7) or a claim for damages for breach of covenant. The claim may be brought in the county court or the High Court. In Rent Act cases, the county court has a very wide jurisdiction and such cases should always be started there otherwise costs may not be recoverable. Proceedings in the county court are normally quicker and cheaper than in the High Court.

Other remedies

6. Introduction. By statute there are two special and ancient remedies available to a landlord against a tenant holding over. In practice they are rarely used. They are:

(a) *An action for double value* under the Landlord and Tenant Act 1730, s. 1 which provides that a landlord may sue for double the yearly value of the land where he gives notice under the Act (before the expiry of the tenancy) requiring the tenant to give up possession but the tenant then wilfully holds over. This action is not available where the tenant holds over by reason of statutory protection; nor is it available against weekly, monthly, or quarterly, tenants.
(b) *An action for double rent* under the Distress for Rent Act 1737, s. 18; this is available where a tenant gives a valid notice to quit and holds over after its expiry. Double rent can be recovered regardless of whether there is statutory protection.

7. Action for mesne profits. If the tenant remains in possession of the demised premises at the end of his tenancy (other than in right of some statutory protection) the landlord is entitled to recover from him 'mesne profits' for the time that he so occupies the premises. Mesne profits are, in effect, a form of damages for the loss of the use of the land which the landlord has suffered by reason of the tenant's failure to give up possession. The way in which they are normally calculated is to consider what is the market rental of the land, since this is the benefit of which the landlord has been deprived.

> NOTE: Mesne profits can only be claimed from the date when the tenant ceases to hold the premises as a tenant and holds them as a trespasser. Until that time the appropriate claim would be for rent.

8. Time-limits. A landlord must re-enter the land or bring his proceedings for possession within 12 years from the time when the right to re-enter or to bring proceedings accrued: Limitation Act 1980, s. 15(1). When the land is let under a written lease the landlord's right to possession accrues when the lease ends. When the land is let under an oral periodic tenancy the landlord's right to possession is deemed to have accrued at the end of the first year, or other period, of the tenancy or at the last time rent was received, whichever is the later. Accordingly if the landlord fails to bring proceedings for possession within the 12 years and there is no acknowledgement of the landlord's title by the tenant, the landlord's right of action will be barred and he will be unable to recover possession.

Examples ————————————————————————————————

(1) L lets land to T on an oral yearly tenancy from 1st January 1960. The last receipt of rent by L is on 1st January 1962. In 1978 L tries to recover possession from T. L would not succeed because the limitation period for his claim expired on 1st January 1974, i.e. 12 years after the last receipt of rent.

(2) L lets land to T for a term of seven years from 1st January 1960. There is no renewal of the term and T remains in possession without paying any rent. In 1978 L tries to recover possession from T. L should succeed because the limitation period would not expire until 1st January 1979 i.e. 12 years after the expiry of the term.

Tenant's rights

9. The tenant's rights on termination. At the end of a tenancy the main question which concerns a vacating tenant is whether he can remove articles which he has fixed to the demised premises.

10. Fixtures, generally. The general rule is that any article fixed to the land becomes part of the land and belongs to the owner of the land. This rule is expressed in the maxim *quicquid plantatur solo, solo cedit* – whatever is attached to the land becomes part of it. Consequently a tenant who attaches things to the demised premises may make them into a part of the land itself and they may thereby become the property of the landlord.

Terminology. Two expressions often used are 'landlord's fixtures' and 'tenant's fixtures'. The former means fixtures which have been attached by the landlord and fixtures which have been added by the tenant but which he is not entitled to remove; the latter means fixtures which have been attached by the tenant and which he is entitled to remove in accordance with the following rules.

11. The difference between fixtures and chattels. A fixture is any article which is so attached to the land as to form in law a part of the land. If an article is not so attached to the land as to form in law a part of the land, then it remains a chattel. In many cases it will be clear whether or not an article is a fixture, e.g. a fireplace. There are, however, many cases where it is difficult to decide if an article is a fixture or a chattel. There are two tests to decide this question:

(a) the degree of annexation; and
(b) the purpose of annexation.

12. The degree of annexation. This test must be considered first. If the article has some actual connection to the land, prima facie it is a fixture, e.g. a fireplace or panelling. If the article has no such connection, prima facie it is not a fixture, e.g. a free standing greenhouse, machinery resting on its own weight. The degree of annexation is not by itself decisive of the question whether any item is a fixture or chattel. It is necessary also to look at the object or purpose of the annexation.

13. The purpose of annexation. This test involves deciding whether the article has been affixed for its more convenient use as a chattel, in which case it remains a chattel, or for the more convenient use of the land to which it is attached. The leading case illustrates this.

> *Leigh* v. *Taylor* (1902). T owned some valuable tapestries. He fixed them to the wall of a house. He nailed strips of wood to the wall, he then stretched canvas over the strips, and the tapestry was fastened by tacks to the strips. Finally the tapestry was surrounded by a moulding. On T's death the question arose whether the tapestries were fixtures and passed with the house. HELD: the tapestries had not become fixtures. *Per* Vaughan Williams LJ: 'In my judgment it is obvious that everything which was done here can be accounted for as being absolutely necessary for the enjoyment of the tapestry.'

14. The right to remove fixtures. If an article is a chattel the tenant can remove it; if it is a fixture it cannot be removed from the land and must be left for the owner of the land. There are exceptions to this last rule in so far as it affects landlord and tenant. Originally the rule was that all fixtures were landlord's fixtures and had to be left for the landlord. The law has mitigated this rule and there are now three exceptions. The following are tenant's fixtures:

(a) *Trade fixtures.* These are fixtures attached by the tenant for the purpose of his business or trade. They can be removed at any time during the term but not after the term has ended (*Poole's Case* (1703)).

(b) *Ornamental and domestic fixtures.* This covers things like mirrors, blinds, stoves. It is a prerequisite that the removal will not cause substantial injury to the building (*Spyer* v. *Phillipson* (1931)).

(c) *Agricultural fixtures.* These do not fall within (**a**). By virtue of the Agricultural Holdings Act 1986, s. 10, a tenant of an agricultural holding who has attached fixtures to the land can take them away before the end of the term, or within two months after the end. The following conditions must be satisfied:

(*i*) the tenant must have performed or satisfied all his obligations to the landlord;

(*ii*) the tenant must have given the landlord written notice of his intention to remove the fixtures;

(*iii*) the landlord must not have served a counter-notice electing to purchase the fixtures;

(*iv*) the removal must not cause avoidable damage to the premises.

15. Removal of fixtures. The rule is that the tenant must remove the fixtures during the tenancy. If he fails to do so they will become the property of the landlord absolutely at the end of the tenancy. If a tenant surrenders his tenancy and is granted a new one of the same premises he loses his right to remove the fixtures unless there is an express provision to the contrary: *Leschallas* v. *Woolf* (1908).

In *New Zealand Government Property Corporation* v. *H.M. & S. Ltd* (1981), however, it was held that, where there was a surrender of a tenancy by operation of law followed by the grant of a new tenancy to the same tenant, there was a clear inference that it was not the intention of the parties that the tenant should be taken to give up his right to remove the fixtures on the determination of his old tenancy.

Statutory rights

16. Generally. So far this book has been primarily concerned with the position at common law between landlord and tenant. At law the relationship is governed by the combination of contract and land law. The parties are free to agree whatever terms they wish for the letting of land. At the end of the lease the landlord is entitled to possession and can evict the tenant or renegotiate the terms of the tenancy. This means that the landlord will generally be in a superior position. During the nineteenth century, this difference in bargaining power became more apparent with the increase in population and the need for more housing. As a result legislation was passed to try to redress the balance by improving the tenant's position. Such legislation has multiplied and today there are several different schemes affording protection to different types of tenants. The nature of these schemes has varied from time to time but, in essence, they do two things: first, they regulate the rent payable under a tenancy; secondly, they give security of tenure. In the case of much legislation since 1980 the latter has been achieved by giving certain residential tenants the right to acquire their landlord's interest.

17. The nature of the protection. The extent of the protection enjoyed by a tenant will depend on the nature of the use to which he puts the premises and the type of tenancy he has. There are distinct codes of protection in respect of:

(a) business tenancies;
(b) residential tenancies other than long leases;
(c) residential tenancies which are long leases;
(d) agricultural holdings;
(e) public sector tenancies.

These different codes are considered in the following chapters.

18. Summary of the relevant statutes. The following is a chronological list of the main statutes with which students should be familiar.

(a) *Landlord and Tenant Act 1927, Part I:* this deals with a business tenant's entitlement, on leaving the demised premises, to compensation for improvements made to the demised premises.
(b) *Landlord and Tenant Act 1954, Part I:* this gives security of tenure to tenants of residential premises who hold under long leases at low rents.
(c) *Landlord and Tenant Act 1954, Part II:* this gives security of tenure to the tenants of business premises.
(d) *Leasehold Reform Acts 1967 and 1979:* these give tenants of houses under long leases at low rents the right to acquire the freehold of their house.
(e) *Rent (Agriculture) Act 1976:* this gives security of tenure to the occupiers of tied agricultural accommodation.
(f) *Rent Act 1977:* this gives security of tenure to tenants of residential property and controls the amount of rent recoverable from the tenant.
(g) *Housing Act 1985:* this gives security of tenure, and the right to buy, to local authority tenants.

(h) *Agricultural Holdings Act 1986:* this gives tenants of agricultural holdings protection.

(i) *Landlord and Tenant Act 1987:* this gives certain residential tenants a right of first refusal on disposal by their landlord and, in exceptional circumstances, the right to acquire compulsorily their landlord's interest; it also deals with the management of leasehold properties.

(j) *Housing Act 1988:* this commences the phasing out of the Rent Acts and introduces assured tenancies under which there is security of tenure but an open market rent can be charged.

(k) *Leasehold Reform, Housing and Urban Development Act 1993:* this extends the right of tenants of houses under long leases to an enfranchise and gives a similar right to certain tenants of flats.

The above is only an outline of the protection conferred by each statute. Whether protection is available and its extent in any case will depend upon the exact facts and the satisfaction of various, often complicated, conditions.

Progress test 9

1. What were the Statutes of Forcible Entry? **(4)**

2. If a tenant fails to give up possession of premises at the end of his tenancy what remedies does the landlord have? How has statute affected these remedies? **(3, 4)**

3. How can a landlord enforce his right to possession at the end of a tenancy? What restrictions are placed on this right by the Criminal Law Act 1977? **(4)**

4. What is a 'displaced residential occupier'? What defence is available to such an occupier? **(4)**

5. What is the difference between
   (a) an action for double value, and
   (b) an action for double rent? **(6)**

6. How are fixtures and chattels distinguished? What tests are applied to distinguish them? **(11)**

7. By when must fixtures be removed by a tenant? **(15)**

8. What are the exceptions to the common law rules regarding fixtures? **(14)**

9. What are mesne profits? **(7)**

10. How does the Limitation Act 1980 affect a landlord's right to possession at the end of a tenancy? **(8)**

11. When did the statutory regulation of landlord and tenant commence? **(16)**

12. What are the main aims of statutory control? **(16)**

13. What classes of lettings are now protected by statute? **(17)**

Part two
Business tenancies

10

Business tenancies

Introduction

1. Generally. At common law a business tenant had no right to renew his tenancy when his tenancy came to an end. This sometimes resulted in considerable hardship. A tenant might have carried on business at his premises for a number of years during the course of which he might have built up goodwill or regular custom. Additionally, the tenant might have spent substantial sums in improving his premises for the benefit of the business he carried on there.

When his tenancy came to an end, such a tenant might find that his landlord was not prepared to grant him a new tenancy, in which case the tenant would lose the benefit of all his efforts and expenditure on the premises. Alternatively, the tenant might find that his landlord would only grant him a new tenancy at a rent which was higher than the market rent, thus taking advantage of the particular benefit to the tenant of remaining at the premises and, in a sense, forcing the tenant to pay for the benefit of his own efforts.

2. History. Parliament first intervened in an effort to prevent this injustice by Part I of the Landlord and Tenant Act 1927 ('the 1927 Act').

The 1927 Act entitled a business tenant to obtain compensation from his landlord for loss of the goodwill attached to the premises when the tenant was required to quit the premises at the end of his tenancy. Furthermore, in certain cases where the compensation for loss of goodwill would have been inadequate the tenant could oblige his landlord to grant him a new lease.

It was not felt that the 1927 Act gave business tenants adequate protection however, and the renewal of business tenancies is now regulated by Part II of the Landlord and Tenant Act 1954 ('the 1954 Act') which came into force on 1st October 1954.

Various amendments have been made to the 1954 Act. Those amendments made by Part I of the Law of Property Act 1969 ('the 1969 Act') are particularly important.

Recent amendments which are worthy of special mention are those made by

(a) Section 149 of, and Schedule 7 to, the Local Government and Housing Act 1989; (amending the compensation provisions in s. 37 of the 1954 Act);

(b) the Landlord and Tenant (Licensed Premises) Act 1990; (amending s. 43 of the 1954 Act so as to apply the 1954 Act to premises licensed for the sale of intoxicating liquor for consumption on the premises);

(c) The High Court and County Courts Jurisdiction Order 1991 (S.I. 1991 No. 724); (amending s. 63 of the 1954 Act so as to extend the County Court's jurisdiction to entertain applications under the 1954 Act, irrespective of the rateable value of the premises in question).

The Landlord and Tenant Act 1954

3. The object of the 1954 Act. The object of this Act is '. . . to enable tenants occupying property for business, professional or certain other purposes to obtain new tenancies in certain cases'.

4. Tenancies to which the 1954 Act applies. Section 23(1) of the 1954 Act provides that: 'Subject to the provisions of this Act this Part of this Act applies to any tenancy (A) where the property comprised in the tenancy is or includes premises (B) which are occupied by the tenant (C) and are so occupied for the purposes of a business carried on by him or for those and other purposes (D)'.

The letters A to D in brackets have been inserted for ease of identification of the main elements of s. 23(1) and each of those elements will now be considered in turn.

(A) *'any tenancy'*
4.1 Section 69(1) of the 1954 Act defines 'tenancy' as follows:

'. . . a tenancy created either immediately or derivatively out of the freehold whether by a lease or underlease by an agreement for a lease or underlease or by a tenancy agreement or in pursuance of any enactment (including this Act) but does not include a mortgage term or any interest arising in favour of a mortgagor by his attorning tenant to his mortgagee and references to the granting of a tenancy and to demised property shall be construed accordingly.'

The 1954 Act does not apply to occupation of premises pursuant to a licence: *Shell-Mex and BP Ltd* v. *Manchester Garages Ltd* (1971).

The nature of a tenancy and the distinctions between a tenancy and a licence have been considered in **2:15.**

NOTES: (1) Payment of rent is not an essential characteristic of a tenancy: *Ashburn Anstalt* v. *Arnold and Another* (1987). The 1954 Act applies to a tenancy irrespective of the fact that no rent or a low rent is payable thereunder.

(2) It has been held that an unlawful sub-tenancy (i.e. one created in breach of a covenant in the headlease against sub-letting) is a tenancy protected by the 1954 Act: *D'Silva* v. *Lister House Developments Ltd* (1971).

(B) *'premises'*
4.2 The word should be given its ordinary meaning and this includes land, buildings and other corporeal hereditaments. The 1954 Act does not apply to grants of incorporeal hereditaments alone, such as a right of way: *Land Reclamation Co. Ltd* v. *Basildon District Council* (1979).

(C) *'occupied by the tenant'*
4.3 Personal occupation by the tenant is not essential. Occupation through an agent or manager is sufficient but the occupation must be genuine and not a sham: *Teasdale* v. *Walker* (1958). A common sense approach must be adopted in establishing whether or not the premises are occupied. Thus the mere storage of files, for example, in premises demised for use as a storeroom may amount to occupation, even though the tenant only visits the premises at irregular intervals. Similarly, continuous occupation is not essential so long as there is a 'thread of continuity' in the business user as in the case of a seasonal business: *Teasdale* v. *Walker* (supra). See also *Wandsworth LBC* v. *Singh* (1991) where the tenant's maintenance of the premises as a park was held to amount to occupation.

In order to obtain the protection afforded by the 1954 Act the tenant must show that he is in occupation of the premises for the purposes of a business carried on by him or, if events over which he has no control have caused him to absent himself from the premises, e.g. a fire, that he continues to exert and claim his right to occupy: *Morrison*

Holdings Ltd v. *Manders Property (Wolverhampton) Ltd* (1976); compare *Aspinall Finance Ltd* v. *Lord Chelsea* (1988) where the tenant deliberately vacated the premises in order to obtain a gaming licence in respect of other premises and lost protection. See also *Demetriou* v. *Poolaction Ltd* (1991) where the tenant's business was the sub-letting of rooms. Due to the state of repair of the premises there had been no sub-lettings for several years. The tenant argued that the responsibility for the repairs lay with the landlord and that his non-occupation therefore resulted from the landlord's failure to comply with its repairing obligations. It was found that the landlord was not liable for the repairs, and thus that the need for the repairs could not be relied upon by the tenant as justifying his non-occupation.

The fact that the tenant shares occupation of the premises, e.g. with a licensee or sub-tenant of part, does not prevent the tenancy from being one to which the 1954 Act applies provided that the tenant retains and occupies some part of the premises himself: *Lee-Verhulst (Investments) Ltd* v. *Harwood Trust* (1972) and *Graysim Holdings Ltd* v. *P & O Property Holdings Ltd* (1994), compare *Trans-Britannia Properties Ltd* v. *Darby Properties Ltd* (1986).

NOTE: Occupation through a company, even if the tenant is the beneficial owner of all or the majority of the issued shares, does not constitute occupation by the tenant: *Nozari-Zadeh* v. *Pearl Assurance plc* (1987).

Two special cases of occupation need to be considered in connection with the meaning of the phrase 'occupied by the tenant'.

(*i*) By virtue of s. 41 of the 1954 Act, where a tenancy is held on trust, occupation by all or any of the beneficiaries under the trust and the carrying on of a business by all or any of the beneficiaries is treated as occupation by the tenant (i.e. the trustees) for the purposes of s. 23.

(*ii*) By virtue of s. 42 of the 1954 Act, if a tenancy is held by a company, occupation by another company within the same group of companies and the carrying on of a business by that other company is treated as occupation by the tenant for the purposes of s. 23.

NOTES: (1) Two companies are members of the same group of companies if one is a subsidiary of the other or both are subsidiaries of a third company.

(2) The word 'subsidiary' has the same meaning as that assigned to it by Section 736 of the Companies Act 1985 (as amended), i.e. company A is a subsidiary of company B if

(a) company B holds a majority of the voting rights in company A; or

(b) company B is a member of company A and has the right to appoint or remove a majority of company A's board of directors; or

(c) company B is a member of company A and controls alone, pursuant to an agreement with other shareholders or members, a majority of the voting rights in company A.

If company B is itself a subsidiary of company C, company A is also a subsidiary of company C.

(D) *'for the purposes of a business carried on by him or for those and other purposes.'*

4.4 A tenant may use premises for two purposes, one being a business user and the other a non-business user and the tenancy will still be one to which the 1954 Act applies, e.g. there may be a shop on the ground floor and a flat upstairs. The business use must, however, be a significant purpose of the tenant's occupation of the premises; it is not sufficient if the business use is merely incidental to the main activity carried on at the premises. Two cases illustrate this principle. In *Cheryl Investments Ltd* v. *Saldanha* (1979) it was held that the 1954 Act applied to a tenancy of a flat in which the tenant resided, it having been established that the tenant had installed office equipment and conducted a considerable volume of trade from the premises. In *Royal Life Saving Society* v. *Page* (1979) where a doctor took a tenancy of a maisonette near his consulting rooms and very occasionally saw a patient there in emergencies, it was held that the 1954 Act did not apply to the tenancy.

See also *Gurton* v. *Parrott* (1991) where, after having lived at the premises for many years and continuing to do so, the tenant carried on the activities of kennelling, grooming and breeding dogs. It was held that these activities were merely incidental to the tenant's occupation of the premises as her home and that the 1954 Act did not apply.

> NOTE: If, when a lease is granted, it falls within the 1954 Act and not within the Rent Act, the tenant cannot subsequently assert that the cessation of the business use and his occupation for purely residential purposes brings the tenancy within the Rent Act: *Trustees of Henry Smith's Charity* v. *Wagle & Anor* (1988).

5. Business use. Section 23(2) of the 1954 Act states that 'business' includes a trade, profession or employment and includes any activity carried on by a body of persons whether corporate or unincorporate'. It should be noted that when the 'business' is not carried on by a body of persons whether corporate or unincorporate (i.e. when the 'business' is carried on by an individual), the 'business' must amount to a trade, profession or employment if the tenancy is to be one to which the 1954 Act applies. In the case of a body of persons corporate or unincorporate the 'business' may be 'any activity'.

Whether or not a particular activity constitutes a business is a question of fact and degree in each case. In *Town Investments Ltd* v. *Department of the Environment* (1978) it was said that ' "business" embraces almost anything which is an occupation as distinguished from a pleasure – anything which is an occupation or a duty which requires attention is a business'.

Some examples of uses which have been held to be within or outside the definition of 'business' in s. 23(2) assist in understanding the definition.

(a) *Examples of uses within the definition*

(*i*) the activities of the governors of a hospital in administering the premises: *Hills (Patents) Ltd* v. *University College Board of Governors* (1956);

(*ii*) the carrying on of a members' tennis club: *Addiscombe Garden Estates Ltd* v. *Crabbe* (1958);

(*iii*) meetings after church services and religious instruction and the making available of recreational facilities to the elderly and young people on a charitable basis: *Parkes* v. *Westminster Roman Catholic Diocese Trustee* (1978);

(*iv*) use as government offices: *Town Investments Ltd* v. *Department of the Environment* (1978);

(*v*) letting of furnished and serviced rooms where the tenant has the right of access to all parts of the building in order to provide services: *Lee-Verhulst (Investments) Ltd* v. *Harwood Trust* (1972); see also *Graysim Holdings Ltd* v. *P & O Property Holdings Ltd* (1994);

(*vi*) the maintenance of an open space as a park for local residents: *Wandsworth LBC* v. *Singh* (1991).

(b) *Examples of uses outside the definition*

(*i*) use of a loft by an individual for a weekly Sunday school; no charge was made, but subscriptions were invited which the tenant gave to a Scripture Mission: *Abernethie* v. *A.M. & J. Kleiman Ltd* (1970);

(*ii*) use of premises as a temporary dumping ground for spoil from building works: *Hillil Property & Investment Co. Ltd v. Naraine Pharmacy* (1979);

(*iii*) taking in of lodgers where the purpose of so doing was to enable the tenant to meet her obligations under the tenancy as opposed to commercial gain: *Lewis* v. *Weldcrest Ltd* (1978);

(*iv*) sub-letting of premises for profit where the whole or substantially the whole of the premises had in fact been sub-let and the parts of the premises retained by the tenant, namely a caretaker's rooms, boiler rooms, storerooms, fuel stores and the common parts could not, considered alone, be said to be used for the purposes of any business carried on by the tenant: *Bagettes Ltd* v. *G.P. Estates Ltd* (1956).

6. Business use in breach of covenant. Section 23(4) of the 1954 Act deals with the question of whether or not a tenant who is carrying on a business at the premises in breach of the user covenant in his lease, has the protection afforded by the 1954 Act. The effect of s. 23(4) is as follows:

(a) if the user covenant is in general terms, e.g. a covenant against any business, trade, profession or employment, a business use in breach will not have the effect of bringing the tenancy within the 1954 Act (for an interesting, modern illustration, see *The Trustees of the Methodist Secondary Schools Trust Deed* v. *O'Leary* (1992));
(b) if the covenant is against use for a specific business, e.g. not to use a shop for the purposes of the trade or business of a butcher, use in breach will not take the tenancy outside the 1954 Act;
(c) if the covenant is against use for any business except a particular business, use in breach will not take the tenancy outside the 1954 Act;
(d) in a case where the landlord or his predecessor in title has consented to the breach or the landlord has acquiesced in the breach, the tenancy will be one to which the 1954 Act applies.

7. Interaction of the 1954 Act with the Rent Act 1977 and the Housing Act 1988. Where there is a tenancy with a mixed use, i.e. part business use and part residential, difficult questions may arise about whether the tenancy is protected by the Rent Act 1977 or by the 1954 Act. In essence, the rule is that a tenancy of premises put to such a mixed use will normally be protected by the 1954 Act unless the business use is insignificant.

Furthermore, if, at its inception, the tenancy was one to which the 1954 Act applied, the subsequent cesser of the business use does not enable the tenant to claim the protection of the Rent Act 1977 (*Pulleng* v. *Curran* (1982) and *Trustees of Henry Smith's Charity* v. *Wagle & Anor* (1988)).

Presumably the same principle would apply if the tenant claimed to be an assured tenant under the Housing Act 1988. Section 1 of, and paragraph 4 of Schedule 1 Part 1 to, the Housing Act 1988 make it clear that a tenancy to which the 1954 Act applies cannot also be an assured tenancy.

8. Tenancies to which the 1954 Act does not apply. These are:

(a) tenancies at will, either express (*Manfield & Sons Ltd* v. *Botchin* (1970) or implied (*Wheeler* v. *Mercer* (1957);

(b) tenancies of agricultural holdings (s. 43(1)(a));

(c) tenancies created by mining leases (s. 43(1)(b));

(d) tenancies granted by reason of, and ceasing with the termination of, some office, appointment or employment provided the tenancy was granted by an instrument in writing which expressed the purpose for which the tenancy was granted (s. 43(2));

(e) tenancies granted for a term certain not exceeding six months unless the tenancy contains provision for renewing the term or extending it beyond six months or the tenant has been in occupation for a period exceeding twelve months (s. 43(3));

(f) 'contracted out' tenancies, namely a tenancy to which the landlord and the tenant agree that ss. 24–28 of the 1954 Act shall not apply and granted after an order of the court, authorising the agreement to exclude those sections, has been obtained under s. 38(4) of the Act;

(g) where the landlord and the tenant agree for the grant of a future tenancy on terms and from a date specified in the agreement, the current tenancy continues to that date, but no longer and ceases to be a tenancy to which the 1954 Act applies (s. 28).

NOTES: (1) The Landlord and Tenant (Licensed Premises) Act 1990 repealed Section 43(1)(d) of the 1954 Act. In consequence, tenancies of premises licensed for the sale of intoxicating liquor for consumption on the premises (e.g. public houses) now attract the protection of the 1954 Act.

(2) Where the interest of the landlord or any superior landlord is held by a government department, a local authority, statutory undertaker or a development corporation, the Minister or board in charge of any government department may certify that it is requisite for the purposes of that department or, as the case may be, of the authority, undertaker or corporation that the use or occupation of the premises or a part of the premises shall be changed by a certain date (s. 57).

The general effect of the issue of such a certificate is that either the tenant cannot make an application to the court for a new tenancy or that the tenant cannot be granted a new tenancy beyond the date specified in the certificate and any new tenancy so granted will not be a tenancy to which the 1954 Act applies. Section 58 contains similar provisions for cases where for reasons of national security it is necessary that the use or occupation of the property should be discontinued or changed.

(3) Section 60 contains similar provisions to s. 58 in cases where the landlord is the Minister of Technology or the Urban Regeneration Agency.

(4) Sections 60A and 60B contain similar provisions to s. 58 where the Welsh Development Agency or the Development Board for Rural Wales is the landlord.

9. Contracting out. The 1954 Act contains provisions to prevent the parties contracting out. Section 38(1) provides that any agreement will be void in so far as it purports to preclude a tenant from making an application for a new tenancy or it provides for the termination of his tenancy or penalises him if he should make such an application. Section 38(4) was added by the Law of Property Act 1969 in order to enable parties to contract out with the leave of the court. Section 38(4)(a) provides that on the joint application of the parties, the court may authorise the grant of a tenancy which will not be subject to the provisions of the Act regarding security of tenure. The proposed tenancy must be for a term of years certain: see *Re: Land and Premises at Liss, Hants* (1971) and *Nicholls* v. *Kinsey* (1994). Further, s. 38(4)(b) provides that on the joint application of the parties, the court may authorise an agreement to surrender the tenancy at any time. The effect of an order under s. 38(4)(a) is that on the contractual termination of the tenancy, the tenancy will not be continued and the tenant's right to occupy will end. An agreement to surrender a business tenancy is void under s. 38(1) unless it is sanctioned by the court under s. 38(4)(b): *Joseph* v. *Joseph* (1967). Where a term of the lease requires the tenant to offer a surrender before he is entitled to licence to assign, the resulting agreement to surrender is unenforceable: *Allnatt London Pties Ltd* v. *Newton* (1984).

> NOTE: The court's authority under s. 38(4)(a) must be obtained *before* the tenancy is granted *see Evenlex Ltd* v. *Essexcrest Ltd* (1988).

Progress test 10

1. Which of the following interests is protected by Part II of the Landlord and Tenant Act 1954?
   (a) a tenancy at no rent;
   (b) a licence;
   (c) an unlawful sub-tenancy. **(4)**

2. Is a lease of a right of way protected by the 1954 Act? **(4)**

3. What are the requirements for protection under the 1954 Act? **(4)**

4. Which of the following are businesses for the purposes of the 1954 Act:
   (a) a bank;
   (b) a Post Office;
   (c) a weekly Sunday school carried on by an individual;
   (d) a members' tennis club? **(5)**

5. A butcher takes a lease of a building with a shop on the ground floor (where he carries on the trade of a butcher) and a flat above (where he lives with his wife and children). Is his tenancy of the building one to which the 1954 act applies? **(4, 7)**

6. A doctor has a tenancy of a flat near his surgery and sometimes sees patients at the flat. Is his tenancy one to which the 1954 Act applies? **(4)**

7. In what circumstances, if any, is a business use in breach of covenant protected by the 1954 Act? **(6)**

8. To which of the following leases does the 1954 Act apply?
(a) a lease of a suite of offices for three months;
(b) a lease of a restaurant;
(c) a lease of a public house;
(d) a lease of a block of flats which the tenant rents out as serviced apartments? **(5, 8)**

9. What special rules apply to:
(a) a tenancy held by a member of a group of companies;
(b) a tenancy held by a trustee on behalf of beneficiaries? **(4)**

10. Are there any circumstances in which the status of the landlord can affect the protection enjoyed by a business tenant? **(8)**

11

Security of tenure

Introduction

1. Generally. The preceding chapter was concerned with the scope of Part II of the Landlord and Tenant Act 1954. It is now necessary to consider how the 1954 Act works. Broadly, it protects the tenant in the following ways:

(a) it limits the ways in which a tenancy may come to an end;

(b) unless the tenancy is ended in one of the specified ways it will continue automatically;

(c) it gives to the business tenant the right to apply for a new tenancy at the end of his current tenancy;

(d) if the landlord wishes to oppose the grant of a new tenancy to the tenant, he can only do so if he establishes one, or more, of certain specified grounds;

(e) a tenant who has to leave may be entitled to compensation.

Continuation

2. Automatic continuation. Section 24(1) of the 1954 Act provides that 'A tenancy to which this Part of this Act applies shall not come to an end unless terminated in accordance with the provisions of this Part of this Act and subject to the provisions of section twenty-nine of this Act, the tenant under such a tenancy may apply to the court for a new tenancy.' The basic principles of the 1954 Act are embodied in this sub-section.

The effect of s. 24(1) is that notwithstanding determination of the contractual term, the tenancy continues at the same rent and subject to the same covenants and conditions as are in force at the expiration of the contractual term, until the tenancy is brought to an end by one of the methods recognised or prescribed by the 1954 Act. In the absence of an express contractual provision to the contrary, the only rights and obligations continued by Section 24 are those of the particular landlord and tenant during the period of statutory continuation of the tenancy. So, in *The City of London* v. *Fell* (1993), the original tenants were not liable for rent which accrued during the period of statutory continuation and which had not been paid by the company to whom they had assigned the tenancy before the expiry of the contractual term.

Methods of termination

3. The common law methods of termination. Section 24 does not prevent the tenancy coming to an end by:

(a) notice to quit given by the tenant (a notice given by one of two or more joint tenants may suffice; see *Hammersmith and Fulham LBC* v. *Monk* (1991));
(b) surrender;
(c) forfeiture;
(d) forfeiture of a superior tenancy.

In cases **(a)** and **(b)**, the notice or surrender will be ineffective if given or made before the tenant has been in occupation of the premises in right of the tenancy for at least one month. This provision is designed to prevent evasion of the Act by a landlord granting a tenancy on condition that the tenant executes a surrender of it or gives notice to quit before he has occupied the premises as tenant for one month.

4. The statutory methods of termination. These are:

(a) by a landlord's notice under s. 25;
(b) by a tenant's request for a new tenancy under s. 26;
(c) by tenant's notice under s. 27.

Before considering each of the statutory methods of termination it will be helpful to consider identification of the parties by or upon whom a notice to terminate the tenancy or a request for a new tenancy may be served.

5. The 'competent' landlord. The landlord entitled to serve a notice to terminate under s. 25 or upon whom a tenant's request under s. 26 should be served is the landlord who at the relevant time satisfies the following conditions:

(a) that he is the owner of an interest in the premises in reversion expectant, whether immediately or not, on the termination of the current tenancy; and

(b) that interest is either:

    (*i*) the fee simple; or

    (*ii*) a tenancy which will not come to an end within 14 months by effluxion of time; and if it is such a tenancy, that no notice has been given by virtue of which it will come to an end within 14 months or any further time by which it may be continued under s. 36(2) or s. 64 and is not itself in reversion expectant (whether immediately or not) on an interest which fulfils those conditions: s. 44(1) of the 1954 Act.

The landlord who from time to time satisfies these conditions is commonly referred to 'the competent landlord'.

In cases where there is a chain of tenancies, there may be more than one landlord who satisfies the conditions laid down in s. 44. In such cases it is the landlord lowest down in the chain of tenancies, who satisfies the conditions laid down in s. 44, who is the competent landlord.

The operation of s. 44 is best illustrated by some examples:

(a) L is the freeholder and lets premises to T who occupies the premises for business purposes. At the relevant time T's contractual tenancy has 12 months to run. L is the competent landlord.

(b) L is the freeholder and lets premises to T for 10 years. T immediately underlets the whole of the premises to UT (who occupies for business purposes) for 5 years. At the relevant time UT's contractual tenancy has 12 months to run.

T is the competent landlord so far as UT is concerned as his tenancy has another 6 years to run and will not therefore come to an end within 14 months by effluxion of time.

(c) L is the freeholder and lets premises to T for 10 years. T then underlets the whole of the premises to UT (who occupies for business purposes) for 10 years less 3 days. At the relevant time UT's contractual tenancy has 12 months to run.

L is the competent landlord so far as UT is concerned. T cannot be the competent landlord as his tenancy will come to an end within 14 months by effluxion of time.

(d) L is the freeholder and lets premises to T for 10 years. T occupies part of the premises for business purposes and sub-lets the remainder to ST (who also occupies for business purposes) for 10 years less 3 days. At the relevant time ST's contractual tenancy has 12 months to run.

T is the competent landlord so far as ST is concerned as his own business tenancy will continue under s. 24 for more than 14 months unless determined in accordance with the provisions of the Act.

(e) L is the freeholder and lets premises to T for 10 years. T occupies part of the premises for business purposes and sub-lets the remainder to ST (who also occupies for business purposes) for 10 years less 3 days. At the relevant time ST's contractual tenancy has 11 months to run and L has served a notice to terminate T's tenancy under s. 25.

L is the competent landlord so far as ST is concerned. T cannot be the competent landlord as he has received a s. 25 notice by virtue of which his tenancy will come to an end within 14 months or any further time by which it may be continued under s. 36(2) or s. 64.

> NOTE: It will be appreciated that the identity of the competent landlord can change (possibly on several occasions) within a short space of time. In *Shelley* v. *United Artists Corporation Ltd* (1989) the Court of Appeal stated that a landlord who serves a s. 25 notice is making a representation that he is the competent landlord, which becomes a misrepresentation which should be corrected when he ceases to be the competent landlord.

6. Procedure for identifying the business tenant and the competent landlord. In cases where there is a chain of tenancies, it can sometimes be difficult to identify the business tenant or the landlord on whom it is necessary to serve any notice to terminate the tenancy or request for a new tenancy.

Section 40(1) entitles the landlord to serve a notice (in the prescribed form) upon his tenant or upon any undertenant requiring the recipient of the notice to notify him in writing:

(a) whether the tenant (or undertenant as the case may be) occupies the premises or any part of the premises for the purposes of a business; and
(b) whether the tenant has any sub-tenant and if so,
    (*i*) the premises comprised in the sub-tenancy;
    (*ii*) if the sub-tenancy is for a fixed term, what the term is, or, if the sub-tenancy is terminable by notice, by what notice it can be terminated;
    (*iii*) what rent the sub-tenant pays;
    (*iv*) the sub-tenant's full name;
    (*v*) if the sub-tenant occupies the whole or part of the premises sub-let to him and, if not, what is the sub-tenant's address.

By s. 40(2) a tenant who holds a tenancy granted for a term of years certain exceeding one year or a tenancy granted for a term of years certain and thereafter from year to year is entitled to serve upon his landlord or any superior landlord a notice (in the prescribed form) requiring the recipient to notify him in writing:

(a) if he is the freeholder of the whole or part of the premises:
(b) if he is not the freeholder,
(*i*) the name and address of his immediate landlord;
(*ii*) the length of his tenancy;
(*iii*) the earliest date (if any) at which his tenancy can be terminated by notice to quit given by his immediate landlord;
(c) if there is a mortgagee in possession of his interest and if so, his name and address;
(d) if there is a receiver appointed by the mortgagee or by the court, his name and address also.

A similar notice may, if appropriate, be served upon a mortgagee in possession.

The notice may not be served more than two years before either the tenancy comes to an end by effluxion of time or the earliest date on which the tenancy could be brought to an end by a notice to quit (s. 40(4)). The recipient of such a notice must provide the information requested within one month.

NOTE: For prescribed forms under the 1954 Act generally, see the Landlord and Tenant Act 1954, Part II (Notices) Regulations 1983, as amended by the Landlord and Tenant Act 1954, Part II (Notices) (Amendment) Regulations 1989 and the High Court and County Courts Jurisdiction Order 1991.

7. Termination of a business tenancy by the competent landlord – s. 25. The competent landlord may terminate a tenancy to which the 1954 Act applies by the service of a notice complying with the requirements of s. 25. The requirements of a valid 'Section 25 Notice' (as it is commonly known) are as follows:

(a) The notice must be in the prescribed form; *see* s. 25(1). The form currently prescribed is Form 1 in Schedule 2 to the Landlord and Tenant 1954 Part II (Notices) Regulations 1983 (as amended) but it has been held that a form substantially to the like effect is adequate. In *Sun Alliance and London Assurance Co. Ltd* v. *Hayman* (1975) it was held that a form taken from regulations previously in force was substantially to the like effect as the form prescribed by the regulations then current. (*See also Morris v. Patel and Others* (1987), *Bridgers v. Stanford* (1991) and *Baglarbasi v. Deedmethod Ltd* (1991)).

(b) The termination date specified in the notice must be not less than 6 months nor more than 12 months prior to the date on which the notice is given; *see* s. 25(2).

(c) The date of termination specified in the notice must be not earlier than the date on which the tenancy will end at common law or the earliest date on which the tenancy could be brought to an end at common law; *see* s. 25(3) and (4).

The following examples help to explain the workings of s. 25(3) and (4) in more detail:

(*i*) *In the case of a tenancy for a fixed term,* the termination date specified must be no earlier than the date upon which the term will expire by effluxion of time.

NOTE: A term expressed to run 'from' a certain date ends at midnight on the appropriate anniversary of that date (*Re Crowhurst Park, Sims-Hilditch* v. *Simmons* (1974)). This presumption is rebuttable (see *Whelton Sinclair* and *Meadfield Properties*)

(*ii*) *In the case of a yearly tenancy running from 1st January* at common law, not less than 6 months' notice determining the tenancy on 31st December or 1st January is required. Thus a s. 25 notice served on 5th April in one year should not specify an earlier termination date than 31st December in that year. However, as the requirement is that the termination date specified in the s. 25 notice must be 'not earlier' than the earliest date on which the tenancy could be brought to an end at common law, a s. 25 notice specifying any termination date between 31st December in the year the notice is served and 5th April in the following year (i.e. up to 12 months hence) would be valid.

(*iii*) *In the case of periodic tenancies* the termination date specified need not be the last day of a period of the tenancy; *see Commercial Properties Ltd* v. *Wood* (1968);

(d) The notice should adequately describe the premises in question. A notice relating to part only of the premises comprised in the tenancy will be invalid (*Dodson Bull Carpet Co. Ltd* v. *City of London Corporation* (1975); *Herongrove Ltd* v. *Wates City of London Properties plc* (1988); *M&P Enterprises (London) Ltd* v. *Norfolk Square Hotels Ltd* (1994)). For an exceptional case where this rule did not apply, *see Gordon Moss* v. *Mobil Oil Co. Ltd* (1988).

It has, however, been held that a single s. 25 notice can determine two or more tenancies of different premises (*Tropis Shipping Co. Ltd* v. *Ibex Property Corporation Ltd* (1967)).

(e) The notice must require the tenant to notify the landlord in writing within two months after the giving of the notice, whether or not the tenant will be willing to give up possession at the termination date; *see* s. 25(5).

(f) The notice must state whether or not the landlord will oppose an application to the court by the tenant for the grant of a new tenancy and, if so, state which of the grounds set out in s. 30(1) the landlord will rely upon; *see* s. 25(6).

A landlord who wishes to oppose the grant of a new tenancy should take care to ensure that he states which of the grounds set out in s. 30(1) he will rely upon, as he cannot subsequently amend his notice so as to add or substitute a ground of opposition (*Nursey* v. *P. Currie (Dartford) Ltd (1959)*).

(g) The notice must be given by the competent landlord. In *Morrow* v. *Nadeem* (1986) the notice indicated that the landlord was Arthur Danzig who was in fact the controlling shareholder in the landlord company. It was held that the notice was invalid. See also *Yamaha-Kemble Music (U.K.) Ltd* v. *ARC Properties Ltd* (1989) and, more generally, *Divall* v. *Harrison* (1992).

The prescribed form contemplates that the notice will be signed by the competent landlord himself or by his properly authorised agent, e.g. his solicitor (*Tennant* v. *LCC* (1957)).

8. Contractual termination provisions and section 25 notices. As can be seen, a landlord cannot terminate a business tenancy prior to the date on which a tenancy for a fixed term will expire by effluxion of time or, in the case of a periodic tenancy, on a date which is earlier than the earliest date on which the tenancy could be brought to an end by notice to quit. In addition a lease may contain a break clause entitling the landlord to determine the tenancy by notice at or after a specified point in time. The rule is that a single notice will be sufficient to operate such a clause and also to satisfy s. 25, provided it satisfies the requirements of s. 25 and the contract; *see Scholl Manufacturing Co. Ltd* v. *Clifton (Slim-line) Ltd* (1967).

If the landlord gives a common law notice to quit or a notice pursuant to a break clause which complies with the contractual requirements but not the requirements of s. 25, the effect will be to determine the contractual tenancy but the tenancy will then continue under s. 24. If the landlord then wishes to end the tenancy he will have to serve a separate s. 25 notice.

The following example helps to illustrate the preceding text:

L grants to T a lease for a term of 15 years with a break clause at the end of the fifth and tenth years. At the end of the fifth year L serves a notice pursuant to the break clause. Unless the notice pursuant to the break clause also complies with s. 25 the tenancy will be continued by s. 24 until it is terminated by a s. 25 notice or one of the other methods of termination permitted by the 1954 Act. A landlord may use this to his advantage; thus in this example, suppose L knows that he will want to redevelop the premises in the eighth year. L can end the tenancy in that year by serving a notice pursuant to the break clause in the fifth year; the tenancy will then continue under s. 24 and in the seventh or eighth year the landlord can serve a s. 25 notice to end the continued tenancy.

9. Continuation tenancy. As has already been seen (*see* **2** above), and as is apparent from the last example, when a tenancy is continued under s. 24 it must still be terminated by one of the methods prescribed by the Act. In such a case the landlord may select any date of termination subject only to the rule that it must not be more than twelve months nor less than six months from the date of service of the notice. For example, if a tenancy is granted for five years expiring 1st May 1985 and continues under s. 24 of the Act, then, if the landlord serves a s. 25 notice on 1st July 1989, it may specify as the date of termination any date between 1st January 1990 and 1st July 1990.

10. The effect of a section 25 notice – action by the tenant. When a tenant receives a s. 25 notice he must decide whether or not to apply for a new tenancy.

(a) If he decides that he does wish to apply for a new tenancy, he must notify the landlord in writing, within two months of the giving of the s. 25 notice, that he is not willing to give up possession. This notification, commonly referred to as 'the tenant's counternotice', is an essential pre-requisite to the tenant's right to apply to the court for a new tenancy (s. 29(2)).

There is no prescribed form for the tenant's counternotice but the counternotice must provide a sufficient indication of the tenant's unwillingness to give up possession of the premises. Compare *Smale* v. *Meakers* (1957) where on the failure of negotiations T wrote to L saying '. . . in view of the above I regret that I have no alternative but to ask for an extension of the vacating day' which was held to be a good counternotice, with *Taylor* v. *Michel* (1960) where T's solicitor wrote to L's solicitor saying that his client '. . . would like if possible to negotiate for a lease . . .' on certain specified terms '. . . and would if possible like to settle this matter to avoid any further worry' which was held not to constitute counternotice.

NOTE: Both s. 25(5) and the prescribed form of s. 25 notice contemplate that the tenant can serve a counternotice that he is willing to give up possession. It is difficult to understand what purpose such a counternotice serves. It should be borne in mind that it has been held that such a counternotice is irrevocable: *De Havilland (Antiques) Ltd* v. *Centrovincial Estates (Mayfair) Ltd* (1971).

(b) Between two and four months after the giving of the s. 25 notice he must apply to the court for a new tenancy (s. 29(3)).
(c) Within two months of the date of issuing his application to the court for a new tenancy, the tenant must serve the application on the landlord (Order 97 of the Rules of the Supreme Court and Order 43

of the County Court Rules – *see also* Chapter 12). The court has only limited power to extend this time.

If the tenant fails to take any of these steps, he will lose the right to apply to the court for a new tenancy and his current tenancy will come to an end on the termination date specified in the s. 25 notice.

11. Termination of a business tenancy by the business tenant – tenant's request for a new tenancy under section 26 of the 1954 Act. This is the first of the methods prescribed by the 1954 Act by which a business tenant can bring his own tenancy to an end. In practice a tenant may wish his tenancy to continue because he will then continue paying the existing rent which, because of inflation, may be lower than the current market rent. If the existing rent payable by the tenant is higher than the current market rent however, the tenant may wish to obtain a new tenancy at the earliest opportunity. There may also be cases where the tenant prefers to regularise his position by obtaining a new lease for a fixed term, e.g. for reasons of financial planning or if he has long term plans for improving the premises. In such cases he can serve a tenant's request for a new tenancy under s. 26.

The tenant's request procedure under s. 26 is not available to all business tenants however. A tenant can only make a request for a new tenancy under s. 26 when his current tenancy was granted for:

(*i*) a term of years certain exceeding one year, whether or not continued under s. 24; or

(*ii*) a term of years certain and thereafter from year to year (s. 26(1)).

The requirements of a valid request under s. 26 are as follows:

(a) the request must be in the prescribed form (Form 8, Sch. 2, Landlord and Tenant Act 1954, Part II (Notices) Regulations 1983, as amended, or in a form substantially to the like effect (s. 26(3));

(b) the request must specify a date for the commencement of the new tenancy which is not less than six months nor more than twelve months hence and which is not in any event a date earlier than the date upon which the tenancy will end by effluxion of time, or could be brought to an end by notice to quit given by the tenant (s. 26(2));

(c) the request must set out the tenant's proposals as to:

(*i*) the property to be comprised in the new tenancy (being either the whole or part of the property comprised in his current tenancy);

(*ii*) the rent to be payable under the new tenancy;

(*iii*) the other terms of the new tenancy (s. 26(3)).

NOTE: Once a tenant has made a valid request for a new tenancy, he cannot withdraw it and serve a fresh request at a later date (*Polyviou* v. *Seeley* (1980)).

12. Effect of a tenant's request under section 26 – action by the landlord and the tenant. When the landlord receives the tenant's request, he must decide whether or not he will oppose the grant of a new tenancy. A landlord who wishes to oppose the grant of a new tenancy must, within two months of the giving of the tenant's request, serve notice on the tenant that he will oppose the grant of a new tenancy and state which of the grounds set out in s. 30(1) he will rely upon (s. 26(6)). There is no form prescribed for the landlord's 'counternotice'. The tenant must:

(a) apply to the court for a new tenancy between two and four months after he has given the request under s. 26 (s. 29(3));
(b) serve his application to the court for a new tenancy upon the landlord within two months of the date upon which the application is issued (Order 97 RSC and Order 43 CCR). The court has only limited power to extend this time.

The effect of a tenant's request is to terminate his current tenancy immediately before the date specified in the request for the commencement of the new tenancy (s. 26(5)). Provided that the tenant has taken the steps described at **(a)** and **(b)** above, his current tenancy will in fact continue beyond that date, but if he fails to take either of these steps he loses his right to apply for a new tenancy and the landlord can recover possession of the premises. (*See* Chapter 12.)

> NOTE: If the landlord fails to serve a counternotice, within two months of the making of the tenant's request, that he will oppose the grant of a new tenancy, he loses the right to oppose the grant of a new tenancy.

13. Termination by a tenant's notice under section 27. A tenancy to which the 1954 Act applies will continue under s. 24 until it is terminated by one of the methods prescribed by the 1954 Act. It may be the case, however, that the tenant does not wish his tenancy to continue, or that he only wishes the tenancy to continue under s. 24 for a certain period. Section 27 deals with these situations.

(a) Where the tenancy is for a term of years certain and the tenant gives to his immediate landlord, not less than three months before the tenancy will expire by effluxion of time, a notice in writing that he does not desire the tenancy to be continued, s. 24 will not apply and the tenancy will thus come to an end when the contractual term expires (s. 27(1)).

(b) Where a tenancy for a term of years certain is continuing by virtue of s. 24, the tenant may bring it to an end on any quarter day by giving to his immediate landlord not less than three months notice in writing (s. 27(2)). The notice can be given either before or after the period of continuation under s. 24 has commenced.

> NOTES: (1) In both cases the tenant must give the notice to his immediate landlord whether or not his immediate landlord is the competent landlord.
> (2) No form of notice is prescribed in either case.
> (3) Service of a notice under s. 27 precludes the tenant from applying for a new tenancy.

14. Priority of notices under the 1954 Act. Generally, the first valid notice or request served to terminate the tenancy, whether by the landlord or the tenant, is operative and any notice or request subsequently served is of no effect. The position is dealt with in s. 26(4) and can be summarised as follows:

(a) if the landlord serves a valid s. 25 notice, the tenant cannot subsequently serve a valid tenant's request under s. 26;
(b) if the tenant has served a valid notice to quit, he cannot subsequently serve a valid request for a new tenancy under s. 26;
(c) if the tenant has served a valid notice under s. 27(1) or (2), he cannot subsequently serve a valid request for a new tenancy under s. 26;
(d) if the tenant has served a valid s. 26 request, the landlord cannot subsequently serve a valid s. 25 notice.

> NOTE: The tenant can terminate his tenancy under s. 27 after the landlord has served a valid s. 25 notice: *Long Acre Securities Ltd* v. *Electro Acoustics Ltd* (1989).

15. Effect of the 1954 Act ceasing to apply to a tenancy. There is another important aspect of termination which remains to be considered, i.e. the effect of the 1954 Act ceasing to apply to a tenancy. An example of this arises if the premises cease to be used for business purposes. Section 24(3) contains special provisions dealing with this and their effect is as follows:

(a) In the case of a term of years certain, if the 1954 Act ceases to apply to it before its expiry there will be no continuation under s. 24 because the tenancy is not one to which the 1954 Act applies. The decision in *Long Acre Securities* v. *Electro Acoustics Ltd* (1989) leaves open the question of how long before the contractual expiry date the tenant must have ceased to occupy for business purposes before the 1954 Act ceases to apply.

(b) In the case of a periodic tenancy to which the 1954 Act ceases to apply, the tenancy can be brought to an end by a common law notice to quit. Even if the tenancy becomes one to which the 1954 Act applies after the notice to quit has been given, e.g. because the tenant goes back into occupation for business purposes, the validity of the notice to quit is unaffected and the tenancy will end on the date specified in the notice to quit.

(c) If a tenancy was granted for a term of years certain and ceases to be a tenancy to which the 1954 Act applies after it has been continued under s. 24, it will not come to an end by reason only of its ceasing to be a tenancy to which the 1954 Act applies. However the landlord can then terminate the tenancy be giving to the tenant not less than three nor more than six months' notice in writing. There is no prescribed form for such a notice.

16. Service of notices under the 1954 Act. It is obviously important to ensure that any notice, request or counternotice required by the 1954 Act is properly served upon the intended recipient. By virtue of s. 66(4) of the 1954 Act, the provisions of s. 23 of the 1927 Act apply. Section 23 of the 1927 Act provides that any notice may be served on the person to whom it is addressed either:

(a) personally; or

(b) by leaving it for him at his last known place of abode in England or Wales. The business address of the intended recipient is included in the expression 'last known place of abode' (*Price* v. *West London Investment Building Society Limited* (1964)); or

(c) by sending it through the post in a registered letter addressed to him there (by virtue of the Recorded Delivery Act 1962, service by recorded delivery post is also now sufficient); or

(d) in the case of a local or public authority or a statutory or public utility company, by sending the notice to the secretary or other proper officer at the principal office of such authority or company.

> NOTES: (1) Service on a limited company should be effected at the company's registered office.
>
> (2) The methods of service prescribed by s. 23 of the 1927 Act are permissive, not exhaustive, so that service by some other means is sufficient if the notice actually reaches the intended recipient (*Stylo Shoes* v. *Prices Tailors Ltd* (1960) and *Galinski* v. *McHugh* (1988)).
>
> (3) It is good practice to use the recorded delivery service (see *Chiswell* v. *Griffon Land and Estates Ltd* (1975) and *Lex Service plc* v. *Johns* (1990)).

Progress test 11

1. On what terms does a business tenancy continue under section 24? (2)

2. Which of the following methods of termination bring a business tenancy to an end without the necessity for service of any notice under the 1954 Act:
   (a) forfeiture;
   (b) effluxion of time;
   (c) notice to quit served by the landlord;
   (d) surrender;
   (e) notice to quit given by the tenant? (3)

3. L grants T a lease of premises for 5 years. T underlets the whole of the premises to UT for 5 years less 3 days. UT's contractual term has 12 months to run. Who is the competent landlord so far as UT is concerned? (5)

4. What is a s. 25 notice? (7)

5. L grants a yearly tenancy of business premises to T. The tenancy runs from 1st March 1975. In August 1978 L decides that he wishes to end the tenancy. What is the earliest date at which L can end the tenancy and why? Would your answer be any different if it was in October 1978 that he decided? (7)

6. How can a business tenant establish the identity of the competent landlord? (5)

7. T has a periodic quarterly tenancy. Can he serve a tenant's request for a new tenancy? (11)

8. What steps should be taken by:
   (a) a business tenant who receives a section 25 notice; and
   (b) a landlord who has received a tenant's request and who wishes to oppose the grant of a new tenancy? (10, 12)

9. L lets premises to T for a term of seven years from 1st January 1981; T occupies the premises for business purposes. At the end of the term T wishes to leave. What formalities, if any, must T comply with? Would your answer be different if:
   (a) T had not decided to leave until after the contractual term had ended, or

(b) T did not occupy the premises when the contractual term ended? **(13)**

10. How should a section 25 notice be served? **(16)**

12

The tenant's application to the court for a new tenancy

Introduction

1. Generally. The effect of the notice procedure described in Chapter 11 is that the parties can see where they stand in relation to each other. The landlord may be willing to grant a new tenancy to the tenant, in which case he will say so in his notice under s. 25 of the 1954 Act, or it will be apparent that he is willing to grant a new tenancy from the fact that he has not served a counter-notice to the tenant's request for a new tenancy under s. 26.

Whether or not the landlord has stated that he will oppose the grant of a new tenancy, the tenant is entitled to apply to the court for the grant of a new tenancy. If the landlord is willing to grant a new tenancy, the tenant is entitled to an order for the grant of a new tenancy as of right, provided he has taken the necessary steps to protect his position. In most cases, however, the landlord and the tenant are able to agree the terms of the new tenancy and the tenant's application to the court is only heard by the court when negotiations have broken down. The tenant must always apply to the court within the prescribed period no matter how near to agreement the parties are, for if he fails to do so he will lose his right to a new tenancy.

If the landlord has stated that he will oppose the grant of a new tenancy, the tenant will be entitled to a new tenancy only if he makes an application to the court within the prescribed period and the landlord cannot prove the ground or grounds set out in s. 30(1) upon which he has stated he will oppose the grant of a new tenancy.

Application

2. The tenant's application to the court. As appears from Chapter 11, a tenant's right to apply to the court for the grant of a new tenancy depends on:

(a) the landlord having served a s. 25 notice or the tenant having served a s. 26 request;

(b) if the application follows a s. 25 notice, the tenant having notified the landlord within two months after the giving of the notice that he is unwilling to give up possession, i.e. a tenant's 'counter-notice' (s. 29(2));

(c) the tenant having applied to the court not less than two months and not more than four months after the giving of the s. 25 notice or the s. 26 request (s. 29(3));

(d) the tenant having served his application to the court upon the landlord within two months of the date on which the application was issued (Order 97 RSC and Order 43 CCR).

It is important that the tenant should have complied strictly with all the time limits; any failure to comply will deprive the tenant of his right to a new tenancy. There are only two exceptions:

(*i*) the landlord can expressly or impliedly waive the time limits (*Kammins Ballroom Co. Ltd* v. *Zenith Investments Torquay Ltd* (1971)); and

(*ii*) in the case of the time limit mentioned in **(d)** above only, the court has a discretionary power to extend the tenant's time for serving his application to the court upon the landlord (*Lewis* v. *Wolking Properties* (1978) and *Ward-Lee* v. *Linehan* (1993)). The court exercises its discretion sparingly however (*Ali* v. *Knight* (1984)).

3. The court. The tenant's application is made either to the High Court (Chancery Division) or the county court (s. 63(2) as amended by the High Court and County Courts Jurisdiction Order 1991). There are no longer any rateable value limits to determine if the application should be made to the High Court or the county court. The county court now has jurisdiction in all cases and in practice, most applications under the 1954 Act are issued and dealt with in the county court. CCR Order 4, rule 8 applies as regards venue. In practice most applications under the 1954 Act are issued in the county court for the district in which the premises are situated.

If the tenant's application is made to the county court, in certain circumstances either party may seek an Order for the transfer of the proceedings to the High Court or vice versa (s. 63(4)(b)). CCR Order 16 deals with the transfer of proceedings from one county court to another. If the application is inadvertently made to the wrong court, the tenant's position is nonetheless protected but the proceedings will be transferred to the correct court (s. 63(4)(a)).

In the High Court the application is made by way of originating summons. In the county court the application is made by way of originating application. The rules of procedure governing such applications are set out in Order 97 RSC and Order 43 CCR respectively.

NOTES: (1) The provisions for service of notices under the 1954 Act considered in Chapter 11 do not apply to service of a tenant's application to the court. Service of the tenant's application must be effected by one of the methods prescribed by the Rules of the Supreme Court or the county court Rules as appropriate.

(2) In the county court the landlord is required to file and serve an Answer to the tenant's originating application within fourteen days of service of the originating application upon him. If the landlord fails to do so he may lose his right to oppose the grant of a new tenancy (*Desbroderie Ltd* v. *Segalov* (1956)).

4. Special cases: joint tenancies and partnerships. The application to the court must be made by the tenant. Where there are joint tenants the old rule was that all the tenants must apply whether or not they were still active in the business (*Jacobs* v. *Chaudhuri* (1968)). This rule has now been altered in certain situations by s. 41A of the 1954 Act which was added by the 1969 Act. The main provisions of s. 41A can be summarised as follows:

(a) where the tenancy is held jointly by two or more persons ('the joint tenants'); and

(b) at one time a business was carried on in partnership by all the joint tenants (either with or without other partners); and

(c) the tenancy was then partnership property; and

(d) the business is now being carried on by one or some only of the joint tenants whether alone or in partnership with other persons (the joint tenants who still carry on the business and those other persons, if any, being known as 'the business tenants'); and

(e) the other joint tenants do not occupy any part of the premises comprised in the tenancy for the purposes of a business they carry on; then:

(*i*) the business tenants on their own may make a request for a new tenancy pursuant to s. 26 or serve notice to terminate the tenancy pursuant to s. 27 (s. 41A(3));

(*ii*) the landlord may address his s. 25 notice to the business tenants only (s. 41A(4));

(*iii*) the business tenants on their own may apply to the court for a new tenancy (s. 41A(5)).

Section 41A is designed to deal with cases where, for example, four individuals who are carrying on business in partnership take a lease of premises to be occupied for the purposes of the partnership's business and by the time the lease expires some of those individuals have retired from the partnership. Section 41A enables the individuals who are still carrying on business at the premises to apply for a new tenancy in their own right.

5. The procedure on a tenant's application. If the parties agree terms for the grant of a new tenancy, the parties may consent to an Order by the court for the grant of a new tenancy on the terms agreed. Often however the parties simply enter into a new lease on the agreed terms without the necessity for any Order by the court. Thereafter it is common for the tenant to withdraw his application to the court.

If the parties are unable to agree terms the matter will go to trial and the court will decide the terms that the parties have not agreed. Each party will put forward his evidence in support of the terms he proposes (e.g. evidence from a surveyor as to the open market rental value of the premises if the amount of the rent which should be paid under the new tenancy is in dispute) and the judge will decide on that evidence what terms are appropriate.

If the landlord opposes the grant of a new tenancy the court will normally order that the ground of opposition be tried as a preliminary issue (*Dutch Oven Ltd* v. *Egham Estates and Investment Co. Ltd* (1968)). If the landlord succeeds, the question of the terms of a new tenancy will not arise for consideration and thus costs will not have been incurred unnecessarily in arguing what the terms of any new tenancy should be.

6. Interim continuation of tenancies. Provided that the tenant has made his application to the court for a new tenancy in good time and served the application to the court upon the landlord in good time, his current tenancy will continue beyond the termination date specified in the landlord's s. 25 notice or the date specified in the tenant's request under s. 26 as the case may be.

Section 64 of the 1954 Act provides that the tenant's current tenancy will then continue until the date which is three months after the date upon which the tenant's application to the court is finally disposed of and any time for appealing has expired.

The time limit for service of notice of appeal to the Court of Appeal is four weeks (Order 59 Rule 4 of RSC).

The effect of s. 64 is therefore as follows:

(a) when the terms of the new tenancy are determined by the court, the current tenancy will come to an end three months and four weeks after the date of the court's judgment;

(b) if either party serves notice of appeal within four weeks of the date

of the judgment, the current tenancy will come to an end three months and four weeks after the date of the Court of Appeal's judgment;
(c) if the tenant withdraws his application for a new tenancy, the current tenancy will end three months after the date upon which the application is withdrawn (as no question of any appeal arises, it is not appropriate to add a further four weeks as in cases **(a)** and **(b)** above).

NOTE: If an 'appeal' is invalid because it is made out of time, the current tenancy will end three months and four weeks after the date of the original judgment (*Shotley Point Marina (1986) Ltd* v. *Spalding* (1989)).

When the tenancy continues under s. 64, it does so on the same terms as were in force at the termination of the contractual tenancy. The landlord may, however, apply for an interim rent.

7. Interim rent. In view of the provisions of s. 64 considered at **6** above, it is possible that the current tenancy may continue for many months or even years beyond the termination date specified in the landlord's s. 25 notice or the date specified in the tenant's request under s. 26. This might be because protracted negotiations take place before the parties conclude that an agreement will not be reached and that the court should be asked to determine the terms of the new tenancy or because one of the parties appeals against the court's decision at first instance.

If, for example, the current tenancy was created many years ago and reserved a rent which is dramatically less than the current open market rental value of the premises, the landlord could be seriously prejudiced and the tenant could derive a substantial, unjustifiable benefit if the landlord could only recover the 'old' rent until the new tenancy commences. Section 24A of the 1954 Act was added by the 1969 Act to cover this situation.

Under s. 24A the court may, on the application of the landlord, determine a rent which it will be reasonable for the tenant to pay while his current tenancy continues. The rent so payable is commonly referred to as 'interim rent'. Interim rent is payable from:
(*i*) the date of termination specified in the s. 25 notice or s. 26 request; or
(*ii*) the date upon which the application for an interim rent is made to the court,
whichever is the later.

The summons or notice of application for determination of an interim rent should be served promptly, however, and may be struck out by the court if it is not (*Texaco Ltd* v. *Benton & Bowles Holdings Ltd* (1983) and *Coates Brothers Plc* v. *General Accident Life Assurance Ltd*

(1991)). The court has a discretion as to whether or not it should determine an interim rent, but that discretion is usually exercised affirmatively. If an interim rent is determined:

(a) the court assumes that the tenant has an annual tenancy of the premises, i.e. determinable on six months' notice;
(b) the interim rent is determined having regard to rental values prevailing at the commencement of the 'interim' period, which will usually be the date specified in the landlord's s. 25 notice, or the tenant's request under s. 26 (*English Exporters (London) Ltd* v. *Eldonwall Ltd* (1973));
(c) the interim rent is determined having regard to the actual condition and state of repair of the premises, notwithstanding the fact that the premises are in a poor state of repair because of breaches of the parties' repairing obligations (*Fawke* v. *Viscount Chelsea* (1980));
(d) the interim rent fixed is the open market rent determined in accordance with s. 34 (rent payable under the new tenancy, *see* Chapter 13), but the court is required to have regard to the rent payable under the current tenancy and in so doing will usually 'cushion' the tenant from the shock of having to pay an increased rent (*English Exporters (London) Ltd* v. *Eldonwall Ltd* (1973) and *see also Charles Follett Ltd* v. *Cabtell Investment Co. Ltd* (1987)).

The result of this exercise is that the interim rent is usually somewhat less than the open market rent for the premises.

> NOTE: Although the tenant is only entitled to a new tenancy of 'the holding', i.e. that part of the premises comprised in his tenancy which he occupies, (*see* Chapter 13), the interim rent is payable in respect of the whole of the premises comprised in the current tenancy. This is because under both ss. 24 and 64 the tenant's current tenancy of the whole of the premises originally demised to him continues.

Progress test 12

1. When may a tenant apply to the court for a new tenancy? (2)

2. The tenant issues his application for a new tenancy in the county court and asks the county court to effect service on the landlord. The court fails to effect service due to an administrative error. What is the tenant's position? (2)

3. When and in what manner should the tenant's application for a new tenancy be served? (2)

4. Which is the appropriate court to hear applications under the 1954 Act? **(3)**

5. The landlord lets property to A, B, C and D who are partners in a business. D dies and B leaves the business. Who should make application to the court for a new tenancy? **(4)**

6. The landlord is opposing the tenant's application to the court on one of the grounds set out in section 30(1). How will the tenant's application usually proceed and why? **(5)**

7. The tenant's application to the court is determined by the court on 1st December 1988. When will the tenant's current tenancy come to an end? Would your answer be any different if the tenant withdrew his application to the court on 1st December 1988? **(6)**

8. The tenant's application to the court is determined by the county court on 1st December 1988. The tenant is dissatisfied with the county court's decision. By what date must the tenant serve notice of appeal and when will his current tenancy end if he does so? **(6)**

9. How may a landlord protect himself during the currency of proceedings under the 1954 Act? **(7)**

10. On what basis is an interim rent determined by the court? **(7)**

Terms of new tenancy ordered to be granted by the court

Introduction

1. Generally. Under the 1954 Act the court is only asked to determine the tenant's application for a new tenancy if the parties are unable to reach agreement. In practice the parties will often be able to agree. There are two main ways in which the court may become involved. First, if the landlord opposes the grant of a new tenancy, his ground of opposition will normally be tried as a preliminary issue. If the landlord fails in his opposition, the court will usually adjourn the proceedings to give the parties the opportunity to agree the terms of the new tenancy to which the tenant will then be entitled. If the parties are unable to agree terms, the proceedings are restored and the terms are determined by the court. Secondly, if the landlord does not oppose the grant of a new tenancy but the parties cannot agree terms, the court will be asked to determine the terms.

The terms of a new tenancy

2. The terms which the court has jurisdiction to determine. These terms are:

(a) the property (s. 32);
(b) the duration (s. 33);
(c) the rent (s. 34);
(d) other terms (s. 35).

3. The property. Section 32(1) provides that the new tenancy will be of 'the holding' as at the date of the court's Order. The 'holding' is defined in s. 23(2) as being the property comprised in the current tenancy excluding any part which is not occupied by the tenant or a person employed by the tenant for the purposes of the tenant's business.

There are two exceptions to the rule that the new tenancy will be of the holding:

(a) where the landlord opposes the grant of a new tenancy on the ground set out at s. 30(1)(*f*) and the court orders the grant of a tenancy of part of the premises only (*see* 14:**11**);

(b) where the landlord exercises the power given to him by s. 32(2) to require the new tenancy to be of the whole of the premises comprised in the current tenancy, e.g. including parts of the premises which have been sublet.

Where the current tenancy includes rights enjoyed by the tenant in connection with the holding, these will be included in the new tenancy unless the parties agree otherwise or the court so determines (s. 32(3)). In *Re No 1 Albermarle Street* (1959) the court determined that the right to display advertising signs on the premises which the tenant enjoyed under his current tenancy should be included in the new tenancy.

4. The duration of the new tenancy. Section 33 provides that the tenancy will be of such duration as the parties may agree or, in default of agreement, such as the court shall determine in all the circumstances to be reasonable (*Leonard Becker* v. *Hill Street Properties Ltd* (1990)). When the court determines the duration, there is an upper limit of 14 years on the term that may be ordered.

In cases where the tenant only requires a short term, the court must balance the tenant's desire for flexibility and reluctance to accept the obligations imposed by a tenancy for a longer term than he desires, against the landlord's desire for certainty (*CBS United Kingdom Ltd* v. *London Scottish Properties Ltd* (1985)). The court may also order the grant of a short term at the landlord's request when the landlord intends to redevelop the premises in the near future (*Reohorn* v. *Barry Corporation* (1956)) or if the landlord intends to occupy the premises himself but cannot oppose the grant of a new tenancy on the ground set out under s. 30(1)(*g*) (*see* Chapter 14) because he has not been the landlord for five years (*Upsons Ltd* v. *E. Robins Ltd* (1956)).

As an alternative to ordering the grant of a new tenancy for a short term if it appears likely that the landlord may require the premises for redevelopment in the future, the court may order the insertion of a break clause in the new tenancy (*McCombie* v. *Grand Junction Co. Ltd* (1962)).

NOTES: (1) The court is entitled to order the grant of a periodic tenancy.

(2) The new tenancy will commence (in the absence of agreement) three months and four weeks after the date of the court's judgment.

5. Rent. Section 34(1) provides that, in the absence of agreement, the rent will be that at which, having regard to the other terms of the new tenancy, the holding might reasonably be expected to be let in the open market by a willing lessor after disregarding certain factors. The other terms of the new tenancy must first be determined as those terms may well have an effect upon the open market rental value of the premises (*Cardshops Ltd* v. *Davies* (1971)). The factors which the court must disregard in determining the rent are:

(a) any effect on rent of the fact that the tenant or his predecessors in title have been in occupation;

(b) any goodwill attached to the holding by reason of the carrying on of the tenant's business;

(c) any effect on rent of an improvement carried out by a person who was at the time the tenant of the premises (otherwise than in pursuance of an obligation to the landlord), and either

(*i*) it was carried out during the current tenancy; or

(*ii*) it was completed not more than 21 years before the application to the court is made and, at all times since, the holding has been comprised in tenancies to which the 1954 Act applies and the tenant did not quit the premises at the termination of each of those tenancies;

(d) where the holding comprises licensed premises, any addition in value due to the licence held by the tenant.

There is authority for the proposition that, in determining the rent, the court will disregard any breaches of the tenant's repairing obligations (*Family Management* v. *Gray* (1979) and *Crown Estate Commissioners* v. *Town Investments Ltd* (1992)). The rent will be determined having regard to rental values prevailing at the date of trial but the court can also take into account matters relevant to the amount of the rent which can reasonably be expected to happen between the date of trial and the date when, having regard to s. 64, the tenancy will commence (*Lovely & Orchard Services Ltd* v. *Daejan Investments Ltd* (1977)).

Under s. 34(3) the court has power to include provisions for review of the rent payable under the new tenancy; these may provide for the rent to be reviewed downwards as well as upwards (*Stylo Shoes Ltd* v. *Manchester Royal Exchange Ltd* (1967); *Janes (Gowns) Ltd* v. *Harlow Development Corporation* (1979)). Where the current lease includes provision for the rent to be reviewed upwards only however, the court may follow the form of the clause in the current lease (*Charles Follett Ltd* v. *Cabtell Investment Co. Ltd* (1987)). Nonetheless the current trend in the county court is to order upwards and downwards reviews.

The court will usually determine the rent on the basis of evidence given as to the rental values of comparable properties. Where premises have an uncommon use however, such as an hotel, a petrol filling station, a theatre or a racecourse and the rental evidence available on comparable premises is inadequate, the profitability of the business carried on at the premises may be relevant. The rule now appears to be that the court will allow evidence of the profitability of the business, such as trading accounts, if that evidence is publicly available but that the court will not order the tenant to give discovery of private trading records and accounts which are not publicly available (*Cornwall Coast Country Club* v. *Cardgrange Ltd* (1987)).

NOTES: (1) In *Simonite* v. *Sheffield City Council* (1992) the court was concerned with the renewal of the tenancies of numerous stalls in a market which all expired at about the same time. It was held that it could not be assumed, in dealing with any particular stall, that all other stalls were, or soon would be, vacant. In determining the rent, the 'supply' of stalls was not assumed to be large and should be considered in the context that most other stalls were already let. This principle could be extended to more common situations, such as a building in multiple occupation or a shopping centre, where the tenancies all expire at about the same time.

(2) In *Land Securities PLC* v. *City of Westminster* (1993) it was held that an arbitrator's rent review award is not admissible in evidence.

(3) While evidence of without prejudice negotiations between the landlord and the tenant is inadmissible, evidence of without prejudice negotiations between other parties, in different proceedings, was held to be admissible in the county court case of *Percy Bartram Ltd* v. *Standard Life Assurance Company* (1990).

6. Other terms. Section 35 of the 1954 Act provides that the other terms of the new tenancy shall be such as may be agreed by the parties or determined by the court and that in determining those terms the court shall have regard to the terms of the current tenancy and to all relevant circumstances.

In *O'May* v. *The City of London Real Property Company Ltd* (1983) the landlord of a block of offices sought to impose service charge obligations on the tenants which would have transferred responsibility for the cost of repair and maintenance of the exterior of the premises and other common parts from the landlord to the tenant. The House of Lords held that the landlord was not entitled to do so and gave important guidance upon the operation of s. 35. In particular, the court held that it is a matter for the party seeking a variation in the terms of the tenancy to justify the variation and that the variation proposed must be fair and reasonable in all the circumstances.

In *Charles Clements (London) Ltd* v. *Rank City Wall Ltd* (1978) the court refused to relax the user clause against the tenant's will when the landlord was seeking the variation solely in order to enable him to obtain a higher rent. Similarly in *Gold* v. *Brighton Corporation* (1956) where the tenant had traded in new and secondhand clothes and the landlord sought to have included a term preventing the tenant from carrying on the sale of secondhand clothes, the Court of Appeal held that it would be wrong to introduce this clause into the new tenancy as it would limit the business which the tenant had previously carried on.

The court has power to insert a break clause for redevelopment (*Adams* v. *Green* (1978): *National Car Parks Ltd* v. *Paternoster Consortium Ltd* (1989)).

In *Cairnplace Ltd* v. *CBL (Property Investment) Co. Ltd* (1984) it was held that the court has power to order a term that the tenant provide guarantors. However, in that case it was also held that it cannot order the tenant to pay the costs of preparing the lease.

7. Carrying out of the order for a new tenancy. If the court makes an order for the grant of a new tenancy and the tenant decides that he does not wish to accept a tenancy on the terms determined by the court, he may apply to the court for revocation of the order within 14 days. The current tenancy will then come to an end at such date either agreed by the parties or determined by the court, as will allow the landlord a reasonable opportunity for re-letting or otherwise disposing of the premises (s. 36(2)).

Unless the tenant applies for revocation of the order for the grant of a new tenancy under s. 36(2), the landlord is bound to execute, and the tenant is bound to accept a lease or agreement for a tenancy embodying the terms set out in the court's order. Furthermore, if the landlord requires him to do so, the tenant must execute a counterpart or duplicate of the lease or agreement for a tenancy.

Progress test 13

1. What is the holding? **(3)**

2. In what circumstances can a tenant be required to accept a new tenancy of premises other than the holding? **(3)**

3. What is the maximum duration of a new tenancy ordered to be granted by the Court?   **(4)**

4. L anticipates that he may wish to redevelop the premises in three years time. T has applied to the court for a new tenancy. Advise L.   **(4)** and **(6)**

5. What factors will the court disregard in determining the rent payable under the new tenancy?   **(5)**

6. What evidence will the court consider in determining the new rent?   **(5)**

7. What provisions for rent review may the court include in the new tenancy?   **(5)**

8. T carries on the business of the sale of stationery, confectionery and tobacco. L is revolted by all forms of smoking. Can the landlord prevent the tenant from selling tobacco under the new tenancy?   **(6)**

9. T feels that he will be unable to pay the rent which the court has ordered will be payable under the new tenancy. What steps should T take?   **(7)**

Opposing the tenant's application for a new tenancy

Introduction

1. Generally. The object of the 1954 Act is to provide business tenants with security of tenure and to entitle them to obtain a new tenancy of their premises. Parliament recognised, however, that either because of the conduct of the tenant or the landlord's own plans for the premises, it would be justifiable to enable the landlord to recover possession at the end of the current tenancy in certain circumstances.

A landlord may therefore state in his s. 25 notice, or in his counternotice to a tenant's request for a new tenancy under s. 26, that he will oppose an application to the court for the grant of a new tenancy and if he does so, he must also specify the ground or grounds upon which the tenant's application will be opposed.

Grounds for opposing the tenant's application

2. The grounds of opposition. These are set out in s. 30(1) of the 1954 Act. It should be remembered that the landlord can only rely on the grounds he has specified in his s. 25 notice or his counternotice to a tenant's request under s. 26. Similarly, if a landlord sells his interest after having served a s. 25 notice, the purchaser landlord can only rely upon the grounds specified in the vendor landlord's notice. The grounds are as follows:

(a) where under the current tenancy the tenant has any obligations as respects the repair and maintenance of the holding, that the tenant ought not to be granted a new tenancy in view of the state of repair of the holding, being a state resulting from the tenant's failure to comply with the said obligations;

(b) that the tenant ought not to be granted a new tenancy in view of his persistent delay in paying rent which has become due;

(c) that the tenant ought not to be granted a new tenancy in view of other substantial breaches by him of his obligations under the current tenancy or for any other reason connected with the tenant's use or management of the holding;

(d) that the landlord has offered, and is willing to provide or secure, the provision of alternative accommodation for the tenant, that the terms on which the alternative accommodation is available are reasonable having regard to the terms of the current tenancy and to all other relevant circumstances and that the accommodation and the time at which it will be available are suitable for the tenant's requirements (including the requirement to preserve goodwill) having regard to the nature and class of the business and to the situation and extent of and facilities afforded by the holding;

(e) where the current tenancy was created by the sub-letting of part only of the property comprised in a superior tenancy and the landlord is the owner of an interest in reversion expectant on the termination of that superior tenancy, that the aggregate of the rents reasonably obtainable on separate lettings of the holding and the remainder of that property would be substantially less than the rent reasonably obtainable on a letting of the property as a whole, that on the termination of the current tenancy the landlord requires possession of the holding for the purpose of letting or otherwise disposing of the said property as a whole and that in view thereof the tenant ought not to be granted a new tenancy;

(f) that on the termination of the current tenancy the landlord intends to demolish or reconstruct the premises comprised in the holding, or a substantial part of those premises, or to carry out substantial work of construction on the holding or part thereof and that he could not reasonably do so without obtaining possession of the holding;

(g) that on the termination of the current tenancy the landlord intends to occupy the holding for the purposes, or partly for the purposes, of a business to be carried on by him therein, or as his residence.

It should be noted that grounds **(a)**, **(b)**, **(c)** and **(e)** are discretionary in that even if the facts are established the court has to consider whether in the circumstances 'the tenant ought not to be granted a new tenancy'. In relation to the other grounds, if the facts are established, the court must find for the landlord.

3. Ground (a) – failure to repair. The onus is on the landlord to prove that the premises are in a state of disrepair as a result of the tenant's failure to comply with his repairing obligations under the current tenancy.

This is one of the discretionary grounds and, as the new tenancy will impose similar repairing obligations upon the tenant and the landlord will be entitled to seek forfeiture of the new tenancy if the tenant does not put the premises into repair promptly, the court may incline to the view that the landlord's position will be adequately protected, whereas the tenant could be severely prejudiced if he does not obtain a new tenancy.

4. Ground (b) – persistent delay in paying rent. In relying upon this ground of opposition, the landlord is required to prove that there has been 'persistent delay' in paying rent. It is not sufficient to show that at the date of service of the s. 25 notice, or the date of trial, there are large current arrears. This is another of the discretionary grounds. The following two cases illustrate that it is difficult to predict how the court will exercise its discretion:

(i) *Hurstfell Ltd* v. *Leicester Square Property Co. Ltd* (1988). The tenant had failed to pay on time the rent and insurance payments due on 11 consecutive quarter days and the landlord was constantly chasing him for payment. Cheques had been dishonoured and proceedings for recovery of arrears had been issued twice. As the current tenancy drew to an end, however, the tenant promptly made payment of the rent due from him. The trial judge was persuaded that the tenant's past record was largely due to business difficulties but that the tenant's financial position was improving. The ground of opposition failed and the Court of Appeal refused to interfere with the trial judge's exercise of his discretion.

(ii) *Rawasdeh* v. *Lane* (1988). Between 1981 and 1987 the tenant had never paid rent on time and the delay in making payment was sometimes several weeks. Cheques had been dishonoured and the landlords had twice issued proceedings for recovery of rent. The ground of opposition succeeded.

A tenant can improve his position by offering to subject himself to conditions such as payment of interest on arrears, the provision of a rent deposit and sureties.

5. Ground (c) – other substantial breaches or other reasons connected with the tenant's use or management of the holding. This is another of the discretionary grounds. The court will have to consider the nature of the obligations and the extent of the breach. The landlord is also entitled to rely upon conduct by the tenant in relation to the use or management of the holding which does not constitute a breach of covenant (*Beard (formerly Coleman)* v. *Williams* (1986)).

6. Ground (d) – alternative accommodation. The alternative accommodation must be provided or secured by the landlord and the terms must be reasonable having regard to the terms of the current tenancy. The accommodation must be suitable to the tenant's requirements, bearing in mind the nature and class of his business and the situation and extent of his holding.

7. Ground (e) – letting of property as a whole. This ground is rarely used in practice, since it is very difficult for the requisite circumstances to arise and it is not therefore considered here.

8. Ground (f) – the landlord requires possession to demolish or reconstruct. This is one of the most important grounds. It comprises the following elements which are considered in the following paragraphs:

(*i*) the landlord intends (*see* **9**);

(*ii*) to demolish or reconstruct the premises comprised in the holding, or a substantial part of those premises, or to carry out substantial work of construction on the holding or part thereof (*see* **10**);

(*iii*) and that he could not reasonably do so without obtaining possession of the holding (*see* **11**).

9. The landlord intends. The following points should be noted:

(a) The intention must be established at the time the court hears the application (*Betty's Cafes Ltd* v. *Phillips Furnishing Stores Ltd* (1959)).

(b) A landlord can rely upon a s. 25 notice served by himself or by his predecessor in title. If he relies on a notice served by a predecessor in title, it does not matter that the notice was served by a predecessor who then had no intention himself (*Marks* v. *British Waterways Board* (1963)).

(c) In order to establish 'intention', it must be shown that there is a firm and settled intention to do something which there is a reasonable prospect of bringing about (*Reohorn* v. *Barry Corporation* (1956); *Cunliffe* v. *Goodman* (1950) and *Edwards* v. *Thompson* (1990));

(d) A landlord cannot rely on ground **(f)** (*see* **8**) if he merely wishes to sell the premises with vacant possession to a purchaser who will carry out the works (but an intention to redevelop with a view to an eventual sale is permissible; see *Turner* v. *Wandsworth LBC* (1994)).

(e) A landlord will succeed, however, if his intention is to grant a building lease of the premises to a developer (*Gilmour Caterers Ltd* v. *St. Bartholomew's Hospital Board of Governors* (1956); *Spook Erection Ltd* v. *BRB* (1988)).

(f) A landlord can have the necessary intention even if he has no full understanding of the proposed method of development and has entrusted the whole matter to his advisers (*P.F. Ahern & Sons Ltd* v. *Hunt* (1988)).

(g) If such matters as planning permission and consent under the building regulations are needed, it will assist the landlord's case if he has secured the grant of them by the time of the hearing; not having them by then will not necessarily be fatal provided the Court is satisfied that there is a reasonable chance of getting them (*Gregson* v. *Cyril Lord* (1963)).

(h) The court has stated that an undertaking by the landlord to carry out the works compels 'fixity of intention' (*London Hilton Jewellers Ltd* v. *Hilton International Hotels Ltd* (1990)).

10. To demolish or reconstruct the premises or carry out substantial work of construction. Whether this requirement is satisfied in any case will be a question of fact. It is important to note that the landlord must prove that he intends to carry out the works to the holding. Works to, e.g., other parts of the building in which the holding is situated are not relevant.

The court will look at the position as a whole and compare the holding in its existing condition with the premises as they will appear after the proposed works have been carried out. Some examples may show how the courts treat such cases:

Joel v. *Swaddle* (1957). L intended to change a small shop with two storage rooms into part of a large hall to be used as an amusement area. It was HELD that there was an intention to reconstruct within the scope of ground **(f)**.

Percy E. Cadle & Co. Ltd v. *Jacmarch Properties Ltd* (1957). L intended to convert three floors, which had been occupied separately, into a single unit by installing new internal staircases. It was HELD that this did not satisfy ground **(f)**.

Atkinson v. *Bettison* (1955). The mere installation of a new shop front was HELD not to be reconstruction of a substantial part of the premises or the carrying out of substantial works.

NOTES: (1) Works of 'reconstruction' must primarily be works of rebuilding involving a substantial interference with the structure of the building, but 'structure' is not necessarily confined to external or other load-bearing walls. (*Romulus Trading Co. Ltd* v. *Henry Smith's Charity Trustees* (1990); see also *City Offices (Regent Street) Ltd* v. *Europa Acceptance Group PLC* (1990)).

(2) Work of 'construction' requires some form of building which involves the structure (*Barth* v. *Pritchard* (1990)).

11. He could not reasonably do so without obtaining possession.
In order to succeed under ground **(f)**, the landlord must prove that he requires legal, as opposed to merely physical, possession of the holding. Accordingly if the landlord has power under the terms of the current tenancy to enter upon the premises to execute works and those powers are sufficient to enable him to carry out his proposed works, he will be unable to rely on ground **(f)**.

In *Heath* v. *Drown* (1973) T occupied premises for the purposes of a business under two leases, each of which reserved to L the right to enter and carry out necessary repairs. L served notices on T under s. 25 relying on ground **(f)** to resist the grant of a new tenancy to T. The House of Lords held that it was not reasonably necessary for L to obtain possession of the holding as it was conceded that he could carry out the works under the reservations and therefore L could not bring himself within the words of s. 30(1)**(f)**.

If the current tenancy does not give the landlord sufficient rights of access to carry out his proposed works, the landlord may still be unable to succeed in his opposition to the grant of a new tenancy if the tenant invokes the provisions of s. 31A of the 1954 Act which provides that the court shall not hold that the landlord could not reasonably carry out the intended works without obtaining possession of the holding if:

(a) the tenant agrees to the inclusion in the new tenancy of terms giving to the landlord access and other facilities for carrying out the work intended, and the landlord could thereby reasonably carry out the work without obtaining possession of the holding and without interfering to a substantial extent or for a substantial time with the tenant's use of the holding, or
(b) the tenant is willing to accept a tenancy of an economically separable part of the holding and either
    (*i*) condition **(a)** above is satisfied with respect to that part; or
    (*ii*) possession of the remainder of the holding would be reasonably sufficient to enable the landlord to carry out the intended work.

In considering whether the intended works will involve interference with the tenant's use of the holding to a substantial extent, or for a substantial time, the court will look at the physical effect of the work on the tenant's use of the holding, as opposed to the effect upon the tenant's business. In *Redfern* v. *Reeves* (1978) the fact that the tenant could carry on her business at other premises for the period of 2–4 months which it would take to carry out the landlord's works to the holding, was held to be irrelevant to the issue to be decided under s. 31A(1)**(a)**.

The tenant will obtain a new tenancy unless the intended works will result in interference which is substantial and which will continue for a substantial time (*Cerex Jewels Ltd* v. *Peachey Property Corporation plc* (1986) and *Blackburn* v. *Hussain* (1988)).

Any of the intended works which the landlord can carry out under a power of entry in the tenancy will be disregarded in assessing the extent and the length of the interference with the tenant's use of the holding (*Cerex Jewels Ltd* v. *Peachey Property Corporation* (1986)).

Section 31A(2) provides that in cases where the tenant is prepared to give up possession of part of the holding so as to enable the landlord to carry out the intended works, the part of the holding retained by the tenant will only be 'an economically separable part', if the aggregate of the rents obtainable, after the completion of the intended works, for the retained part and the remainder of the premises affected by the work or resulting from the work, will not be substantially less than the rent which would then be reasonably obtainable on a letting of those premises as a whole.

12. Ground (g) – the landlord intends to occupy the holding. The landlord must show a firm intention to occupy the premises for the purpose of his own business or as his residence. Many of the matters discussed above (*see* 9) will be relevant to a consideration of intention.

Other points to note are:

(a) the landlord can rely on this ground even though he intends

(*i*) to use the premises in partnership with someone else (*Clift* v. *Taylor* (1948)) even if the landlord will not be moving into the premises himself or taking any active part in the business to be carried on there (*Skeet* v. *Powell – Sheddon* (1988));

(*ii*) to occupy by an agent or manager (*Parkes* v. *Westminster Roman Catholic Diocese Trustee* (1978) and *Teesside Indoor Bowls Ltd* v. *Stockton on Tees Borough Council* (1990));

(*iii*) to occupy by an organisation for which the landlord provides services, including accommodation (*Willis* v. *Association of Universities of the British Commonwealth* (1965));

(*iv*) to give possession to a company in which he has a controlling interest and which will carry on business from the premises (s. 30(3));

(b) the landlord may rely on ground **(g)** where it is a company in a group and another member of the group is to occupy the premises (s. 42(3));

(c) the intention to occupy must be for a period which is more than minimal (*Willis* v. *Association of Universities for the British Commonwealth* (1965));

(d) the ground applies where the holding is to be used partly for the purposes of a business;

(e) it is not necessary for the landlord to occupy the same buildings as are occupied by the tenant (*Leathwoods Ltd* v. *Total Oil (GB)* (1984) and *J.W. Thornton Ltd* v. *Blacks Leisure Group plc* (1987));

(f) the landlord need not occupy the whole of the holding (*Cam Gears Ltd* v. *Cunningham* (1981));

(g) the ground also applies where the landlord intends to use the premises as his residence;

(h) it may assist the landlord's case if he is willing to give an undertaking to the court that he will occupy (*Chez Gerard Ltd* v. *Greene Ltd* (1983) and *London Hilton Jewellers Ltd* v. *Hilton International Hotels Ltd* (1990)).

13. The exclusion of ground (g). A landlord cannot rely upon ground **(g)** if his interest was purchased or created within the period of five years prior to the termination of the current tenancy, and at all times since the purchase or creation of that interest, the holding has been comprised in a tenancy to which the 1954 Act applies (s. 30(2)).

Effect of opposition

14. Successful opposition by landlord. The rules are as follows:

(a) If the landlord succeeds in his opposition, the court cannot make an order for the grant of a new tenancy (s. 31(1)). The tenant will have four weeks within which to appeal to the Court of Appeal if he considers he has grounds for an appeal. If he appeals, his tenancy will be continued until three months and four weeks after the Court of Appeal's decision. If he serves notice of appeal to the Court of Appeal, but subsequently withdraws his appeal, his current tenancy will come to an end three months after the date of such withdrawal (s. 64). If the tenant does not serve notice of appeal, his current tenancy will end three months and four weeks after the date of the court's Order dismissing his application for a new tenancy (s. 64).

(b) If the landlord relies on one or more of grounds **(d)**, **(e)** and **(f)** (*see* **6–8**) and the court is not satisfied that the ground has been established but would have been satisfied if the date specified in the s. 25 notice, or the tenant's request under s. 26, had been a date up to a year later, the court will make a declaration to that effect specifying the later date at which it considers that all the requirements of grounds **(d)**, **(e)** or **(f)** as the case may be, will be satisfied and will not make an order for the grant of a new tenancy.

The tenant may then apply within 14 days for the declared date to be substituted for the date specified in the s. 25 notice or s. 26 request, in which case the tenancy will continue until that date. If the tenant does not so apply, the current tenancy ends three months and four weeks after the date of the court's judgment.

15. The tenant's right to compensation. Where the landlord successfully opposes an application for a new tenancy on grounds **(e)**, **(f)** or **(g)**, compensation will be payable to the tenant under s. 37. Where the landlord serves a s. 25 notice specifying one or more of these grounds but not any other ground the tenant will be entitled to compensation whether or not he makes an application to the court for a new tenancy and whether any application for a new tenancy he may issue is withdrawn or dismissed by the court.

By virtue of s. 37(2) the amount of the compensation will be the product of 'the appropriate multiplier' and the rateable value of the holding or in cases where the tenant has carried on business at the premises during the whole of the fourteen years preceding the termination of the current tenancy, twice that amount.

The following points should be noted.

(*i*) The rateable value is the rateable value of the holding as at the date the s. 25 notice is given or the tenant's request pursuant to s. 26 is made (s. 37(5)).

(*ii*) It is the extent of the holding as at the date the s. 25 notice is given or the tenant's request pursuant to s. 26 is made, which is relevant (*Edicron Ltd* v. *William Whiteley Ltd* (1983)).

(*iii*) The date of termination of the current tenancy is the date specified in the s. 25 notice or tenant's request pursuant to s. 26 (s. 37(7)).

(*iv*) 'The appropriate multiplier' is one (Landlord and Tenant Act 1954 (Appropriate Multiplier) Order 1990) so that a tenant who has carried on business at the premises for less than fourteen years is entitled to compensation equivalent to the rateable value of the holding, and a tenant who has carried on business at the premises for more than fourteen years is entitled to compensation equivalent to two times the rateable value of the holding.

(*v*) In order to be entitled to compensation equivalent to two times the rateable value of the holding, the tenant must have carried on business for the whole of the fourteen years preceding the termination of the current tenancy. Thirteen years and 364 days is not sufficient (*Secretary of State for the Environment* v. *Royal Insurance Company plc* (1987)).

(*vi*) The tenant is entitled to two times the rateable value of the holding, even though he has not himself carried on business at the premises for more than 14 years, provided that **(a)** he is the successor to the business carried on by the previous occupier, and **(b)** the periods during which T and his predecessor have been in occupation together exceed 14 years. E.g. where A has carried on business at the premises for twelve years and then assigns the tenancy and the business to T, the period of A's occupation is included for the purposes of s. 37 in the calculation of the period that T has carried on business at the premises (s. 37(2) and (3)).

(*vii*) Any agreement to exclude or reduce the tenant's entitlement to compensation is void, unless the tenant has carried on business at the premises for less than five years.

NOTE: If the tenant is the successor to the business carried on at the premises, the period of his predecessor's occupation will also be included in calculating whether or not the tenant has carried on business for five years.

16. Local Government and Housing Act 1989. Section 149 of, and Schedule 7 to, this Act introduced special compensation provisions to deal with situations where the whole or part of the holding comprises 'domestic property'. These provisions are consequent upon the abolition of rateable values for domestic property.

'Domestic property' has the meaning assigned to it by s. 66 of the Local Government Finance Act 1988 namely, property which 'is used wholly for the purposes of living accommodation'.

17. Compensation where part of the holding is domestic property. In these circumstances the tenant is entitled to compensation equivalent to one or two times (depending on whether or not the tenant has occupied for less than 14 years) the rateable value of the pure business premises (namely, that part of the holding which has a rateable value after 1st April 1990), plus a sum equivalent to the tenant's reasonable expenses in removing from the domestic property (s. 37(5A)).

An example of a situation in which s. 37(5A) would apply is where a tenant has a lease of a shop with a flat above.

18. Compensation where the whole of the holding is domestic property. An example of a situation where the whole of the holding was domestic property is provided by *Groveside Properties Ltd* v. *Westminster Medical School* (1983). In that case the tenant used a flat for the provision of living accommodation for its students. It was found that this fostered a corporate or collegiate spirit which furthered the students' medical education and that the tenant occupied the flat, through the students, for business purposes.

Where the whole of the holding is domestic property a notional rateable value is ascribed to the holding and the compensation will be one or two times that notional rateable value depending on whether or not the tenant has occupied for less than fourteen years (s. 37(5C)).

The notional rateable value is taken to be the rent at which it is estimated the holding might reasonably be expected to be let from year to year, if the tenant undertook to pay all usual tenant's rates and taxes and to bear the cost of the repairs and insurance and other expenses (if any) necessary to maintain the holding in a state to command that rent.

Section 37(5D) contains provisions for determination of the notional rateable value in case of any dispute and also provides that the date by reference to which the determination is to be carried out is the date of the landlord's s. 25 notice or counternotice under s. 26(6).

19. 'The special basis of compensation'. Paragraph 4 of Schedule 7 to the Local Government and Housing Act 1989 provides that the tenant is entitled to 'the special basis of compensation' if

(a) the tenancy was entered into before 1st April 1990 (or after that date in pursuance of a contract made before that date); and
(b) the landlord's s. 25 notice or counternotice under s. 26(6) is given before 1st April 2000; and
(c) between two and four months after the giving of the s. 25 notice or tenant's s. 26 request, the tenant gives notice to the landlord that he wants the special basis of compensation provided for by Paragraph 4.

In these circumstances the tenant is entitled to compensation equivalent to eight or sixteen times the rateable value of the holding on 31st March 1990, depending on whether or not the tenant has been in occupation for less than fourteen years (see paragraph 4(b) of the Landlord and Tenant Act 1954 (Appropriate Multiplier) Regulations 1990 which prescribes an appropriate multiplier of eight where the special basis of compensation is claimed).

NOTE: Some doubt has been expressed as to whether or not a tenant whose holding comprises purely business premises, with no domestic property, can claim the special basis of compensation. In the county court case of *Busby* v. *Co-Operative Insurance Society Ltd* (1994) it was held that he cannot.

Progress test 14

1. Which are the discretionary grounds of opposition? In what way are they discretionary? **(2)**

2. What are the elements of ground **(f)**? **(8–11)**

3. At what date must the landlord have the necessary intention for the purposes of ground **(f)**? **(9)**

4. L proposes to sell his interest to a third party who wishes to redevelop the land. Can L rely on ground **(f)** Would your answer be different if L proposed to grant the third party a building lease of the land? **(9)**

5. T occupies one floor of a multi storey office block. L plans to convert the floor occupied by T and the two floors immediately above into a single unit by installing new internal staircases. Will this satisfy ground **(f)**? **(10)**

6. What is the effect of s. 31A on ground **(f)**? **(11)**

7. L, a limited company, wishes to obtain possession of T's premises so that its wholly owned subsidiary X Ltd can carry on business there. Can L rely on ground **(g)**? **(12)**

8. L purchased the freehold of premises occupied by T for business purposes two years before the termination date specified in his s. 25 notice. Can L rely on ground **(g)**? **(13)**

9. What is the appropriate multiplier for the purpose of calculating compensation under s. 37? **(15)** and **(19)**

10. In what circumstances is a tenant entitled to compensation equivalent to two times the rateable value of the holding? **(15)**

15

Business tenancies: compensation for improvements

1. Generally. Part I of the Landlord and Tenant Act 1927 (ss. 1–17, excluding ss. 4–7 which have been repealed) and Part III of the Landlord and Tenant Act 1954 (ss. 47–50) make provision for the payment of compensation to the tenant of business premises, upon quitting the premises, for improvements made by him to the demised premises. The following points have to be considered:

(a) the premises (*see* **2**):
(b) the improvements (*see* **3**):
(c) pre-conditions to a claim (*see* **4**):
(d) the claim for compensation (*see* **5**):
(e) the amount of compensation (*see* **6,7**):
(f) the rights of mesne landlords (*see* **8**).

2. The premises. Part I of the 1927 Act applies to any premises used wholly or partly for trade, professional or business purposes. The provisions do not apply to mining leases or to leases in writing where the tenant is expressed to be the holder of an office or employment under the landlord. The premises to which Part I of the 1927 Act apply and those to which Part II of the 1954 Act apply are not entirely the same (s. 17). In particular the business of sub-letting flats is expressly excluded from the operation of the 1927 Act but such a business tenancy may be protected by Part II of the 1954 Act (*see* **10:5**).

3. The improvements. By s. 1 of the 1927 Act a tenant can claim compensation for any improvement made by him or his predecessors in title which adds to the letting value of the holding at the end of the tenancy. The following points must be noted about this:

(a) improvements include the erection of any building but not any trade or other fixture which the tenant is by law entitled to remove: s. 1(1);

(b) the right to compensation does not apply to improvements made before 1927: s. 2(1)(*a*);

(c) the Act does not apply to improvements which the tenant was under an obligation to make in pursuance of a contract entered into for valuable consideration: s. 2(1)(*b*);

(d) whether or not works constitute an improvement must be considered from the tenant's point of view (*F.W. Woolworth & Co. Ltd* v. *Lambert* (1937) and (1938)).

4. Pre-conditions to making a claim. Section 3 of the 1927 Act provides that in order to make a claim for compensation:

(a) the tenant must have served on the landlord notice of his intention to carry out the improvements together with a specification and plan showing the proposed improvement and the part of the existing premises affected; and

(b) if the landlord gave notice of objection within three months, the tenant must have obtained a certificate from the court that the improvement was a proper one (such a certificate will not be granted if the landlord proves that he has offered to carry out the improvements himself in consideration of a reasonable increase in rent paid);

(c) the tenant must have carried out the improvements within the time agreed with the landlord or fixed by the court.

NOTE: The court cannot grant a certificate that the improvement is a proper one if the improvement has been completed by the time the application for a certificate is heard; *Hogarth Health Club* v. *Westbourne Investments Ltd* (1989).

5. The claim for compensation. The claim must be made by the tenant within the period prescribed by the Landlord and Tenant Act 1954, s. 47. That period varies with the manner in which the tenancy is ended.

(a) if the tenancy is ended by the giving of notice to quit or notice under Part II of the 1954 Act, a claim may be made at any time within three months beginning on the date on which the notice is given: s. 47(1);

(b) if the tenancy comes to an end by effluxion of time, a claim may be made at any time not more than six months and not less than three months before the coming to an end of the tenancy: s. 47(2);

(c) if the tenancy is terminated by forfeiture or re-entry, a claim may be made at any time within the period of three months from the effective date of the possession order by the court or the date of the re-entry: s. 47(3).

NOTES: (1) Where a tenancy is terminated by a tenant's request for a new tenancy under s. 26 of the 1954 Act, the time for making the claim for compensation is three months from the date of the landlord's counternotice under s. 26(6) of the 1954 Act or if no such counternotice is given, within 5 months of the date on which the tenant's request under s. 26 is given (s. 47(1) of the 1954 Act).

(2) The effective date of the possession order means the date on which the order is stated to take effect, or the date on which it ceases to be subject to appeal whichever is the later: s. 47(4) of the 1954 Act.

6. The amount of compensation. By s. 1(1) of the 1927 Act the amount to be paid as compensation must not exceed the lesser of:

(a) the net addition to the value of the holding as a whole which is the direct result of the improvement; or

(b) the reasonable cost of carrying out the improvement at the end of the tenancy, subject to a deduction of an amount equal to the cost (if any) of putting the works constituting the improvements into a reasonable state of repair.

In practice this may be limited by s. 1(2) which provides that in determining item **(a)**, regard must be had to the purposes for which it is intended to use the premises at the end of the tenancy. If it is shown that it is intended to demolish or alter the premises or change the use, regard must be had to the effect of these acts on the additional value due to the improvement and to the length of time likely to elapse between the end of the tenancy and the demolition, alteration or change of use.

NOTE: In practice, s. 1(2) of the 1927 Act will often operate to reduce the amount of compensation to which a tenant is entitled.

7. Determination of disputes. Sections 1(3) and 21 of the 1927 Act provides that, in the absence of any agreement between the parties, questions as to the right to compensation or the amount must be determined by the court.

By s. 63(2) of the 1954 Act both the High Court and county court have jurisdiction but see articles 4–8 of the High Court and County Court Jurisdiction Order 1991 as to the trial of any such dispute and enforcement of any judgment or Order.

8. Mesne landlords. There are special provisions dealing with the position where there is a chain of tenancies. By s. 8 of the 1927 Act, a mesne landlord (i.e. a landlord who is himself a tenant) who has paid or is liable to pay compensation under the 1927 Act is entitled, at the end of his own term, to compensation from his immediate landlord in like manner and on the same conditions as if he had himself made the improvements in question. This right is conditional on the mesne landlord, at the prescribed time, having served on his immediate landlord copies of all documents sent to him and relating to proposed improvements and claims under the Act. Where a mesne landlord has served on a superior landlord copies of such documents, the superior landlord has the same rights of opposing a proposed improvement or a claim for compensation as the mesne landlord. By these provisions where there is a chain of tenancies a landlord, who satisfies the relevant conditions, may pass on his liabilities under the 1927 Act.

> NOTE: Where a mesne landlord's own tenancy comes to an end by effluxion of time, he may make a claim for compensation against his own landlord not earlier than six, nor later than two months, before the coming to an end of his tenancy (s. 8(1)).

9. Contracting out. Section 9 of the 1927 Act, as amended by s. 49 of the 1954 Act, prevents the landlord and tenant from entering into any agreement that the provisions of the 1927 Act shall not apply.

10. Interaction of the 1927 Act with covenants against improvements. Leases often contain a covenant by the tenant that he will not carry out any alterations to the demised premises, or that he will not carry out any such alterations without the landlord's consent. Section 19(2) of the 1927 Act (*see* **5:36**) provides that any covenant against the making of improvements without consent is deemed to be subject to a proviso that such consent is not to be unreasonably withheld.

The combined effect of s. 3(4) (landlord's right to object to the improvements proposed by the tenant) and s. 9 (restriction on contracting out) of the 1927 Act is that even if the lease contains an absolute covenant against the carrying out of improvements, the tenant can lawfully carry out improvements, without subjecting himself to any risk of forfeiture of his lease or any claim for damages for breach of covenant, by following the procedure laid down by s. 3.

Progress test 15

1. What are the main differences between premises to which Part II of the 1954 Act applies and those to which the 1927 Act applies? **(2)**

2. What improvements are excluded from the compensation provisions? **(3)**

3. How does a tenant make his claim for compensation under the 1927 Act? **(4)**

4. What are the statutory limits on the amount of compensation? **(6)**

5. Which court determines disputes regarding compensation under the 1927 Act? **(7)**

6. L lets property to T who sub-lets it to S who makes improvements to it. At the end of his tenancy S claims compensation under the 1927 Act from T. Advise T of his rights against L and S. **(8)**

Part three
Private sector residential tenancies

16

Residential tenancies: the Rent Act 1977

History

1. Introduction. The relevant history starts in 1915. It is a long and complex history which originated with the housing shortage brought about by the First World War and which constantly reflects political change. An understanding of the history is helpful in securing a clear understanding of the protection as there have been different types of protection with their origins in different Acts.

Terminology

2. Historical table. The following are the main Acts since 1915 and summaries of some of their effects.

(a) *Increase of Rent and Mortgage Interest (War Restriction) Act 1915.* This Act introduced control for the first time. It restricted the rent chargeable and the landlord's right to possession. It applied only to houses in certain rental and rateable value brackets.

(b) *Increase of Rent and Mortgage Interest (Restriction) Act 1920.* This replaced the 1915 Act and contained the same system of protection.

(c) *Rent and Mortgage Interest Restrictions Act 1923; Rent and Mortgage Interest Restrictions Act (Amendment) Act 1933; Increase of Rent and*

Mortgage Interest (Restriction) Act 1938. These three Acts provided for a certain measure of de-control.

(d) *Rent and Mortgage Interest Restriction Act 1939.* This ended the period of de-control and started what was called 'new' control.

(e) *Rent Act 1957.* This provided for immediate de-control of dwellings over a certain rateable value and a gradual de-control thereafter as old tenancies ended and new tenancies were granted. It also provided a new method of calculating rents for dwellings still subject to control.

(f) *Rent Act 1965.* This brought back controls on dwellings de-controlled by the 1957 Act. It also provided for a new method of calculating rents. Tenancies deriving their protection from this Act, or its later re-enactments, are called regulated tenancies.

(g) *Rent Act 1968.* Prior to this Act the law was contained in a number of Acts running back to 1920. This Act consolidated the bulk of the earlier provisions.

(h) *Housing Finance Act 1972.* This provided for automatic conversion of controlled to regulated tenancies.

(i) *Rent Act 1974.* This brought furnished tenancies fully within the protection of the Rent Acts for the first time.

(j) *Rent Act 1977.* This consolidated the earlier Acts, and forms the basis of the present law.

(k) *Protection from Eviction Act 1977.* This brought together in one Act various provisions relating to notices to quit, restrictions on enforcing rights of re-entry in relation to residential property and other restrictions on the recovery of possession of residential property.

(l) *Housing Act 1980.* This gave security of tenure and the right to buy to tenants of local authorities and other bodies.

(m) *Housing Act 1985.* This re-enacts provisions first introduced in the Housing Act 1980.

(n) *Housing Act 1988.* This commences the phasing out of protected tenancies and introduces assured tenancies under which there is security of tenure but a market rent may be charged and assured shorthold tenancies with minimal security of tenure under which a market rent may be charged.

(o) *The References to Rating (Housing) Regulations 1990.* These regulations deal with the effect of the abolition of domestic rating with effect from 1st April 1990.

3. Terminology. Before considering the nature of the protection under the legislation it is important to be clear about the names given to different types of tenancies involved. There are two important distinctions:

(a) *between controlled and regulated tenancies.* This has already been touched upon in the history: essentially it distinguishes between tenancies enjoying the old style protection under the pre-1957 Acts and those enjoying the protection created by the Rent Act 1965. Its significance was greatly reduced by the Housing Act 1980.

(b) *between protected and statutory tenancies.* A protected tenancy is a contractual tenancy which is within the Rent Act. Thus, for instance, a monthly tenancy or a tenancy for a fixed term, being a contractual tenancy, will be a protected tenancy (provided it satisfies various conditions). A statutory tenancy is a tenancy which arises, by virtue of the Rent Act, at the end of a contractual (protected) tenancy and which continues as long as the tenant continues to reside in the dwelling-house.

Examples _____

(1) L lets a dwelling to T on a monthly tenancy. The letting is within the Rent Act. L serves notice to quit on T but T continues to reside in the house. Until the notice to quit takes effect, T has a protected tenancy; from the date it takes effect T has a statutory tenancy.

(2) L lets a dwelling to T for a term of seven years from 1st January 1970. The tenancy is within the Rent Act and T continues to reside there at the end of the term. Until 31st December 1977 T has a protected tenancy and thereafter he has a statutory tenancy so long as he occupies the dwelling as his residence.

Protected tenancies

4. Introduction. Section 1 of the 1977 Act provides that a tenancy under which a dwelling-house (which may be a house or part of a house) is let as a separate dwelling is a protected tenancy. In addition, the rateable value of the dwelling-house must come within certain limits and the tenancy must not fall within certain specified exceptions. There are therefore five matters to be considered:

(a) there must be a tenancy (*see* **5**);
(b) of a dwelling-house (*see* **6,7**);
(c) which is let as a separate dwelling (*see* **8** *et seq.*);
(d) whose rateable value is within the limits (*see* **12** *et seq.*);
(e) and the tenancy does not fall within the exceptions (*see* **18** *et seq.*).

Further, the tenancy must have been entered into before 15th January 1989: Housing Act 1988, s. 34(1). On or after that date the tenancy cannot be a protected tenancy unless it falls within the limited exceptions contained in s. 34(1) (a) to (d).

5. A tenancy. It is first necessary to ensure that there is in fact a tenancy. If there is not then there can be no question of the Rent Act applying. The distinction between tenancies and licences has already been considered in 2: **15**. Provided there is a tenancy there can be Rent Act protection whatever the form of the tenancy. A tenancy granted for 99 years can in principle be a protected tenancy as much as can a weekly tenancy. Even a tenancy at will can be a protected tenancy for the purposes of the Rent Act: *Francis Jackson Developments Ltd* v. *Stemp* (1943).

6. Of a dwelling-house. The Rent Act 1977, s. 1 provides that a dwelling-house may be a house or part of a house. There is no other definition of a dwelling-house in the Act. There have been various cases on the meaning of the words and they show that the court has considered whether the premises are the 'home' of the tenant, i.e. the place where he carries on his ordinary domestic life. A flat is a dwelling-house for the purposes of the Rent Act. A single room may also be one.

7. Let as a dwelling. This is closely connected to the preceding requirement. If a dwelling-house is not let as a dwelling-house, it will not be protected. If there is a user covenant in the tenancy, it will determine how the dwelling is let. If the user covenant is for use other than as a residence, the premises will not be let as a dwelling and the tenancy will not be protected. If there is no user covenant, the court looks at the circumstances of the letting. The position was summarised by Denning LJ in *Wolfe* v. *Hogan* (1949) in the following terms:

> 'In determining whether a house or part of a house is "let as a dwelling" within the meaning of the Rent Acts, it is necessary to look at the purpose of the letting. If the lease contains an express provision as to the purpose of the letting, it is not necessary to look further, but, if there is no express provision, it is open to the court to look at the circumstances of the letting. If the house is constructed for use as a dwelling-house, it is reasonable to infer that the purpose was to let it as a dwelling, but if, on the other hand, it is constructed for use as a lock-up shop, the reasonable inference is that it was let for business purposes. If the position were neutral, it would be proper to look at the actual user. It is not a question of implied terms. It is a question of the purpose for which the premises were let.'

See also *Henry Smith's Charity Trustees* v. *Wagle* (1989).

8. Let as a separate dwelling. This paragraph is concerned with the use of the word 'separate' in s. 1. The effect of this word is that the dwelling must be exclusive to the tenant and not involve any sharing with some other person. What is required was helpfully summarised by MacKinnon LJ in *Cole* v. *Harris* (1945) in the following terms:

> 'It is, I think, difficult to formulate any principle of law which separates what I have called the contrasted conceptions of (1) a demise of part of a house as a separate dwelling, and (2) an agreement to share the use and occupation of a house. But I think Morton LJ provides the best formula by saying that to create (1) there must be an agreement by which the occupier has the exclusive use of the essential *living* rooms of a separate dwelling-house. After all, a dwelling-house is that in which a person dwells or lives, and it seems reasonable that a separate dwelling should be one containing essential living rooms. A w.c. may be essential in modern days, but I do not think it is a living room, whereas a kitchen, I think, is.'

The cases show that, in deciding whether a room is or is not an 'essential living room' within the meaning of the words of MacKinnon LJ, the courts have distinguished between rooms such as a bedroom, sitting room or kitchen where people spend a good deal of their time and rooms such as a lavatory, bathroom or garage which are not used such a great deal. So if a tenant has to share any of the rooms in the former category there will be no separate dwelling; but if he has to share any of the rooms in the latter category that sharing will not prevent there being a separate dwelling. If there is a separate dwelling the tenancy can (if it satisfies the other conditions) be a protected tenancy; if there is no separate dwelling there can be no protected tenancy.

9. Special cases. The rules described in the preceding paragraph have been altered by the Act in two special cases. They are where:

(a) the tenant has exclusive occupation of some accommodation and shares the other accommodation with his landlord (s. 21); and
(b) the tenant has exclusive occupation of some accommodation and shares other accommodation with persons other than his landlord (s. 22).

> NOTE: The word 'accommodation' here means the essential living rooms as defined in the preceding paragraph.

10. Tenant sharing with his landlord. Section 21 of the 1977 Rent Act provides that where under any contract:

(a) a tenant has the exclusive occupation of any accommodation, and
(b) the terms on which he holds it include the use of other accommodation in common with his landlord or in common with his landlord
and other persons, and
(c) by reason of (b) the accommodation in (a) is not a dwelling-house
let on a protected tenancy,

the contract has the status of a 'restricted contract'. This is a special
form of protection which gives the tenant a limited or restricted form
of security of tenure only and not the full Rent Act security. It is considered in Chapter 20.

11. Tenant sharing with person other than landlord. Section 22
provides that where a tenant has the exclusive occupation of accommodation ('the separate accommodation') and

(a) the terms as between the tenant and his landlord on which he
holds the separate accommodation include the use of other accommodation ('the shared accommodation') in common with another
person or other persons, not being or including the landlord; and
(b) by reason of the circumstances in (*a*), the separate accommodation would not be a dwelling-house let on or subject to a protected or
statutory tenancy,

the separate accommodation is deemed to be a dwelling-house let on
a protected tenancy or, as the case may be, subject to a statutory tenancy. This means that in relation to the separate accommodation the
tenant has full Rent Act protection. This protection is secured by two
special provisions in s. 22. They are as follows:

(a) a possession order cannot be made in respect of the shared accommodation unless an order is also made in respect of the separate
accommodation: s. 22(5);
(b) while the tenant is in possession of the separate accommodation,
any term of the contract of tenancy modifying or providing for the
modification of his right to the use of any of the shared accommodation will be ineffective: s. 22(3).

12. The rateable value. The policy of the Rent Acts has always been
to exclude from protection dwelling-houses of a comparatively high
rateable value. This is dealt with in s. 4(1) of the 1977 Act which provides that a tenancy is not a protected tenancy if the dwelling-house
falls within one of the three classes in s. 4(2). These classes specify
various rateable value limits on certain days. In order to decide into
which class a house falls (and therefore whether the rateable value is

within the limits) it is first necessary to consider what is the 'appropriate day' in relation to the dwelling-house. When the appropriate day is determined, the house can be placed in one of the three classes and it can be seen whether the rateable value is within the limits.

NOTE: Domestic rating was abolished with effect from 1st April 1990. In the case of a tenancy entered into on or after that date, otherwise than in pursuance of a contract made before that date, it is not a protected tenancy if under it the rent payable for the time being is payable at a rate exceeding £25,000: s. 4(4) as amended by The Reference to Rating (Housing) Regulations 1990. The actual rent is to be considered and not any sum payable by the tenant which is expressed to be payable in respect of rates, services, repairs, maintenance or insurance. In view of the reforms introduced by the Housing Act 1988 this provision will be of limited effect: *see* **4** above.

13. The appropriate day. Section 25(3) defines the appropriate day in the following way:

(a) where the dwelling-house had a rateable value shown in the valuation list on 23rd March 1965, that is the appropriate day;
(b) in relation to any other dwelling, it means the date on which a rateable value was first shown in the valuation list, i.e. it will be a date after 23rd March 1965.

Examples

(1) A house is built in 1945 and is then entered in the valuation list. The appropriate day is 23rd March 1965.
(2) A house is built in 1969 and is entered in the valuation list on 1st January 1970. The appropriate day is 1st January 1970.

NOTE: The significance of 23rd March 1965 is that it was the date on which the Bill which became the Rent Act 1965 was introduced into the House of Commons. It was that Act which created the new form of protection given to regulated tenancies.

14. The rateable value limits. Having considered the meaning of the 'appropriate day', it is now possible to consider the limits. A tenancy is not a protected tenancy if the dwelling-house falls within one of the classes set out below. Where alternative values are mentioned, the higher value applies if the dwelling-house is in Greater London and the lower value if it is elsewhere.

(a) *Class A.* The appropriate day in relation to the dwelling-house falls or fell on or after 1st April 1973 and the dwelling-house on the appropriate day has or had a rateable value exceeding £1,500 or £750.
(b) *Class B.* The appropriate day in relation to the dwelling-house fell

on or after 22nd March 1973, but before 1st April 1973, and the dwelling-house

   (*i*) on the appropriate day had a rateable value exceeding £600 or £300; and

   (*ii*) on 1st April 1973 had a rateable value exceeding £1,500 or £750.

(c) *Class C*. The appropriate day in relation to the dwelling-house fell before 22nd March 1973 and the dwelling-house

   (*i*) on the appropriate day had a rateable value exceeding £400 or £200; and

   (*ii*) on 22nd March 1973 had a rateable value exceeding £600 or £300; and

   (*iii*) on 1st April 1973 had a rateable value exceeding £1,500 or £750.

15. Historical explanation of the limits. At first sight these limits are complicated; it will assist students to know the historical explanation for them:

(a) 23rd March 1965 is the date on which the Rent Bill 1965 was first introduced in the House of Commons.

(b) 22nd March 1973 was the date on which the Counter-Inflation Act 1973 was passed. This Act increased the limits so as to take account of the effect of inflation on the assessment of rateable values.

(c) 1st April 1973 was the date on which a new valuation list came into effect, following a generous re-assessment of premises for rating purposes.

16. Operation of the limits. With this historical explanation in mind, it is now necessary to consider how the limits operate. There are the following steps:

(a) determine the appropriate day; then

(b) determine, by reference to the appropriate day, which of the three classes the dwelling-house falls into; then

(c) consider whether the rateable value on each day specified in the class was exceeded.

   If the rateable value on any of the days specified in the relevant class is not exceeded the dwelling-house comes within the limits.

17. Examples. The following examples illustrate the way in which the limits operate.

Examples
_____

(1) A flat built in Mayfair in the nineteenth century. It has the following values on the following dates: 23rd March 1965: £450; 22nd March 1973: £650;

1st April 1973: £1,200. This flat would be within the limits. The appropriate day would be 23rd March 1965 (*see* **13** above). The class to consider is therefore class C. In that class conditions (**a**) and (**b**) are satisfied but condition (**c**) is not satisfied. Therefore the flat is within the rateable value limits. If the flat was in Bristol it would be outside the limits.

(2) A house in Manchester, built in 1972 and first appearing in the valuation list on 22nd March 1973. It has the following rateable values on the following dates: 22nd March 1973: £450; 1st April 1973: £800. The house is outside the rateable value limits. The appropriate day is 22nd March 1973. The class to consider is class B. In that class both conditions (**a**) and (**b**) are satisfied in so far as the lower values are concerned. If the house was in London with the same rateable values, it would be within the limits since condition (**b**) would not be satisfied, the value being under £1,500.

(3) A house built in London in 1978 and first appearing in the list on 1st January 1979. The appropriate day is that date. If the rateable value is £1,500 or less, the house will be within the limits; if it is above £1,500, the house will be outside the limits. If the house was in Liverpool the relevant limit would be £750.

Exceptions to protection

18. Introduction. If there is a tenancy of a separate dwelling whose rateable value is within the limits, the final question to consider is whether the tenancy falls within any of the exceptions. Those exceptions are as follows:

(**a**) tenancies at low rents: s. 5 (*see* **19–20**);
(**b**) certain shared ownership leases: s. 5A (*see* **21**);
(**c**) dwelling-houses let with other land: s. 6 (*see* **22**);
(**d**) payments for board or attendance: s. 7 (*see* **23**);
(**e**) lettings to students: s. 8 (*see* **24**);
(**f**) holiday lettings: s. 9 (*see* **25**);
(**g**) agricultural holdings: s. 10 (*see* **26**);
(**h**) licensed premises: s. 11 (*see* **27**);
(**i**) resident landlords: s. 12 (*see* **28–29**);
(**j**) landlord's interest belonging to the Crown: s. 13 (*see* **30**);
(**k**) landlord's interest belonging to a local authority: s. 14 (*see* **31**);
(**l**) landlord's interest belonging to a housing association: s. 15 (*see* **32**);
(**m**) landlord's interest belonging to a housing co-operative: s. 16 (*see* **33**).

19. Tenancies at a low rent. A tenancy is not a protected tenancy if under it either no rent is payable or the rent payable is less than two-thirds of the rateable value on the appropriate day: Rent Act 1977, s. 5(1). A tenancy falling within s. 5 is called a tenancy at a low rent, and such tenancies have always been outside the Rent Acts. The reason for this is to exclude leases at a ground rent (i.e. leases where the rent only represents a payment for the use of the site and not the building on it).

Examples _____
(1) L lets a flat to T for no rent. The tenancy is within s. 5 and it is excluded from protection.
(2) L lets a house to T for £60 per year. On the appropriate day the rateable value was £100. The rent is therefore less than two-thirds of the rateable value and the tenancy is not protected.

In calculating whether a long tenancy (i.e. a tenancy granted for a term of more than 21 years) is a tenancy at a low rent, s. 5(4) requires that sums payable by the tenant in respect of rates, services, repairs, maintenance or insurance must be disregarded.

NOTE: Domestic rating was abolished with effect from 1st April 1990. In the case of a tenancy entered into on or after that date, otherwise than in pursuance of a contract made before that date, it is not a protected tenancy if either (i) no rent is payable or (ii) the rent is £1,000 or less a year if the dwelling-house is in Greater London or (iii) the rent is £250 or less a year if the dwelling-house is outside Greater London: s. 5(2A) as added by the References to Rating (Housing) Regulations 1990. In view of the reforms introduced by the Housing Act 1988 this provision will be of limited effect: see **4** above.

20. Qualifications to the operation of s. 5. There is an important limit on the working of s. 5, which applies where the appropriate day in relation to a dwelling-house fell before 22nd March 1973 and on the appropriate day the dwelling-house had a rateable value exceeding £400 in Greater London and £200 elsewhere: s. 5(2). The qualification is that in those circumstances s. 5(1) (*see* **19**) applies as if the reference to the appropriate day were a reference to 22nd March 1973. The reason for the qualification is as follows. Prior to the changing of the rateable value limits under the Counter-Inflation Act 1973, a tenancy may have been outside the protection of the Rent Act by reason of its high rateable value. The 1973 Act may have brought that tenancy within the limits and the protection. In such a case, a concession is made to the landlord because, in determining if a tenancy is at a low rent, s. 5(2) requires that the comparison be between the rent and the rateable value on the 22nd March 1973. This means that if, as is probable, the rateable value increased between the appropriate day and 22nd March 1973, s. 5(2) may operate to exclude the tenancy from protection by making the tenancy one at a low rent.

21. Certain shared ownership leases. Section 5A of the Rent Act 1977 provides that a tenancy is not a protected tenancy if it is a qualifying shared ownership lease, i.e. (*a*) a lease granted in pursuance of the right to be granted a shared ownership lease under Part V of the Housing Act 1985 or (*b*) a lease granted by a housing association complying with various conditions specified in s. 5A(2).

22. Dwelling-houses let with other land. A tenancy is not a protected one if the dwelling-house which is subject to it is let together with land other than the site of the dwelling-house: Rent Act 1977, s. 6. This provision has to be read together with s. 26 which provides that any land or premises let together with a dwelling-house is, unless it is agricultural land of more than two acres, to be treated as part of the dwelling-house. The effect of the two provisions is that it is first necessary to consider if either,

(a) the dwelling-house is let with other land, or

(b) other land is let with the dwelling-house.

The way in which to carry out this exercise is to consider the relative significance of the land and the house: *Pender* v. *Reid* (1948). If it is the land which is the more significant part of the letting, then the case falls within s. 6 and the letting is not protected by the Rent Act. If, on the other hand, it is the house which is the more significant part, the case falls within s. 26 and the land is treated as part of the house and the letting will be protected, provided all other necessary conditions are satisfied.

Feyereisel v. *Turnidge* (1952). A camping site was let together with a small bungalow. The Court of Appeal HELD: the bungalow was let as an adjunct to the camping site and therefore the letting was not protected.

Pender v. *Reid* (1948). A dwelling was let as a part of a coal yard used for a coal merchant's business. The house occupied less than one-third of the whole area. The tenant claimed the protection of the Rent Acts. HELD: the dwelling was merely an adjunct to the rest of the yard and was therefore let together with other land and was not protected by the Rent Acts.

23. Payments for board or attendance. A tenancy is not a protected one if the dwelling-house is bona fide let at a rent which includes payment in respect of board or attendance: Rent Act 1977, s. 7. Any amount of 'board' which is more than *de minimis* will suffice; thus the bona fide provisions of a daily 'continental breakfast' (two bread rolls, butter, jam and marmalade, and tea or coffee with sugar and milk) was held to constitute board in *Otter* v. *Norman* (1988). 'Attendance' means services personal to the tenant performed by an attendant provided by the landlord, e.g. delivering letters. It does not include the provision of the services normally provided in large blocks of flats: *see Property Holding Co. Ltd* v. *Mischeff* (1948).

In the case of attendance, s. 7(2) provides that a dwelling-house is not bona fide let at a rent which includes payments in respect of attendance unless the amount of rent which is fairly attributable to attendance forms a substantial part of the whole rent having regard to the value of the attendance to the tenant. The effect is that the court must consider what value the attendance is to the tenant in relation to the rent.

24. Lettings to students. A tenancy is not a protected one if it is granted to a person who is pursuing or intends to pursue a course of study provided by a specified educational institution and is so granted by that institution: Rent Act 1977, s. 8. 'Specified' here means specified by the Secretary of State by regulations in a statutory instrument. Regulations have been made and the specified institutions include:

(a) universities;
(b) teacher training colleges;
(c) polytechnics (the new universities).

25. Holiday lettings. A tenancy is not a protected one if its purpose is to confer on the tenant the right to occupy the dwelling-house for a holiday: Rent Act 1977, s. 9. Where the parties to an agreement expressly say that it is a holiday letting, that is prima facie evidence that it is so, although it can be displaced by evidence that the expressed purpose was not the true one: *Buchmann* v. *May* (1978).

Buchmann v. *May* (1978). B let to M a house on a series of short furnished tenancies. In late 1974 M sought a short renewal saying that she would be leaving England at its end. M signed an agreement for a new three month tenancy. It provided that 'the letting hereby made is solely for the purpose of (M's) holiday'. After the tenancy ended M remained in the house. B sued for possession claiming that the tenancy was outside the Rent Acts because it was a holiday letting. The judge took the view that the 'purpose of the tenancy' had to be determined by the reality of the situation and held that the tenancy was not a holiday letting. B appealed to the Court of Appeal which HELD: where a tenancy agreement expressly stated that the purpose for which it was made was for a holiday letting, that would be taken by the court as evidence of the purpose of the parties unless the tenant could show that the true purpose was different. In this case there was no such evidence by the tenant and it was therefore a holiday letting. B was entitled to possession.

26. Agricultural holdings. A tenancy is not a protected one if the dwelling-house is comprised in an agricultural holding within the meaning of the Agricultural Holdings Act 1986 and is occupied by the person responsible for the control (whether as tenant or as servant or agent of the tenant) of the farming of the holding: Rent Act 1977, s. 10.

27. Licensed premises. A tenancy of a dwelling-house which consists of or includes premises licensed for the sale of intoxicating liquors for consumption on the premises is not a protected one: Rent Act 1977, s. 11.

28. Resident landlords. Section 12 (as amended by the Housing Act 1980, s. 65) deals with the 'resident landlord' exception. This was introduced by the 1974 Act which, it will be recalled (*see* **2**), gave furnished tenancies protection under the Rent Acts. At the same time, it introduced this new exception designed to assist landlords who 'live in'. The section provides that a tenancy is not a protected one if,

(a) it was granted on or after 14th August 1974; and
(b) the dwelling-house forms part only of a building and the building is not a purpose-built block of flats; and
(c) the tenancy was granted by a person who, at the time he granted it, occupied as his residence another dwelling-house which also formed part of the building;
(d) at all times since the tenancy was granted the interest of the landlord under the tenancy has belonged to a person who, at the time he owned that interest, occupied as his residence another dwelling-house which also formed part of that building.

A person is treated as occupying a dwelling-house as his residence if he fulfils the same conditions as have to be fulfilled by a statutory tenant (*see* Chapter 17). Where there is a resident landlord, the tenant will not be a protected tenant but will be entitled to the more limited protection given to restricted contracts: *see* Chapter 20.

Conditions (**a**)–(**d**) above apply to tenancies granted before 28th November 1980. The effect of the wording of the conditions, however, was possibly to prevent the resident-landlord exception from applying to a person who owned a flat in a purpose-built block of flats and who let part of his flat but resided in the rest of it. The Housing Act 1980, s. 65(1), substituted for the last three conditions (above) the following conditions, and they will apply to lettings after 28th November 1980:

(**a**) the dwelling-house forms part of a building and, except in a case where the dwelling-house also forms part of a flat, the building is not a purpose-built block of flats: and

(**b**) the tenancy was granted by a person who, at the time when he granted it, occupied as his residence another dwelling-house which

(*i*) in the case mentioned in (**a**) above, also forms part of the flat; or

(*ii*) in any other case, also forms part of the building; and

(**c**) at all times since the tenancy was granted, the interest of the landlord under the tenancy has belonged to a person who, at the time he owned that interest, occupied as his residence another dwelling-house which

(*i*) in the case mentioned in (**a**) above, also formed part of the flat; or

(*ii*) in any other case, also formed part of the building.

NOTE: The Rent Act 1977, Sch. 2, contains detailed provisions dealing with, primarily, the satisfaction of the residence condition where the interest of the landlord under the tenancy is transferred to a new landlord or is vested in personal representatives, trustees or the probate judge. The provisions of the Schedule were considered by the House of Lords in *Landau* v. *Sloan* (1981). It was as a result of the decision of the Court of Appeal in that case that the terms of Sch. 2 were amended. The provisions of that Schedule are complex and outside the scope of this book.

29. Exceptions to s. 12. This section does not apply to:

(**a**) tenancies granted before 14th August 1974; or

(**b**) a tenancy of a dwelling-house which forms part of a building if it is granted to someone who, before it was granted, was a protected or statutory tenant of the same dwelling-house or another dwelling-house in the same building.

Exception (**a**) has already been examined (*see* **28**(*a*)). Exception (**b**) prevents a landlord moving into a building, granting new tenancies to the existing tenants and then trying to rely on s. 12 to get them out.

30. Landlord's interest belonging to Crown. A tenancy is not a protected or statutory one at any time when the interest of the landlord belongs to Her Majesty in right of the Crown or to a government department or is held in trust for Her Majesty for the purposes of a government department: Rent Act 1977, s. 13(1) (as substituted by the Housing Act 1980, s. 73). The effect of this provision and of s. 13(2) is that tenants of the Crown who are tenants of (*a*) the Duchy of Lancaster, or (*b*) the Duchy of Cornwall, or (*c*) the Crown Estate Commissioners, can now be regulated tenants if they satisfy the other necessary conditions (*see* **4**).

31. Landlord's interest belonging to a local authority. The Rent Act 1977, s. 14 provides that a tenancy is not a protected one at any time when the interest of the landlord belongs to:

(a) a county council; or
(b) a district council; or
(c) the London Borough Councils or the City of London; or
(d) ILEA; or
(e) a joint authority under Part IV of the Local Government Act 1985; or
(f) the Commission for New Towns; or
(g) a development corporation; or
(h) the Development Board for Rural Wales; or
(i) an urban development corporation.

Such tenancies may, however, be secure tenancies (*see* Chapter 32).

32. Landlord's interest belonging to housing association. The Rent Act 1977, s. 15 provides that tenancies held from the following organisations are not protected:

(a) the Housing Corporation;
(b) a housing trust which is a charity;
(c) a housing association which is a registered association;
(d) a housing association which is a co-operative housing association.

Such tenancies may, however, be secure tenancies (*see* Chapter 32).

33. Landlord's interest belonging to a housing co-operative. The Rent Act 1977, s. 16 provides that tenancies held of certain housing co-operatives are not protected.

Regulated and controlled tenancies

34. Generally. So far this chapter has been concerned with the general conditions which must be satisfied for a tenancy to be a protected tenancy. Until 28th November 1980 a protected tenancy could be either a regulated or a controlled tenancy. There were detailed provisions for determining which of the two categories a tenancy fell into. In summary, a controlled tenancy was one granted prior to 6th July 1957 in respect of a house erected before 24th August 1954 whose rateable value did not exceed £40 in London (£30 elsewhere) on 7th November 1956. If a tenancy was a controlled one there was a special basis for assessing the maximum rent lawfully recoverable.

Two attempts were made to convert controlled tenancies into regulated ones. First, there was provision in the Housing Finance Act 1972 for automatic conversion by reference to rateable value; the automatic conversion was, however, only partially implemented. Secondly, there was provision under Part VIII of the 1977 Rent Act for conversion where a dwelling was in good repair and provided with all the standard amenities.

35. Housing Act 1980, s. 64(1). This provision came into operation on the 28th November 1980 when 'every controlled tenancy shall cease to be a controlled tenancy and become a regulated tenancy'. Some controlled tenancies, however, were so classified notwithstanding that they had a business element in them. Section 64(2) of the 1980 Act provides that if the controlled tenancy is one to which Part II of the 1954 Act would apply, on ceasing to be a controlled tenancy (i.e. on 28th November 1980) it is treated as a tenancy continuing by virtue of s. 24 of the 1954 Act.

Interaction of Rent Act 1977 and Part II of the 1954 Act

36. Interaction of above Acts. The Rent Act protects the occupier of residential property; Part II of the Landlord and Tenant Act 1954 (*see* Chapter 11) protects the occupier of business property. Now, after the operation of the Housing Act 1980, s. 64 (*see* **35**), where a property has a mixed business and residential user the tenancy will normally be protected by Part II of the 1954 Act: *see* the Rent Act 1977, s. 24(3).

Protected shorthold tenancies and assured tenancies under the Housing Act 1980

37. Introduction. In order to try to induce landlords or prospective landlords to let residential property, the Housing Act 1980 introduced two types of protection under which the landlord might let his property and be sure of recovering possession. The two types were:

(a) protected shorthold tenancies: ss. 51–55 of the Housing Act 1980;
(b) assured tenancies: ss. 56–58.

The first type enabled a landlord to recover possession but the tenant might apply to have a registered rent. The second type enabled the landlord to charge a market rent and recover possession.

38. Protected shorthold tenancies. It should be noted that a protected shorthold tenancy was still a protected tenancy. There was, however, a new Case added to the Rent Act 1977, Sch. 15, Part II (the mandatory grounds for possession) which enabled the landlord to recover possession at the end of a shorthold letting: *see* Case 19.

39. Conditions to be satisfied. In order for a tenancy to be a protected shorthold tenancy the following had to be satisfied: s. 52:

(a) there had to be a protected tenancy granted after 28th November 1980;
(b) the grant had to be for a term certain of not less than one year nor more than five years;
(c) the tenancy had to be incapable of being brought to an end by the landlord except in pursuance of a provision for re-entry or forfeiture for non-payment of rent or breach of any other obligation of the tenancy;
(d) before the grant the landlord had to have given the tenant a valid notice in the prescribed form stating that the tenancy was to be a protected shorthold tenancy.

NOTES: (1) A tenancy of a dwelling-house was not a protected shorthold tenancy if it was granted to a person who, immediately before it was granted, was a protected or statutory tenant of that dwelling-house; s. 52(2).

(2) A protected shorthold tenancy continued to be one if it was for a term certain as above, followed, at the tenant's option, by a further term, or for a term certain as above and thereafter from year to year or some other period; s. 52(5).

(3) In proceedings for possession, if the court was of the opinion that, although (*d*) above was not satisfied, it was just and equitable to make an

order for possession, the court could treat the tenancy as a protected short-hold tenancy: s. 55(2).

40. Right of tenant to end protected shorthold tenancy. By s. 53(1) a protected shorthold tenancy could be brought to an end by the tenant giving written notice to the landlord. The period of the notice was:

(a) one month if the term certain is two years or less;
(b) three months if the term is more than two years.

41. Assignment or sub-letting. By virtue of s. 54(2), a protected shorthold tenancy was not capable of being assigned. By s. 54(1), where the tenant under a protected shorthold tenancy sub-let the whole or part of the dwelling-house, the landlord became entitled as against the tenant to possession of the premises. He was also entitled to possession against the sub-tenant and the 1977 Act, s. 137 (*see* 18: **38**) did not apply.

42. Effect of Housing Act 1988. The Housing Act 1988 provides that a tenancy entered into after the commencement of that Act (i.e. 15th January 1989) cannot be a protected tenancy except in special cases: s. 34(1) of the 1988 Act. However, s. 20 of the same Act provides for assured shorthold tenancies (*see* 21:**2**). What this means is that after 15th January 1989, except in a limited number of special cases, there cannot be granted a new protected shorthold tenancy; instead there can be granted an assured shorthold tenancy. The provisions of the Housing Act 1980, ss. 51 to 55 will therefore be of diminishing significance. There are transitional provisions in s. 34 of the 1988 Act.

43. Assured tenancies. An assured tenancy was one which satisfied the following conditions:

(a) the interest of the landlord since the creation of the tenancy had to have belonged to an 'approved body'; and
(b) before the tenant first occupied the dwelling-house under the tenancy no part of it had been occupied by any person as his residence except under an assured tenancy: and either
(c) the dwelling-house had to have been, or formed part of, a building which was erected (and on which construction work first began) after the passing of the 1980 Act (i.e. 8th August 1980); or
(d) qualifying works had been carried out to the dwelling-house.

NOTES: (1) 'Approved body' meant a body or one of a description of bodies for the time being specified in an order made by the Secretary of State: s. 56(4).

(2) Section 56 did not apply if, before the grant of the tenancy, the landlord gave the tenant a valid notice in the prescribed form that the tenancy was to be a protected tenancy or a housing association tenancy and not an assured tenancy.

(3) 'Qualifying works' were defined in s. 56B.

44. Effect of landlord ceasing to be an approved body. When the landlord under an assured tenancy ceased to be an approved body by reason of a variation in the bodies specified in an order under s. 56(4), in relation to that tenancy and any further tenancy granted by the landlord to the person who immediately before the grant was in possession of the dwelling-house as an assured tenant, the landlord was treated as continuing to be an approved body: s. 57(1). If, for any period, the reason for such cesser was other than above, then in determining whether condition 43(*a*) above was satisfied, any period of less than three months would be disregarded.

45. Protection given to assured tenants. The protection given to assured tenants was that of Part II of the Landlord and Tenant Act 1954 (*see* Chapters 10–15) subject to the exceptions and modifications specified in Sch. 5 to the 1980 Act.

46. Schedule 5. The main exceptions and modifications were:

(a) s. 23 did not apply (i.e. definition of business tenancy);

(b) s. 43 did not apply (i.e. exceptions from protection);

(c) 'the holding' meant the property comprised in the tenancy;

(d) for ground (*d*) of s. 30(1), there was substituted 'the landlord has offered and is willing to provide or secure the provision of suitable alternative accommodation for the tenant'.

There were other alterations for which reference should be made to Sch. 5.

47. Effect of Housing Act 1988. Section 37 of the 1988 Act provides that a tenancy which is entered into after 15th January 1989 cannot be an assured tenancy for the purposes of ss. 56–58 of the Housing Act 1980. Section 1(2) of the 1988 Act provides that, subject to certain special exceptions, at 15th January 1989 any subsisting assured tenancy for the purposes of ss. 56–58 of the 1980 Act becomes an assured tenancy for the purposes of the 1988 Act.

Progress test 16 .

1. Outline the history of the Rent Acts. **(2)**

2. What is the difference between:
  (a) a controlled and a regulated tenancy;
  (b) a statutory tenancy and a protected tenancy;
  (c) a resident and a non-resident landlord? **(3, 28)**

3. What conditions must a tenant satisfy to be a protected tenant? **(4)**

4. Which of the following comprises a dwelling-house for the purposes of the Rent Act;
  (a) a cave;
  (b) Noah's Ark;
  (c) a cottage;
  (d) a flat;
  (e) a garden shed? **(6–8)**

5. Are the occupiers of the following premises protected by the Rent Act:
  (a) a YMCA room;
  (b) a shop with a flat over it;
  (c) a shop alone;
  (d) a flat;
  (e) a tied cottage? **(6–11)**

6. When are premises let as a dwelling? **(7)**

7. What is an essential living room? **(8)**

8. What protection does T have in the following cases:
  (a) T shares a bathroom with L, his landlord, but he has the exclusive use of two other rooms;
  (b) T shares accommodation with L's daughter but not with L;
  (c) T lives in a flat in the same house as L. **(9, 28)**

9. Explain how the rateable value limits operate. What is the difference between premises in and outside London? **(12)**

10. What is the appropriate day in relation to
  (a) a house built in 1936;
  (b) a flat built in June 1973;
  (c) a shop built in 1978? **(13)**

11. What is the significance of the following dates:
   (a) 23rd March 1965;
   (b) 22nd March 1973;
   (c) 1st April 1973;
   (d) 14th August 1974?   **(13, 15, 28)**

12. How does one determine whether a tenancy of mixed commercial and residential premises is protected by Part II of the 1954 Act or the Rent Act?   **(36)**

13. What is a tenancy at a low rent? What special rules apply to determining whether a long tenancy is at a low rent?   **(19)**

14. L lets to T a factory with a dwelling-house in its grounds. T lives in the dwelling and runs his business from the factory. Is T's occupation of the dwelling protected by the Rent Act?   **(22)**

15. What are
   (a) board, and
   (b) attendance?   **(23)**

16. What is the effect of a letting with
   (a) substantial board, and
   (b) substantial attendance?   **(23)**

17. The Oxbridge university lets one dwelling to S, a student at the university, and one to L, a lecturer there. At the end of the summer term L and S refuse to leave the dwellings. Advise the university. Would your answer be different if L had sub-let his entire dwelling to three students at the university?   **(24)**

18. What conditions must be satisfied if the resident landlord exception is to apply?   **(28)**

19. What are the exceptions to the resident landlord exception?   **(29)**

20. What is the effect of a letting by
   (a) a landlord whose interest belongs to one of the following bodies; and
   (b) a tenant whose landlord is one of the following bodies: (*i*) the Crown; (*ii*) a local authority, (*iii*) a housing association?   **(30, 31)**

Security of tenure

Statutory tenancies

1. Introduction. The Rent Act gives security of tenure in two ways:

(a) a tenancy will be continued beyond its contractual date of termination so long as the tenant occupies the dwelling-house as his residence; this statutory continuation is called a 'statutory tenancy';
(b) a landlord's right to recover possession can only be enforced by means of a court order, and this can only be granted in specific cases; to get such an order a landlord must establish one of the specified grounds for possession (*see* Chapter 18).

2. Statutory tenancies and tenants. A statutory tenancy may arise in one of two ways:

(a) upon the determination of a previous protected tenancy; or
(b) by succession.

A statutory tenancy has been aptly described as a 'status of irremovability'.

3. Statutory tenancy by virtue of a previous protected tenancy.
Section 2(1)(*a*) of the 1977 Rent Act provides that after the termination of a protected tenancy of a dwelling-house, the person who immediately before that termination was the protected tenant of it, if and so long as he occupies it as his residence, will be the statutory tenant of it.

A statutory tenancy is therefore a form of protection which arises at the end of a protected tenancy and continues so long as the residential condition is satisfied. Section 2(1)(*a*) breaks down into the following requirements, all of which will have to satisfied for a statutory tenancy to exist:

(a) there must be a protected (i.e. contractual) tenancy; and
(b) that tenancy must have ended; this may be by notice to quit, forfeiture or any of the other common law methods of termination; and

(c) there must be a person who was a protected tenant before the termination; and
(d) that person must continue to occupy the dwelling-house as his residence.

Of these four elements the first three have already been considered in previous chapters. It is therefore only the last condition which has to be considered now. First it is necessary to deal with companies.

4. Companies. A company can be a protected tenant, but it cannot be a statutory tenant because it cannot satisfy the requirement that it occupies the dwelling-house as its residence: *Hiller* v. *United Dairies* (1934). Consequently, while a company may be a protected tenant, on the termination of its tenancy it will not become a statutory tenant and will therefore lose its Rent Act protection. Hence there is nowadays a practice for landlords to let dwelling-houses to companies only. The directors or other employees of the company are then allowed to occupy the premises as licensees. Where the intention of the parties is that the flat should be let to the company and occupied by a director as the company's nominee and that is the reality of the situation the Court will not treat the tenancy granted to the company as a sham: *Hilton* v. *Plustile Ltd* (1988).

5. Occupation as residence. This is the central requirement of a statutory tenancy. The rule is that a non-occupying tenant loses his status as a statutory tenant. It may, however, be difficult to decide if a tenant has ceased to occupy. The classic statement of the law was by the Court of Appeal in *Brown* v. *Brash* (1948); the judgment contains the following significant passage:

> '. . . absence of the [tenant] may be sufficiently prolonged or unintermittent to compel the inference, prima facie, of a cesser of possession or occupation. The question is one of fact and of degree . . . Notwithstanding an absence so protracted [i.e. five years or more] the authorities suggest that its effect may be averted if the tenant has an intention to return and if he couples and clothes his inward intention with some formal, outward and visible sign of it.'

In summary therefore, when a tenant is not himself physically occupying the premises, his statutory tenancy will continue so long as

(a) the tenant intends to return to the dwelling-house; and
(b) there is an outward physical sign of that intention.

There is no principle of law to prevent a person occupying two dwelling-houses as his residence at the same time and being a statutory tenant of either or both; *see Hampstead Way Investments Ltd* v. *Lewis-Weare* (1985). This may arise, for example, where a person lives in the country, but his work requires him to live in a city; both places may then be his residence or home.

6. Statutory tenancy by succession – death before 15th January 1989. A statutory tenancy may be transmitted to another person on the death of the statutory tenant by virtue of a previous protected tenancy ('the original tenant'). Schedule 1 to the Rent Act 1977 contains provisions which provide for two transmissions on death provided certain conditions are satisfied. The effect of the provisions is that:

(a) the surviving spouse (if any) of the original tenant, if residing in the dwelling-house immediately before the death of the original tenant, will, after the death, be the statutory tenant if and so long as he or she occupies the dwelling-house as his or her residence;
(b) where **(a)** does not apply, but a person who was a member of the original tenant's family was residing with him at the time of and for the period of six months immediately before his death, after the death, that person (or, if there is more than one such person, such one of them as may be decided by agreement, or in default of agreement, decided by the county court) will be the statutory tenant if and so long as he occupies the dwelling-house as his residence.

A person who becomes a statutory tenant under these provisions is called the first successor. There may also be a second transmission under Sch. 1, para. 5. as follows:

(a) the surviving spouse (if any) of the first successor, if residing in the dwelling-house immediately before the death of the first successor, after the death will be the statutory tenant if and so long as he or she occupies the dwelling-house as his or her residence;
(b) if **(a)** does not apply, there are similar provisions to those in **(b)** above to determine who, if anyone, will be the statutory tenant. The provisions are the same, except that for the words 'original tenant' there are substituted the words 'first successor'.

There can only be two transmissions on death of the statutory tenancy. When the successor to the first successor dies, the right to occupy the dwelling-house under a statutory tenancy ends and any members of that person's family will have to leave.

7. Succession – death after 15th January 1989. The Housing Act

1988, s. 39 and Sch. 4, modify the succession provisions in relation to deaths after 15th January 1989 in the following way:

(a) where it is the original tenant who dies then there may be two successions to an assured tenancy of the dwelling-house instead of to a statutory tenancy;

(b) where it is the first successor who dies, there may be one succession to an assured tenancy instead of to a statutory tenancy;

(c) it is now made clear that the 'surviving spouse' includes a person who was living with the original tenant as his or her wife or husband; where there is more than one person who fulfils the conditions applicable to a surviving spouse, in default of agreement, the county court will decide who is to be treated as the surviving spouse;

(d) the residence condition for members of the original tenant's family, or for members of the successor's family, is now that the member 'was residing with him in the dwelling-house for the period of 2 years immediately before his death';

(e) in order for there to be a second succession the person must not only satisfy the residence requirement just described, but must also (*i*) have been a member of the original tenant's family immediately before that tenant's death, and (*ii*) have been a member of the first successor's family immediately before the first successor's death;

(f) where an original tenant or first successor dies within 18 months beginning on 15th January 1989 then if a person was residing with him for six months before 15th January 1989, and up to the death, then the two year period of residence is deemed to be satisfied.

8. Death after 15th January 1989 – nature of succession tenancy.
Where there is a succession to an assured tenancy, it is a periodic tenancy arising by virtue of s. 39. By s. 39(6) the tenancy is one:

(a) taking effect in possession immediately after the death of the protected or statutory tenant on whose death the successor became so entitled;

(b) deemed to have been granted to the successor by the person who, immediately before the death of the predecessor, was the landlord of the predecessor under his tenancy;

(c) under which the premises which are let are the same dwelling-house as, immediately before his death, the predecessor occupied under his tenancy;

(d) under which the periods of the tenancy are the same as those for which rent was last payable by the predecessor under his tenancy;

(e) under which the other terms are the same as those on which, under his tenancy, the predecessor occupied the dwelling-house immediately before his death; and

(f) which is treated as a statutory periodic tenancy.

9. Death after 15th January 1989 – miscellaneous provisions. If, immediately before death, the landlord could have recovered possession under Case 19 in Sch. 15 to the Rent Act 1977, the assured periodic tenancy of the successor is an assured shorthold tenancy (*see* 16:**42**). Where before his death the predecessor was a tenant under a fixed term tenancy, s. 6 of the 1988 Act (fixing terms of periodic tenancy) applies to the assured periodic tenancy which arises on possession.

The provisions regarding the recovery of possession from an assured tenant are modified in the case of an assured tenancy arising by succession: *see* Sch. 4, Pt. III of the 1988 Act.

10. Meaning of 'family'. The word 'family' as it is used in Sch. 1 of the Rent Act is not defined in that Act. The cases show that it includes:

(a) children, brothers and sisters of the deceased; and
(b) adopted children.

There have been several cases concerning mistresses: *see Gammans* v. *Ekins* (1950); *Dyson Holdings* v. *Fox* (1975). These cases are now only relevant to deaths before 15th January 1989. The Housing Act 1988 makes clear that persons living with the original tenant as his or her wife or husband shall be treated as the spouse of the original tenant.

It has been established that two adults who live together in a platonic relationship can never establish a familial nexus for the purposes of Sch. 1.

> *Carega Properties* v. *Sharratt* (1979). S, a young man, lived for 18 years with an elderly widow to whom he was not related. The relationship was platonic and filial and S looked after her in her last years. When she died S claimed to be entitled to remain in her rented flat as a statutory tenant by succession. The House of Lords HELD: the word 'family' was to be given its ordinary natural meaning and did not here have the same meaning as the word 'household'. There was here no recognisable familial nexus, S was not therefore a member of the widow's family and was not entitled to become the statutory tenant by succession.

11. The nature of a statutory tenancy. A statutory tenancy is a purely personal right. It cannot be assigned or sold and it does not pass to the personal representatives of a deceased statutory tenant;

nor will it pass to a trustee in bankruptcy. The reason is that it is dependent upon the occupation of the tenant himself and ceases to exist when he ceases to occupy the dwelling-house as his residence. Similarly, a statutory tenant cannot sub-let the entire dwelling-house, for his tenancy will then end.

12. The terms and conditions of a statutory tenancy. Section 3(1) of the Rent Act 1977 provides that so long as he retains possession, a statutory tenant must observe and will be entitled to the benefit of all the terms and conditions of the original contract of tenancy so far as they are consistent with the provisions of the Act. This means that the terms of the previous tenancy (e.g. as to repairs) will normally continue into the statutory tenancy. Some terms, however, will not so continue, since they are repugnant to the status of irremovability that is conferred by a statutory tenancy (e.g. a provision allowing the landlord to determine the tenancy on the tenant ceasing to retain a certain employment).

Section 3(3) provides that a statutory tenant is entitled to give up possession of the dwelling-house if, and only if, he gives such notice as would have been required under the original contractual tenancy or if no notice would have been so required, on giving not less than three months' notice.

13. Termination of a statutory tenancy. There are only two ways in which a statutory tenancy can come to an end:

(a) by the court making a possession order against the tenant;
(b) by the tenant unequivocally giving up possession.

14. Husband and wife. For the purpose of continuation of a statutory tenancy, possession by the wife of the matrimonial home is possession by the husband so that the husband's statutory tenancy will continue through the wife's residence so long as the marriage lasts: *Brown* v. *Draper* (1944). A mistress's occupation does not suffice for these purposes: *Colin Smith Music Ltd* v. *Ridge* (1975). Reference should be made to the Matrimonial Homes Act 1983 which affects the position as between husband and wife and provides for transfer of a statutory tenancy on divorce. The detailed provisions are outside the scope of this book.

Progress test 17

1. What is a statutory tenancy?   **(3)**

2. What is the difference between:
   (a) a statutory tenancy by virtue of a previous tenancy; and
   (b) a statutory tenancy by succession?   **(3, 6)**

3. What conditions must be satisfied for there to be a statutory tenancy?   **(3)**

4. Why cannot a company be a statutory tenancy?   **(4)**

5. Who may succeed to a statutory tenancy? What conditions must a person satisfy in order to qualify as a successor?   **(6)**

6. How many successors can there be to a statutory tenancy?   **(6)**

7. Which of the following, if any, can succeed to a statutory tenancy:
   (a) a mistress;
   (b) a platonic friend;
   (c) a step-child;
   (d) a widower?   **(10)**

8. In what ways may a statutory tenancy end?   **(13)**

9. Under what terms does a statutory tenant hold?   **(12)**

18

Recovery of possession of dwelling-houses subject to the Rent Act

Introduction

1. Generally. One of the two main ways in which the Rent Act protects tenants is that it restricts the landlord's right to recover possession. This is done in two ways. The first is the statutory tenancy which (*see* Chapter 17) gives to the tenant the right to stay in possession even though his tenancy has ended providing he continues to reside in the demised premises. The second way is that if the landlord does wish to recover possession, he must establish, to the satisfaction of the court, one of certain specified grounds or cases for possession. The Act prohibits the court from making a possession order except on those specified grounds.

2. Establishing a right to possession. It must always be borne in mind that the protection given by the Rent Act is in addition and not in substitution for the ordinary contractual rights of tenants. Consequently a landlord who seeks an order for possession has to get over two hurdles. First, he must show that as a matter of contract the tenancy is ended. Secondly, he must establish one of the grounds for possession under the Rent Act 1977. For example, if the tenancy is a periodic one the landlord must determine it contractually by service of a notice to quit or other appropriate means before there can be any question of his entitlement to possession. Of course, once the tenancy has been determined as a matter of contract and has become a statutory one it is only the statutory grounds for possession which have any relevance.

However where a tenancy agreement was rescinded on the grounds of fraudulent misrepresentation, the statutory tenancy which sprang from it was brought to an end with the result that the statutory grounds for possession had no relevance: *Killick* v. *Roberts* (1991).

Grounds for possession

3. Introduction. Section 98(1) of the Rent Act 1977 provides that a court must not make an order for possession of a dwelling-house which is let on a protected tenancy or is subject to a statutory tenancy unless the court considers it reasonable to make such an order and either:

(a) it is satisfied that suitable alternative accommodation is available for the tenant or will be available for him when the order takes effect; or
(b) the circumstances are as specified in any of the Cases in Part I of Sch. 15 to the Act.

The cases specified in Sch. 15, Part I are discretionary in that the court must consider if it is reasonable to make an order. There are in addition certain cases which are mandatory in that if the landlord makes them out the court must make an order: *see* s. 98(2). These cases are contained in Part II of Sch. 15.

4. Effect of s. 98. The following matters arise out of s. 98, and must be considered:

(a) suitable alternative accommodation (*see* **5,6**);
(b) the discretionary cases in Part I of Sch. 15 (*see* **7** *et seq.*);
(c) the mandatory cases in Part II of Sch. 15 (*see* **20** *et seq.*);
(d) the powers of the court generally (*see* **32** *et seq.*).

Suitable alternative accommodation

5. Introduction. The provisions relating to suitable alternative accommodation are contained in the Rent Act 1977, Sch. 15, Part IV. There are two ways in which the landlord may satisfy the requirements relating to suitable alternative accommodation:

(a) if the housing authority issues a certificate that it will provide suitable alternative accommodation for the tenant by a specified date; or
(b) if the court deems the accommodation to be suitable.

Only the second of these requires further consideration. The first is little used in practice since the local authority is understandably reluctant to issue certificates.

6. Deemed suitable by the court. The Rent Act 1977, Sch. 15, paras. 4 and 5 provide that accommodation is to be deemed to be suitable when:

(a) the accommodation comprises premises to be let on a protected tenancy or with reasonably equivalent security of tenure; and
(b) it is similar as regards rental and extent to the accommodation offered by the housing authority in the area for persons whose needs are similar, or is reasonably suitable to the means and needs of the tenant as regards extent and character; and
(c) it is reasonably suitable as regards proximity to place of work.

Discretionary cases

7. The Cases in Schedule 15. Part I of this Schedule contains ten cases where the court may order possession. The landlord must satisfy the court that:

(a) it is reasonable to make the order; and
(b) he has made out the case.

In the following paragraphs these cases are considered. In each paragraph the case is set out and, where appropriate, comments are made on it. In summary, it may be said that Cases 5, 8 and 9 concern the landlord's needs while the remaining cases concern misbehaviour by the tenant. A landlord may rely on two or more cases. Sometimes the same facts may permit reliance on two cases, e.g. Cases 1 and 2.

Where there is before the court a claim that the defendant is entitled to the benefit of the Rent Acts, the court may not make an order for possession unless it is satisfied, either by evidence or by admission by or on behalf of the defendant, that he is not entitled to that protection or that the necessary grounds for possession exist: *R. v. Bloomsbury and Marylebone CC ex p Blackburne* (1985).

8. Case 1. Where any rent lawfully due from the tenant has not been paid or any obligation of the protected or statutory tenancy has been broken or not performed.

This case is the one most commonly relied upon by a landlord. It covers a breach of any of the obligations of the tenancy except the covenant to give up possession of the premises at the end of the term.

9. Case 2. Where the tenant or any person residing or lodging with him or any sub-tenant of his has been guilty of conduct which is a nuisance or annoyance to adjoining occupiers, or has been convicted of using the dwelling-house or allowing the dwelling-house to be used for immoral or illegal purposes. Nuisance or annoyance here covers such things as noise, offensive activities, and using premises as a brothel.

10. Case 3. Where the condition of the dwelling-house has, in the opinion of the court, deteriorated owing to acts of waste by, or the neglect or default of, the tenant or any person residing or lodging with him or any sub-tenant of his and, in the case of any act of waste by, or the neglect or default of, a person lodging with the tenant or a sub-tenant of his, where the court is satisfied that the tenant has not, before the making of the order in question, taken such steps as he ought reasonably to have taken for the removal of the lodger or sub-tenant, as the case may be.

11. Case 4. Where the condition of any furniture provided for use under the tenancy has, in the opinion of the court, deteriorated owing to ill-treatment by the tenant or any person residing or lodging with him or any sub-tenant of his and, in the case of any ill-treatment by a person lodging with the tenant or a sub-tenant of his, where the court is satisfied that the tenant has not, before the making of the order in question, taken such steps as he ought reasonably to have taken for the removal of the lodger or sub-tenant as the case may be.

12. Case 5. Where the tenant has given notice to quit and, in consequence of that notice, the landlord has contracted to sell or let the dwelling-house or has taken any other steps as the result of which he would, in the opinion of the court, be seriously prejudiced if he could not obtain possession.

Notice to quit here means the service of a proper notice; it does not mean informally agreeing to leave: *Standingford* v. *Bruce* (1926).

13. Case 6. Where, without the consent of the landlord, the tenant has at any time assigned or sub-let the whole of the dwelling-house or sub-let part of it, the remainder being already sub-let. This case can be relied upon against both the tenant and the sub-tenant: *Leith Properties Ltd* v. *Springer* (1982).

14. Case 7. This case was repealed by the Housing Act 1980.

15. Case 8. Where the dwelling-house is reasonably required by the landlord for occupation as a residence for some person engaged in his whole-time employment, or in the whole-time employment of some tenant from him or with whom, conditional on housing being provided, a contract for such employment has been entered into, and the tenant was in the employment of the landlord or a former landlord, and the dwelling-house was let to him in consequence of that employment and he has ceased to be in that employment.

16. Case 9. Where the dwelling-house is reasonably required by the landlord for occupation as a residence for either:

(a) himself; or
(b) any son or daughter of his over 18 years of age; or
(c) his father or mother; or
(d) if the dwelling-house is let on or subject to a regulated tenancy, the father or mother of his wife or husband; and the landlord did not become landlord by purchasing the dwelling-house or any interest therein, after either:
　(*i*) 7th November 1956, in the case of a tenancy which was then a controlled tenancy;
　(*ii*) 8th March 1973, in the case of a tenancy which became a regulated tenancy by virtue of the Counter-Inflation Act 1973, s. 14;
　(*iii*) 24th May 1974, in the case of a regulated furnished tenancy; or
　(*iv*) 23rd March 1965, in the case of any other tenancy.

17. Case 9 explained. Case 9 is of some importance. It is often relied on by a landlord who is trying to recover possession of a dwelling-house for his own use or for the use of his immediate family. The following points should be noted:

(a) the dwelling-house must be reasonably required; this means that there must be a genuine need for the house;
(b) the landlord must not be a landlord by purchase, i.e. if a landlord grants a tenancy to a tenant and then sells his own interest to another person, that other person is a landlord by purchase and cannot rely on this case;
(c) the court has to consider the question of greater hardship when considering a claim under Case 9.

18. Case 9 and greater hardship. In considering a claim for possession under Case 9 the court must have regard to the question of greater hardship: Rent Act 1977, Sch. 15, Part III. In particular, the court must not make an order by reason of Case 9 if it is shown that, having regard to all the circumstances of the case, including the question whether other accommodation is available to the landlord or the tenant, greater hardship would be caused by granting the order than by refusing to grant it: Sch. 15, para. 1. The following points should be noted in regard to the question of greater hardship:

(a) the tenant must prove greater hardship;
(b) the mere fact that a tenant must move is not of itself evidence of greater hardship;
(c) the court considers all the factors as at the time of the hearing.

19. Case 10. Where the court is satisfied that the tenant has sub-let part of the dwelling at a rent in excess of the maximum rent recoverable under the Rent Act.

Schedule 15, Part II

20. The mandatory cases in Part II. These are the case in which the court must order possession where the dwelling-house is subject to a regulated tenancy. There is no discretion in the court and the question of reasonableness does not apply.

21. Case 11. Where a person who let the dwelling-house on a regulated tenancy had, at any time before the letting, occupied it as his residence ('the owner-occupier'), and:

(a) not later than the relevant date the landlord gave written notice to the tenant that possession might be recovered under this Case; and
(b) the dwelling-house has not, since
  (*i*) 22nd March 1973, in the case of a tenancy which became a regulated tenancy by virtue of the Counter-Inflation Act 1973, s. 14;
  (*ii*) 14th August 1974, in the case of a regulated furnished tenancy; or
  (*iii*) 8th December 1965, in the case of any other tenancy;
been let by the owner-occupier on a protected tenancy with respect to which the condition mentioned in paragraph (**a**) above was not satisfied; and
(c) the court is of the opinion that any of the conditions in the Rent Act 1977, Sch. 15, Part V, paras. (*a*), (*c*)–(*f*), is satisfied (for the conditions *see* **24**, below).
   This case enables an owner-occupier who previously occupied a house as his residence at any time before the letting and then let it, to recover possession where the court is satisfied that the house is required for one of the reasons specified in the Act (*see* **24** below). One of two

joint owner-occupiers may rely on this case: *Tilling* v. *Whiteman*(1980).

NOTE: A protected shorthold tenancy or a Case 20 letting granted between 16th November 1984 and 22nd July 1985 is treated as satisfying condition (b) above. This period covers the period of uncertainty following the decision in *Pocock* v. *Steel* (1985) now covered by the Rent (Amendment) Act 1985.

22. Meaning of relevant date. As can be seen above notice must have been given to the tenant not later than the 'relevant date' that possession might be recovered under this Case. The relevant date is defined by Sch. 15, Part III, para. 2 and is:

(a) in the case of a tenancy created before 8th December 1965, 7th June 1966;
(b) in the case of a tenancy becoming protected by virtue of the Counter-Inflation Act 1973, s. 14, and created before 22nd March 1973, 22nd September 1973;
(c) in the case of a regulated furnished tenancy created before 14th August 1979, 13th February 1975;
(d) in any other case, the date of commencement of the tenancy.

23. The court's discretion to dispense with notice. Where notice has not been served, if it considers it just and equitable to make an order for possession, the court may dispense with the requirements under paragraph (*a*) or (*b*) of Case 11.

24. Schedule 15, Part V. This was added to the Rent Act 1977 by s. 66 of the Housing Act 1980, and defines the Cases which an occupier may rely on to recover possession where he has served the appropriate notice. Paragraphs (*a*) and (*c*)–(*f*) apply to Case 11. Paragraphs (*b*)–(*e*) apply to Case 12. Paragraphs (*c*)–(*f*) apply to Case 20. The relevant provisions of Part V are as follows.

(a) The dwelling-house is required as a residence for the owner or any member of his family who resided with the owner when he last occupied the dwelling-house as a residence.
(b) The owner has retired from regular employment and requires the dwelling-house as a residence.
(c) The owner has died and the dwelling-house is required as a residence for a member of his family who was residing with him at the time of his death.
(d) The owner has died and the dwelling-house is required by a successor in title as his residence or for the purpose of disposing of it with vacant possession.

(e) The dwelling-house is subject to a mortgage, made by deed and granted before the tenancy, and the mortgagee

(*i*) is entitled to exercise a power of sale conferred on him by the mortgage or by the Law of Property Act 1925, s. 101; and

(*ii*) requires the dwelling-house for the purpose of disposing of it with vacant possession in exercise of that power.

(f) The dwelling-house is not reasonably suitable to the needs of the owner, having regard to his place of work, and he requires it for the purpose of disposing of it with vacant possession and of using the proceeds of that disposal in acquiring, as his residence, a dwelling-house which is more suitable to those needs.

25. Case 12. Where a person ('the owner') intends to occupy the dwelling-house as his residence at such time as he might retire from regular employment and has let it on a regulated tenancy before he has so retired and

(a) not later than the relevant date the landlord gave written notice to the tenant that possession might be recovered under this Case; and

(b) the dwelling-house has not, since 14th August 1974, been let by the owner on a protected tenancy with respect to which the condition mentioned in paragraph (*a*) above was not satisfied; and

(c) the court is of the opinion that any of the conditions in the Rent Act 1977, Sch. 15, Part V, paras (*b*)–(*e*) is satisfied (*see* **24,** above for the conditions).

This case concerns retirement homes bought and then let out pending retirement. Again, as in Case 11, the court has a discretion to dispense with the requirement under (*a*) or (*b*).

26. Case 13. Where the dwelling-house is let under a tenancy for a term of years certain not exceeding eight months and

(a) not later than the relevant date the landlord gave written notice to the tenant that possession might be recovered under this Case; and

(b) the dwelling-house was, at some time within the period of 12 months ending on the relevant date, occupied under a right to occupy it for a holiday.

For the purposes of this Case a tenancy will be treated as being for a term of years certain notwithstanding that it is liable to determination by re-entry or on the happening of any event other than the giving of notice by the landlord to determine the term.

This Case concerns short lettings which follow holiday lettings and it operates as follows. If there is a holiday letting and within 12 months of it the landlord lets the property for a short term of less than eight months, he may serve notice at the start of that short term that he relies on this case. It is therefore intended to apply to those who own property which is normally let on holiday lettings but who let it out of season for short periods.

27. Case 14. Where the dwelling-house is let under a tenancy for a term of years certain not exceeding 12 months and

(a) not later than the relevant date the landlord gave written notice to the tenant that possession might be recovered under this Case; and
(b) at some time within the period of 12 months ending on the relevant date, the dwelling-house was subject to such a tenancy as is referred to in the Rent Act 1977, s. 8(1).

This case concerns short lettings which follow lettings to students within s. 8 of the Act (*see* 16: **24**), and is intended to enable those who let to students under s. 8 to let the property for short periods of up to one year and then to recover possession.

28. Case 15. Where the dwelling-house is held for the purpose of being available for occupation by a minister of religion as a residence from which to perform the duties of his office and

(a) not later than the relevant date the tenant was given written notice that possession might be recovered under this Case; and
(b) the court is satisfied that the dwelling-house is required for occupation by a minister of religion as such a residence.

29. Cases 16–18. These cases all concern the recovery of dwelling-houses occupied by persons employed on, or responsible for, the control of agricultural units. They are particularly complicated even by the standards of the law of landlord and tenant and are outside the scope of this book.

30. Case 19. Where the dwelling-house was let under a protected shorthold tenancy (or is treated under the Housing Act 1980, s. 55 as having been so let) and

(a) there either has been no grant of a further tenancy of the dwelling-house since the end of the protected shorthold tenancy or, if there was such a grant, it was to a person who immediately before the grant was in possession of the dwelling-house as a protected or statutory tenant; and
(b) the proceedings for possession were commenced after appropri-

ate notice by the landlord to the tenant and not later than three months after the expiry of the notice.

A notice is appropriate for this Case if

(a) it is in writing and states that proceedings for possession under this Case may be brought after its expiry; and

(b) it expires not earlier than three months after it is served nor, if, when it is served, the tenancy is a periodic tenancy, before that periodic tenancy could be brought to an end by a notice to quit served by the landlord on the same day;

(c) it is served

(*i*) in the period of three months immediately preceding the date on which the protected shorthold tenancy comes to an end; or

(*ii*) if that date has passed, in the period of three months immediately preceding any anniversary of that date; and

(d) in a case where a previous notice has been served by the landlord on the tenant in respect of the dwelling-house, and that notice was an appropriate notice, it is served not earlier than three months after the expiry of the previous notice.

31. Case 20. This case was added to the Rent Act 1977 by the Housing Act 1980, s. 67, and deals with lettings by servicemen. Where the dwelling-house was let by a person ('the owner') at any time after 28th November 1980, and

(a) at the time when the owner acquired the dwelling-house he was a member of the regular armed forces of the Crown;

(b) at the relevant date the owner was a member of the regular armed forces of the Crown;

(c) not later than the relevant date the owner gave written notice to the tenant that possession might be recovered under this Case;

(d) the dwelling-house has not since 28th November 1980 been let by the owner on a protected tenancy with respect to which the condition mentioned in paragraph (**c**) above was not satisfied; and

(e) the court is of the opinion that either:

(*i*) the dwelling-house is required as a residence for the owner; or

(*ii*) that any of the conditions in the Rent Act 1977, Sch. 15, Part V, paras (*c*) – (*f*) is satisfied (*see* **24** above for the conditions).

If the court is of the opinion that, notwithstanding that the condition in paragraph (**c**) or (**d**) above is not complied with, it is just and equitable to make an order for possession of the dwelling-house, it may dispense with the requirements of either or both of these paragraphs, as the case may require.

32. The court's powers to make possession orders. Proceedings for possession are normally brought in the county court. When the landlord relies on one of the discretionary cases in Part I of Schedule 15 on the making of an order for possession the court may

(a) stay or suspend the execution of the order; or
(b) postpone the date of possession;

for such period as it thinks fit: Rent Act 1977, s. 100(3).

NOTES: (1) Under the Housing Act 1980, s. 75(2), where the court exercises its power in (a) or (b) above, it must impose conditions with regard to payment by the tenant of arrears of rent (if any) and current rent or mesne profits and may impose such other conditions as it thinks fit.

(2) Under the Housing Act 1980, s. 89, in dealing with the cases under Part II of Schedule 15 (the mandatory cases) the court must not postpone possession more than 14 days unless there is exceptional hardship, in which case the maximum is six weeks.

(3) There is a special speedy procedure in the county court for recovery of possession of a dwelling-house under:
   (a) Cases 11, 12 or 20, provided
      (*i*) the dwelling-house is required as a residence for the owner or for any member of the owner's family who resided with him at his death or, where the proceedings are brought under Case 11, for any member of the owner's family who resided with him when he last occupied the dwelling-house as a residence; and
      (*ii*) the requisite notice was given; and
   (b) Cases 13-19 (inclusive).

Miscellaneous provisions concerning security of tenure

33. Miscellaneous matters. The main provisions of the Rent Act concerning security of tenure have now been considered. There are however two miscellaneous matters which can be conveniently dealt with here. They are:

(a) unlawful eviction and harassment of residential occupiers (*see* **34–37**);
(b) sub-lettings (*see* **38–48**).

34. Unlawful eviction and harassment. Section 1(2) of the Protection from Eviction Act 1977 makes it an offence if any person unlawfully deprives a residential occupier of any premises of his occupation of the premises or any part of them, or if he attempts to do so, unless he proves that he believed, and had reasonable cause to believe, that the residential occupier had ceased to reside in the premises. Section 1(3) makes it an offence if any person, with intent to cause the residential occupier of any premises

(a) to give up the occupation of the premises or any part of them,
(b) to refrain from exercising any right or pursuing any remedy in respect of the premises or any part of them,

does acts calculated likely to interfere with the peace or comfort of the residential occupier or members of his household, or persistently withdraws or withholds services reasonably required for the occupation of the premises as a residence.

Section 1(3A) added by the Housing Act 1988 makes it an offence if the landlord of a residential occupier, or an agent of such a landlord (*a*) does acts likely to interfere with the peace or comfort of the residential occupier or members of his household, or (*b*) persistently withdraws or withholds services reasonably required for the occupation of the premises in question as a residence, and (in either case) he knows, or has reasonable cause to believe, that that conduct is likely to cause the residential occupier to give up the occupation of the whole or part of the premises or to refrain from exercising any right or pursuing any remedy in respect of the premises.

The reference to a 'residential occupier' means a person occupying premises as a residence whether under a contract or by virtue of any enactment or rule of law giving him the right to remain in occupation or restricting the right of any other person to recover possession of the premises: Protection from Eviction Act 1977, s. 1(1). This is a wide definition and it covers not only protected tenants but also occupants under restricted contracts, residential licensees and service licensees. It is therefore intended to protect all lawful residential occupiers in their enjoyment of their occupation.

35. Unlawful eviction; civil proceedings. The preceding paragraph was concerned with criminal proceedings. Where a landlord harasses or evicts a residential occupier, that occupier will normally also have a civil remedy. He may seek an injunction to restrain the landlord from harassing him or may sue him for damages for the losses he has suffered. It has been held that where a landlord unlawfully evicts a protected tenant from his home, that tenant may recover what are called 'exemplary damages'.

Drane v. *Evangelou* (1978). D rented a flat from E. D applied to the rent officer for a review of his rent. The rent officer reduced the rent. Soon after this, while D was out of the premises E entered the flat, put D's belongings out in the yard and stopped him going back in. D applied to the court for an injunction putting him back in the flat. The court granted it and eventually E complied with it. D then went on and sued E for the loss he had suffered. The Court of Appeal HELD: this was a suitable case for an award of exemplary damages because it was a case where it was 'necessary to teach a wrongdoer that tort does not pay'. Damages totalling £1,000 were awarded.

36. Housing Act 1988, Sections 27 and 28. If, at any time after 9th June 1988, a landlord, or any person acting on his behalf, unlawfully deprives the residential occupier of any premises of his occupation of the whole or part of the premises, then under s. 27(1) the landlord is liable to pay to the former residential occupier, in respect of his loss of the right to occupy the premises, damages assessed on the basis set out in s. 28. This liability also arises if, at any time after 9th June 1988, the landlord or any person acting on his behalf attempts unlawfully to deprive the residential occupier of any premises of his occupation of the whole or part of the premises or, knowing or having reasonable cause to believe that the conduct is likely to cause the residential occupier (*i*) to give up occupation or (*ii*) to refrain from exercising any right or pursuing any remedy, does acts likely to interfere with the peace or comfort of the residential occupier or members of his household, or persistently withdraws or withholds services, and, as a result, the residential occupier gives up his occupation: s. 27(2).

The liability is in tort and is in addition to any other liability. It does not arise where the former residential occupier is reinstated or a court makes an order as a result of which he is reinstated: s. 27(6). Damages may be reduced where (*a*) the conduct of the former residential occupier was such that it is reasonable to mitigate the damages or (*b*) before proceedings were begun, the landlord offered to reinstate the former residential occupier and it was unreasonable to refuse the offer: s. 27(7). It is a defence for the landlord to prove that he reasonably believed that the residential occupier had ceased to reside in the premises at the relevant time.

NOTES: (1) 'Residential occupier' has the same meaning as in **34** above.
(2) Section 27 applies where a statutory tenant is subject to a possession order but the landlord forcibly evicts the tenant before the warrant is executed by the court bailiff: *Haniff* v. *Robinson* (1992).

37. Measure of damages. The basis for the assessment of damages under s. 27 is the difference in value, as at the time immediately before the residential occupier ceased to occupy the premises, between (*a*) the value of the interest of the landlord assuming that the residential occupier continued to have the same right to occupy and (*b*) the value of that interest assuming that the residential occupier had ceased to have that right: s. 28(1). For the purposes of that valuation, it is assumed that (*a*) the landlord is selling on the open market to a willing buyer, (*b*) neither the residential occupier nor any member of his family wishes to buy and (*c*) it is unlawful to carry out any substantial development of any of the land in which the landlord has an interest or to demolish the whole or any part of any building on that land. 'Substantial development' is defined in s. 28(6).

38. Sub-lettings. A sub-tenancy which satisfies all the conditions of a protected tenancy will be a protected tenancy, notwithstanding the fact that it is a sub-tenancy. At common law, when the head tenancy ends the sub-tenancy ends with it. The Rent Acts have therefore always contained special provisions to protect sub-tenants who are protected or statutory tenants. The present provision is s. 137 of the 1977 Act. There are two situations which have to be considered:

(a) where the head tenancy is a protected or statutory tenancy (*see* **39**);
(b) where the head tenancy is not a protected or statutory tenancy (*see* **40**).

39. Sub-lettings where the head tenancy is a protected or statutory tenancy. In this situation there are two rules:

(a) If a court makes an order for possession of a dwelling-house from a protected or statutory tenant on one of the specified grounds in the Act, nothing in that order will affect the right of any sub-tenant to whom the dwelling-house or any part of it has been lawfully sub-let, nor will the order operate to give a right of possession against any sub-tenant: Rent Act 1977, s. 137(1).
(b) Where a protected or statutory tenancy is determined whether as a result of an order for possession or for any other reason, any sub-tenant to whom the dwelling-house or part of it has been lawfully sub-let will be deemed to become the tenant of the landlord on the same terms as if the tenant's statutory or protected tenancy had continued: *ibid.* s. 137(2).

Examples _____

(1) L lets a house to T who sub-lets part to S. When T fails to pay his rent he is taken to court by L who gets a possession order against him. The order does not operate against S: s. 137(1).

(2) L lets a house to T who sub-lets part to S. When T surrenders his interest

to L, S is deemed to become L's tenant on the same terms as he held from T: s. 137(2).

NOTE: The sub-letting must be a lawful one. This means that if the sub-letting was created in breach of covenant and the landlord has not, by his conduct or expressly, accepted the sub-letting, the sub-tenant will not be protected by s. 137. The strict common law rules as to waiver of forfeiture (*see* 8: **10**) do not apply to s. 137; in each case it is a question of fact whether the landlord's conduct amounts to an acknowledgement that the sub-tenancy is lawful: *Trustees of Henry Smith's Charity* v. *Willson* (1983).

40. Sub-lettings where the head tenancy is not a protected or statutory tenancy. Section 137(3) of the Rent Act 1977 deals with the situation where the head tenancy is not a protected or a statutory tenancy under that Act. It provides that where a dwelling-house both:

(a) forms part of premises which have been let as a whole on a superior tenancy but do not constitute a dwelling-house let on a protected or statutory tenancy; and
(b) is itself subject to a protected or statutory tenancy,

from the coming to an end of the superior tenancy, the Rent Act applies in relation to the dwelling-house as if, in lieu of the superior tenancy, there had been separate tenancies of the dwelling-house and of the remainder, for the like purposes as under the superior tenancy and at the rents equal to the just proportion of the rent under the superior tenancy.

NOTE: Where the head tenancy is of business premises part of which are used for residential purposes, then these are not 'premises' for the purposes of s. 137(3) and a sub-tenancy of the residential part is not protected when the head tenancy ends: *Pittalis* v. *Grant* (1989).

41. Sub-lettings where the head tenancy is a long lease at a low rent. In order to complete the protection given to sub-tenants, the Rent Act 1977, s. 137(5) provides that where there is a superior long tenancy of a dwelling-house which is at a low rent and which, but for the fact that it was at a low rent, would have been a protected tenancy or an assured tenancy within the meaning of Part I of the Housing Act 1988, it is to be treated as a protected tenancy for the purposes of s. 137(2). This means that where a sub-tenant who is a protected tenant holds from an unprotected long leaseholder at a low rent, the sub-tenant will have the same protection under s. 137(2) (*see* **39**(*b*) above) as he would have had if the head tenancy had been a protected tenancy.

42. Effect on furnished sub-tenancy of the determination of a superior unfurnished tenancy. Section 138 of the Rent Act 1977 deals with the situation where there is a superior tenancy which was unfurnished and a sub-tenancy which was furnished and the superior tenancy comes to an end. In such a situation the landlord under the superior tenancy has the right, within six weeks from the day on which the superior tenancy ends, to serve notice on the sub-tenant that he requires s. 138 to apply to the sub-tenancy. The effect is that the terms on which the sub-tenant is (by virtue of s. 137(2)) deemed to become the tenant of the landlord will not include any terms as to the provision by the landlord of furniture or services: s. 138(1).

43. Obligation to notify sub-lettings. In conclusion on this section on sub-tenancies, students should note that s. 139 provides that if the tenant of a dwelling-house let on or subject to a protected or statutory tenancy sub-lets any part of the dwelling-house on a protected tenancy, within 14 days after the sub-letting he must supply the landlord with a written statement giving particulars of the sub-letting. Failure to do so or the supplying of a false statement is an offence.

Progress test 18

1. What constitutes suitable alternative accommodation? **(5)**

2. Why are the Cases in Part I of the Rent Act 1977, Sch. 15 discretionary? How does the court exercise its discretion? **(7)**

3. Which Case is most commonly relied upon by a landlord seeking to recover possession? **(8)**

4. In what way can Cases 5, 8 and 9 be distinguished from the remaining cases in Part I? **(7)**

5. What are the elements of Case 9? **(16–18)**

6. How does the court consider the question of greater hardship? **(18)**

7. L lets premises to T on a protected tenancy. L sells his interest to X who wishes to have his daughter live in the premises. How, if at all, can X do this? **(16)**

8. Which Cases should a landlord rely upon in the following instance to recover possession from T, the tenant of a flat:

(a) T uses the flat as a brothel;
(b) T sub-lets the flat at an excessive rent;
(c) T damages the furniture;
(d) T damages the flat? **(2, 9, 11, 10)**

9. How may an owner-occupier let his house and be certain of recovering possession of it when he wishes to return to live there? **(21)**

10. What is the position of an owner-occupier who wishes to rely upon Case 11 but who has failed to give the necessary notice? **(22)**

11. Which are the mandatory Cases for possession? **(20)**

12. L lets flats to tourists in London on short holiday lettings. At the end of one of these, L lets a flat to T on a letting which is not a holiday letting and which is for six months. How can L recover possession from T? Would your answer be different if the letting to T was for nine months? **(26)**

13. Which court normally deals with possession proceedings? **(32)**

14. L lets a flat to T on a protected tenancy. L sells his interest to X Ltd, a property company, which cuts off T's electricity and water supplies, and bars his entrance to the flat. Advise X. **(34, 35)**

15. L lets a flat to X Ltd which sub-lets it to S, one of its directors. X's tenancy comes to an end. Advise S. **(39)**

16. L lets a house to T on a lease for 99 years at a rent of £1 per year. T sub-lets the house to S at a full rent. T's lease comes to an end. Advise S. **(41)**

Rent control

Rents under regulated tenancies

1. Rents under regulated tenancies. There are two main situations to consider, and they are:

(a) where a rent is registered under the Rent Act 1977, Part IV; and
(b) where no rent is registered.

The actual process and mechanics of registration are dealt with later (*see* **13** *et seq.*). This section is concerned with the actual limits on the rent a landlord may recover under a regulated tenancy according to whether a rent is registered (*see* **2–4**) or not (*see* **5** *et seq.*).

2. The limit where a rent is registered. There are two cases to consider:

(a) when the tenancy is a contractual tenancy; i.e. the rent limit during contractual periods (*see* **3**); and
(b) when the tenancy is a statutory tenancy, i.e. the rent limit during statutory periods (*see* **4**).

3. Limit of rent during contractual periods. The Rent Act 1977, s. 44(1) provides that where a rent is registered the rent recoverable during any contractual period of a regulated tenancy is limited to the rent so registered. Section 44(2) provides that where any rent payable under the tenancy exceeds the limit it is irrecoverable from the tenant.

   Where the registered rent exceeds the contractual rent the landlord is unable to recover the excess so long as the contractual tenancy continues and the tenant will be bound only to pay the sum registered.

Examples

(1) L lets a flat to T at a contractual rent of £30 per week. A fair rent of £25 per week is registered. The rent limit is therefore £25 and the landlord cannot lawfully charge or recover more than that.

(2) L lets a flat to T at a contractual rent of £30 per week. The tenancy is for two years. A fair rent of £40 per week is registered. For the duration of the

tenancy L cannot recover more than £30 because that is the maximum recoverable under the contract. L cannot increase the rent until the end of the two years unless the contract provides for an increase.

4. Limit of rent during statutory periods. During statutory periods the rent limit is the registered rent: Rent Act 1977, s. 45(2). The landlord cannot recover more than the registered rent: s. 45(2). During a statutory period, however, if the rent is less than the registered rent, the landlord can increase it up to the registered rent by means of a notice of increase. Where a rent was registered for an unfurnished letting and the same premises were later let furnished without any new rent being registered, the recoverable rent was limited to the registered rent despite the fact that the later letting was furnished: *Rakhit* v. *Carty* (1990).

5. Where no rent is registered. The relevant provisions are contained in the Rent Act 1977, ss. 51, 52, 54. Their effect can be summarised in the following way:

(a) where the tenant is a new tenant, there is no limit on rent payable under a contractual tenancy;

(b) where the tenant was tenant under a regulated tenancy and is granted a new tenancy of the same premises the rent limit is the amount payable at the end of the former tenancy;

(c) where the tenant is the tenant under a subsisting tenancy, the limit is the rent payable under that tenancy, i.e. the contractual rent under it;

(d) in the case of a statutory period, the limit is the rent payable during the last contractual period.

6. Lawful increases in the recoverable rent. The rent which the landlord can lawfully recover is subject to the above limits where no rent is registered. The Rent Act 1977, s. 51(1), however, gives the landlord a lawful means whereby he may increase the rent *provided* the tenant agrees and the agreement is in a specified form. The agreement is called a 'rent agreement with a tenant having security of tenure', and means either:

(a) an agreement increasing the rent payable under a regulated tenancy; or

(b) the grant to the tenant under a regulated tenancy of another tenancy of the dwelling-house at a rent exceeding the rent under the previous tenancy: s. 51(1).

7. Form of the rent agreement. The Rent Act 1977, s. 51(3), (4) requires the rent agreement to be in a specified form. Failure to comply with this requirement means that any increase in rent (other than an increase on account of rates payable by the landlord) is irrecoverable from the tenant: s. 54(1). The requirements are:

(a) the agreement must be in writing signed by the landlord and the tenant; and

(b) the document containing the agreement must contain a statement in characters not less conspicuous than those used in other parts of the agreement:

    (*i*) that the tenant's security of tenure under the Act will not be affected if he refuses to enter into the agreement; and

    (*ii*) that if the agreement were not made but instead a rent were registered under Part IV of the Act, part only of any increase over the rent previously recoverable by the landlord would be payable by the tenant during the first year (this is a new provision and was enacted by the Housing Act 1980, s. 68(1)); and

    (*iii*) that entry into the agreement will not deprive the tenant or landlord of the right to apply to the rent officer for the registration of a fair rent, or words to that effect; and

(c) the statement in **(b)** must be set out at the head of the agreement.

8. Limit of rent during statutory periods. Section 45 provides that the rent payable for any statutory period is not to exceed the rent recoverable for the last preceding contractual period. Accordingly, to determine the rent limit for any statutory period, it is necessary to consider (*see* **3–7**) what was the rent limit under the contractual tenancy; that will be the limit in the statutory period. This limit may be increased or decreased by permitted adjustments. They are:

(a) adjustments with respect to rates: s. 46;

(b) adjustments with respect to the provision of services and furniture: s. 47.

The increase under s. 46 can only be made in pursuance of a notice of increase served by the landlord on the tenant (*see* **10**).

9. Miscellaneous matters. Before the system of registration is considered, there remain several miscellaneous matters to consider. They are:

(a) notices of increase (*see* **10**);

(b) phasing (*see* **11**); and

(c) the recovery of over-payments (*see* **12**).

10. Notices of increase. Notices of increase are required in certain circumstances to increase the rent to a new limit. A notice of increase must be in the prescribed form: Rent Act 1977, s. 49(2). Where a notice of increase is served during a contractual period and the protected tenancy could have been ended before the date specified in the notice of increase by notice to quit given by the landlord at the same time, the notice of increase operates to convert the protected tenancy into a statutory tenancy: s. 49(4). Notices of increase are required:

(a) under s. 46: *see* **8** above;
(b) when a rent is registered and it is desired to increase the rent up to the registered rent.

11. Phasing. This was a process whereby certain rent increases were staged or phased over two years. The relevant provisions were repealed, subject to very limited exceptions, with effect from 4th May 1987. For the exceptions, see Schedule 2 to the Rent (Relief from Phasing) Order 1987.

12. Recovery of over-payment. Section 57 of the Rent Act 1977, enables a tenant who has paid rent in excess of the rent limit to recover it from the landlord or his personal representatives. Alternatively the tenant may set it off against future rent due to the landlord. It is only recoverable for up to two years after it was paid. In the case of a breach of s. 54(1) (*see* **7** above), the period is one year.

The system of registration of fair rents

13. Registration of rents under regulated tenancies. This system was set up by the 1965 Act; the provisions are now contained in Part IV of the 1977 Act. There are separate registration areas each with its own rent officer and rent assessment committee. Applications are made first to the rent officer and can then be referred to the committee.

14. The register of rents. Section 66 of the Rent Act 1977 requires the rent officer for any area to prepare and keep up to date a register of rents available for inspection. It must contain:

(a) the rent payable;
(b) certain prescribed particulars;
(c) a specification of the dwelling-house.

15. Application for registration. Under sections 67 and 68 an application for the registration of a fair rent may be made to the rent officer by:

(a) the landlord;
(b) the tenant;
(c) jointly by landlord and tenant; or
(d) the local authority.

The application must be made in the prescribed form and contain certain prescribed particulars. An application cannot be made within two years from the date on which the existing registration took effect or was confirmed, save that the landlord may apply in the last three months of that two year period. An application may be made in that two year period on the ground that there has been a change, such as to make the registered rent no longer a fair rent, in

(a) the condition of the dwelling-house;
(b) the terms of the tenancy;
(c) the quantity, quality or condition of any furniture provided;
(d) any other circumstances considered when the rent was registered: s. 67(3).

16. Procedure on application to rent officer. Schedule 11 to the Rent Act 1977 contains the detailed provisions for procedure on an application. In outline, it is as follows. The rent officer has power to, and may, require the giving of further information by the parties. Then he must give notice of the application to them and specify a period during which representations can be made to him. Thereafter he may, if necessary, consider in consultation with the parties (who may be represented) what rent ought to be registered. Then he must either determine a fair rent and register it or confirm the existing rent in the register and notify the parties of his decision. They can then object to it within 28 days. If they do object, the rent will automatically be referred to a rent assessment committee.

17. Determination by rent assessment committee. The committee consists of a chairman and one or two other members. The procedure before the committee is similar to that before the rent officer. The committee may first require the parties to give further information. Thereafter the landlord or the tenant may make representations in writing or request leave to make oral representations. Where a party requests leave to make oral representations the committee must give him an opportunity to be heard. Thereafter the committee will decide either to confirm the rent fixed by the rent officer or, if it does not appear to it that it is a fair rent, it will determine a fair rent. The land-lord and tenant are then notified. The decision of the committee must be in writing, signed and contain the reasons for the decision. The decision may be challenged on a point of law in the High Court.

18. Certificate of fair rent. Section 69 of the Rent Act 1977 provides that a person intending either to provide a dwelling-house by the erection, conversion or improvement of any premises, or to let on a regulated tenancy a dwelling-house which is not the subject of such a tenancy and for which no rent is registered or has been registered in the last two years, may apply to the rent officer for a certificate specifying the rent, which in the opinion of the rent officer, would be a fair rent. There are detailed provisions in Sch. 12 concerning certif-icates and applications for them. When a certificate has been issued, an application for registration in accordance with the certificate may be made within two years of the date of the certificate. In such a case the procedure on an application for registration is different and enquiry is directed to ensuring that:

(a) any works required by the certificate to be carried out have been carried out; or
(b) the condition of the house is the same as it was at the date of the issue of the certificate; or
(c) if furniture is provided it accords with the particulars given in the application for a certificate as being furniture to be provided when a letting takes place.

19. Determination of a fair rent. A 'fair rent' is not defined. Section 70(1) provides that in determining a fair rent regard must be had to all the circumstances (other than personal circumstances) and in particular to:

(a) the age, character, locality and state of repair of the dwelling-house;
(b) the quantity and quality and condition of any furniture which is provided; and
(c) any premium lawfully required on the grant, renewal, continu-ance or assignment of the tenancy.

No account is taken of scarcity of accommodation in assessing a fair rent: s. 70(2). By s. 70(3) there is also disregarded, in assessing a fair rent, the following:

(a) disrepair due to a failure by the tenant to carry out his obligations;
(b) improvements carried out by the tenant, other than those carried out in pursuance of an obligation;

(c) any improvement to the furniture by the tenant or any deterioration due to ill-treatment by the tenant.

20. Effect of registration of rent. The Rent Act 1977, s. 72 (as substituted by the Housing Act 1980, s. 61) provides that the registration of a rent takes effect as follows:

(a) if the rent is determined by the rent officer, from the date when it is registered;
(b) if the rent is determined by the rent assessment committee, from the date when the committee makes its decision;
(c) if the rent is confirmed by the rent officer, from the date when it is noted in the register;
(d) if confirmed by the rent assessment committee, from the date when the committee makes its decision.

Premiums

21. Introduction. The provisions of the Rent Act concerning premiums are designed to prevent the evasion of the other provisions concerning rent restriction by the landlord or some other person demanding a capital sum for the grant of assignment of a protected tenancy. These provisions prohibit the taking of a premium in two situations:

(a) on the grant, renewal or continuance of a protected tenancy: Rent Act 1977, s. 119;
(b) on the assignment of a protected tenancy: s. 120.

22. Definition. A premium is defined as including

(a) any fine or other like sum;
(b) any other pecuniary consideration in addition to the rent; and
(c) any sum paid by way of a deposit, other than one which does not exceed one-sixth of the annual rent and is reasonable in relation to the potential liability in respect of which it is paid: Rent Act 1977, s. 128.

The usual form which a premium will take is that of a capital sum. By s. 123 of the Act, however, where the purchase of any furniture has been required as a condition of the grant, renewal, continuance or assignment of a protected tenancy, if the price exceeds the reasonable price for the furniture the excess is treated for the purposes of the Act as if it were a premium required to be paid as a condition of the grant, renewal, continuance or assignment of the interest.

23. Premiums on the grant, renewal or continuance of a protected tenancy. Section 119 provides that 'any person' who, as a condition of the grant, renewal or continuance of a protected tenancy, requires in addition to the rent the payment of any premium or the making of any loan will be guilty of an offence. It extends also to any person who in connection with the grant, etc., receives any premium. The court by which the person is convicted may order the repayment of the premium to the person by whom it was paid.

24. Exceptions to s. 119. There are exceptions to the rule contained in s. 119. They are dealt with in s. 127 (as amended by the Housing Act 1980, s. 78 and the Housing Act 1988, s. 115). The exceptions concern tenancies which are both a long tenancy and a protected tenancy. The detailed provisions are outside the scope of this book and reference should be made to other books on this point.

25. Premiums on the assignment of a protected tenancy. Section 120 of the Rent Act 1977 provides that 'any person' who, as a condition of the assignment of a protected tenancy, requires the payment of any premium or the making of any loan will be guilty of an offence. It also extends to any person who in connection with the assignment of a protected tenancy receives any premium. There are, however, certain sums which, by virtue of s. 120(3), an assignor of a protected tenancy is entitled to require or receive from the assignee:

(a) outgoings paid by the assignor and referable to any period after the assignment takes effect;
(b) a sum not exceeding the amount of any expenditure reasonably incurred by the assignor in carrying out any structural alteration of the dwelling-house;
(c) where the assignor acquired the tenancy by an assignment, the amount of any sum he paid to his assignor under (b) above;
(d) if part of the premises are used for a business, payment for goodwill.

26. Exceptions to s. 120. There are three main exceptions to the rule (*see* **25**) in s. 120; they are:

(a) where a premium was lawfully required or received at the commencement of the tenancy: s. 120(5);
(b) where a premium was lawfully required on the grant, renewal or continuance of a regulated tenancy
  (*i*) which was granted before 8th March 1973; and
  (*ii*) which was brought into protection by the increasing of the rateable value by the Counter-Inflation Act 1973;

(c) on the assignment of a tenancy which satisfies the conditions in s. 127 (*see* **24** above).

As can be seen, the first two situations cover tenancies not originally subject to the restrictions on premiums (i.e. because the tenancy was not at the time of payment of the premium protected by the legislation) but which have subsequently become subject to the restrictions. In these circumstances it would obviously be unfair on the person who paid the lawful premium (at the time when the tenancy was not protected) to prevent him from receiving a payment for the tenancy. The Act therefore allows the tenant to require a premium calculated in accordance with the detailed provisions contained in Sch. 18. Broadly speaking this enables the tenant to require a premium which is a proportion of the lawful premium originally required. The proportion is, in effect, equal to the proportion which the residue of the term at the time of the assignment bears to the whole of the term.

27. The meaning of the words 'any person'. The words used in the Rent Act 1977, ss. 119, 120 are 'any person who . . . requires the payment of any premium'. The meaning of these words has been considered by the House of Lords, in the following case:

Farrell v. *Alexander* (1976). A had a protected tenancy of a flat which she wished to assign to F for £4,000 for 'fixtures and fittings'. The landlords were entitled under the terms of the tenancy to require a surrender of the tenancy but they were prepared to grant a new tenancy to F. An agreement was made between A and F that F would pay A £4,000 on the grant of the new lease. This duly took place. F then sued A to recover the amount by which the £4,000 exceeded the reasonable price of the furniture. The question arose whether A fell within the words 'any person' or whether those words were confined to the landlord, in which case it would not affect this transaction. There were two earlier decisions of the Court of Appeal which supported the narrower construction. The House of Lords HELD: the words 'any person' were not restricted to a landlord but included anyone who, as a condition of the grant of a tenancy, required the payment of a premium. It therefore extended to A who would have to pay back to F the difference between the £4,000 and the reasonable cost of the furniture.

28. The recovery of unlawful premiums. As can be seen (*see* **27**) from *Farrell* v. *Alexander*, it is possible to recover an unlawful premium by an action in the courts. This is the result of the Rent Act 1977, s. 125 which provides that where under any agreement any premium is paid and the whole or any part of it could not lawfully be required then the amount of it or, so much of it as could not lawfully be required, is recoverable by the person by whom it was paid. The normal way of recovering it will be by an action in the county court.

Progress test 19

1. What details does the register of rents contain? **(14)**

2. Who may make an application for the registration of a fair rent? **(15)**

3. What is the procedure adopted on the determination of an application for the registration of a fair rent? **(16)**

4. What means is there of challenging a fair rent assessed by the rent officer? **(17)**

5. What criteria are adopted in determining a 'fair rent'? **(19)**

6. What is a certificate of fair rent? **(18)**

7. For how long is a registered rent effective? **(15)**

8. What is the rent limit when a tenancy is a contractual tenancy? **(3)**

9. What is a rent agreement with a tenant having security of tenure? How does it limit the recoverable rent? What form must it take? **(17)**

10. What is the rent limit during statutory periods of a regulated tenancy? **(8)**

11. How may a landlord increase the rent payable by a regulated tenant up to the rent limit? **(8)**

12. How may a tenant recover rent which he has paid to his landlord over the rent limit? **(12)**

13. What is a premium? **(22)**

14. What restrictions apply to the taking of a premium on the grant or assignment of a protected tenancy? **(23, 25)**

15. In what circumstances may a landlord take a premium on the grant or assignment of a protected tenancy? **(24)**

16. What is the importance of the decision in *Farrell* v. *Alexander*? **(27)**

20

Restricted contracts

Introduction

1. History. Until 1974 a tenancy could not be a protected one if the dwelling-house was let at a rent which included payments in respect of board, attendance or the use of furniture. A system was evolved to protect tenants under such tenancies, providing rent limits and a measure of security of tenure. Under the 1968 Act these contracts and other lettings where the tenant shared accommodation with his landlord were called 'Part VI Contracts', Part VI being the Part of that Act in which they were dealt with.

In 1974 furnished tenancies were brought into line with unfurnished tenancies and given protection. At the same time the resident-landlord exception was created and tenancies falling within that exception were given the old Part VI protection. In the 1977 Act the contracts falling within the old Part VI were given a new name – restricted contracts.

A tenancy or contract entered into after 15th January 1989 cannot be a restricted contract for the purposes of the Rent Act 1977: *see* s. 36 of the Housing Act 1988. Thus, restricted contracts will be gradually phased out by virtue of the 1988 Act.

2. Definition. Section 19 of the Rent Act 1977 provides that a restricted contract is one whereby one person grants to another person, in consideration of a rent which includes payment for the use of furniture or for services, the right to occupy a dwelling as a residence (s. 19(1)). This is a wide definition and might appear to cover a large number of contracts including regulated tenancies. It is subject, however, to a number of exceptions and a contract is not a restricted contract if:

(a) it creates a regulated tenancy: s. 19(5)(*a*);
(b) the interest of the landlord belongs to a local authority or other body mentioned in s. 14 (*see* 16: **31**): s. 19(5)(*aa*);
(c) the interest of the landlord belongs to the Crown or a Government Department but not the Duchy of Lancaster, the Duchy of Cornwall nor the Crown Estate Commissioners: s. 19(5)(*b*);

(d) the rent includes payment for board and the value of the board to the tenant is a substantial proportion of the whole rent: s. 19(5)(*c*);

(e) it creates a qualifying shared ownership lease within the meaning of s. 5A (*see* 16: **21**): s. 19(5)(*cc*);

(f) it is a protected occupancy under the Rent (Agriculture) Act 1976: s. 19(5)(*d*);

(g) it is a housing association tenancy: s. 19(5)(*e*);

(h) it creates an assured tenancy within the meaning of s. 56 of the Housing Act 1980;

(i) it is a holiday letting: s. 19(7);

(j) the occupier does not have exclusive occupation of some part of the dwelling-house: s. 19(6);

(k) it is outside the rateable value limits (*see* **3**).

3. The rateable value limits. A contract is not a restricted one if it falls within one of the classes in the Rent Act 1977, s. 19(4). These are as follows:

(a) *Class D*. The appropriate day in relation to the dwelling falls or fell on or after 1st April 1973 and the dwelling on the appropriate day has or had a rateable value exceeding £1,500 or £750.

(b) *Class E*. The appropriate day in relation to the dwelling fell before 1st April 1973 and the dwelling had a rateable value exceeding:

    (*i*) on the appropriate day £400 or £200; and

    (*ii*) on 1st April 1973, £1,500 or £750.

The meaning of 'the appropriate day' has already been considered in relation to protected tenancies (*see* 16:**13**).

4. Where a restricted contract arises. The preceding two paragraphs contain what is, with its detailed exceptions, a complicated definition. It will most assist students simply to know what are the main situations where a restricted contract may arise. They are where:

(a) there is a resident landlord under the Rent Act 1977, s. 12 (*see* 16:**28**);

(b) the tenant shares accommodation with the landlord and comes within s. 21 (*see* 16:**10**);

(c) certain residential licences have been granted.

The resident landlord exception and sharing under s. 21 have already been considered. It is therefore only necessary to consider which residential licences are restricted contracts. It should be noted that, unlike the general protection given by the Rent Act, the protection given to restricted contracts applies to licences as well as to tenancies.

5. Residential licences. Section 19 requires that there be a contract whereby one person is granted the right to occupy a dwelling as a residence. This may apply to a lodger or other residential licensee.

Luganda v. *Service Hotels Ltd* (1968). A student had a furnished room in an hotel. He had his own key to the room which was a bed-sittingroom with a gas-ring. The room was cleaned by the hotel owners. HELD: The student was a contractual licensee who came within the (old) Part VI protection.

R. v. *South Middlesex Rent Tribunal, ex p. Beswick* (1976). B lived in a single furnished room at a YWCA hostel. The room was her home and she was a permanent resident. She had the use of various communal facilities. HELD: she was a residential licensee and was entitled to the protection of Part VI of the 1968 Act.

6. The protection given to restricted contracts. The general scheme of protection is that:

(a) there is control of rents;
(b) there is a limited security of tenure.

The body responsible for assessing rents and deciding if a tenant should have security of tenure is the rent assessment committee which, when constituted to carry out these functions, is known as a rent tribunal.

Rent control

7. Rents under restricted contracts. A restricted contract may be referred to the rent tribunal for the appropriate district by the lessor, the lessee or the local authority: Rent Act 1977, s. 77. Where a restricted contract is referred to a rent tribunal and the reference is not, before the tribunal has entered upon consideration of it, withdrawn by the party or authority who made it, the tribunal must consider it: s. 78. After making appropriate enquiries and giving the parties an opportunity to be heard the tribunal may approve, reduce or increase the rent payable as they think is reasonable and must notify the parties of its decision. If a rent has already been registered under Part IV (i.e. registered rents under regulated tenancies) the rent tribunal cannot reduce the rent below that registered sum. It is the duty of the president of every rent assessment panel to keep an up-to-date register of rents under restricted contracts where the tribunal has considered the rent: s. 79. The register must contain details of the rent, the contract and the dwelling.

8. Reconsideration of registered rent. Where the rent payable for a dwelling has been entered in the register under the Rent Act 1977, s. 79, the lessor, lessee or local authority may refer the case to the tribunal for reconsideration of the rent entered. Where a rent has been entered within the last two years however, the tribunal cannot be required to hear a further reference in the two-year period unless either:

(a) the application is made jointly by the lessor and lessee; or
(b) there has been a change in:
    (*i*) the condition of the dwelling;
    (*ii*) the furniture or services provided;
    (*iii*) the terms of the contract; or
    (*iv*) any other circumstances taken into consideration when the rent was last considered,

so as to make the registered rent no longer a reasonable rent: s. 80. In this context 'lessor' and 'lessee' indicate the owner and occupier of the property when the contract is a licence only.

9. Effect of registration of rent. Where the rent for any dwelling is entered in the register under the Rent Act 1977, s. 79, it is not lawful to require or receive on account of rent for that dwelling under a restricted contract payment of any sum in excess of the rent so registered: s. 81. Where any rent has been paid in contravention of s. 81, the amount of the excess is recoverable by the person by whom it was paid. It is also a criminal offence for any person to require or receive any payment in contravention of s. 81. Proceedings may only be commenced by the local authority.

10. Premiums. Section 122 of the Rent Act 1977 provides that where a rent is registered under s. 79, any person who as a condition of the grant, renewal, continuance or assignment of rights under a restricted contract requires the payment of any premium will be guilty of a criminal offence. This does not prevent a person from requiring the payment of:

(a) outgoings referable to any period after the grant or assignment takes place; or
(b) a reasonable amount in respect of the goodwill of a business trade or profession where the goodwill is transferred in connection with the grant or assignment.

Security of tenure

11. Introduction. In relation to restricted contracts entered into before 28th November 1980, the statutory provisions operate in the following way. Where a notice to quit is served by the landlord, the operation of that notice may be deferred by the rent tribunal for one or more periods of up to six months depending upon the circumstances of the case. This means that the security of tenure provisions apply only to periodic tenancies, not to tenancies for a fixed term. There are two situations to be considered in relation to security of tenure. They are where notice to quit is served:

(a) after a reference is made to the rent tribunal (*see* **12**); and
(b) before a reference is made but where reference is made before the notice to quit expires (*see* **13**).

12. Notice to quit served after reference to tribunal. Notice to quit served after reference to tribunal.

Section 103 of the Rent Act 1977 provides that if after a reference by the lessee or the local authority the lessor gives notice to the lessee at any time before the decision of the tribunal is given or within the period of six months thereafter then the notice will not take effect before the end of that period. This is subject to two exceptions:

(a) notice to quit served by an owner-occupier; and
(b) where the period of notice is reduced under s. 106.

13. Notice to quit served by an owner-occupier. Section 105 of the Rent Act 1977 provides that s. 103 does not apply where a person who has occupied the dwelling as a residence ('the owner-occupier') has, by a restricted contract, granted the right to occupy the dwelling to another person, and

(a) at or before the time when the right was granted the owner-occupier had given written notice that he was the owner-occupier; and
(b) if the dwelling is part of a house, the owner-occupier does not occupy any other part of the house as his residence; and
(c) at the time the notice is to take effect, the dwelling is required as a residence for the owner-occupier or any member of his family who resided with him when he last occupied the dwelling as a residence.

14. Reduction of the period of notice on account of the lessee's default. Section 106(2) provides that where it appears to the tribunal on an application by the lessor for a direction that:

(a) the lessee has not complied with the terms of the contract; or

(b) the lessee or any person residing or lodging with him has been guilty of conduct which is a nuisance or annoyance to adjoining occupiers or has been convicted of using the dwelling or allowing the dwelling to be used for an immoral or illegal purpose; or

(c) the condition of the dwelling has deteriorated owing to any act or neglect of the lessee or any person residing or lodging with him; or

(d) the condition of any furniture provided for the use of the lessee has deteriorated owing to any ill-treatment by the lessee or any person residing or lodging with him;

the tribunal may reduce the period for the operation of the notice to quit.

15. Application to tribunal. In a case where:

(a) notice to quit a dwelling subject to a restricted contract has been served; and

(b) the restricted contract has been referred to a rent tribunal; and

(c) the period of the notice to quit has not expired,

the lessee may apply to the tribunal for the extension of the period of the notice to quit: Rent Act 1977, s. 104(1). On an application by a lessee under s. 104, after making appropriate enquiries and giving the parties an opportunity of being heard, the tribunal may direct that the notice to quit have no effect until the end of such period as it may direct. The period cannot exceed six months from the date on which the notice to quit would have taken effect. At the end of the extended period a further application for a further extension can be made. Thus indefinite security of tenure can be given. If the tribunal refuses to make a direction the lessee cannot make a further application. It should be noted that an application by a lessee under s. 104 is subject to s. 106 (*see* **14**) and so the landlord may apply for a direction reducing the period on the grounds specified in that section. If such a direction is made then no further application can be made by the lessee.

16. Recovery of possession. In order to recover possession of a dwelling which is subject to a restricted contract, the landlord must first serve notice to quit (assuming the tenancy is a periodic one). The tenant may then apply for security of tenure to the rent tribunal. If the tribunal directs that the notice is not to take effect for a specified period the landlord must await the expiry of that period. At the end of that period (or any further extended period) he can recover possession. To recover possession, however, he will normally have to bring proceedings in the courts. This is the effect of the Protection from Eviction Act 1977, s. 3, which provides that it is not lawful for an owner to enforce his right to possession otherwise than by proceedings in the court.

17. Security of tenure under contract entered into after 28th November 1980. In relation to these contracts, the rent tribunal will have no jurisdiction to defer the operation of a notice to quit. Instead, in proceedings for possession, the court is given power to postpone the date for possession for up to three months: Rent Act 1977, s. 106A (added by the Housing Act 1980, s. 69(2)).

18. Housing Act 1988, s. 36. A tenancy or other contract entered into after 15th January 1989 cannot be a restricted contract for the purpose of the Rent Act 1977 unless it is entered into pursuant to a contract made before that date: *see* s. 36 of the Housing Act 1988.

Progress test 20

1. What were Part VI contracts? What effect did the Rent Act 1977 have upon them? **(1)**

2. What are the rateable value limits in relation to restricted contracts? **(3)**

3. In what main situations do restricted contracts arise? **(4)**

4. Is a holiday letting capable of being a restricted contract? **(2)**

5. In what ways does the protection given to an occupier under a restricted contract differ from that given to a tenant under a protected tenancy? **(15–17)**

6. What is a rent assessment committee? What is a rent tribunal, how is it constituted and what are its functions? What is the difference between these bodies? **(6)**

7. May a resident landlord charge a premium on the grant of a tenancy of a dwelling-house in the same building as that in which he lives? **(10)**

8. L lets a flat to T on a weekly tenancy. L is a resident landlord and serves notice to quit on T. Advise L what rights T has. What would be the position if T had a tenancy for a fixed term which had expired? **(15–17)**

9. How may a landlord recover possession of a dwelling subject to a restricted contract? **(16)**

Assured tenancies under the Housing Act 1988

1. Introduction. The Rent Act legislation and its history have been considered in Chapter 16. The primary purpose of the Rent Act legislation has always been to provide tenants of residential accommodation with security of tenure and to protect such tenants from the effects of market forces, particularly in times of housing shortage, by regulating the level of the rents payable by such tenants.

The Rent Act legislation was, however, the subject of considerable criticism over the course of many years (not the least for its complexity). In particular, in more recent times it was argued that the existence of the Rent Acts had the reverse effect to that intended. Many landlords of residential accommodation were reluctant to grant tenancies which would be protected tenancies under the Rent Act legislation because:

(a) they might be unable to recover possession of the premises for many years (indeed the landlord might be unable to recover possession in his lifetime in view of the succession provisions) irrespective of the length of the term originally agreed between the landlord and the tenant; and

(b) irrespective of the amount of the rent agreed between the landlord and the tenant, there are restrictions upon the amount of rent recoverable from a protected or statutory tenant; in particular, when rents payable under protected or statutory tenancies are determined by a rent officer, it is assumed that the demand for rented residential accommodation is not substantially greater than the residential accommodation which is available for rent. The result in many cases is that the 'fair rent' registered by the rent officer is considerably less than the amount which would otherwise be the market rent for the accommodation in question.

The reluctance of private sector landlords to let residential accommodation for these reasons, coupled with the substantial increase in house prices since the early 1970s, led to an increasing burden upon the public sector. In an effort to encourage private sector landlords to release residential accommodation onto the market, a new species of tenancy – the protected shorthold tenancy – was created by the Housing Act 1980. Enthusiasm for the protected shorthold tenancy was muted however, as although the landlord under such a tenancy could recover possession at the end of the term, the rent recoverable was restricted in the same way as rents payable under Rent Act protected or statutory tenancies.

The Housing Act 1980 also introduced a new species of tenancy of residential accommodation known as an 'assured tenancy' (not to be confused with the assured tenancy which is the creature of the Housing Act 1988 and which is the subject considered in this chapter) which was governed not by the Rent Acts but by a modified version of Part II of the Landlord and Tenant Act 1954 (*see* 16:**43**).

The Housing Act 1980 assured tenancies had a limited impact on the housing market however as:

(a) they could only be granted by certain 'approved bodies' such as housing associations;
(b) assured tenancies could only be granted if either:
(*i*) dwelling-houses on which work of construction first began after 8th August 1980; or
(*ii*) dwelling-houses created by the conversion of premises or made fit for human habitation by the expenditure of certain minimum sums, during the two years immediately preceding the grant of the first relevant tenancy.

2. The Housing Act 1988. The most important features of the Housing Act 1988 ('the Act') are that:

(a) it created a new species of tenancy of residential accommodation known as 'an assured tenancy'; an assured tenancy provides the tenant with security of tenure but enables the landlord to recover a market rent (Ch. I of the Act);
(b) it created a new species of tenancy of residential accommodation known as an 'assured shorthold tenancy' under which the tenant has very limited security of tenure and under which the landlord can again recover a market rent provided it is not 'excessive' (*see* Ch. II of the Act);
(c) it created 'assured agricultural occupancies' (*see* Ch. III of the Act);
(d) save in exceptional circumstances, it is not possible to create a protected tenancy under the Rent Act legislation after the commencement of the Act;
(e) it is not possible to grant a protected shorthold tenancy after the commencement of the Act: s. 34(3);

(f) it is not possible to grant an old style Housing Act 1980 assured tenancy after the commencement of the Act: s. 34(3).

Part I of the Act (Chs. I–VI, ss. 1–45) came into force on 15th January 1989: s. 141(3).

3. Relevance of the Rent Act legislation. In this chapter Ch. I of Part I of the Act (ss. 1–19) is considered. Much of the terminology used in Ch. I of the Act is similar to the terminology used in the Rent Act legislation. Accordingly, many of the cases decided under the Rent Act legislation will be of assistance in interpreting and understanding the provisions of Ch. I of the Act (*see* Chapters 16 *et seq.*).

4. Assured tenancies. Section 1 of the Act provides that any tenancy under which a dwelling-house is let as a separate dwelling is an assured tenancy if and so long as:

(a) the tenant (or, in the case of joint tenants, each of them) is an individual – so that lettings to, for example, a limited company cannot constitute an assured tenancy; and
(b) the tenant or, as the case may be, at least one of the joint tenants, occupies the dwelling-house as his only or principal home – this requirement should be contrasted with the requirement under s. 2 of the Rent Act 1977 that a statutory tenant under the Rent Act 1977 must occupy the dwelling-house 'as his residence';
(c) the tenancy is not in one of the excepted categories of tenancy which cannot be an assured tenancy (*see* **5**).

It should be noted that s. 1 only applies to tenancies and thus licensees do not have the protection afforded by Ch. I of the Act.

The expression 'dwelling-house' is not defined in the Act although s. 45(1) expressly provides that a dwelling-house may be a house or part of a house. By analogy with the Rent Act legislation, there can be no doubt that a flat in a purpose-built block of flats is a dwelling-house (*Langford Property Co. Ltd* v. *Goldrich* (1949)). In *Curl* v. *Angelo* (1948), Lord Greene MR said that the question of whether or not premises constitute a dwelling-house depends on whether or not it can be said '. . . as a fair and reasonable construction of simple words in the English language, that these premises were the "home" to anybody.'

It should also be noted that the purpose for which the dwelling-house has been let must have been for occupation as a dwelling. So that if premises are let for business purposes but are subsequently occupied as a dwelling only, the tenancy will not be an assured tenancy (*Wolfe* v. *Hogan* (1949)). See also *Henry Smith's Charity Trustees* v. *Wagle* (1989).

The requirement that the dwelling-house must be let as a 'separate' dwelling is considered below.

NOTE: Generally, any old style assured tenancy under the Housing Act 1980 is now an assured tenancy for the purposes of the Housing Act 1988: ss. 1(3), 37.

5. Tenancies which cannot be assured tenancies.   Most, but not all, tenancies which cannot be assured tenancies are described in Part I of Sch. 1 to the Act.

The tenancies which cannot be assured tenancies include:

(1)   Tenancies entered into before the commencement of the Act or pursuant to a contract made before the commencement of the Act (see *Proma Ltd* v. *Curtis* (1990) concerning similar wording in the Leasehold Reform Act 1967).

(2)   Tenancies at high rents or rateable values, namely:

(a)   tenancies entered into on or after 1st April 1990 (otherwise than, where the dwelling-house had a rateable value on 31st March 1990, in pursuance of a contract made before 1st April 1990) under which the rent payable for the time being is payable at a rate exceeding £25,000 a year; and

(b)   tenancies entered into before 1st April 1990 (or on or after that date in pursuance of a contract made before that date) under which the dwelling-house had a rateable value exceeding £1500, if in Greater London, or £750, if elsewhere.

(3)   Tenancies at low rents, namely

(a)   tenancies under which for the time being no rent is payable; and

(b)   tenancies entered into on or after 1st April 1990 (otherwise than, where the dwelling-house had a rateable value on 31st March 1990, in pursuance of a contract made before 1st April 1990) under which the rent payable for the time being is payable at a rate of £1000 or less a year (if the dwelling-house is in Greater London) or £250 or less a year (if the dwelling-house is elsewhere);

(c)   tenancies entered into before 1st April 1990 (or, where the dwelling-house had a rateable value on 31st March 1990, on or after 1st April in pursuance of a contract made before that date) under which the rent for the time being payable is less than two-thirds of the rateable value of the dwelling-house on 31st March 1990.

(4)   Business tenancies.

(5)   Tenancies of premises licensed for the sale of intoxicating liquor for consumption on the premises, e.g. public houses.

(6) Tenancies under which agricultural land exceeding two acres is let with the dwelling-house.

(7) Tenancies of a dwelling-house comprised in an agricultural holding.

(8) Student lettings.

(9) Holiday lettings.

(10) Lettings by resident landlords.

(11) Tenancies granted by the Crown.

(12) Tenancies granted by local authorities, certain statutory bodies such as the Commission for New Towns, fully mutual housing associations and housing action trusts.

(13) Transitional cases:

(a) a protected tenancy within the meaning of the Rent Act 1977;

(b) a housing association tenancy within the meaning of Part VI of the Rent Act 1977;

(c) a secure tenancy (mainly tenancies granted by local authorities and housing associations prior to the commencement of the Act);

(d) a tenant who is a protected occupier of a dwelling-house under the Rent (Agriculture) Act 1976.

(14) Certain tenancies granted under arrangements with a local housing authority in pursuance of that authority's duty to house homeless persons: s. 1(6), (7).

NOTES: (1) Paragraphs (2) and (3) above result from amendments made by the References to Rating (Housing) Regulations 1990.

(2) *See* 7 below concerning lettings of a dwelling-house together with other land.

6. Phasing out of the Rent Acts. This is such a radical effect that it merits specific mention. Section 34(1) of the Act provides that a tenancy entered into on or after the commencement of the Act cannot be a protected tenancy under the Rent Act 1977 except in the limited cases mentioned below, namely:

(a) when the tenancy is entered into in pursuance of a contract made before the commencement of the Act (s. 34(1)(*a*) and para. 1 of Part I of Sch. 1 to the Act);

(b) when it is granted to a person (alone or jointly with others) who was a Rent Act protected or statutory tenant of the dwelling-house in question immediately before the new tenancy is granted *and* the new tenancy is granted by the landlord who was the landlord (or one of the joint landlords) under the Rent Act protected or statutory tenancy immediately before the new tenancy is granted: s. 34(1)(*b*).

(c) when it is granted to a person against whom an Order for possession has been obtained on the ground that suitable alternative accommodation is available and the new tenancy is of such alternative accommodation found to be suitable but the court considered that the grant of an assured tenancy of the suitable alternative accommodation would not afford the required security and directed that the tenancy would be a protected tenancy: s. 34(1)(*c*);

(d) when it was granted by a new town corporation and the landlord's interest is transferred to the private sector by 31st March 1996: s. 34(1)(*d*) and SI 1990 No 1980.

7. **Letting of a dwelling-house together with other land.** Section 2 provides that if, under a tenancy, a dwelling-house is let together with other land, it will be treated as an assured tenancy if the main purpose of the letting was, and remains, the provision of a home for the tenant or, in the case of joint tenants, at least one of them. If, however, the main purpose of the letting was not to provide a home for the tenant, the tenancy is not treated as being a tenancy under which a dwelling-house is let as a separate dwelling and hence (because of the provisions of s. 1(1)) the tenancy will not be an assured tenancy.

8. **'Separate dwelling' and shared accommodation.** The   requirement that the dwelling-house should be let as a separate dwelling prima facie means that the tenant must have exclusive occupation of the accommodation that constitutes the dwelling. Section 3(1) of the Act provides that where a tenant has exclusive occupation of any accommodation (the 'separate accommodation') and under the terms of his tenancy he has the use of any other accommodation (the 'shared accommodation') in common with another person or persons (except the landlord), the separate accommodation is deemed to be a dwelling-house let on an assured tenancy. Furthermore s. 3(3) provides that while the tenant has possession of the separate accommodation, any term of the tenancy terminating or modifying or providing for the termination or modification of the tenant's right to the use of any of the shared accommodation which is living accommodation is of no effect. Any term of the tenancy which provides that the persons with whom the tenant shares the shared accommodation may be varied or that the number of persons using the shared accommodation may be increased is effective however: s. 3(4).

'Living accommodation' is defined in s. 3(5). Essentially, it means any accommodation which, taken together with the separate accommodation, would constitute a dwelling-house.

Section 3 thus covers situations where a tenant is granted exclusive occupation of a bedroom together with the use of, for example, a sitting-room, kitchen and bathroom/w.c. in common with other persons.

9. Special provisions applicable to shared accommodation.

Section 10(2) provides that while the tenant is in possession of the separate accommodation no order for possession of any of the shared accommodation can be made unless an order for possession of the separate accommodation has already been made or is made at the same time. This is the case whether the application for an order for possession of any part of the shared accommodation is made by the landlord or any person under whom the landlord derives title, e.g. a superior landlord. Presumably, this provision is designed to protect the tenant in circumstances where, for example, the landlord holds the separate accommodation and the shared accommodation under different leases and the landlord's lease of the shared accommodation is forfeited. But for s. 10(2), the position at common law in such circumstances would be that the tenant's interest in the shared accommodation would also come to an end by the forfeiture. Furthermore, s. 10(2) provides that the provisions of s. 6 (which deals with the fixing of the terms of statutory periodic tenancies – considered at 12 below) shall have effect accordingly.

Section 10(3) empowers the court, on the application of the landlord, to make such order as it thinks just either:

(a) terminating the tenant's right to use the whole or any part of the shared accommodation other than living accommodation; or
(b) modifying the tenant's right to use the whole or any part of the shared accommodation, whether by varying the persons or increasing the number of persons entitled to use the shared accommodation or otherwise.

The court cannot make an order under s. 10(3) unless the terms of the tenancy (whether the terms of the contractual tenancy or, in an appropriate case, the terms of a statutory periodic tenancy as varied under s. 6) provide for the termination or modification of the tenant's right to use the shared accommodation: s. 10(4). It will be remembered that s. 3(3) of the Act provides that while the tenant is in possession of the separate accommodation any term of the tenancy terminating or modifying or providing for the termination or modification of his right to the use of any of the shared accommodation which is living accommodation shall be of no effect. Presumably s. 3(3) should be regarded as the general rule to which s. 10(3) and (4) provides an exception.

10. Effect of sub-letting.
If the tenant sub-lets the whole of the dwelling-house, he will cease to occupy the dwelling-house, and thus his tenancy will no longer be an assured tenancy.

Section 4 of the Act provides that if the tenant sub-lets part of the dwelling-house, then, as against his landlord or any superior landlord, no part of the dwelling-house shall be treated as excluded from being a dwelling-house let on an assured tenancy by reason only that the terms of the sub-tenancy include the use of accommodation in common with other persons.

11. Termination of assured tenancies otherwise than by order of the court. An assured tenancy may be either a 'fixed term tenancy' or a 'periodic tenancy'.

A fixed term tenancy is any tenancy other than a periodic tenancy: s. 45(1).

A periodic tenancy cannot be brought to an end by a notice to quit served by the landlord: s. 5(1).

A contractual (as opposed to statutory) periodic tenancy may however be brought to an end:

(a) by the service of a notice to quit by the tenant;
(b) by surrender.

A fixed term tenancy can be brought to an end:

(a) by surrender: s. 5(2);
(b) by 'other action on the part of the tenant', e.g. the exercise by the tenant of an option to determine the tenancy: s. 5(2);
(c) by the exercise of a power for the landlord to determine the tenancy in certain circumstances, e.g. an option to determine – but the exercise of that power will only end the contractual tenancy. As mentioned below, the tenant will have the right to remain in possession under a statutory periodic tenancy: s. 5(2);
(d) by effluxion of time – but once again the tenant will be entitled to remain in possession under a statutory periodic tenancy.

> NOTE: Strictly speaking, a landlord cannot bring a fixed term tenancy to an end by forfeiture; s. 45(4) expressly provides that any reference to 'a power for a landlord to determine a tenancy', such as the reference in **(c)** above, does not include a power of re-entry or forfeiture for breach of any term or condition of the tenancy. However, if the tenancy provides for re-entry, forfeiture or determination by notice or otherwise on grounds corresponding to Grounds 2 or 8 in Part I of Sch. 2, or any of the Grounds in Part II of Sch. 2 (apart from Grounds 9 or 16), the landlord is entitled to apply for an order for possession, in accordance with the provisions of the Act, during the fixed term tenancy if any of those grounds arise (s. 7(6)).

12. Statutory periodic tenancies. When a fixed term tenancy expires by effluxion of time or by the exercise of a power for the landlord to determine the tenancy in certain circumstances, e.g. an option to determine, the tenant is entitled to remain in possession by virtue of the statutory periodic tenancy which automatically then arises: s. 5(2).

The periods of the statutory periodic tenancy are fixed by reference to the manner in which rent was last payable under the fixed term tenancy, e.g. if the rent was paid weekly, the statutory periodic tenancy will be a weekly tenancy, or if the rent was paid monthly, the statutory periodic tenancy will be a monthly tenancy and so on: s. 5(3)(*d*).

The terms of the statutory periodic tenancy are the same as those of the fixed term tenancy immediately before the latter came to an end. However, any provision for determination by the landlord or the tenant applicable to the fixed term tenancy is of no effect so long as the statutory periodic tenancy remains an assured tenancy: s. 5(3)(*e*).

The terms of the statutory periodic tenancy as ascertained in accordance with s. 5(3)(*e*) are known as the 'implied terms'.

Section 6 set out provisions for varying the implied terms. At any time up to the first anniversary of the date on which the fixed term tenancy came to an end, the landlord or the tenant may serve upon the other a notice in the prescribed form proposing that the terms of the statutory periodic tenancy, including the rent if the landlord or the tenant as the case may be considers it appropriate, shall be terms other than the implied terms: s. 6(2).

If the recipient of the notice does not refer the notice to a rent assessment committee within three months, the terms proposed in the notice shall be terms of the statutory periodic tenancy in substitution for any of the implied terms dealing with the same subject matter. The variation of the terms of the statutory periodic tenancy takes effect from such date as may be specified in the notice provided that such date is more than three months after the date of service of the notice: s. 6(3)(*b*).

13. Determination of terms of statutory periodic tenancies by a rent assessment committee. If the recipient of the notice objects to the terms proposed by the notice, he must refer the notice to a rent assessment committee by making an application in the prescribed form within three months of the date of service of the notice upon him. The rent assessment committee will consider the terms proposed and then determine whether those terms, or some other terms dealing with the same subject matter, might reasonably be expected to be found in an assured periodic tenancy of the dwelling-house which:

(a) begins on the coming to an end of the fixed term tenancy; and

(b) is granted by a willing landlord on the same terms as those of the statutory periodic tenancy other than those terms which relate to matters in respect of which the notice proposes different terms: s. 6(4).

Whether or not the notice proposes any adjustment of the rent payable under the statutory periodic tenancy, the rent assessment committee has power to adjust the rent payable to take account of the other terms it determines: s. 6(5).

In determining any terms of the statutory periodic tenancy or any adjustment of the rent, the rent assessment committee must disregard any effects on those terms or the rent, attributable to the fact that the hypothetical tenancy referred to in s. 6(4) may be a tenancy granted to a sitting tenant: s. 6(6).

In the absence of agreement between the landlord and the tenant, the terms of the statutory tenancy determined by the rent assessment committee take effect in substitution for any of the implied terms dealing with the same subject matter on such date as the rent assessment committee may direct. However, in the case of any adjustment of the rent payable, the rent assessment committee may not direct that the same shall be effective on a date which is earlier than the date specified in the s. 6(2) notice: s. 6(7).

14. Rents under assured tenancies. An assured periodic or fixed term tenancy may contain provisions for increasing the rent payable from time to time. The landlord's ability to increase the rent pursuant to any such provisions is not restricted by the Act in any way.

In the cases of a periodic tenancy which does not contain any such provisions and a statutory periodic tenancy, the rent payable may be increased in accordance with ss. 13 and 14.

The landlord may serve a notice upon the tenant in the prescribed form and proposing that the new rent specified in the notice should be payable with effect from the beginning of the new period of the tenancy specified in the notice. The landlord should not specify the beginning of a new period of the tenancy which is earlier than:

(a) the 'minimum period' after the date of service of the notice, the minimum period being:

   (i) six months in the case of a yearly tenancy;

   (ii) a period equal to a period of the tenancy in the case of periodic tenancies for periods of more than one month;

   (iii) one month in any other case: s. 13(3); and

(b) the first anniversary of the date on which the first period of the tenancy began (except in the case of a statutory periodic tenancy): s. 13(2)(*b*); and

(c) the first anniversary of the date on which the rent was last increased by the service of a landlord's notice under s. 13 or by a determination by a rent assessment committee under s. 14: s. 13(2)(*c*).

Unless the tenant refers the notice proposing an increase in rent to a rent assessment committee before the beginning of the new period of the tenancy specified in the notice, the new rent proposed will take effect from the beginning of that new period.

15. Determination of rents by rent assessment committees. If the notice is referred to a rent assessment committee, the committee will determine the rent at which a willing landlord might reasonably expect to let the dwelling-house in the open market on an assured tenancy:

(a) which is a periodic tenancy with the same periods as the tenancy to which the landlord's notice relates;

(b) which begins at the beginning of the new period of the tenancy specified in the landlord's notice;

(c) which is on the same terms (other than as to the amount of the rent) as the tenancy to which the landlord's notice relates;

(d) in respect of which any notices in fact given by the landlord under Grounds 1 to 5 of Sch. 2 to the Act (being Grounds upon which the court must make an order for possession) have been given: s. 14(1).

In making their determination the rent assessment committee must disregard:

(a) any effect on the rent attributable to the granting of the tenancy to a sitting tenant: s. 14(2)(*a*);

(b) any increase in the value of the dwelling-house attributable to certain improvements carried out by a tenant: s. 14(2)(*b*) and (3);

(c) any reduction in the value of the dwelling-house attributable to a failure by the tenant to comply with any terms of the tenancy, e.g. an obligation to keep the dwelling-house in repair: s. 14(2)(*c*).

Unless the landlord and the tenant otherwise agree, the rent determined by the rent assessment committee takes effect from the beginning of the new period of the tenancy specified in the landlord's notice. However, if the rent assessment committee considers that this would cause undue hardship to the tenant, it may direct that the new rent will take effect from a later date which is not itself later than the date of their determination: s. 14(7).

16. Alienation. Leases or tenancy agreements often contain provisions restricting the tenant's ability to assign his tenancy or to sublet or otherwise part with possession of the whole or part of the premises. Such provisions may take the form of an absolute restriction on assignment or subletting or a qualified restriction so that, for example, the tenant may only assign or sublet with his landlord's consent.

In the case of assured tenancies which are fixed term tenancies, the tenant's ability to assign or sublet will be governed by the terms of the lease or tenancy agreement and the rules of law considered in Chapter 6 apply accordingly.

In the case of assured tenancies which are periodic tenancies, it is an implied term of the tenancy that the tenant shall not, without the landlord's consent, assign the tenancy (in whole or in part) or sublet or part with possession of the whole or any part of the dwelling-house: s. 15(1). However, s. 19 of the Landlord and Tenant Act 1927 (which provides that when the tenant may only assign or sublet, etc. with the landlord's consent, the landlord may not unreasonably withhold his consent) does not apply to this implied term: s. 15(2).

When the periodic tenancy is a contractual as opposed to a statutory periodic tenancy, there is no such implied term if

(a) there is any provision applicable to the tenancy which either prohibits or permits (absolutely or conditionally) assignment, subletting or parting with possession: s. 15(3)(*a*); or

(b) a premium is required to be paid on the grant or renewal of the tenancy: s. 15(3)(*b*).

> NOTE: 'Premium' includes: (*a*) any fine or other like sum; (*b*) any other pecuniary consideration in addition to the rent; (*c*) any deposit in excess of one-sixth of the annual rent payable under the tenancy immediately after it is granted or renewed: s. 15(4).

17. Access for repairs. It is an implied term of every assured tenancy that the tenant shall give to the landlord access to the dwelling-house and reasonable facilities to enable the landlord to execute any repairs in the dwelling-house the landlord is entitled to execute: s. 16.

18. Succession to assured periodic tenancy by spouse. Generally on the death of a tenant who holds a contractual tenancy, whether it be for a fixed term or periodic, the tenancy will form part of his estate and devolve upon his beneficiaries in accordance with the terms of his will or the law of intestacy. On the death of a tenant who holds a fixed term assured tenancy, this general rule applies. However,

s. 17(1) of the Act provides that an assured periodic tenancy will vest in the deceased tenant's spouse if:

(a) the deceased tenant was the sole tenant; and
(b) immediately before his death the deceased tenant's spouse was occupying the dwelling-house as his or her only or principal home; and
(c) the deceased tenant was not himself a successor as defined in s. 17(2), (3).

> NOTES: (1) A person who was living with the deceased tenant as his or her wife or husband is treated as the deceased tenant's spouse: s. 17(4). (2) If on the tenant's death, there is more than one person who fulfils the condition in **(b)** above, they may agree which one of them is to succeed to the assured tenancy or, in default of agreement, the county court may determine which one of them is to succeed to the assured tenancy.

As mentioned above, an assured periodic tenancy will only vest in the deceased tenant's spouse if the deceased tenant was not himself a successor. Section 17(2) provides that a tenant is a successor if:

(a) the tenancy vested in him by virtue of s. 17 or under the will or intestacy of a previous tenant; or
(b) at some time before the tenant's death, the tenancy was a joint tenancy held by the deceased and one or more other persons and prior to his death, the deceased became the sole tenant by survivorship; or
(c) the deceased tenant became entitled to the tenancy in the circumstances mentioned in s. 39(5) of the Act, i.e. succession to an assured tenancy under the Rent Act 1977 or the Rent (Agriculture) Act 1976.

Section 17(3) deals with the situation where a successor is granted a new tenancy of the same or substantially the same dwelling-house as that to which he succeeded. Such a person is a successor in relation to the new tenancy.

19. Reversions to assured tenancies. If the landlord of a lawful assured tenant is himself a tenant and his superior tenancy comes to an end, the superior landlord becomes the assured tenant's direct landlord and the assured tenancy continues unless by reason of the superior landlord's status, e.g. the superior landlord's interest is held by the Crown or a local authority, the tenancy cannot be an assured tenancy: s. 18(1) and (2).

Furthermore, if an assured periodic tenancy (whether contractual or statutory) continues beyond the commencement of any reversionary tenancy which was granted so as to commence on or after:

(a) the date on which any previous fixed term tenancy would come to an end as a matter of common law by effluxion of time; or
(b) a date on which the periodic tenancy could have been brought to an end by notice to quit by the landlord save for the provisions of Part I of the Act;

the reversionary tenancy has effect as if it had been granted subject to the periodic tenancy: s. 18.

> NOTE: Section 18 is similar to certain provisions of s. 137 of the Rent Act 1977.

20. Proceedings for possession of dwelling-houses let on assured tenancies. The court will only entertain proceedings for possession of a dwelling-house let on an assured tenancy if the landlord (or one or more of the joint landlords) has served upon the tenant a notice complying with the provisions of s. 8 of the Act and the proceedings are begun within the time limits set out in s. 8. The court may however dispense with the requirement for service of a s. 8 notice if it considers it just and equitable to do so (s. 8(1)) but not if the Ground for possession relied upon by the landlord is Ground 8 in Sch. 2 to the Act: s. 8(5). The notice must:

(a) be in the prescribed form;
(b) specify one or more of the Grounds for possession set out in Sch. 2 to the Act (*see* below) although by s. 8(2) the landlord may with leave of the court alter or add to the Grounds specified in his notice. In order to be valid, the s. 8 notice must at least set out the full substance of the Ground or Grounds relied upon: *Mountain* v. *Hastings* (1993);
(c) specify particulars of the Ground or Grounds for possession relied upon;
(d) inform the tenant that the landlord intends to begin proceedings for possession on one or more of the Grounds specified in the notice;
(e) inform the tenant that the proceedings will not begin earlier than a date specified in the notice which (subject as mentioned below) must not be earlier than two weeks after the date of service of the notice;
(f) inform the tenant that the proceedings will not begin later than 12 months after service of the notice: s. 8(2), (3).

If the notice specifies any of Grounds 1, 2, 5 to 7, 9 and 16 in Sch. 2 to the Act (*see* below) whether with or without other grounds, the date specified in the landlord's notice as being the earliest date on which the proceedings will begin must be not earlier than:

(a) two months from the date of service of the notice; and

(b) in the case of a periodic tenancy, the earliest date upon which the landlord could bring the tenancy to an end by a notice to quit served on the same date as the s. 8 notice, if apart from s. 5(1) the tenancy could be brought to an end by notice to quit: s. 8(4).

21. Grounds for possession (mandatory). The court can only make an order for possession on one or more of the Grounds set out in Sch. 2 to the Act: s. 7(1).

Subject to the special rules applicable to fixed term tenancies set out in s. 7(6) and briefly considered in **11**, the court must make an order for possession if the landlord establishes any of the Grounds set out in Part I of Sch. 2 to the Act: s. 7(3). These Grounds are:

Ground 1 – that the dwelling-house was formerly occupied by the landlord or one of joint landlords as his only or principal home and is required by the landlord as his or his spouse's only or principal home.

NOTES: (1) Unless the Court dispenses with this requirement, the landlord must have given the tenant notice in writing that possession might be recovered on this Ground by no later than the beginning of the tenancy.

(2) This Ground is not available to a landlord who acquired the reversion for money or money's worth.

Ground 2 – that a mortgagee under a mortgage granted before the beginning of the tenancy is entitled to exercise a power of sale and requires vacant possession in order to dispose of the dwelling-house pursuant to that power.

NOTE: Unless the Court dispenses with this requirement, the landlord must have given the tenant notice in writing that possession might be recovered on this Ground by no later than the beginning of the tenancy.

Ground 3 – that the tenancy is a fixed term tenancy for a term not exceeding eight months and at some time within the period of twelve months ending with the beginning of the tenancy, the dwelling-house was occupied under a right to occupy it for a holiday.

NOTES: (1) The landlord must have given the tenant notice in writing that possession might be recovered on this Ground by no later than the beginning of the tenancy.

(2) This Ground relates to out-of-season lettings of holiday accommodation.

Ground 4 – that the tenancy is a fixed term tenancy for a term not exceeding 12 months and, at some time within the period of 12 months ending with the beginning of the tenancy, the dwelling-house was subject to a student letting of the type described in para. 8 of Sch. 1 to the Act.

NOTE: The landlord must have given the tenant notice in writing that possession might be recovered on this Ground by not later than the beginning of the tenancy.

Ground 5 – that the dwelling-house is held for the purpose of being available for a minister of religion as a residence from which to perform the duties of his office and the court is satisfied that the dwelling-house is required for occupation by a minister of religion as such a residence.

NOTE: The landlord must have given the tenant notice in writing that possession might be recovered on this Ground by not later than the beginning of the tenancy.

Ground 6 – that the landlord who is seeking possession, or, if that landlord is a registered housing association or charitable housing trust, a superior landlord intends to demolish or reconstruct the whole or a substantial part of the dwelling-house or to carry out substantial works on the dwelling-house or any part thereof or any building of which it forms part and certain specified conditions are fulfilled.

Ground 7 – that the tenancy is a periodic tenancy (including a statutory periodic tenancy) which has devolved under the will or intestacy of the deceased tenant and the proceedings for possession are begun not later than 12 months after the death of the tenant or, if the court so directs, the date on which the landlord or any one of joint landlords, in the opinion of the court, became aware of the death of the tenant.

NOTES: (1) The Ground provides that the acceptance of rent from the new tenant upon whom the tenancy has devolved, after the death of the former tenant, does not have the effect of creating a new periodic tenancy unless the landlord agrees in writing to any change in the terms of the tenancy.

(2) As this Ground only applies to a periodic tenancy which has devolved under the will or intestacy of the deceased tenant, it follows that this Ground does not apply where the tenancy has vested in the deceased tenant's spouse under s. 17 (*see* **18**).

Ground 8 – that both at the date of the s. 8 notice and the date of the hearing of the proceedings for possession:

(a) if rent is payable weekly or fortnightly – at least 13 weeks' rent is unpaid;

(b) if rent is payable monthly – at least three months' rent is unpaid;

(c) if rent is payable quarterly – at least one quarters' rent is more than three months in arrears;

(d) if rent is payable yearly – at least three months' rent is more than three months in arrears.

NOTES: (1) Generally, by virtue of s. 9 of the Act, the court has a discretion to adjourn proceedings for possession of dwelling-houses let on assured tenancies, to postpone the date for possession on making an order for possession or to stay or suspend execution of the order for possession. The court has no such discretion if the court is satisfied that the landlord is entitled to possession on any of the mandatory Grounds.

(2) Where the landlord seeks possession on Grounds 1, 3, 4 or 5, he may use the accelerated possession procedure provided by County Court Order 49 rule 6. This enables the landlord to obtain an order for possession (only) without any hearing before the court.

22. Grounds for possession (discretionary). Section 7(4) provides that if any of the Grounds specified in Part II of Sch. 2 to the Act is established, the court may make an order for possession if it considers it reasonable to do so.

The Grounds set out in Part II of Sch. 2 are as follows:

Ground 9 – that suitable alternative accommodation is available for the tenant or will be available for him when the order for possession takes effect.

NOTE: 'Suitable alternative accommodation' is defined by Part III of Sch. 2 which contains provisions similar to those in Part IV of Sch. 15 to the Rent Act 1977.

Ground 10 – that some rent lawfully due from the tenant is unpaid on the date on which the proceedings for possession are begun and that some rent lawfully due was in arrears at the date of service of the s. 8 notice (unless pursuant to s. 8(1)(*b*) the court considers it just and equitable to dispense with the requirement for service of a s. 8 notice).

Ground 11 – that the tenant has persistently delayed paying rent which has become lawfully due.

NOTE: This Ground may be used whether or not any rent is in arrears on the date upon which the proceedings for possession are begun.

Ground 12 – that any obligation of the tenancy (other than one related to the payment of rent) has been broken or not performed.

Ground 13 – that the condition of the dwelling-house or any of the common parts has deteriorated due to acts of waste by, or the neglect or default of, the tenant or any other person residing in the dwelling-house.

NOTES: (1) 'Common parts' means any part of a building comprising the dwelling-house and any other premises which the tenant is entitled to use under the terms of his tenancy in common with the occupiers of other dwelling-houses, in which the landlord has an estate or interest.

(2) In the case of an act of waste by, or the neglect or default of a person lodging with the tenant or a sub-tenant of his, this Ground is only available to the landlord if the tenant has failed to take such steps as he ought reasonably to have taken for the removal of the lodger or sub-tenant.

Ground 14 – that the tenant or any other person residing at the dwelling-house has been guilty of conduct which is a nuisance or annoyance to adjoining occupiers, or has been convicted of using the dwelling-house or allowing the dwelling-house to be used for immoral or illegal purposes.

Ground 15 – that the condition of any furniture provided for use under the tenancy has in the opinion of the court deteriorated owing to ill-treatment by the tenant or any other person residing in the dwelling-house.

NOTE: In the latter case, this Ground is only available to the landlord if the tenant has failed to take such steps as he ought reasonably to have taken for the removal of the lodger or sub-tenant.

Ground 16 – that the dwelling-house was let to the tenant in consequence of his employment by the landlord seeking possession or a previous landlord under the tenancy and the tenant has ceased to be in that employment.

23. Prescribed Forms. These are to be found in The Assured Tenancies and Agricultural Occupancies (Forms) Regulations 1988 (SI 1988 No. 2203) and The Assured Tenancies and Agricultural Occupancies (Forms) (Amendment) Regulations 1989 (SI 1989 No. 146), 1990 (SI 1990 No. 1532) and 1993 (SI 1993 No. 654).

Progress test 21

1. What are the three essential attributes of an assured tenancy? **(4)**

2. What are the rateable value and/or rent limits within which a dwelling-house must fall if a tenancy of the dwelling-house is to be an assured tenancy? **(5)**

3. Can the status of the landlord affect the question of whether or not a tenancy of a dwelling-house is an assured tenancy? **(5)**

4. T is granted a tenancy of a room in a house under which he has the right to share the kitchen, bathroom and dining room with other persons. Is his tenancy an assured tenancy? **(8)**

5. T holds an assured periodic tenancy of a dwelling-house. He receives a notice to quit from his landlord. What is the effect of that notice? **(11)**

6. By what procedure may the terms of a statutory periodic tenancy be altered? **(12, 13)**

7. By what means can a landlord increase the rent payable under an assured periodic tenancy? Would your answer be different if the terms of the tenancy provided that the rent would automatically increase by 10% every quarter? **(14, 15)**

8. Who may succeed to an assured periodic tenancy on the death of the tenant? **(18)**

9. What are the requirements of a valid Section 8 notice? **(20)**

10. L is the owner of number of holiday flats for which there is little demand out of season. T approaches L with a suggestion that L should let one of the flats to him from month to month until L requires the flat for lettings to holiday makers. Advise L. **(21)**

Assured shorthold tenancies under the Housing Act 1988

1. Introduction. In the introduction to the preceding chapter, some of the criticisms of the Rent Act legislation were considered and mention was made of the attempt to persuade owners of residential accommodation to release that accommodation onto the market by the introduction of protected shorthold tenancies. This new species of tenancy was created by the Housing Act 1980 but did not prove to be an overwhelming success. The main reasons for this were that although protected shorthold tenants enjoyed little security of tenure compared with Rent Act protected or statutory tenants, the provisions for registration of a fair rent under the Rent Act 1977 were equally applicable to protected shorthold tenancies. Furthermore, if the landlord failed to serve the appropriate notice (stating that proceedings for possession would be brought after its expiry) during the three months preceding the expiry of the contractual term, he was obliged to wait until the corresponding three-month period in the following year or any subsequent year before he could serve the appropriate notice and thereafter bring proceedings for possession.

Since 15th January 1989, when Part I of the Housing Act 1988 came into force, it has not been possible to create a protected shorthold tenancy: s. 34(3).

2. Assured shorthold tenancies. There can be little doubt that private sector landlords would be rather more willing to let residential accommodation if they could be satisfied that they could recover possession of the dwelling-house at the expiry of the tenancy or any time thereafter and that the rent they agree with the tenant, or at least a market rent which is not 'excessive', will be recoverable. Ch. II of the Housing Act 1988 (ss. 20–23) therefore introduced a particular type of assured tenancy known as an 'assured shorthold tenancy' which satisfies these conditions.

NOTE: It should be remembered that an assured shorthold tenancy is an assured tenancy so that, subject to the provisions of ss. 20–23 of the Act considered below, the provisions of Ch. I of the Act (considered in the preceding chapter) are equally applicable to assured shorthold tenancies.

3. Essential elements for the creation of an assured shorthold tenancy. The tenancy must be an assured tenancy:

(a) which is a fixed term tenancy for a term certain of at least six months: s. 20(1)(*a*) – see *Bedding* v. *McCarthy* (1993);
(b) in respect of which there is no power for the landlord to determine the tenancy at any time during the first six months of the term: s. 20(1)(*b*);
(c) in respect of which a notice is served as mentioned in s. 20(2): s. 20(1)(*c*).

NOTES: (1) It does not appear to be possible to grant an assured shorthold tenancy to a tenant of the dwelling-house in question who is already a protected or statutory tenant of the dwelling-house under the Rent Act 1977.

(2) An assured shorthold tenancy cannot be granted to a tenant who was an assured tenant of the dwelling-house immediately before the grant of the new tenancy (s. 20(3)).

(3) The requirement in s. 20(1)(*b*) that there should be no power for the landlord to determine the tenancy during the first six months of the term does not exclude or invalidate any power of re-entry or forfeiture for breach of any term or condition of the tenancy: s. 45(4). However s. 7(6) of the Act restricts the landlord's ability to obtain an order for possession pursuant to such a power of re-entry or forfeiture (*see* 21:**11**).

4. Notice to be served before the tenancy is entered into. The notice referred to in s. 20(1)(*b*) must comply with the requirements of s. 20(2), namely:

(a) the notice must be in the prescribed form (Form No 7 in the Schedule to the Assured Tenancies and Agricultural Occupancies (Forms) Regulations SI 1988 No. 2203 as amended);
(b) it must be served before the tenancy is entered into; there is no minimum period which must elapse between service of the notice and the tenancy being entered into: *Murugamoorthy* v. *Jackson* (1991) – see also *Bedding* v. *McCarthy* (1993);
(c) it must be served by the person who is to be the landlord under the assured tenancy on the person who is to be the tenant under that tenancy;
(d) it must state that the assured tenancy to which it relates is to be a shorthold tenancy.

NOTE: Care should be taken to ensure that the notice is correctly completed. In *Panayi* v. *Roberts* (1993) the date on which the tenancy would end (contractually) was incorrectly stated in the notice with the result that the tenancy was held to be an assured (as opposed to assured shorthold) tenancy.

5. Renewal of tenancies and statutory continuation. If, on the coming to an end of an assured shorthold tenancy (including a tenancy which was an assured shorthold tenancy but ceased to be assured before it came to an end), a new tenancy of the same or substantially the same premises comes into being under which the same persons who were the landlord and tenant respectively at the end of the previous tenancy are, once again, the landlord and tenant respectively, that new tenancy will be an assured shorthold tenancy whether or not it satisfies the conditions set out in s. 20(1)(*a*)–(*c*), provided that the new tenancy satisfies the requirements of an assured tenancy: s. 20(4).

Similarly, the statutory periodic tenancy which will come into being at the end of the fixed term (by virtue of s. 5) will automatically be an assured shorthold tenancy.

NOTES: (1) If the landlord (or one of two or more joint landlords) serves notice on the tenant that the new tenancy or, as the case may be, the statutory periodic tenancy, is not to be an assured shorthold tenancy and that notice is served before the new tenancy is entered into or the statutory periodic tenancy arises, the new or the statutory periodic tenancy will not be an assured shorthold tenancy but will be an assured tenancy: s. 20(5).

(2) If a new tenancy is granted to a protected shorthold tenant, the new tenancy will be an assured shorthold tenancy whether or not it fulfils the conditions set out in s. 20(1) (*a*)–(*c*) unless, before the tenancy is entered into, the landlord serves notice on the tenant that it is not to be an assured shorthold tenancy. In the event of service of such a notice, the new tenancy will be an assured tenancy: s. 34(3).

6. Reference of excessive rents to a rent assessment committee.
The rent payable under an assured shorthold tenancy is the rent agreed by the landlord and the tenant. However, the notice pursuant to s. 20(2) will advise the tenant of his right to make an application to a rent assessment committee pursuant to s. 22 of the Act if he considers that the rent agreed is excessive. The application to a rent assessment committee must be in the prescribed form and is an application for a determination of a rent which in the committee's opinion the landlord might reasonably be expected to obtain under the assured shorthold tenancy: s. 22(1).

Section 22(3) provides that a rent assessment committee shall not make any such determination unless it considers:

(a) that there is a sufficient number of similar dwelling-houses in the locality let on assured tenancies (whether shorthold or not); and

(b) that the rent payable under the assured shorthold tenancy in question is significantly higher than the landlord might reasonably be expected to be able to obtain under the tenancy having regard to the level of rents payable under the tenancies of similar dwelling-houses in the locality let on assured or assured shorthold tenancies.

If the rent assessment committee makes such a determination, the reduced rent will be payable from such date as the committee may direct, not being earlier than the date of the tenant's application: s. 22(4)(*a*). As from the date upon which the rent assessment committee's determination takes effect, the difference between the rent originally agreed between the landlord and the tenant and the rent determined by the rent assessment committee, is not recoverable from the tenant: s. 22(4)(*b*).

NOTES: (1) Once a rent assessment committee has made a determination under s. 22, no further application for such a determination can be made: s. 22(2)(*a*).

(2) Furthermore, if on the coming to an end of the assured shorthold tenancy a new assured shorthold tenancy is granted by the same landlord to the same tenant, or a statutory periodic tenancy arises, no application to a rent assessment committee can be made under s. 22 in respect of the rent payable under that new or statutory periodic tenancy: s. 22(2)(*b*).

7. Statutory periodic assured shorthold tenancies. As has been emphasised, assured shorthold tenancies are a particular species of assured tenancy so that, subject to the particular provisions concerning assured shorthold tenancies set out in Ch. II of the Act, the provisions of Ch. I of the Act, which deal with assured tenancies generally, are equally applicable to assured shorthold tenancies (*see* preceding chapter).

Thus, on the coming to an end of the fixed term of an assured shorthold tenancy:

(a) a statutory periodic tenancy (which will also be an assured shorthold tenancy) arises (*see* s. 5 of the Act and 21:**12**);

(b) the terms of the statutory periodic tenancy may be altered (*see* s. 6 of the Act and 21:**12, 13**);

(c) the landlord may serve a notice upon the tenant pursuant to s. 13(2) of the Act proposing that a new rent shall be payable under the statutory periodic tenancy and a rent assessment committee may determine the rent payable under the statutory periodic tenancy if the tenant refers the landlord's notice to it (*see* ss. 13, 14 of the Act and 21: **14, 15**).

NOTES: (1) In relation to assured shorthold tenancies, s. 14(1) of the Act (determination of rents by rent assessment committees) is to be read as if the reference to an 'assured tenancy' were a reference to an 'assured shorthold tenancy'.

(2) If a rent assessment committee makes a determination of the rent payable under an assured shorthold tenancy pursuant to s. 22 of the Act (*see* 6 above) the landlord cannot serve a notice pursuant to s. 13(2) of the Act proposing that a new rent should be payable under the statutory periodic tenancy until after the first anniversary of the date on which the rent assessment committee's determination takes effect: s. 22(4)(*c*).

8. Recovery of possession of dwelling-houses let on an assured shorthold tenancy. If the landlord wishes to recover possession at the end of the fixed term of an assured shorthold tenancy, he must give the tenant at least two months' notice stating that he requires possession. The notice must be given before or on the day the fixed term tenancy comes to an end.

Provided that the landlord has served such a notice and no further assured tenancy has come into being (other than an assured shorthold periodic tenancy, whether statutory or not – and it will be recalled that in the ordinary course of events such a statutory tenancy will automatically arise on the expiry of the fixed term), the court must make an order for possession of the dwelling-house in proceedings brought for this purpose on or after the expiry of the fixed term: s. 21(1) and (2).

An order for possession will be made notwithstanding the fact that a statutory periodic tenancy has arisen and without the necessity for service of any further notice. The statutory periodic tenancy will come to an end on the date the court's order for possession takes effect: s. 21(3).

If the landlord does not serve a notice complying with the requirements of s. 21(2), the landlord may nonetheless determine the statutory periodic tenancy which will then have arisen (or any assured shorthold periodic tenancy which comes into being by virtue of s. 20(4)) by serving a notice upon the tenant under s. 21(4). The notice under s. 21(4) must state that after a date specified in the notice, possession of the dwelling-house is required by virtue of s. 21(4). The date so specified in the notice must be

(a) at least two months after the date upon which the notice is given (s. 21(4)(*a*));
(b) not earlier than the last day of the next ensuing full period of the tenancy;
(c) the last day of a period of the tenancy.

For example, if the statutory periodic tenancy is a quarterly tenancy, a landlord giving a notice under s. 21(4) on 1st February 1994 cannot specify a date earlier than 23rd June 1994.

> NOTES: (1) The landlord's ability to seek possession at the end of the fixed term of an assured shorthold tenancy or during a statutory periodic tenancy by the procedures mentioned above, is expressly without prejudice to his right to seek possession on any of the Grounds set out in Sch. 2 to the Act. In practice however, in view of the relative simplicity of, and the certainty afforded by the procedures laid down in s. 21 of the Act, it seems likely that the occasions on which a landlord will seek possession on any of those Grounds, will be rare.
>
> (2) Section 8 has no application to a notice under s. 21: *Panayi* v. *Roberts* (1993).

9. Where the landlord is seeking possession of a dwelling-house let on an assured shorthold tenancy after service of a notice under s. 21, he may use the accelerated possession procedure provided by County Court Order 49 rule 6A. This enables the landlord to obtain an order for possession (only) without any hearing before the court.

Progress test 22

1. What are the characteristics of an assured shorthold tenancy? **(3)**

2. L grants T a tenancy of a dwelling-house for a term of nine months which it was agreed should be an assured shorthold tenancy. L forgot to serve a notice complying with s. 20(2) upon T before granting the tenancy. Advise L. **(4)**

3. In the absence of the grant of a new tenancy and any steps taken by the landlord to recover possession, what happens when the fixed term of an assured shorthold tenancy comes to an end? **(5)**

4. T has just been granted an assured shorthold tenancy of a flat within a block and discovers that the rent he is paying is twice as much as the rent being paid by other tenants of flats within the block. Advise T. **(6)**

5. Are there any circumstances in which the terms of an assured shorthold tenancy (other than the rent) can be altered? **(7)**

6. What steps must a landlord take if he wishes to recover possession of a dwelling-house let on an assured shorthold tenancy at the end of the fixed term? **(8)**

7. When is it appropriate for a landlord to serve a s. 21(4) notice?   **(8)**

8. T holds a quarterly statutory periodic assured shorthold tenancy. He receives a s. 21(4) notice on 1st March 1994 stating that possession of the dwelling-house is required after 1st April 1994. Advise T.   **(8)**

Tenants' right of first refusal: Pt I, Landlord and Tenant Act 1987

1. Introduction. Under the terms of tenancies of residential flats in multi-occupied buildings, such as blocks of flats, the landlord is usually responsible for the provision of some or all of the following services:

(a) the repair and maintenance of the structure and exterior of the building;
(b) the repair and maintenance of the common parts of the building;
(c) the repair and maintenance of plant and machinery such as lifts and hot-water and central-heating boilers.

Each of the tenants will usually have a reciprocal obligation to pay 'a service charge' to the landlord, this being a fixed percentage or a fair proportion of the landlord's expenditure in providing those services.

On the face of it, this is an eminently sensible arrangement. The responsibility for the provision of such services is centralised and devolves upon the only party who has the necessary rights of possession, control and access – namely the landlord – and the cost of providing those services is ultimately borne by the parties who benefit from the provision of the services, namely the tenants. In practice however this type of arrangement has been the subject of considerable criticism from both tenants and landlords.

Complaints which have frequently been made by tenants are that

(a) the landlord is too remote and has no interest in maintaining the building and providing services;
(b) the landlord has delegated his obligations to managing agents who have no direct responsibility to the tenants and who view the collection of rents as their primary role;
(c) the enforcement of the landlord's obligations is often a complex, time-consuming and expensive process.

A complaint frequently made by landlords is that fixed 'on account' service charge payments result in the landlord being obliged to fund the provision of services out of his own pocket until service charge accounts have been prepared and the process of demand and collection of the tenants' full service charge contributions has been completed at the end of each service charge year.

These and similar complaints were investigated by a Committee of Inquiry under the chairmanship of Edward Nugee QC which reported in November 1985. A point which clearly emerged from the Nugee Report was that, generally, where tenants were responsible for management of the buildings of which their flats formed part the incidence of complaints was significantly lower.

The Landlord and Tenant Act 1987 ('the Act') implemented many of the recommendations made by the Nugee Report, and by Parts I and III of the Act tenants were given the right to acquire their landlords' interest in certain circumstances. A number of amendments have been made to the Act by the Housing Act 1988. Minor amendments were made by the Leasehold Reform, Housing and Urban Development Act 1993.

Most of the decisions on the Act are decisions of Leasehold Valuation Tribunals ('LVT'). Reference is made to some of these decisions in this Chapter but it should be borne in mind that these decisions do not have the same binding or persuasive force as decisions of the court.

2. The right conferred by Part I of the Act. In this chapter we shall deal with the provisions of Part I of the Act, which came into force on 1st February 1988. In summary, Part I of the Act provides that before a landlord can dispose of any interest (with certain exceptions) in premises containing two or more flats which have been let for residential purposes, he must offer to sell that interest to the 'qualifying tenants' of the flats on terms which are no more onerous than the terms upon which he proposes to dispose of that interest to any third party. A straightforward example would be a case where the landlord of a block of residential flats proposes to sell his freehold interest to a third party for £100,000. Before he can sell the freehold to any third party the landlord must give the tenants of the block the opportunity to purchase the freehold for not more than £100,000.

3. Premises to which Part I of the Act applies. Part I of the Act applies to premises if:

(a) the premises consist of the whole or part of a building or (accord-

ing to the LVT in *30 Upperton Gardens Management Ltd* v. *Akano* (1990))
a building scheme; and
(b) the premises contain two or more flats held by qualifying tenants;
and
(c) the qualifying tenants hold more than 50% of the total number of
flats contained in the premises: s. 1(2).

Part I of the Act will not apply if more than 50% of the internal floor
area of the premises is occupied or is intended to be occupied otherwise than for residential purposes, the internal floor area of any
common parts being disregarded for the purposes of this calculation:
s. 1(3).

> NOTES: (1) Section 60(1) defines a 'flat' as being a separate set of premises,
> whether or not on the same floor, which
> > **(a)** forms part of a building, and
> > **(b)** is divided horizontally from some other part of that building, and
> > **(c)** is constructed or adapted for use for the purposes of a dwelling.
>
> (2) The word 'building' is not to be construed too literally and is not
> confined to the bricks and mortar of which it is constructed. The 'building'
> extends to gardens and other appurtenances expressly or impliedly
> included in a demise of a flat to a tenant: *Denetower Ltd* v. *Toop* (1991).

4. Landlord for the purposes of Part I of the Act. The landlord is
the immediate landlord of the qualifying tenants of the flats contained
in the premises or, where any of those tenants is a statutory tenant
under the provisions of the Rent Act 1977, the person who would be
entitled to possession of the flat in question apart from the statutory
tenancy: s. 2(1).

If the immediate landlord is himself a tenant whose tenancy is for
a term of less than seven years or for a longer term which is determinable within the first seven years at the option of the superior landlord,
the superior landlord is also the landlord for the purposes of Part I of
the Act. Where there is a chain of mesne landlords the landlord for
the purposes of Part I of the Act is all landlords in the chain, up to and
including the landlord lowest down the chain who is either the freehold owner or holds a tenancy for a term of more than seven years
which is not determinable within the first seven years at the option
of his own landlord.

Examples _____
(1) IL is the freehold owner of the premises – IL is the landlord for the purposes of Part I of the Act.
(2) IL holds a lease for a term of 5 years granted to him by the freehold owner,
SL – the landlord for the purposes of Part I of the Act is both IL and SL.

(3) IL holds a lease for a term of 5 years granted to him by ML. ML holds a lease granted to him by SL, the freehold owner, for a term of 21 years but containing a provision entitling SL to determine the lease at the end of the fifth year of the term – the landlord for the purposes of Part I of the Act is IL, ML and SL.

5. Exempt landlords. Part I of the Act does not apply to the eleven categories of landlord set out in s. 58(1) of the Act: s. 1(4). These exempt landlords are mainly statutory or local authorities (such as the Commission for the New Towns and District, County or London Borough Councils) or charitable housing trusts or housing associations.

6. Resident landlords. Part I of the Act does not apply if the premises are not and do not form part of a purpose-built block of flats and the landlord has occupied a flat contained in the premises as his only or principal residence for more than 12 months: ss. 1(4), 58(2). A 'purpose-built block of flats' means a building which contained as constructed, and contains, two or more flats: s. 58(3).

7. Qualifying tenants and the requisite majority. The right of first refusal is only conferred upon tenants of flats whose tenancies are not:

(a) protected shorthold tenancies under the Housing Act 1980;
(b) business tenancies to which Part II of the Landlord and Tenant Act 1954 applies;
(c) tenancies terminable on the cessation of the tenant's employment;
(d) assured tenancies or assured agricultural occupancies under Part I of the Housing Act 1988: s. 3(1).

Certain tenants are excluded from the definition of 'qualifying tenant'. These are:
(*i*) a tenant of three or more flats in the premises in question whether under a single tenancy or a number of tenancies: s. 3(2);
(*ii*) any tenant of a flat whose immediate landlord is a qualifying tenant of that flat, e.g. a sub-tenant: s. 3(4).

NOTE: s. 3(3) provides that for the purposes of s. 3(2) a tenant of a flat who is a body corporate is to be treated as the tenant of any other flat in the premises in question which is let to an associated company: *see* s. 20(1).

Reference is made throughout Part I of the Act to the 'requisite majority' of qualifying tenants. The 'requisite majority' of qualifying tenants means the qualifying tenants of those flats (the 'constituent flats') with over 50 per cent of the available votes. The 'constituent flats' are those flats contained in the premises which the landlord proposes to dispose of, which are let to qualifying tenants. It is envisaged that the qualifying tenants of the constituent flats will conduct a vote to decide whether or not to accept the landlord's offer, on the basis of one vote per constituent flat which is let to a qualifying tenant, i.e. even if the tenancy of a constituent flat is held by joint tenants, only one vote will be attributed to the tenants of that flat: ss. 5(6), 5(8).

8. Relevant disposals. Section 1 of the Act provides that a landlord shall not make a 'relevant disposal' affecting any premises to which Part I applies, unless he has served an offer notice upon the qualifying tenants in accordance with s. 5 and the disposal is made in accordance with the requirements of ss. 6–10 of the Act.

Section 4 of the Act provides that a 'relevant disposal' is the disposal of any estate or interest (whether legal or equitable) in the premises by the landlord, including the disposal of any such estate or interest in any common parts of the premises in question. A 'disposal' means a disposal whether by the creation or the transfer of an estate or interest including the surrender of a tenancy and the grant of an option or right of pre-emption but excluding any disposal under the terms of a will or under the law relating to intestacy: s. 4(3).

A number of categories of disposals are excluded from the definition of 'relevant disposals'. These are detailed in s. 4(2) and include:

(a) certain involuntary disposals, such as a disposal to a trustee in bankruptcy or liquidator or pursuant to a compulsory purchase order;

(b) a disposal consisting of the creation of an estate or interest by way of security for a loan, e.g. by way of mortgage;

(c) disposals by way of gift to a member of the landlord's family or to a charity;

(d) a disposal pursuant to any option or right of pre-emption binding on the landlord (whenever granted) or any other obligation binding on the landlord created before 1st February 1988;

(e) a disposal to the Crown;

(f) where the landlord is a body corporate, a disposal to an associated company;

(g) a disposal of any freehold or leasehold interest pursuant to Chapter 1 of Part 1 of the Leasehold Reform, Housing and Urban Development Act 1993.

Section 4(1)(a) makes it clear that the grant of a tenancy of a single flat is not a relevant disposal.

NOTE: Where the landlord's interest has been mortgaged and the mortgagee proposes to make a disposal in exercise of a power of sale or leasing, the disposal by the mortgagee is treated as a relevant disposal and the mortgagee must observe the requirements of ss. 5–10 of Part I of the Act (s. 4(1A)).

9. The landlord's offer notice. Before a landlord can make a relevant disposal he must serve an offer notice upon the qualifying tenants in accordance with the provisions of s. 5 of the Act. Ideally, the offer notice should be served upon all qualifying tenants but an offer notice will still be valid notwithstanding the fact that it has not been served upon all qualifying tenants provided that:

(a) the offer notice has been served upon not less than 90% of the qualifying tenants; or
(b) if there are less than ten qualifying tenants, the offer notice has been served upon all but one of them: s. 5(4).

The landlord's offer notice must:
(*i*) be in writing: s. 54(1)(*a*);
(*ii*) set out the principal terms of the proposed disposal including the property to which it relates, the estate or interest proposed to be disposed of and the consideration required by the landlord: s. 5(2)(*a*);
(*iii*) state that the offer notice constitutes an offer by the landlord to dispose of the premises on those terms which may be accepted by the 'requisite majority' of the qualifying tenants: s. 5(2)(*b*);
(*iv*) specify a period within which the offer may be accepted, such period being not less than two months from the date of service of the notice: s. 5(2)(*c*);
(*v*) specify a further period of not less than two months from the expiration of the period within which the offer may be accepted (thus being not less than four months from the date of service of the offer notice) within which the qualifying tenants may nominate a person or persons to whom the interest in the premises which the landlord proposes to dispose of should be transferred (or as the case may be): s. 5(2)(*d*).

Section 5(5) of the Act deals with cases where the landlord wishes to dispose of an estate or interest in more than one building. If, for example, the landlord proposes to sell by way of a single transaction his interest in two buildings, one of which comprises a block of flats let to qualifying tenants and the other of which comprises business premises, he must sever the transaction for the purposes of s. 5 by serving an offer notice upon the qualifying tenants of the block of flats setting out the terms upon which he is willing to dispose of his interest in the block of flats alone.

NOTES: (1) By s. 54(3) of the Act the Secretary of State may prescribe the form of any notices required or authorised to be served under the Act and the particulars which any such notices shall contain. However no forms have been prescribed.

(2) By s. 54(1)(*b*) of the Act any notice required or authorised to be served under the Act may be sent by post.

(3) It would seem that any issue as to the validity of any notice served under Part I of the Act is to be determined by the court as opposed to the LVT (*Denetower Ltd* v. *Toop* (1991)).

10. Action by the qualifying tenants following receipt of the landlord's offer notice. When the landlord has served an offer notice upon the qualifying tenants in accordance with s. 5 of the Act, there are three options open to the qualifying tenants, namely:

(a) to take no action;
(b) to accept the landlord's offer;
(c) to make a counter-offer.

11. The qualifying tenants take no action. If the 'requisite majority' of qualifying tenants take no action following receipt of the landlord's offer notice, the landlord is free to dispose of the interest in the premises which he has offered to the qualifying tenants at any time during the period of 12 months commencing on the expiration of the qualifying tenants' time for accepting the offer: s. 7(1). A simple example illustrates the operation of s. 7(1). Let us assume:

(a) that the landlord serves an offer notice upon all qualifying tenants on 1st January 1989 offering to dispose of his freehold interest for £100,000 and specifying a period of two months within which the offer may be accepted; and
(b) that the 'requisite majority' of qualifying tenants have not served any notice upon the landlord by 1st March 1989.

The landlord will be free to dispose of his freehold interest to any other party at any time between 2nd March 1989 and 1st March 1990.

NOTES: (1) The landlord may not dispose of his interest for less than the consideration specified in his offer notice: s. 6(3)(*a*).

(2) The other terms of the disposal to a third party must correspond with the terms specified in the offer notice: s. 6(3)(*b*).

(3) The landlord is only entitled to dispose of the interest which he has offered to the qualifying tenants. Thus, if the landlord has offered to sell his freehold interest to the qualifying tenants as in the example above, he can only dispose of his freehold interest to any third party. If the landlord wished to grant a long lease of the premises to a third party he would

have to serve a fresh offer notice upon the qualifying tenants offering the qualifying tenants the opportunity to take the long lease: s. 6(4).

12. The qualifying tenants accept the landlord's offer. If the 'requisite majority' of qualifying tenants wish to accept the offer made by the landlord's offer notice, they must serve what is termed an 'acceptance notice' upon the landlord within the period (of not less than two months) specified in the landlord's offer notice. The effect of service of an acceptance notice by the requisite majority of qualifying tenants is as follows:

(a) If the requisite majority of qualifying tenants fail to nominate a person or persons to whom the landlord should transfer the interest referred to in the offer notice ('the protected interest' – s. 6(9)) within the period for making such nomination specified in that offer notice (which period cannot be less than four months from the date of service of the landlord's offer notice as mentioned above), the landlord may at any time within 12 months from the expiration of that period dispose of the protected interest to a third party (but subject to the provisions of s. 6(3), 6(4) noted above).

Example
(1) The landlord serves an offer notice upon the qualifying tenants on 1st January 1989. **(2)** The offer notice specifies a period of two months within which the offer may be accepted. **(3)** The requisite majority of qualifying tenants serve an acceptance notice upon the landlord on 1st February 1989. **(4)** The offer notice specifies a period of two months within which the requisite majority of qualifying tenants must nominate a person or persons to whom the protected interest is to be transferred (or as the case may be), i.e. expiring on 1st May 1989. **(5)** The requisite majority of qualifying tenants fail to nominate such a person or persons by 1st May 1989.

The landlord may dispose of the protected interest to any third party at any time between 2nd May 1989 and 1st May 1990: ss. 6(2)(*a*), 6(3).

(b) If the requisite majority of qualifying tenants duly nominate a person or persons to whom the protected interest is to be transferred, but a binding contract has not been entered into within three months after the expiration of the nomination period specified in the landlord's offer notice, the landlord may at any time within 12 months after the expiration of those three months dispose of the protected interest to a third party (but again subject to the provisions of s. 6(3), 6(4) noted above).

Example

(1) The landlord serves an offer notice upon the qualifying tenants on 1st January 1989. **(2)** The offer notice specifies a period of two months within which the offer may be accepted. **(3)** The requisite majority of qualifying tenants serve an acceptance notice upon the landlord on 1st February 1989. **(4)** The offer notice specifies a period of two months within which the requisite majority of qualifying tenants must nominate a person or persons to whom the protected interest is to be transferred (or as the case may be), i.e. expiring on 1st May 1989. **(5)** The requisite majority of qualifying tenants nominate such a person or persons on 1st May 1989. **(6)** The landlord and the nominated person(s) do not enter into a binding contract by 1st August 1989.

The landlord can serve a notice on the nominated person, pursuant to s. 10(4), whereupon the landlord may dispose of the protected interest to any third party at any time between 2nd August 1989 and 1st August 1990: s. 6(2)(*b*), 6(3).

(c) if the requisite majority of qualifying tenants duly nominates a person or persons to whom the protected interest is to be transferred and the landlord and the person(s) so nominated enter into a binding contract within three months of the expiration of the nomination period specified in the offer notice, the sale thereafter proceeds in the usual way.

NOTES: (1) If the landlord cannot dispose of the protected interest unless the consent of some other person is obtained, e.g. a superior landlord where the landlord is himself a tenant, the landlord is obliged to use his best endeavours to secure that consent and, if it appears to him that consent is being unreasonably withheld, he must issue proceedings for a declaration to that effect: s. 6(7).

(2) If the landlord unsuccessfully applies for any consent required from some other person and cannot obtain a declaration that such consent is being unreasonably withheld, or the nominated person has not entered into a binding contract with the landlord within three months after the expiration of the nomination period, the landlord may serve a notice on the nominated person pursuant to s. 10(4). Thereupon the landlord may dispose of the protected interest to any third party during the period of 12 months commencing three months after the expiration of the nomination period. Any disposal to a third party must however be on terms corresponding to those agreed with the qualifying tenants and for a consideration which is not less than that agreed with the qualifying tenants (s. 9(2)).

(3) If a binding contract has not been entered into in the circumstances described in Note (2) above and the landlord has served a notice pursuant to s. 10(4) on the nominated person on that ground, the landlord can recover all costs he has reasonably incurred in connection with the disposal to the nominated person during the period commencing four weeks after

the commencement of the nomination period and expiring on the date of service of his notice under s. 10(4): s. 10(5).

13. The qualifying tenants make a counter-offer. Within the period specified in the landlord's offer notice for acceptance of the offer made by the offer notice, the requisite majority of qualifying tenants may serve a notice upon the landlord making him a counter-offer for such estate or interest as is specified in their notice (which need not necessarily be the estate or interest specified in the landlord's offer notice). The notice making the counter-offer must specify the terms of the counter-offer, including those relating to the consideration payable and the name and address of a person on whom the landlord must serve a notice stating whether he accepts or rejects the counter-offer: s. 7(3).

There are three courses of action open to a landlord who has received a notice making a counter-offer, namely:

(a) to reject the counter-offer;
(b) to accept the counter-offer;
(c) to reject the counter-offer but to make a fresh offer at the same time.

14. The landlord rejects the counter-offer. If the landlord serves a notice simply rejecting the qualifying tenants' counter-offer, he may dispose of the protected interest to a third party within the period of 12 months following the period specified in his offer notice for acceptance of the offer made thereby (but subject to the provisions of s. 6(3), 6(4) noted above). If, however, the landlord's notice rejecting the counter-offer is served after the expiration of the period specified in his offer notice for acceptance of the offer made thereby, the period of 12 months during which the landlord may dispose of the protected interest to a third party commences on the date of service of his notice rejecting the counter-offer: s. 7(5).

Examples _____
(1)(*i*) The landlord serves an offer notice upon the qualifying tenants on 1st January 1989; (*ii*) The offer notice specifies a period of two months within which the offer may be accepted (i.e. expiring on 1st March 1989); (*iii*) The requisite majority of qualifying tenants serves a notice making a counter-offer upon the landlord on 1st February 1989; (*iv*) The landlord serves a notice rejecting the counter-offer on 15th February 1989. The landlord may dispose of the protected interest to any third party at any time between 2nd March 1989 and 1st March 1990.

(2)(*i*), (*ii*) and (*iii*) as per (1); (*iv*) The landlord serves a notice rejecting the counter-offer on 17th March 1989. The landlord may dispose of the protected interest to any third party at any time between 17th March 1989 and 16th March 1990.

15. The landlord accepts the counter-offer. If the landlord accepts the counter-offer, the matter proceeds in the same way as if the requisite majority of qualifying tenants had served an acceptance notice upon the landlord following receipt of an offer notice offering to dispose of the estate or interest specified in the tenants' counter-notice on the terms specified in the tenants' counter-notice: s. 7(4) and *see* **12** above. In other words, the qualifying tenants must still nominate a person(s) to whom the estate or interest is to be transferred within the nomination period specified in the offer notice and the restrictions on the landlord's ability to dispose of the estate or interest in question are the same as those described at **12** above. If, however, the landlord serves his notice accepting the counter-offer after the acceptance period specified in his offer notice, the nomination period begins on the date of service of the landlord's notice accepting the counter-offer and all subsequent time-limits are adjusted accordingly: s. 7(4)(*c*).

Examples

(1)(*i*) The landlord serves an offer notice upon the qualifying tenants on 1st January 1989. (*ii*) The offer notice specifies a period of two months within which the offer may be accepted (i.e. expiring 1st March 1989). (*iii*) The offer notice specifies a nomination period of two months (i.e. expiring 1st May 1989). (*iv*) The requisite majority of qualifying tenants serves a notice making a counter-offer upon the landlord on 1st February 1989. (*v*) The landlord serves a notice accepting the counter-offer on 17th March 1989. The nomination period begins on 17th March 1989 and if the majority of the qualifying tenants does not nominate a person or persons to whom the estate or interest in question is to be transferred by 17th May 1989, the landlord may dispose of the estate or interest in question to any third party at any time between 18th May 1989 and 17th May 1990.

(2)(*i*) to (*v*) as *per* (1); (*vi*) The majority of the qualifying tenants nominates a person to whom the estate or interest in question is to be transferred on 1st May 1989. The landlord and the tenant should enter into a binding contract by 17th August 1989 and if they do not, the landlord may (subject to service of a notice pursuant to s. 10(4)) dispose of the estate or interest in question to any third party at any time between 18th August 1989 and 17th August 1990.

16. The landlord rejects the counter-offer but makes a fresh offer at the same time. Instead of serving a notice which simply rejects the counter-offer, the landlord may serve a notice pursuant to s. 8(1) rejecting the counter-offer and

(a) stating that it constitutes a fresh offer by the landlord to dispose of an estate or interest in the property specified in his original offer notice, which may be accepted by the requisite majority of qualifying tenants of the constituent flats;

(b) setting out the principal terms of the proposed disposal, the estate or interest proposed to be disposed of and the consideration required;

(c) specifying a period within which the fresh offer may be accepted (which should presumably be not less than two months beginning with the date of service of the notice under s. 8(1) having regard to s. 5(1)(*c*)).

The consequences of service of such a notice are as follows:

(A) If the requisite majority of qualifying tenants of the constituent flats serves a notice upon the landlord accepting the fresh offer within the period specified in the landlord's notice under s. 8(1), the provisions of s. 6 apply as if the landlord's fresh offer was the offer made by the landlord's original offer notice (*see* **12** above). However, if the qualifying tenants' notice accepting the fresh offer is served after the acceptance period specified in the landlord's original offer notice has expired, the nomination period begins on the date of service of the qualifying tenants' notice accepting the fresh offer.

Example

(*i*) The landlord serves an offer notice upon the qualifying tenants on 1st January 1989. (*ii*) The offer notice specifies a period of two months within which the offer may be accepted (i.e. expiring 1st March 1989). (*iii*) The offer notice specifies a period of two months within which the requisite majority of qualifying tenants must nominate a person to whom the protected interest is to be transferred (i.e. expiring 1st May 1989). (*iv*) The requisite majority of the qualifying tenants serves a notice making a counter-offer on 1st February 1989. (*v*) The landlord serves a notice rejecting the counter-offer but making a fresh offer pursuant to s. 8(1) on 17th March 1989 and specifying a period of two months within which the fresh offer may be accepted (i.e. expiring 17th May 1989). (*vi*) The requisite majority of qualifying tenants serve a notice accepting the fresh offer on 16th May 1989.

The nomination period of two months specified in the landlord's original offer notice is deemed to commence on 16th May 1989 (i.e. expiring 16th July 1989) and a binding contract should therefore be entered into by 16th October 1989.

(B) If the landlord's fresh offer is not accepted within the period specified in the landlord's notice under s. 8(1), the landlord may dispose of the estate or interest specified in his notice under s. 8(1) to any third party within the period of 12 months beginning with the end of that period. Any disposal to a third party must be on terms corresponding to those specified in the landlord's notice under s. 8(1) and for a consideration which is not less than the consideration required by the notice under s. 8(1): s. 8(3).

(**C**) If within the period specified in the landlord's notice under s. 8(1) the requisite majority of the qualifying tenants of the constituent flats serve a notice upon the landlord stating that they are making a further counter-offer for the acquisition of an estate or interest in the property specified in the landlord's original offer notice, the landlord may:

(**a**) reject the counter-offer (*see* **14** above);
(**b**) accept the counter-offer (*see* **15** above);
(**c**) reject the counter-offer and make a further fresh offer at the same time (in which event the matter proceeds in one of the ways discussed in **16**, including this sub-paragraph (**C**)).

17. Replacement of the nominated person. When any offer or counter-offer is accepted in accordance with any of the provisions discussed above and the requisite majority of qualifying tenants have nominated one person only for the purposes of s. 6, i.e. as the person to whom the protected interest is to be transferred, that person may only be replaced by another person nominated by the requisite majority of the qualifying tenants if he has (for any reason, e.g. death) ceased to be able to act as a person so nominated: s. 6(5).

If two or more persons have been nominated and any of them ceases to act without being replaced as mentioned above, the remaining person or persons so nominated are entitled to continue to act as the nominated person(s) on his/their own: s. 6(6).

18. Withdrawal of either party from transaction. At any time after an offer or counter-offer has been accepted in accordance with the provisions discussed above and a person has been duly nominated as the person to whom the protected interest is to be transferred, the nominated person may serve a notice upon the landlord pursuant to s. 9(1) indicating that he no longer intends to proceed with the acquisition of the protected interest.

During the period of 12 months beginning with the date of service of the nominated person's notice under s. 9(1) the landlord may dispose of the protected interest to any third party on terms corresponding to those agreed with the qualifying tenants and for a consideration which is not less than that agreed with the qualifying tenants. Indeed if the nominated person becomes aware at any time that the number of qualifying tenants willing to proceed with the acquisition of the protected interest falls below the requisite majority, he is obliged to serve notice upon the landlord in accordance with s. 9(1) that he no longer intends to proceed with the acquisition: s. 9(3). Similarly, the landlord can serve a notice upon the nominated person that he no longer intends to proceed with the transaction at any time after the appointment of the nominated person. In that event, the landlord is not entitled to make any relevant disposal unless he serves a fresh offer notice: s. 9(4).

Section 9(8) makes it clear that the parties are not able to withdraw from the transaction after a binding contract has been entered into. If the landlord withdraws from the transaction later than four weeks after the commencement of the period for nomination, he is responsible for all costs reasonably incurred by the nominated person and the qualifying tenants whom he represents between the expiration of the period of four weeks from the commencement of the period for nomination and the date of service of the notice of intention to withdraw from the transaction. The nominated person and the qualifying tenants whom he represents are similarly responsible for the landlord's costs if the nominated person serves a notice of intention to withdraw from the transaction later than four weeks after the commencement of the nomination period: s. 9(6). The liability of the nominated person and the qualifying tenants whom he represents, for the landlord's costs, is joint and several: s. 9(7).

19. Lapse of landlord's offer. If at any time after the landlord has served an offer notice the premises cease to be premises to which Part I applies (e.g. because the number of flats held by qualifying tenants falls below 50% of the total number of flats contained in the premises), he may serve a notice on the qualifying tenants pursuant to s. 10(1) of the Act stating that the premises have ceased to be premises to which Part I applies and that the offer notice, and anything done in consequence of it, is to be of no effect. Thereafter the landlord may dispose of any interest in the premises as he sees fit. If the landlord fails to serve a notice pursuant to s. 10(1), Part I of the Act will continue to apply notwithstanding the fact that the premises are no longer premises to which Part I applies: s. 10(3). If a binding contract is entered into by the landlord and the nominated person and the landlord lawfully rescinds the contract (e.g. because the nominated person fails to complete) the landlord is entitled to dispose of the protected interest to any third party and on such terms as the landlord thinks fit at any time during the period of 12 months beginning with the date of the rescission of the contract: s. 10(6).

Enforcement by tenants of rights against new landlord

20. Duty of new landlord to furnish particulars of disposal made in contravention of Part I. If a landlord has made a relevant disposal without serving an offer notice on the qualifying tenants or in contravention of ss. 6–10 of Part I of the Act, then so long as the premises are still premises to which Part I applies, the requisite majority of qualifying tenants can serve a notice on the new landlord pursuant to s. 11(1) of the Act requiring the new landlord to provide details of the terms of the relevant disposal to a person whose name and address must be specified in the qualifying tenants' notice. The new landlord must then provide such details within one month: s. 11(3). The qualifying tenants' notice under s. 11(1) must be served upon the new landlord within the period of two months beginning with the date by which the requisite majority of qualifying tenants have been served with formal notice of the disposal to the new landlord pursuant to s. 3 of the Landlord and Tenant Act 1985 or the date by which other documents indicating that the disposal has taken place have been served on the requisite majority of qualifying tenants: s. 11(2).

21. Service of a purchase notice by the qualifying tenants. If a landlord has made a relevant disposal of premises to which Part I applies without having served an offer notice on the qualifying tenants or in contravention of ss. 6–10 of the Act and provided that the premises are still premises to which Part I of the Act applies, the requisite majority of qualifying tenants of the constituent flats may serve a notice upon the new landlord pursuant to s. 12(1) of the Act (a 'purchase notice').

The purchase notice requires the new landlord to transfer the estate or interest which was the subject of the original disposal (i.e. the estate or interest transferred by the original landlord to the new landlord) to a person or persons nominated by the requisite majority of the qualifying tenants on the same terms and at the same consideration that the original disposal was made. If the original disposal was of the premises to which Part I of the Act applied together with other premises (e.g. if the original landlord sold his interest in two buildings, one of which comprises a block of flats let to qualifying tenants and the other of which comprises business premises), the purchase notice must require the new landlord to transfer (or as the case may be) the estate or interest he has acquired in the premises to which Part I of the Act applied and to do so on the terms of the original disposal subject to such modifications as are necessary or expedient in the circumstances: s. 12(3)(*a*).

Alternatively the purchase notice may simply require the new land-lord to transfer such estate or interest in the premises to which Part I applied as may be determined by a rent assessment committee on such terms as may be determined by a rent assessment committee: s. 12(3)(*b*).

The purchase notice must be served on the new landlord within three months of the date on which the new landlord provides details of the original disposal pursuant to s. 11(3) or, if no s. 11(1) notice has been served, within five months of the date upon which the requisite majority of the qualifying tenants were served with notice (either for-mally or by information contained in other documents) of the original disposal: s. 12(2).

> NOTES: (1)　A purchase notice pursuant to s. 12(1) may not be served where the relevant disposal by the landlord without service of an offer notice or in contravention of the provisions of ss. 6 to 10, was a surrender of a tenancy held by him. Section 15 contains provisions dealing with this situation which are very similar to the provisions applicable to service of a purchase notice considered above and below.
>
> (2)　A purchase notice which required the new landlord to convey, to the person nominated by the qualifying tenants, the freehold land acquired by the new landlord 'subject only to such modifications as are necessary or expedient in the circumstances', was not invalidated by the fact that the land in question included land which the qualifying tenants were not entitled to acquire (*Denetower Ltd* v. *Toop* (1991)).

22. Terms of the disposal by the new landlord to the qualifying tenants. In a simple case where, for example, the original landlord has sold his freehold interest in the premises to which Part I applies to the new landlord for £100,000, there is usually no difficulty in es-tablishing the estate or interest which the new landlord is obliged to transfer to the person nominated by the qualifying tenants in their purchase notice, the terms of the transfer to the nominated person and the consideration for the transfer. The new landlord will be obliged to transfer the freehold interest to the nominated person for £100,000 and otherwise on terms corresponding to the terms of the original disposal.

Section 12(6) deals with cases where the property to be transferred by the new landlord to the nominated person has increased in mon-etary value owing to any change in circumstances, other than a change in the value of money, since the date of the original disposal. Any increase in value attributable to any change in the value of money, i.e. inflation, is disregarded. Examples of the change in cir-cumstances envisaged by s. 12(6) are a flat becoming vacant and reverting to the landlord or the carrying out of some improvement by the landlord. The effect of s. 12(6) is that the amount payable by the qualifying tenants/the nominated person is the amount that might reasonably have been obtained on a corresponding disposal on the open market at the time of the original disposal on the assumption that the change in circumstances in question had already taken place.

NOTE: In *Crumpton* v. *Unifox Properties Ltd* (1992) there were two dispositions of the freehold in breach of Part I of the Act. The first new landlord had forfeited two of the leases of the flats by peaceable re-entry and the second new landlord had spent substantial sums on refurbishment of those flats. However, by the time of service of the purchase notice, the mortgagees of the two forfeited leases had issued proceedings for relief from forfeiture/a vesting order. In determining the price to be paid by the qualifying tenants, the court held that there had been no great change in circumstances and, thus, that the second new landlord's expenditure on improvements did not result in any increase in the value of the premises.

23. Role of rent assessment committees/leasehold valuation tribunals. In the event of any dispute arising out of a purchase notice as to:

(a) the nature of the estate or interest to be transferred;
(b) the identity of the property;
(c) the consideration for the disposal;
(d) the other terms of the disposal;

or in any case where the purchase notice provides that any of these matters are to be determined by a rent assessment committee in accordance with s. 12(3)(*b*), a rent assessment committee has jurisdiction to hear and determine that dispute or make that determination: s. 13(1).

In exercising the jurisdiction conferred upon it by s. 13, a rent assessment committee is known as a leasehold valuation tribunal ('LVT'). On any application to an LVT the interests of the qualifying tenants are represented by the nominated person and the parties to the application bear their own costs of the application: s. 13(3), 13(4). An appeal lies to the Lands Tribunal.

NOTES: (1) The LVT also has jurisdiction when the first new landlord has sold on his interest and the qualifying tenants are enforcing their rights against that subsequent purchaser (*see* **26** below).

(2) In exercising its jurisdiction, the LVT has decided on several occasions that it has no power to determine de novo a value for the premises as at the date of the original disposal and that it is bound by the terms of the original disposal. However, the LVT has power to make any appropriate adjustment in the price if, for example, the original price was 'incorrect'

due to misdescriptions in auction particulars; see *Cousins* v. *Metropolitan Guarantee Ltd* (1989); *30 Upperton Gardens Management Ltd* v. *Akano* (1990); *Gregory* v. *Saddiq* (1991) and *Davis* v. *Stone* (1992); but see also *Newman* v. *Kay* (1991); (all decisions of the LVT).

(3) The LVT will also determine the price payable by the qualifying tenants for property disposed of to the new landlord as part of a lot, by reference to the price paid for that lot; *Venus* v. *Khan* (1990) and *Sullivan* v. *Safeland Investments Ltd* (1990).

(4) The application to the LVT must be in the prescribed form: see S. I. 1987 No. 2178 as amended.

24. Discharge of charges and other incumbrances. If the new landlord has charged or otherwise encumbered the property which he is required to transfer to the nominated person pursuant to a purchase notice at any time since the original disposal, the provisions of s. 12(4) and 12(5) and Part I of Sch. 1 to the Act apply.

Unless the Court otherwise directs the effect of these provisions is as follows:

(a) If the property has been charged by the new landlord to secure the payment of money or the performance of any other obligation by the new landlord or any other person, the instrument, e.g. the transfer, by virtue of which the property is disposed of by the new landlord to the nominated person, operates to discharge the property from that charge: s. 12(4)(*a*). The nominated person has a duty to apply the consideration payable in or towards redemption of any such charge and if there is more than one charge, then according to the priority of each such charge: Para. 1 of Sch. 1 Part I.

(b) If any difficulty arises in ascertaining how much is payable in respect of any such charge, in finding the holder of the charge, in obtaining a proper discharge from the holder of the charge or for any of the other reasons set out in para. 4 of Part I of Sch. 1 to the Act, the nominated person may pay the whole or part of the consideration into court.

(c) Provided that the nominated person applies the consideration in or towards redemption of any such charges in the first instance or, in an appropriate case, pays the whole or part of the consideration into court, the property will be transferred to the nominated person free of all such charges or incumbrances notwithstanding the fact that the consideration is insufficient to enable the charge or charges to be redeemed in their entirety (para. 2(2) of Part I of Sch. 1 to the Act). Paragraph 5 of Part I of Sch. 1 to the Act preserves the rights of the holders of any such charge, which is not redeemed in its entirety by the nominated person's application of the consideration, over any other property which is subject to the charge. The new landlord's personal liability under the charge is similarly preserved.

(d) In the case of any other incumbrance (e.g. the letting by the new landlord of a flat which was vacant at the date of the original disposal) the consideration payable to the new landlord is reduced by an amount corresponding to the amount by which the existence of the incumbrance reduces the value of the property: s. 12(4)(*b*).

NOTE: A lease of roofspace granted by the new landlord, after a purchase notice had been served, was an 'incumbrance' within s. 12(4)(b) and accordingly the interest acquired by the qualifying tenants was subject to that lease; see *Englefield Court Tenants* v. *Skeels* (1990 – LVT). On the other hand, where the new landlord granted leases, which constituted relevant disposals under Part I of the Act, without having served offer notices under s. 5, the LVT decided that the leases were not incumbrances subject to which the qualifying tenants acquired the freehold; see *Nolan* v. *Eagle Wharf Developments Ltd* (1992 – LVT).

25. Withdrawal of nominated person following service of a purchase notice. If the nominated person serves a notice on the new landlord before a binding contract has been entered into indicating that he no longer intends to proceed with the disposal required by the purchase notice, the new landlord can recover all costs he has reasonably incurred in connection with the disposal: s. 14(1). Those costs may be determined by the court or the Lands Tribunal if at the time of service of such a notice by the nominated person any proceedings relating to the purchase notice are pending before the court or the Lands Tribunal: s. 14(3).

By virtue of s. 12(9) which is made applicable by s. 14(5) any such liability for costs is the joint and several liability of the nominated person and the qualifying tenants by whom the purchase notice was served. The costs recoverable by the new landlord do not include any part of his costs of any application to an LVT s. 14(4).

The nominated person is obliged to serve notice upon the new landlord pursuant to s. 14(1) if he becomes aware that the number of qualifying tenants willing to proceed with the disposal required by the purchase notice has fallen below the requisite majority: s. 14(2).

26. Right of qualifying tenants to compel a sale by a subsequent purchaser. It is not uncommon for an interest in property to change hands on two or more occasions within a very short space of time. Section 16 of the Act deals with these situations.

If the new landlord is served with a s. 11(1) notice (requesting details of the original disposal – *see* **20** above) after he has himself disposed of the estate or interest which was the subject of the original disposal, he must, within one month:

(*i*) provide the person specified in the s. 11(1) notice with particulars of the terms and date on which the original disposal was made; and

(*ii*) serve on that person a notice informing him of the name and address of the subsequent purchaser; and

(*iii*) serve on the subsequent purchaser a copy of the s. 11(1) notice and of his response.

If the new landlord is served with a purchase notice under s. 12(1) he must forthwith:

(*i*) forward the notice to the subsequent purchaser; and

(*ii*) serve on the nominated person a notice informing him of the name and address of the subsequent purchaser: s. 16(1).

Section 16(2) provides that if the new landlord serves a notice providing the name and address of the subsequent purchaser upon the person specified in the qualifying tenants' notice under s. 11(1) or upon the nominated person referred to in any purchase notice served pursuant to s. 12(1), ss. 12–14 shall, instead of applying to the new landlord, apply to the subsequent purchaser as if the subsequent purchaser were the transferee under the original disposal.

The risk taken by a subsequent purchaser who purchases in circumstances where no offer notice has been served on the qualifying tenants is demonstrated by the decision in *Tyson* v. *Carlisle Estates Ltd* (1990 – LVT). The original disposal was at a price of £15,000. Sixteen days later the new landlord sold on to the subsequent purchaser for £20,000. In neither case was an offer notice served. It was decided that the qualifying tenants were entitled to acquire the interest in question from the subsequent purchaser for £15,000.

In *Wilkins* v. *Horrowitz* (1990 – LVT) an LVT appears to have taken the view that where the original landlord had exchanged contracts for the sale of the freehold and the intended purchaser then sold on the benefit of the contract to the new landlord, there was no relevant disposal until completion of the sale by the original landlord to the new landlord.

In a case where the qualifying tenants have only served a notice requesting details of the original disposal pursuant to s. 11(1), they should then serve a purchase notice upon the subsequent purchaser pursuant to s. 12(1) if they wish to compel the subsequent purchaser to transfer (or as the case may be) the property to them.

It is not clear whether it is necessary for the qualifying tenants to serve a fresh purchase notice upon the subsequent purchaser in a case where they have served a purchase notice on the new landlord and the new landlord has forwarded the notice to the subsequent purchaser and provided the name and address of the subsequent purchaser to the nominated person pursuant to s. 16(1)(*b*). It may therefore be prudent for the qualifying tenants to serve a fresh purchase notice upon the subsequent purchaser without prejudice to the validity of the purchase notice served upon the new landlord.

NOTES: (1) If the new landlord has disposed of part or parts of the estate or interest that was the subject matter of the original disposal the provisions discussed above and the provisions of ss. 12–14 (*see* **21** to **25** above) apply with such modifications as are appropriate so that the qualifying tenants can, if they wish, compel a sale by the subsequent purchaser(s) of any part or parts of the estate or interest which was the subject matter of the original disposal and in an appropriate case, may also compel a sale by the new landlord of any part of the estate or interest which was the subject matter of the original disposal which has been retained by him: s. 16(3).

(2) Section 16(1) does not apply if the premises affected by the original disposal have ceased to be premises to which Part I of the Act applies: s. 16(4), but *see* **27** below.

27. Termination of rights against new landlord or subsequent purchasers. Where the premises cease to be premises to which Part I applies at any time after a s. 11(1) notice (requesting details of the original disposal) or a purchase notice has been served, the new landlord (or the subsequent purchaser) may serve a notice upon the qualifying tenants of the constituent flats stating that:

(*i*) the premises have ceased to be premises to which Part I of the Act applies; and

(*ii*) the s. 11(1) notice or the purchase notice or anything done in pursuance of the same are to be treated as not having been served or done: s. 17(1).

NOTE: The s. 17(1) notice must be served on the qualifying tenants of the constituent flats (or at least 90% of them or upon all but one of them in accordance with s. 5(4)). It is not sufficient to serve the s. 17(1) notice upon the person specified in any s. 11(1) notice or the nominated person referred to in any purchase notice.

If the new landlord fails to serve a notice pursuant to s. 17(1), Part I of the Act will continue to apply notwithstanding the fact that the premises are no longer premises to which Part I of the Act applies: s. 17(6).

If a binding contract has not been entered into and no application to the court or to an LVT has been made within three months of the date of service of the purchase notice, the new landlord is entitled to serve a notice upon the nominated person stating that the purchase notice and anything done in pursuance of it is to be treated as not having been served or done: s. 17(3).

If an application has been made to an LVT within three months of the date of service of the purchase notice and a binding contract has not been entered into within two months after the determination of that application, then provided that no application to the court in connection with the purchase notice is pending, the new landlord may serve a notice upon the nominated person stating that the purchase notice and anything done in pursuance of it is to be treated as not having been served or done: s. 17(4).

Miscellaneous provisions

28. Action by prospective purchaser to ensure that the qualifying tenants do not become entitled to serve a purchase notice. Section 18 sets out a procedure by which a prospective purchaser of premises to which Part I of the Act applies can ensure that he will obtain a 'clean title', i.e. that he will not be compelled to dispose of any interest he acquires in the premises to the qualifying tenants.

The prospective landlord may serve a notice pursuant to s. 18(1) upon the tenants of the flats contained in the premises which he proposes to acquire. In order to be valid the s. 18(1) notice must be served on at least 80 per cent of the tenants of the flats affected: s. 18(3).

The requirements of a valid s. 18(1) notice are as follows:

(a) it must inform the tenant of the general nature of the principal terms of the proposed disposal including in particular;

    (*i*) the property to which it would relate and the estate or interest in that property proposed to be disposed of by the landlord; and

    (*ii*) the consideration required by the landlord for making that disposal; and

(b) it must invite the tenant to serve a notice on the prospective purchaser stating:

    (*i*) whether the landlord has served an offer notice upon him or on any predecessor in title of the tenant; and

    (*ii*) if no offer notice has been served, whether the tenant is aware of any reason why he is not entitled to be served with an offer notice by the landlord; and

    (*iii*) if he is not aware of any reason why he is not entitled to be served with an offer notice, whether he would wish to avail himself of the right of first refusal conferred by an offer notice if such a notice were served upon him; and

(c) it must inform the tenant of the effects of s. 18(3) and (4): s. 18(2).

29. Effect of s. 18(1) notice. As mentioned above, in order to be valid, the prospective purchaser's s. 18(1) notice must be served upon at least 80% of the tenants of the flats contained in the premises the landlord proposes to dispose of. Section 18(3) provides that if:

(a) not more than 50% of the tenants so served respond to the notice within 28 days after the date upon which the last s. 18(1) notice was served; or

(b) more than 50% of the tenants so served have responded by serving notices on the prospective purchaser stating that either:

(*i*) they do not regard themselves as being entitled to be served with an offer notice by the landlord; or

(*ii*) they would not wish to avail themselves of the right of first refusal if an offer notice were served upon them,

the premises affected by the disposal shall in relation to the disposal be treated as premises to which Part I of the Act does not apply.

In calculating the percentage of the tenants who do or do not respond to the s. 18(1) notice for the purposes of s. 18(3), each of the flats affected is treated as having one tenant (whether or not the tenancy of that flat is in fact held by joint tenants) and each such tenant counts towards the percentages specified in s. 18(3) whether he is a qualifying tenant or not: s. 18(4).

The advantage to the landlord and the prospective purchaser of the s. 18 procedure is that depending on the number and terms of the tenants' responses to the s. 18(1) notice, they may be free to proceed with the proposed transaction after 28 days. As we have seen, if the offer notice procedure is followed, there could easily be a delay of seven months or more before the landlord is free to dispose of his interest to a third party.

NOTES: (1) If not more than 50% of the tenants served with a prospective purchaser's notice under s. 18(1) respond within 28 days then, as stated above, the premises affected by the disposal shall, in relation to the disposal, be treated as premises to which Part I of the Act does not apply.

This would seem to be the case even if the landlord has in fact served an offer notice. In view of s. 10(3) however, it seems that it would still be necessary for the landlord to serve a notice upon the qualifying tenants pursuant to s. 10(1) before he will be free to proceed with the disposal to the prospective purchaser (*see* **19** above).

(2) The position, in the event that more than 50% of the tenants served with the s. 18(1) notice respond by stating that an offer notice has in fact been served on them, is not clear. This possibility is not expressly contemplated by Part I of the Act.

What is the position if those tenants responding state that they do not regard themselves as being entitled to be served with an offer notice, or that they do not wish to avail themselves of the right of first refusal?

The cautious view must be that the offer notice remains effective, at least until the qualifying tenants' time for accepting the offer made by the offer notice, or to make a counter-offer, has expired.

An alternative view is that, if more than 50% of the tenants upon whom the s. 18(1) notice has been served respond by informing the prospective purchaser

(*i*) that they have received an offer notice; and

(*ii*) that they do not wish to avail themselves of the right of first refusal and the tenants who so respond constitute the 'requisite majority' of qualifying tenants, the landlord and the prospective purchaser should be free to proceed immediately.

While the prospective purchaser might be entitled to resist any purchase notice subsequently received in these circumstances, it is less than clear that a representation of this kind, made by the requisite majority of qualifying tenants to the prospective purchaser, is one upon which the landlord is entitled to rely.

30. Status of offers and counter-offers. Section 20(2) of the Act makes it clear that any reference to an offer, counter-offer or acceptance of an offer or counter-offer in Part I of the Act is to be treated as an offer, counter-offer or acceptance, subject to contract.

31. Enforcement of obligations under Part I. If any party interested in premises to which Part I of the Act applies considers that any other party has made default in complying with any duty imposed by Part I, he may apply to the court for an Order requiring the defaulting party to make good his default: s. 19(1).

Before making any application to the court pursuant to s. 19(1) the applicant must have served on the defaulting party more than 14 days prior to the application to the court, a notice requiring the defaulting party to make good the default: s. 19(2).

By s. 19(3) of the Act the court is given an express power to grant an injunction to restrain a relevant disposal in a case where no offer notice has been served or which is not being made in accordance with s. 6–s. 10. The Order the court is empowered to make under s. 19(1) is effectively a mandatory injunction; so, presumably, s. 19(3) envisages that, for example, the court may additionally wish to restrain an unlawful disposal by way of injunction until such time as any Order made pursuant to s. 19(1) has been complied with.

It is submitted that it is arguable that in certain circumstance default in complying with a duty imposed by Part I of the Act may give rise to an action for damages in the tort of breach of statutory duty.

NOTE: A county court has jurisdiction to hear and determine any question arising under the provisions of Part I of the Act other than a question falling within the jurisdiction of an LVT: s. 52.

Progress test 23

1. What is the right conferred upon qualifying tenants by Part I of the Act? **(2)**

2. L has a lease of a block of flats to which Part I of the Act applies for a term of 99 years but subject to a break-clause entitling his landlord – the freeholder – to bring the lease to an end after five years. Who is the landlord for the purposes of Part I of the Act? **(4)**

3. X Ltd is the tenant of a flat contained in premises to which Part I of the Act applies. X Ltd's wholly owned subsidiaries Y Ltd and Z Ltd hold tenancies of two further flats contained in the premises. Is X Ltd a qualifying tenant? **(7)**

4. What is a relevant disposal? **(8)**

5. What are the requirements of a valid offer notice? **(9)**

6. What is the 'requisite majority' of qualifying tenants for the purpose of service of an acceptance notice? **(7)**

7. What courses of action are open to a landlord who receives a counter-offer? **(13)**

8. The requisite majority of qualifying tenants have served an acceptance notice in good time but have failed to nominate a person or persons to whom the landlord's interest is to be transferred within the period specified in the landlord's offer notice. Advise the landlord. **(12)**

9. The qualifying tenants of flats contained in premises to which Part I applies receive an authority to pay rent to a new landlord. The qualifying tenants have not received any offer notice from their previous landlord. Advise the qualifying tenants. **(20)** and **(21)**

10. What steps may be taken by a prospective purchaser of premises to which Part I applies to ensure that he obtains a 'clean title'? **(28)**

Appointment of managers by the Court: Pt II, Landlord and Tenant Act 1987

1. Introduction. In the introduction to the preceding chapter, reference was made to the difficulties sometimes encountered by tenants of residential flats in multi-occupied buildings, such as blocks of flats, in enforcing the landlord's compliance with his management responsibilities. One solution to this type of problem is to empower a third party to carry out the landlord's management responsibilities and to receive the income from the premises in question for that purpose.

The High Court has power to appoint such a person (a 'receiver') under s. 37 of the Supreme Court Act 1981 and the county court has a similar power under s. 38 of the County Courts Act 1984. The High Court has exercised its power to appoint a receiver on several occasions, e.g. *Hart* v. *Emelkirk Ltd* (1983) and *Daiches* v. *Bluelake Investments Ltd* (1985), but difficulties have arisen in practice, in particular in relation to the execution of any necessary works which do not fall within the responsibilities of either the landlord or the tenants and in relation to the receiver's remuneration (*see* e.g. *Evans* v. *Clayhope Properties Ltd* (1987)).

Part II of the Landlord and Tenant Act 1987 (ss. 21 to 24) seeks to resolve some of these difficulties by empowering the court to appoint a manager in certain circumstances. Part II of the Act provides a complete self-contained code for the appointment of a manager in the cases to which it applies, and s. 21(6) makes it clear that where Part II of the Act applies, the tenants are not entitled to seek the appointment of a receiver or manager under any other power to make such an appointment which the court may have.

Part II of the Act came into force on 18th April 1988.

2. Premises to which Part II of the act applies. Part II applies to premises:

(a) which consist of the whole or part of a building; and

(b) which contain two or more flats: s. 21(2).

Part II will not apply if:

(a) the landlord is an exempt landlord (*see* s. 58(1) of the Act and 23: **5**);
(b) the landlord is a resident landlord (*see* s. 58(2) of the Act and 23: **6**);
(c) the premises are included within the functional land of any charity (*see* ss. 21(3) and 60(1)).

3. By whom can the application for the appointment of a manager be made? The application can be made by any tenant of a flat contained in the premises whose tenancy is not a tenancy to which Part II of the Landlord and Tenant Act 1954 applies: s. 21(1), 21(7). The restrictive definition of a 'qualifying tenant' in Part I of the Act (s. 3) has no relevance for the purposes of Part II.

The tenants of two or more flats contained in the premises can make the application jointly: s. 21(4)(*a*). The application can be made in respect of two or more premises to which Part II applies: s. 21(4)(*b*). So, for example, if two blocks of flats to which Part II applies are owned by the same landlord and the tenants of the flats contained in those blocks benefit from common services provided by the landlord, such as common access roads and communal gardens, the application could be made jointly by a tenant from each block. An application may also be made by one or more of the joint tenants of a flat contained in the premises: s. 21(5).

4. Preliminary notice by tenant. Before making an application for the appointment of a manager the tenant must serve a notice on the landlord which complies with the requirements of s. 22(2).

The notice must:

(a) specify the tenant's name, the address of his flat and an address in England and Wales at which the landlord may serve notices or proceedings in connection with Part II upon him;
(b) state that the tenant intends to apply to the court for an order for the appointment of a manager under s. 24;
(c) specify the premises in respect of which the order will be sought;
(d) state that the tenant will not make the application if the matters complained of in the notice are capable of remedy and the landlord remedies those complaints as required by the notice;
(e) specify the grounds on which the court will be asked to make the order (see s. 24(2) below) and the matters that will be relied upon by the tenant for the purposes of establishing those grounds;

(f) if the matters complained of are capable of remedy,

(*i*) require the landlord to take such steps as are specified in the notice to remedy the matters complained of; and

(*ii*) specify a reasonable period within which the landlord must take the steps specified;

(g) contain such information (if any) as the Secretary of State may by regulations prescribe.

Under s. 22(3) the court may make an order dispensing with the requirement for service of a s. 22 notice if it is satisfied that it would not be reasonably practicable to serve the notice upon the landlord, e.g. because the landlord cannot be found. The court's order may however be made subject to terms that other notices be served or other steps taken (possibly, for example, advertisement of the notice in a newspaper). The application for an order dispensing with service of s. 22 notice may be made prior to or at the hearing of the application for the appointment of a manager.

5. Steps to be taken by the landlord. If a landlord who has been served with a s. 22 notice wishes to avoid the appointment of a manager he must remedy the matters complained of in the notice if they are capable of remedy. The landlord must in any event serve a copy of the notice upon any mortgagee who has an interest in the premises specified in the notice as being the premises in respect of which the tenant will ask the court to appoint a manager and he must do so as soon as reasonably practicable after he has received the notice: s. 22(4).

The purpose of s. 22(4) is to give the mortgagee the opportunity to protect his security and to be joined as a party to the application for the appointment of a manager.

6. The application for appointment of a manager. No application for an order for the appointment of a manager can be made unless:

(a) a s. 22 notice has been served upon the landlord and (if appropriate) the period specified therein for remedying the matters complained of has expired without the landlord having taken the steps specified in the notice to remedy the matters complained of; or

(b) the court has dispensed with the requirement for service of a s. 22 notice on the landlord and any directions given by the court as to the service of notices and the taking of any other steps, have been complied with: s. 23(1).

The application must be made by originating summons in the High Court or originating application in a county court. If a s. 22 notice has been served, a copy must be appended to the originating summons or originating application.

RSC Order 97 Rule 15 and CCR Order 43 Rule 18 require the applicant to serve a copy of the application upon every person known to the applicant who is likely to be affected by the application, including, but not limited to:

(a) the other tenants of the flats contained in the premises;
(b) any mortgagee of the landlord's interest;
(c) any superior landlord;
(d) any tenants' association;
(e) the proposed manager.

Obviously, the application should also be served on the landlord (who will be the defendant to the application) if at all possible.

A notice must also be served upon the parties mentioned at (*a*) to (*d*) above advising them of their right to apply to be made a party to the proceedings.

7. Grounds for appointment of a manager by the court. The court will not make an order for the appointment of a manager unless it is satisfied:

(a)(*i*) that the landlord is in breach of any obligation owed by him to the tenant under the terms of the tenancy relating to the management of the premises in question or any part of those premises; or
(*ii*) that in the case of an obligation dependent on notice the landlord would be in breach of that obligation if notice had been given to him and that it has not been reasonably practicable for the tenant to give the appropriate notice; and
(b) that the circumstances by virtue of which the landlord is (or would be) in breach are likely to continue; and
(c) that it is just and convenient to make the order in all the circumstances of the case: s. 24(2)(*a*).

Alternatively, the court must be satisfied that other circumstances exist which make it just and convenient for the order to be made: s. 24(2)(*b*).

Section 24(11) provides that references in s. 24 to the management of any premises include references to the repair, maintenance or insurance of those premises.

8. Terms of the order. The court will order that a specified person or persons be appointed as manager to carry out such functions in connection with the management of the premises or such functions of a receiver (or both) as the court thinks fit: s. 24(1). The court has power to order that the appointment of the manager is to be in relation to premises which are more or less extensive than the premises specified in the application: s. 24(3). The court may include in its order such directions relating to the manager's exercise of his functions under the order and such incidental or ancillary matters as it thinks fit and such directions can be given on any application for directions subsequently made by the manager: s. 24(4).

In particular, the order may provide:

(a) for rights and liabilities arising under contracts to which the manager is not a party to become rights and liabilities of the manager (e.g. rights and liabilities arising under contracts for the maintenance of lifts etc.);

(b) for the manager to be entitled to prosecute claims in respect of causes of action (whether contractual or tortious) accruing before or after the date of his appointment;

(c) for remuneration to be paid to the manager by the landlord, or by the tenants of the premises in respect of which the order is made or by all or any of those persons;

(e) for the manager's functions to be exercisable by him during either a specified or unlimited period (s. 24(5)).

The order may be conditional, for example, upon the tenants putting the manager in funds, and may be suspended on terms, e.g. on terms that the landlord carries out certain works within a specified period: s. 24(6).

If it thinks fit the court may make an order for the appointment of a manager notwithstanding that:

(a) any period within which the s. 22 notice required the landlord to take specified steps was not reasonable; or

(b) the notice failed to comply with the requirements of s. 22(2) or any regulations made by the Secretary of State applying to s. 22 notices under s. 54(3) of the Act (s. 24(7)).

NOTES: (1) The order for the appointment of a manager can and should be registered under the Land Charges Act 1972 or the Land Registration Act 1925 as the case may be: s. 24(8).

(2) The court may make an interlocutory order for the appointment of a manager: s. 24(1).

(3) See *Howard* v. *Midrome Ltd* (1991) for an example of a case where a manager was appointed on an interlocutory application and the court was prepared to exercise its discretion under s. 24(7) in relation to alleged defects in the s. 22 notice.

9. Discharge of order for the appointment of a manager. If the order provides that the manager's functions will be exercisable during a specified period, the manager's appointment will automatically come to an end when that period expires. Doubtless however, any order for the appointment of a manager will provide that the parties are to be at liberty to apply and accordingly, in an appropriate case, the parties will be able to refer back to the court for an order extending the period of the manager's appointment.

By s. 24(9) the court may on the application of any party interested vary or discharge the order for the appointment of the manager (whether conditionally or unconditionally) and if the order has been protected by an entry registered under the Land Charges Act 1972 or the Land Registration Act 1925, direct that the entry shall be cancelled.

10. The court. A county court has jurisdiction to hear and determine any application to dispense with the requirement for service of a s. 22 notice or for the appointment of a manager.

Progress test 24

1. To what premises does Part II of the Act apply? **(2)**

2. A tenant of premises to which Part II applies seeks an Order for the appointment of a receiver under s. 37 of the Supreme Court Act 1981. Advise the landlord. **(1)**

3. Donald, Huey, Dewey and Louis are joint tenants of a flat contained in premises to which Part II applies. Donald considers that the landlord is in breach of his repairing obligations and wishes to apply for the appointment of a manager. Huey, Dewey and Louis do not wish to become involved. Can Donald take any action? **(3)**

4. What are the requirements of a valid s. 22 notice? **(4)**

5. The tenants of flats contained in premises to which Part II of the Act applies wish to serve a s. 22 notice upon the landlord as a preliminary to making an application for the appointment of a manager. The landlord cannot be found. Advise the tenants. **(4)**

6. What action should a landlord take upon receipt of a s. 22 notice? **(5)**

7. How soon after service of a s. 22 notice can an application be made to the court for the appointment of a manager? **(6)**

8. What are the grounds upon which the court will make an order for the appointment of a manager? **(7)**

9. The tenant's notice under s. 22 required the landlord to carry out certain works within 14 days. Those works could not realistically be carried out in less than three months. The tenant had been pressing the landlord to carry out the works in question in correspondence for many months prior to service of the s. 22 notice. Advise the tenant. **(8)**

10. After his appointment the manager discovers that he does not have access to sufficient funds to enable him to carry out the particular repairs upon which the tenants' application for his appointment was founded. Advise the manager. **(8, 9)**

Compulsory acquisition by tenants of their landlord's interest: Pt III, Landlord and Tenant Act 1987

1. Introduction. In the introduction to Chapter 23 reference was made to the recommendations made in the Nugee Report for alleviating the difficulties suffered by tenants of residential flats contained in multi-occupied buildings in enforcing the landlord's compliance with his management obligations. In particular, it was noted that the Nugee Report found that the incidence of complaints concerning the management of such buildings is significantly lower when the tenants control the management of the building within which such flats are contained and are responsible for the provision of common services.

The Nugee Report's recommendations that tenants should have a right of first refusal when the landlord's interest is being sold or otherwise disposed of and that the tenants should have the ability to appoint their own nominee to exercise the landlord's management functions in certain cases were accepted by Parliament with little qualification and enacted as Parts I and II respectively of the Landlord and Tenant Act 1987 (considered in the two preceding chapters).

Parliament has gone further than the recommendations made by the Nugee Report by giving certain tenants the right to acquire compulsorily their landlord's interest in certain circumstances. This right is conferred by Part III of the Landlord and Tenant Act 1987 (ss. 25–34) which we shall now consider.

Part III of the Act came into force on 18th April 1988 and certain amendments have been made by the Housing Act 1988 and the Leasehold Reform, Housing and Urban Development Act 1993.

2. The right conferred by Part III. The right is '. . . to make an application to the court for an order providing for a person nominated by them to acquire their landlord's interest in the premises without his consent . . .' (s. 25(1)).

3. Premises to which Part III applies. Part III applies to premises if:

(a) they consist of the whole or part of a building; and
(b) they contain two or more flats held by tenants of the landlord who are 'qualifying tenants'; and
(c) the total number of flats held by such tenants is not less than two thirds of the total number of flats contained in the premises (s. 25(2)).

Part III will not apply if more than 50% of the internal floor area is occupied or is intended to be occupied otherwise than for residential purposes, the internal floor area of any common parts being disregarded for the purposes of this calculation: s. 25(4).

4. The landlord for the purposes of Part III of the Act. The landlord referred to in Part III is the immediate landlord of the qualifying tenants of the flats contained in the premises: s. 60(1).

Part III will not apply if:

(a) the landlord is an exempt landlord (*see* s. 58(1) of the Act and 23:5); or
(b) the landlord is a resident landlord (*see* s. 58(2) of the Act and 23:6); or
(c) the premises are included within the functional land of any charity (*see* s. 60(1)): (s. 25(5)).

5. Qualifying tenants and the requisite majority. By s. 26(1) a person is a qualifying tenant if he is the tenant of the flat under a long lease and his tenancy is not a tenancy to which Part II of the Landlord and Tenant Act 1954 applies.

Certain tenants are excluded from the definition of 'qualifying tenant'. These are:

(*i*) tenants of three or more flats in the premises in question whether under a single long lease or a number of long leases: s. 26(2);
(*ii*) any tenant of a flat whose immediate landlord is a qualifying tenant of that flat, e.g. a sub-tenant: s. 26(3).

NOTES: (1) The expression 'long lease' is defined in s. 59(3) of the Act. It will be sufficient for most purposes to note that the lease must have been granted for a term certain exceeding 21 years whether or not it is (or may be) terminable before the end of that term by notice given by the tenant or by re-entry or forfeiture.

(2) Section 26(4) provides that for the purposes of s. 26(2) a tenant of a flat who is a body corporate is to be treated as the tenant of any other flat in the premises in question which is let to an associated company (*see* s. 20(1)).

Reference is made throughout Part III of the Act to the 'requisite majority' of qualifying tenants. The 'requisite majority' of qualifying tenants means qualifying tenants of the flats contained in the premises in question with not less than two thirds of the available votes. It is envisaged that the qualifying tenants will conduct a vote to decide whether or not to apply for an acquisition order on the basis of one vote per flat let to a qualifying tenant (i.e. even if the long lease of a flat contained in the premises in question is held by joint tenants, only one vote will be attributed to that flat): s. 27(4).

6. Preliminary notice by tenants. Before making an application for an 'acquisition order', the requisite majority of qualifying tenants must serve a notice on the landlord which complies with the requirements of s. 27(2).

The notice must:

(a) specify the names of the qualifying tenants by whom it is served, the addresses of their flats and the name and the address in England and Wales of a person on whom the landlord may serve notices and proceedings in connection with Part III, instead of serving such notices and proceedings on the qualifying tenants by whom the notice is served;

(b) state that those tenants intend to apply for an acquisition order;

(c) specify the premises in respect of which the acquisition order will be sought;

(d) state that the tenants will not apply for an acquisition order if the matters complained of in the notice are capable of remedy and the landlord remedies those complaints as required by the notice;

(e) specify the grounds on which the court will be asked to make an acquisition order (*see* s. 29(1) to (3) below) and the matters that will be relied upon by the tenant for the purposes of establishing those grounds;

(f) if the matters complained of are capable of remedy,

(*i*) require the landlord to take such steps as are specified in the notice to remedy the matters complained of; and

(*ii*) specify a reasonable period within which the landlord must take the steps specified;

(g) contain such information (if any) as the Secretary of State may by regulations prescribe.

Under s. 27(3) the court may make an order dispensing with the requirement for service of a s. 27 notice if it is satisfied that it would not be reasonably practicable to serve the notice upon the landlord, e.g. because the landlord cannot be found. The court's order may, however, be made subject to terms that other notices be served or other steps taken (possibly, for example, advertisement of the notice in a newspaper).

7. The application for an acquisition order. No application for an acquisition order can be made unless:

(a) a s. 27 notice has been served upon the landlord and (if appropriate) the period specified therein for remedying the matters complained of has expired without the landlord having taken the steps specified in the notice to remedy the matters complained of; or
(b) the court has dispensed with the requirement for service of a s. 27 notice on the landlord and any directions given by the court as to the service of notices and the taking of any other steps have been complied with (s. 28(2)).

The application must be made by the requisite majority of qualifying tenants: s. 28(1). The qualifying tenants constituting the requisite majority who make the application for an acquisition order need not be the same qualifying tenants who constituted the requisite majority for the purposes of service of the s. 27 notice: s. 27(5).

It is possible for the respective qualifying tenants of two or more premises to which Part III applies to apply to the court for a single acquisition order in respect of both (or as the case may be) those premises. So, for example, if two blocks of flats to which Part III applies are owned by the same landlord and the tenants of the flats contained in those blocks benefit from common services or there is some other good reason why a single acquisition order should be made in respect of both blocks of flats, the qualifying tenants of both blocks can make a joint application for an acquisition order: s. 28(3). Each set of qualifying tenants must, however, have served a s. 27 notice upon the landlord in respect of the block in which their flats are contained unless the requirement for service of a s. 27 notice is dispensed with by the court.

The provisions of s. 28(3) may be of particular importance in view of the provisions of s. 29(5) considered below. The application must be made by originating summons in the High Court or originating application in the county court.

RSC Order 97 Rule 16 of the Rules of the Supreme Court, and CCR Order 43 Rule 19 also require the applicants to serve a copy of the application upon every person known to the applicants who is likely to be affected by the application, including but not limited to:

(*i*) the other tenants of the flats contained in the premises whether or not they could have made an application (i.e. irrespective of whether or not those other tenants are qualifying tenants);

(*ii*) any mortgagee of the landlord's interest;

(*iii*) any superior landlord;

(*iv*) any tenants' association;

(*v*) the person nominated by the qualifying tenants to acquire their landlord's interest if the nominated person is not an applicant (in which event the nominated person must be made a defendant to the application).

Obviously the application should also be served on the landlord (who must be made a defendant to the application) if at all possible. A notice must also be served upon the parties mentioned at (*i*) to (*iv*) above advising them of their right to apply to be made a party to the proceedings.

NOTES: (1) The application for an acquisition order can and should be registered as a pending land action under the Land Charges Act 1972 and the Land Registration Act 1925: s. 28(5).

(2) The applicants are treated as persons having an interest in the premises for the purposes of s. 57 of the Land Registration Act 1925 and may thus register an inhibition prohibiting any dealings with any registered land containing the whole or part of the premises: s. 28(6).

8. Grounds for making an acquisition order. The court will not make an acquisition order unless it is satisfied:

(a) that the premises were at the date of service of the s. 27 notice and the date the application was made, premises to which Part III applies and have not ceased to be premises to which Part III applies since the date the application was made (but *see also* s. 29(7)); and

(b) that it is appropriate to make the order in the circumstances of the case (but *see* s. 29(5) and para. **13** below); and either

(c)(*i*) that the landlord is in breach of any obligation owed by him to the applicants under their leases and relating to the repair, maintenance, insurance or management of the premises in question or any part of those premises; or

(*ii*) that in the case of an obligation dependent upon notice (such as an obligation to repair) the landlord would be in breach of that obligation if notice had been given to him and that it has not been reasonably practicable for the tenants to give him the appropriate notice; and

(*iii*) that the circumstances by virtue of which the landlord is (or would be) in breach are likely to continue; or

(d) both at the date when the application was made and throughout the period of three years immediately preceding that date, there was in force an appointment of a manager under Part II (s. 29(1)–(3)).

NOTE: If it thinks fit the court may make an acquisition order notwithstanding that: (*a*) any period within which the s. 27 notice required the landlord to take specified steps was not reasonable; or (*b*) the notice failed to comply with the requirements of s. 27(2) or any regulations made by the Secretary of State relating to s. 27 notices under s. 54(3) of the Act: s. 29(6).

9. Terms of the acquisition order. Except in a case where the landlord cannot be found the acquisition order will provide for the nominated person to be entitled to acquire the landlord's interest in the premises on such terms as may be determined:

(a) by agreement between the landlord and the qualifying tenants in whose favour the acquisition order is made; or
(b) in default of agreement, by a rent assessment committee under s. 31: s. 30(1).

If the court thinks fit the acquisition order may include any yard, garden or appurtenance belonging to or usually enjoyed with the premises specified in the application or exclude any part of the premises specified in the application: s. 29(4).

The order may be conditional and in particular its operation may be suspended on terms fixed by the court, e.g. the order may be conditional upon the landlord's failure to carry out certain works within a specified period: s. 30(2).

If the landlord cannot dispose of his interest unless the consent of some other person is obtained, e.g. a superior landlord where the landlord is himself a tenant, the landlord is obliged to use his best endeavours to secure that consent and if it appears to him that consent is being unreasonably withheld, he must issue proceedings for a declaration to that effect: s. 30(5)(*a*).

If the landlord unsuccessfully applies for any consent required from some other person and cannot obtain a declaration that such consent is being unreasonably withheld, the acquisition order will cease to have effect: s. 30(5)(*b*).

NOTE: The acquisition order can and should be registered under the Land Charges Act 1972 or the Land Registration Act 1925 as the case may be: s. 30(6).

10. Role of rent assessment committees. If the landlord cannot agree any of the terms upon which his premises are to be acquired by the nominated person pursuant to the acquisition order with the nominated person or the qualifying tenants in whose favour the order was made, those terms may be determined by a rent assessment committee: s. 31(1). Subsections (2), (4) and (5) of s. 13 of the Act apply by virtue of s. 31(5) and thus:

(a) any application to a rent assessment committee must be in the prescribed form: see S. I. 1988 No. 484 as amended.
(b) the parties to an application to a rent assessment committee bear their own costs of the application;
(c) when exercising the jurisdiction conferred upon it by s. 31, a rent assessment committee is known as a leasehold valuation tribunal ('LVT').

On any application to an LVT the interests of the qualifying tenants in whose favour an acquisition order has been made are represented by the nominated person and the qualifying tenants themselves are not parties to the application: s. 31(4).

The LVT determines any terms of the acquisition which are in dispute on the basis of what appears to them to be fair and reasonable: s. 31(1). If an LVT is called upon to determine the consideration payable for the landlord's interest, it must determine the amount which that interest might be expected to realise if sold on the open market by a willing lessor on 'the appropriate terms'. The LVT must assume that none of the tenants of the premises which are the subject of the acquisition order are buying or seeking to buy the landlord's interest. In this way, any particular benefit to any tenant of the premises in acquiring the landlord's interest which might prompt such a tenant to pay more than any other party is disregarded: s. 31(2). The 'appropriate terms' referred to in s. 31(2) are all terms of the acquisition (whether determined by agreement or the LVT), other than those relating to the consideration payable: s. 31(3).

NOTE: In *139 Finborough Road Management Ltd* v. *Mansoor* (1990 –LVT), an LVT expressed the view that the relevant date for valuation of the landlord's interest is the date of the acquisition order.

11. Acquisition orders where the landlord cannot be found.
Where the landlord cannot be found or his identity cannot be ascertained the acquisition order will provide for the premises specified in the order to vest in the nominated person:

(a) on such terms (other than as to payment) as the court thinks fit, being the terms which, in the court's opinion, correspond so far as possible to those on which the landlord's interest might be expected to be transferred if it were being transferred by the landlord;
(b) and upon payment into Court of:
    (*i*) a price certified by a surveyor selected by the President of the

Lands Tribunal as being the amount which, in his opinion, the landlord's interest might be expected to realise if sold on the open market by a willing seller on the terms determined by the court;

(*ii*) any amounts or estimated amounts remaining due to the landlord from any tenants of his of any premises comprised in the premises which are the subject of the acquisition order, being amounts or estimated amounts determined by the court as being due from those persons under the terms of their leases, e.g. rent and service charges: s. 33(1), (2).

The premises which are the subject of the acquisition order vest in the nominated person when the amounts mentioned above are paid into court: s. 33(3).

12. Discharge of mortgages. If the landlord's interest is mortgaged or charged, the instrument by virtue of which it is acquired by the nominated person operates to discharge the premises from any such mortgage or charge on that interest unless s. 32(2) (considered below) applies and subject to Part II of Sch. I of the Act: s. 32(1).

The provisions of Part II of Sch. I to the Act are very similar to the provisions of Part I of that Sch. considered at 23:**24**.

In summary:

(a) the nominated person must apply the consideration payable pursuant to the acquisition order towards discharge of all mortgages and charges over the landlord's interest or, in cases of difficulty, pay the whole or part of that consideration into court;

(b) provided that he does so, the premises will be acquired by the nominated person free of all such mortgages and charges even if the consideration payable pursuant to the acquisition order is insufficient to enable all mortgages and charges to be redeemed in their entirety.

Section 32(2) provides that the foregoing provisions will not apply to any mortgage or charge if:

(a) it has been agreed between the landlord and the nominated person or the qualifying tenants in whose favour the acquisition order was made that the landlord's interest should be acquired subject to the charge; or

(b) the court is satisfied either on the application for the acquisition order or on an application made by the person entitled to the benefit of the mortgage or charge, that in the exceptional circumstances of the case it would be fair and reasonable that the landlord's interest should be acquired subject to the mortgage or charge and the court orders accordingly.

13. Restrictions on the court's power to make an acquisition order.
Section 29(5) provides that, even if the court is satisfied that there are
grounds for making an acquisition order, no acquisition order shall
be made

(a) if the premises to which the application for an acquisition order
relates consist of part only of more extensive premises in which the
landlord has an interest; and
(b) the landlord's interest is not reasonably capable of being severed
even if the court were to exclude any part of the premises specified in
the application for an acquisition order as it is empowered to do by
s. 29(4)(*b*).

An example might be a case where a building contains both premises
to which Part III applies and business premises which have been let
by the landlord on terms requiring the landlord to repair the exterior, structure and common parts of the building. If an acquisition
order were made in respect of the premises to which Part III applies
only, problems (which could be insoluble) might arise in agreeing
arrangements with the landlord of the retained business premises. In
such a situation, it would be sensible for the requisite majority of
qualifying tenants to consider if it is possible for them to make an
application for an acquisition order in respect of the whole building.

**14. Discharge of acquisition order/withdrawal by tenants and costs
consequences.** (A) The court may discharge an acquisition order on
the application of the landlord if it is satisfied:

(a) that the nominated person has had a reasonable time within
which to effect the acquisition of the landlord's interest in pursuance
of the order but has not done so; or
(b) that the number of qualifying tenants who desire to proceed with
the acquisition is less than the requisite majority; or
(c) that the premises have ceased to be premises to which Part III
applies, e.g. because a number of flats have become vacant and re-
verted to the landlord and that in consequence the number of flats
held by qualifying tenants has fallen below the number required by
s. 25(2)(c) (s. 34(1)).

Costs consequences. The landlord may recover such costs incurred by
him in connection with the disposal of his interest pursuant to the
acquisition order as the court may determine. (s. 34(4)).

(B) If a notice pursuant to s. 34(2) is served on the landlord by either:
    (*i*) the qualifying tenants who served the s. 27 notice; or

(*ii*) the qualifying tenants who made the application for an acquisition order; or

(*iii*) the nominated person

indicating an intention no longer to proceed with the acquisition of the landlord's interest, the acquisition order will cease to have effect.

Costs consequences

(a) If there are no proceedings pending before the court or the Lands Tribunal, the landlord can recover any costs reasonably incurred by him in connection with the disposal down to the time when the s. 34(2) notice was served. Those costs will include costs incurred by the landlord in connection with any proceedings under Part III but will not include the costs of any proceedings before an LVT: s. 34(5).

(b) If any proceedings are pending before the court or the Lands Tribunal at the time when the notice is served, the landlord can recover such costs incurred by him in connection with the disposal as the court or (as the case may be) the Lands Tribunal may determine. Once again, those costs may include costs incurred by the landlord in connection with any proceedings under Part III but will not include the costs of any proceedings before an LVT: s. 34(4), (5).

(C) If (whether before or after the making of an acquisition order) the nominated person becomes aware that the number of qualifying tenants willing to proceed with the acquisition has fallen below the requisite majority or that the premises have ceased to be premises to which Part III applies, he must serve a notice upon the landlord pursuant to s. 34(3) indicating an intention no longer to proceed with the acquisition and if an acquisition order has been made, it will cease to have effect.

Costs consequences – as set out at **(B)(a)** and **(b)** above.

(D) If at any time when any proceedings are pending before the court or the Lands Tribunal:

(a) the nominated person indicates that he is no longer willing to act before an acquisition order is made, and nobody is nominated in his place; or

(b) the number of qualifying tenants willing to proceed with the acquisition falls below the requisite majority before an acquisition order has been made and without any notice under s. 34(3) having been served by the nominated person; or

(c) the premises cease to be premises to which Part III applies before an acquisition order is made and without any notice under s. 34(3) having been served by the nominated person,

the landlord will be entitled to apply to strike out those proceedings.

Cost consequences
The landlord can recover such costs incurred by him in connection with the disposal as the court or the Lands Tribunal may determine: s. 34(4).

Those costs may include costs incurred by the landlord in connection with any proceedings under Part III but will not include any costs of any proceedings before an LVT: s. 34(5).

NOTES: (1) If the nominated person indicates that he is no longer willing to act after an acquisition order has been made and nobody is nominated in his place (which would require the approval of the court under s. 30(4) in any event) the landlord can presumably apply to the court for discharge of the acquisition order pursuant to s. 34(1)(*a*) (see (A) above). Possibly however, if the nominated person's 'indication' is in writing, it will constitute notice pursuant to s. 34(2) (see (B) above).

(2) If an acquisition order is discharged or ceases to have effect the court may order that any entry relating to the order which has been registered under the Land Charges Act 1972 or the Land Registration Act 1925 shall be cancelled.

15. Liability for the landlord's costs. Any liability for costs arising under s. 34 is the joint and several liability of:

(a) the tenants by whom the s. 27 notice was served if the liability arises before an application for an acquisition order is made; or
(b) the tenants by whom the application was made if the liability arises after an application is made,

together with (in either case) the nominated person: s. 34(6).

If the liability arises after a tenant who was a party to the s. 27 notice or the application for an acquisition order has disposed of his long lease, e.g. by assignment, his successor in title is jointly and severally liable with the other tenants mentioned above and the nominated person for the costs in question: s. 34(7). This provision is designed to overcome any difficulties the landlord might encounter in seeking to recover costs from a former tenant who may be difficult to trace.

16. The court. A county court has jurisdiction to hear and determine any application or question arising under Part III, other than a question falling within the jurisdiction of an LVT (s. 52).

Progress test 25

1. To what premises does Part III of the Act apply? **(3)**

2. Who is a qualifying tenant? **(5)**

3. A building contains 30 flats let to qualifying tenants. What is the requisite majority for the purposes of Part III? **(5)**

4. How long must elapse between the date of service of a s. 27 notice and the date upon which the application for an acquisition order is made to the court? **(6, 7)**

5. Premises to which Part III of the Act applies are in serious need of repair. The landlord is responsible for those repairs but cannot be found. Advise the tenants. **(6, 7)**

6. How are the terms upon which the qualifying tenants acquire the landlord's interest pursuant to an acquisition order determined? **(9, 10)**

7. How must the nominated person apply the consideration payable pursuant to an acquisition order? **(12)**

8. The qualifying tenants of a building which also contains business tenants, wish to apply for an acquisition order. Advise the tenants. **(13)**

9. In what circumstances will an acquisition order cease to have effect? **(14)**

10. What costs are recoverable by a landlord who has been served with a notice pursuant to s. 34(2) at a time when no proceedings are pending and from whom? **(14)**

Part four
Long leases

26
Long residential leases

Landlord and Tenant Act 1954, Part I

1. Generally. Long residential leases have had a varied history as regards statutory protection. They were not excluded from the early Rent Acts but in practice many were outside those Acts because they were at a low rent. Protection was then given by Part I of the Landlord and Tenant Act 1954 to tenants under long leases at a low rent. In 1957, protection under Part I was extended to all long leaseholders irrespective of the rent; this was as a result of the Rent Act 1957 which, at the same time, excluded *all* long leases from the Rent Act protection. The Leasehold Reform Act 1967 restored the pre-1957 position. The position now is that long leases at a low rent are:

(a) outside the Rent Act because they are at a low rent; and
(b) within Part I of the 1954 Act.

The Local Government and Housing Act 1989, s. 186 and Sch. 10 have effect to amend the provisions of Part I and, in particular, to establish assured periodic tenancies (*see* Chapter 21) when such long tenancies came to an end.

2. Tenancies within Part I. In order to fall within the Landlord and Tenant Act 1954, Part I, a tenancy must be one to which s. 1 of the Act applies. By s. 2 of the Act a tenancy is one to which s. 1 applies if it satisfies the following three conditions:

(a) the tenancy must be a long one (*see* **3**);
(b) the rent must be a low rent (*see* **4**);
(c) the tenancy must fulfil 'the qualifying condition' (*see* **5**).

3. A long tenancy. A long tenancy is one granted for a term of years certain exceeding 21 years: s. 2(4). Where a long tenancy comes to an end and the tenant becomes tenant under another tenancy at a low rent, the second tenancy is deemed to be a long one irrespective of its terms: s. 19(1).

Example

T holds under two successive tenancies at low rents from 1950 to 1975 and from 1975 to 1990. The second tenancy is, by s. 19(1), deemed to be a long tenancy because it follows an earlier long tenancy at a low rent.

---

4. At a low rent. In the case of a tenancy granted before 1st April 1990 this expression means a tenancy where the rent payable is less than two-thirds of the rateable value of the property: Landlord and Tenant Act 1954, s. 2(5) as amended by the References to Rating (Housing) Regulations 1990. The rateable value here is that which would be taken as the rateable value for the purposes of the Rent Act 1977, s. 5 (*see* 16: **19**). It must be remembered that in determining whether a long tenancy is at a low rent, there must be disregarded such part of the sums payable by the tenant as is expressed to be payable in respect of rates, services, repairs, maintenance or insurance: *see* s. 5(4) of the 1977 Act and s. 2(7) of the 1954 Act. In the case of a tenancy granted after 1st April 1990 the test is based on prescribed minimum rental values in accordance with s. 5(2A) of the 1977 Act: *see* 16:**19**.

5. The qualifying condition. The qualifying condition is 'that the circumstances (as respects the property comprised in the tenancy, the use of that property, and all other relevant matters) are such that on the coming to an end of the tenancy at that time the tenant would, if the tenancy had not been one at a low rent, be entitled by virtue of the Rent Act to retain possession of the whole or part of the property comprised in the tenancy': Landlord and Tenant Act 1954, s. 2(1). This means that it is necessary to ask whether, if the tenancy were not at a low rent, it would be protected by the Rent Act 1977. There is required a consideration of the matters in 16: **5** *et seq*. The condition must be satisfied as at the 'term date,' that is to say as at the date of expiry of the term of the long tenancy.

If at any time in the last 12 months before the term date, it appears to the landlord that the qualifying condition is not fulfilled, he can apply to the court for an order declaring that the tenancy is not to be treated as one to which Part I applies; s. 2(2). If the court is satisfied that the tenancy is likely, immediately before the term date, to be a tenancy to which s. 1 does not apply, it must make such an order. The effect of such an order is that the tenant loses the protection of Part I as regards that tenancy.

> NOTE: The qualifying condition requires that the rateable value of the dwelling-house fall within the limits prescribed by s. 4 of the 1977 Act: see 16: **12** to **17**. However in the case of a tenancy granted on or after 1st April 1990 there is substituted a formula based on the length of the term and the premium payable: see s. 2(1A) of the 1954 Act as added by the References to Rating (Housing) Regulations 1990.

6. Automatic continuance of tenancies. A tenancy which is current immediately before the term date and is then one to which Part I applies is automatically continued by the Act of 1954, s. 3 until it is ended in accordance with the provisions of Part I. This means that once the tenancy is continued beyond the term date it will carry on until ended by one of the specified methods of termination.

A distinction is made between the situation where the whole of the premises qualifies for protection and that where only a part so qualifies. The 'premises qualifying for protection' means the premises of which, if the tenancy was not a long one at a low rent, the tenant could have retained possession as a statutory tenant under the Rent Act. Where the whole of the premises qualifies for protection, the tenancy continues on the same terms as before. When only a part qualifies for protection, the continuance is in respect of that part only and is at an apportioned rent and, if necessary, on modified terms.

Methods of termination

7. Termination by the tenant. The tenant may end a tenancy to which the Landlord and Tenant Act 1954, s. 1, applies in the following ways:

(a) by surrender: s. 17;
(b) by giving not less than one month's written notice to the immediate landlord to expire at the term date or later: s. 5.

8. Termination of tenancy by the landlord. The landlord may terminate a tenancy to which the Act of 1954, s. 1 applies by a notice given to the tenant. The notice must:

(a) be in the prescribed form (s. 4(1));
(b) specify the date at which the tenancy is to come to an end ('the date of termination'), and this must be the term date or a later date (s. 4(1));
(c) be given not more than twelve nor less than six months before the date of termination specified (s. 4(2));
(d) specify the premises the landlord believes to be, or to be likely to be, the premises qualifying for protection (s. 4(3)).

The notice will take one of two forms:

(a) a landlord's notice proposing a statutory tenancy (s. 4(3)(*a*): *see* **9**); or
(b) a landlord's notice to resume possession (s. 4(3)(*b*): *see* **10**).

9. Landlord's notice proposing a statutory tenancy. A landlord will serve this form of notice when he wishes to bring up to date the terms upon which the tenant holds the premises but does not wish (or is unable) to recover possession. By virtue of the Act of 1954, s. 7(3), the notice must set out the landlord's proposals for the terms of the statutory tenancy:

(a) the premises;
(b) the rent, the amount and the manner of payment;
(c) the responsibility for initial repairs (*see* below),
(d) responsibility for repairs during the statutory tenancy; and
(e) any other terms.

Following the service of the notice the parties will try to agree terms. If they cannot agree the landlord must apply to the county court to have them determined: Act of 1954, s. 7(1). The application must be made not less than two months after service of the notice and not less than two months before the date of termination: s. 7(2), (5). Failure to comply with this requirement renders the notice invalid.

10. Landlord's notice to resume possession. The landlord will serve this form of notice when he wishes to try to recover possession at the end of the long lease or at some time during its continuation under s. 3 (*see* **6**). The notice must:

(a) be in the prescribed form (s. 4(1));
(b) inform the tenant that, if he is not willing to give up possession at the date of termination, the landlord intends to apply to the court for possession on one or more of the grounds specified in s. 12 (s. 4(3)(*b*));

(c) state the ground or grounds on which he proposes to apply (*ibid.*);
(d) invite the tenant to notify the landlord in writing whether he is willing to give up possession at the date of termination (s. 4(4)).

11. Procedure following notice to resume possession. The effect of a notice to resume possession depends upon the tenant's response to it and whether the qualifying condition remains satisfied. The alternatives are:

(a) if the tenant elects to retain possession within the two months, the landlord must apply to court for an order on the ground(s) in his notice: (Act of 1954, s. 13(1)(*a*));
(b) if the tenant does not elect to retain possession but the qualifying condition is satisfied at the end of the two months, the landlord must apply to court (*ibid.* s. 13(1)(*b*));
(c) if the tenant does not elect to retain possession and the qualifying condition is not satisfied at the end of the two months, the landlord can recover possession without having to establish any of the specified grounds.

12. Application to court for possession. In cases (*a*) and (*b*) above the landlord must apply to the court within two months after the tenant elects to retain possession, or if he does not so elect, within four months of serving the notice: s. 13. The grounds upon which he can apply are those specified in the Landlord and Tenant Act 1954, Sch. 3, or, if the landlord is a local authority or other public body, upon a proposal to demolish or to reconstruct the whole or a substantial part of the premises: Act of 1954, s. 12(1).

13. The grounds in Schedule 3. Subject to the necessary modifications, the grounds in the Landlord and Tenant Act 1954, Sch. 3, correspond with Cases 1–9 of the Rent Act 1977, Sch. 15 (*see* Chapter 18).

14. Making a possession order. On an application by the landlord relying on one of the grounds in the Act of 1954, Sch. 3, if the court is satisfied that the ground is established *and* that it is reasonable to make the order, the court must make the order: s. 13(1).

15. Position where landlord does not obtain order for possession. The rules governing this situation are as follows:

(a) if the landlord does not apply to court in the prescribed time his notice to resume possession will be of no more effect: s. 14(2);

(b) if the landlord makes his application but does not get an order, within one month of the final disposal of the matter he may serve a notice proposing a statutory tenancy and specifying as the date of termination a date not less than three months from the date of giving notice: s. 14(3). This is therefore a provision enabling the landlord to serve a short notice proposing a statutory tenancy.

Statutory tenancies

16. Introduction. A statutory tenancy may arise in one of two ways:

(a) following a landlord's notice proposing a statutory tenancy; or
(b) following a landlord's unsuccessful application to court if he then serves notice under s. 14(3) (*see* **15**(*b*) above).

As has already been seen, the terms of the statutory tenancy will be agreed between the parties or, in default of agreement, determined by the court. Until the terms have been so agreed or determined, the long tenancy will continue until the date of termination or three months after the final disposal of the application by the court and any time for appealing has expired: Landlord and Tenant Act 1954, s. 64.

17. The application to the court to determine the terms. If the parties cannot agree the terms, the landlord must apply to court within a certain specified time to have the court determine the terms. By virtue of the Act of 1954, s. 7(2), the application must be made:

(a) during the currency of the notice proposing the statutory tenancy; and
(b) not during the first two months following service of the notice; and
(c) not during the last two months before the date of termination.

In the case of a short notice following a landlord's unsuccessful application to court, the period in which matters have to be agreed is adjusted. The terms must be agreed in the three months beginning with the service of the notice or application made to the court within that time.

18. Terms of the statutory tenancy: repairs. Under a long tenancy, the tenant will normally be responsible for all repairs. At the end of the term there may be considerable repairs necessary. Section 8 of the

1954 Act provides for the parties to agree or, in default the court to decide, terms for the carrying out of 'initial repairs.'

If the landlord is required to do initial repairs, he is entitled to payment from the tenant for doing them if they are required in consequence of failure by the tenant to fulfil his obligations under the former tenancy. The amount to which he is entitled is the cost reasonably incurred by the landlord in ascertaining what repairs are necessary and in carrying them out: s. 8(1).

A tenant can agree to carry out initial repairs, but the court cannot order him to do so unless he gives his consent: s. 9(3).

19. Rent. Until a rent is registered, the rent is the sum agreed between the parties or, in default of agreement, the rent payable under the former long tenancy. Either party may apply to the Rent Officer to have a rent registered.

20. The nature of the statutory tenancy. By virtue of the Act of 1954, s. 6, the statutory tenancy takes effect as a statutory tenancy arising under the Rent Act 1977. When the statutory tenancy commences, any liability of the tenant under the terms of the former tenancy is extinguished except in so far as it is a liability (*a*) for failure to pay rent or rates or to insure or keep insured, or (*b*) in respect of the use of any premises for immoral or illegal purposes, or (*c*) relating to property other than the dwelling-house: s. 10(1). 'Rent' in this context does not include service charge: *Blatherwick* v. *King* (1991). However an obligation to contribute towards the cost of repairing the building of which the dwelling-house is part is preserved by (*c*) above: *Blatherwick* v. *King*.

Miscellaneous provisions

21. Other provisions of Part I. Section 16 of the 1954 Act gives to tenants under long tenancies at a low rent special protection from forfeiture in addition to any rights to relief under the Law of Property Act 1925, s. 146. The special provisions are as follows.

(a) If a landlord seeks to forfeit the lease or seeks damages for breach of covenant when the tenancy has more than seven months to run, if the tenant applies for relief under s. 16, any order for possession or damages will have no effect except as to costs; the tenancy will then take effect as expiring in seven months.

(b) If a landlord seeks to forfeit the lease or seeks damages for breach of covenant when the tenancy has less than seven months to run and the tenant applies for relief, the court cannot make any order for possession or damages.

The effect of these provisions is that the landlord is prevented from forfeiting the lease *but* the operation of Part I is accelerated because in case (*a*) the tenancy is treated as having only seven months to run.

22. Exceptions to s. 16. The provisions of s. 16 do not apply to a failure to comply with any terms as to,

(a) payment of rent or rates or insuring the premises,
(b) immoral or illegal user (Act of 1954, s. 16(4)).

23. Alternative relief. A tenant should be wary of applying for relief under s. 16 for he may be in a better position if he applies for relief from forfeiture under the general law. If a tenant applies under s. 16, the effect is to reduce his contractual term to seven months; if he obtains relief under the general law, his contractual term will continue unaffected and he will simply have to comply with the terms upon which relief was granted.

24. Contracting out. The provisions of Part I apply notwithstanding any agreement to the contrary. There can therefore be no contracting out of the Act.

25. Comparison with Part II. Part II of the 1954 Act applies to business tenancies. It will be seen, however, that there are several similarities between the two Parts. In particular:

(a) the notice procedure for determining the old tenancy and for agreeing or determining the terms of the new tenancy is similar;
(b) both Parts require strict compliance with the time limits and failure to comply with them may deprive the defaulting party of his statutory rights;
(c) the interim continuation provisions of s. 64 apply to both Parts.

26. Local Government and Housing Act 1989. Section 186 of, and Sch. 10 to, this Act have effect to amend the provisions of Part I. In summary, the main amendments are:

(*i*) long residential leases continue until terminated in accordance with the provisions of Sch. 10;
(*ii*) the landlord may terminate the lease by giving notice (*a*) proposing an assured monthly periodic tenancy or (*b*) specifying a ground for recovering possession;

(*iii*) an interim rent may be payable by the tenant;

(*iv*) the tenant may end the lease by giving notice;

(*v*) the rent and terms of the assured periodic tenancy are determined by the rent assessment committee, if not agreed between the parties;

(*vi*) the rent is to be that at which the dwelling-house might be reasonably expected to be let in the open market by a willing landlord under an assured tenancy subject to certain specified assumptions;

(*vii*) the landlord may seek to recover possession on limited grounds only;

(*viii*) the provisions of Sch. 10 apply to long tenancies at a low rent granted after the day appointed for the coming into force of s. 186;

(*ix*) there is a transitional period until 15th January 1999 during which Part I of the 1954 Act continues to apply although not to tenancies falling within (*viii*).

Progress test 26

1. L lets a flat to T:
    (a) for a term of 25 years at a low rent;
    (b) for a term of 22 years at a rack rent;
    (c) for a term of 10 years at a rack rent;
    (d) for a term of 5 years at a low rent.
By which Act is each lease protected? **(3, 4)**

2. What is a long tenancy? **(3)**

3. What is the test to determine if a long tenancy is at a low rent? **(4)**

4. What is the nature of the protection given to a long lease-holder at a low rent? **(4)**

5. What is the qualifying condition? When must it be satisfied? What is the effect if it is not satisfied within the last year before the end of the tenancy? **(5)**

6. How may a tenant end a tenancy protected by Part I of the Landlord and Tenant Act 1954? **(7)**

7. What is the effect of a notice proposing a statutory tenancy? What requirements must it satisfy? **(9)**

8. What steps must
   (a) the landlord, and
   (b) the tenant, take after the service of a notice proposing a statutory tenancy? **(9)**

9. Upon what grounds may a landlord seek to recover possession of a dwelling-house subject to Part I of the Landlord and Tenant Act 1954? **(13)**

10. What is a landlord's notice to resume possession? What requirements must it satisfy? **(10)**

11. What rent is payable by a tenant under a tenancy protected by Part I of the Landlord and Tenant Act 1954? **(19)**

12. What are initial repairs? Whose responsibility are they? **(18)**

13. In what ways do the interim continuation provisions of the Landlord and Tenant Act 1954, s. 64 affect a tenancy protected by Part I of that Act? **(16, 25)**

14. In what ways does Part I of the Landlord and Tenant Act 1954 affect the landlord's right to forfeit a lease for breach of covenant? **(22)**

15. What similarities are there between Parts I and II of the Landlord and Tenant Act 1954? **(25)**

16. What is the effect of Schedule 10 to the Local Government and Housing Act 1989 on Part I of the 1954 Act? **(26)**

The Leasehold Reform Act 1967

Introduction

1. Generally. The Leasehold Reform Act 1967 ('the 1967 Act') enables certain tenants of houses held on long leases at low rents to acquire the freehold of their house or an extended lease of it by the grant of an additional 50-year term. The 1967 Act came into operation on 1st January 1968. The process whereby a tenant may acquire the freehold is called enfranchisement.

The underlying principle of the 1967 Act is that it applies to long leases at a low (or ground) rent which would normally have been granted for a premium payable to the original landlord. In the case of such a lease the Act's approach is to treat the tenant as being the owner of the building, the landlord being left with the land, hence his entitlement to a ground rent only. Thus, when the compensation provisions in the Act are considered (*see* **21**) it will be seen that the landlord receives compensation assessed on the value of the site disregarding the buildings which are on it.

One of the main reasons for the legislation was that in the later part of the nineteenth century many 99-year leases were granted which have been falling in over the last 30 years or so. The Act was intended to alleviate hardship which might otherwise have been caused by the falling in of these leases and which Part I of the Landlord and Tenant Act 1954 was not able fully to deal with.

2. Leasehold Reform, Housing and Urban Development Act 1993. Sections 63 to 75 of this Act amend the 1967 Act. In particular, they amend those provisions concerning (i) the rateable value limits, (ii) tenancies at a low rent and (iii) estate management schemes. The first two changes operate to extend the scope of the Act and the passage of the Bill through Parliament caused some controversy with the owners of large estates such as the Westminster and Cadogan estates in London. However the Act did introduce a limited exception in relation to charitable housing trusts.

3. The scope of this chapter. The 1967 Act as amended contains many complicated and detailed provisions for giving effect to the process of enfranchisement, for dealing with the different situations that may arise and for dealing with the interaction of the 1967 Act with other Acts such as Part I of the Landlord and Tenant Act 1954. This chapter does not attempt to deal with all these matters and simply gives a very broad picture of the Act's operation.

Statutory conditions

4. The right to enfranchisement or extension. Section 1(1) provides that a tenant of a house who satisfies certain conditions has a 'right to acquire on fair terms the freehold or an extended lease of the house and premises.' The conditions are:

(a) the tenant must be tenant of a leasehold house;

(b) his tenancy must be a long tenancy;

(c) the tenancy must be at a low rent;

(d) the rateable value of the house must be within specified limits;

(e) the tenant must satisfy a residential condition.

5. The tenant of a leasehold house. The word house is defined by s. 2(1) as including: 'any building designed or adapted for living in and reasonably so called, notwithstanding that the building is not structurally detached, or was or is not solely designed or adapted for living in, or is divided horizontally into flats or maisonettes; and

(a) where a building is divided horizontally, the flats or other units into which it is so divided are not separate 'houses,' though the building as a whole may be; and

(b) where a building is divided vertically the building as a whole is not a 'house' though any of the units into which it is divided may be.'

The effect of **(a)** is to exclude individual flats from the 1967 Act but an entire building divided into flats may be a house. The effect of **(b)** is to exclude, say, a terrace of houses or a pair of semi-detached houses although each property in the terrace or each semi may be a house.

6. Premises with a mixed commercial and residential use. The House of Lords has decided that since Parliament clearly intended to extend the benefit of the 1967 Act to tenants of premises which were not exclusively designed or adapted for living in for residential purposes, it is only in exceptional circumstances that a judge will be justified in holding that a building designed or adapted for occupation as a residence is not a house for the purposes of the 1967 Act: *Tandon v. Trustees of Spurgeons Homes* (1982). This means that in all but the most exceptional circumstances, business premises with integral residential premises will be within the 1967 Act.

7. House and premises. In parts of the 1967 Act reference is made to the 'house and premises.' For example, under s. 1(1), the tenant has the right to acquire the freehold or an extended lease of 'the house and premises.' The reference to premises is to be taken as referring to any garage, outhouse, garden, yard and appurtenances which at the relevant time are let to him with the house and are occupied with the house and used for the purposes of the house: s. 2(3).

8. A long tenancy. A long tenancy means one granted for a term of years certain exceeding 21 years: s. 3. The following points should be noted:

(a) A tenancy terminable before the end of such a term by notice given by or to the tenant or by re-entry or forfeiture or otherwise is, notwithstanding these matters, a long tenancy: s. 3(1).

(b) Where a tenant under a long tenancy at a low rent takes a new tenancy of the same property or part of it at the end of the long tenancy, the new tenancy is deemed to be a long one irrespective of its terms: s. 3(2).

(c) Where a tenant under a long tenancy takes another long tenancy of the same property or part of it at the end of the long one, the two long tenancies are treated as a single one running from the start of the first to the end of the second: s. 3(3).

(d) Where a tenancy is granted for 21 years or less, but there is a covenant for renewal, without payment of a premium, and the tenancy is or has been once more renewed so as to bring the total of the term to more than 21 years, the 1967 Act applies as it would if the term originally granted had been one exceeding 21 years: s. 3(4).

> NOTES: (1) It is important to remember that the term must *exceed* 21 years; this means that a term of 21 years will *not* be within the Act.
> (2) Before 1980 one way of avoiding the 1967 Act was to grant a tenancy terminable by notice after a death or marriage so that it was not a long tenancy: sometimes called a 'Prince of Wales' clause. The 1980 Act prevented such devices in future leases. The 1993 Act prevented it in relation to pre-1980 leases: see s. 1B of the 1967 Act added by s. 64 of the 1993 Act.

9. At a low rent. This requirement is designed to limit the leases to which the Act applies to those at a ground rent only. It does this by

s. 4(1), which provides that a tenancy of any property entered into before 1st April 1990 is at a low rent at any time when the annual rent is less than two-thirds of the rateable value of the property on the appropriate day or, if later, the first day of the term. The 'appropriate day' here means 23rd March 1965 or such later date as the house first appeared in the valuation list: s. 4(1)(a). 'Rent' in this context means the rent reserved disregarding any part of the rent expressed to be payable for services to be provided or for repairs, maintenance or insurance to be effected by the landlord. In the case of a tenancy entered into on or after 1st April 1990, it is a tenancy at a low rent at any time when rent is not payable under the tenancy at a yearly rate of more than £1,000 if the property is in Greater London or more than £250 if the property is elsewhere: see s. 4(1) as amended by the References to Rating (Housing) Regulations 1990.

10. The proviso to s. 4(1). There is a proviso to s. 4(1) to the effect that, in the case of a tenancy created between the end of August 1939 and the beginning of April 1963, the tenancy will not be regarded as being one at a low rent if, at its commencement, the rent payable was more than two-thirds of the letting value of the property. This rule does not apply to building leases. The proviso is intended to benefit the landlord and to cover those cases where it might be said that the rateable value on the appropriate day was not a fair indication of the letting value of the house at the start of the tenancy. When any question arises on the operation of the proviso, s. 1(5) provides that it must be presumed in the tenant's favour that the proviso does not apply. This means that it will be for the landlord to bring evidence to prove that the letting value of the property was such that the tenancy should not be regarded as being at a low rent.

11. The time at which there must be a low rent. The above requirement of a low rent must be satisfied for the three years prior to the claim and at the time the claim is made: Act of 1967, s. 1(1).

12. Alternative rent limits. The 1993 Act added an alternative rent limit which applies where a tenancy is not a tenancy at a low rent in accordance with the above provisions: see s. 1A(2) of the 1967 Act added by s. 63 of the 1993 Act. The alternative rent limit is contained in s. 4A of the 1967 Act added by s. 65 of the 1993 Act. The effect of s. 4A is that a tenancy is a tenancy at a low rent if during its first year the rent payable did not exceed a particular figure. There are effectively five classes of tenancy to be considered under these alternative rent limits:

(1) Those entered into before 1st April 1963 where the figure is two-thirds of the 'letting value' (see **10** above) of the house.

(2) Those entered into between 1st April 1963 and 1st March 1990 where the figure is two-thirds of the rateable value on the commencement of the tenancy or, if later, the date on which the house first had a rateable value.

(3) Those entered into after 31st March 1990 in pursuance of a contract made before 1st April 1990 where the figure is as in (2) above.

(4) Other tenancies in Greater London where the figure is £1,000.

(5) Other tenancies outside Greater London where the figure is £250.

13. The rateable value of the house must be within specified limits. The following rules apply where the tenancy was created before 1st April 1990:

(a) The rateable value of the house and premises on the appropriate day (*see* **8**) must not have exceeded £200 (in Greater London, £400): s. 1(1)(*a*).

(b) Where the appropriate day is on or after 1st April 1973:

(*i*) in the case of a tenancy created on or before 18th February 1966, the rateable value must not have exceeded £750 (in Greater London, £1,500); and

(*ii*) in the case of a tenancy created after 18th February 1966, the rateable value must not have exceeded £500 (in Greater London, £1,000).

If in relation to any house

(*i*) the appropriate day fell before 1st April 1973; and

(*ii*) the rateable value on that day exceeded £200 (in Greater London, £400); and

(*iii*) the tenancy was created on or before 18th February 1966; for the purposes of rule (*a*) above, it has effect as if for the sums of £200 (and £400) there were substituted £750 (and £1,500) and for the reference to the appropriate day there were substituted a reference to 1st April 1973.

14. Value in case of tenancy granted on or after 1st April 1990. In the case of a tenancy granted on or after 1st April 1990 the test of value is determined by a mathematical formula concerning the relationship between the premium and the term: see s. 1(1)(a) as amended by References to Rating (Housing) Regulations 1990.

15. Rateable value limits and the 1993 Act. Where the only matter preventing enfranchisement is that the rateable value is too high,

s. 1A(1), added by s. 63 of the 1993 Act, provides that the tenant shall have the right to enfranchise as if the rateable value limit were not exceeded. This means that if a tenant falls outside the limits set out above, he has a right to enfranchise under s. 1A(1) if he fulfils the other conditions.

16. Adjustment of rateable values. By s. 1(4A) of the 1967 Act a tenant may take action to have his property's rateable value adjusted for the purposes of the 1967 Act. This provision applies where the tenant or any previous tenant has made, or contributed to the cost of, any improvements to the premises, provided the improvement amounts to a structural alteration, extension of or addition to the premises. The procedure is for the tenant to serve notice requiring the landlord to agree to a reduction (for the purposes of the 1967 Act only). In default of agreement the county court may determine the matter. The effect of such a national reduction may be to bring premises within the Act which would not otherwise be within it. Despite the amendments made by the 1993 Act (see **15** above) this procedure may still be relevant as it may affect the method of valuation to be relied upon.

Pearlman v. *Harrow School* (1979). T held a long lease at a low rent of a house in London. He removed old style central heating and replaced it by a modern system which was connected to the walls and whose pipes ran through the walls, floors and ceilings to a tank in the roof. When installed the pipes could not be removed. The improvement led to an increase in the rateable value to £1,597 (outside the limits: *see* **11**). T applied to L for their agreement to a reduction under s. 1(4A) to £1,487 on the grounds that the central heating system was an improvement within these provisions. L did not agree and an application was made to the county court. On appeal to the Court of Appeal, it was HELD: that the central heating system, by affecting and being connected to the fabric of the house, was a structural alteration or addition to the house. This meant that the rateable value would be notionally reduced for the purposes of the 1967 Act and that T was entitled to enfranchise.

17. The residential condition. At the time of giving notice of his claim, the tenant must have been occupying the house as his residence for the last three years or for periods amounting to three years in the last ten years: s. 1(1)(*b*) (as amended by the Housing Act 1980, s. 141, Sch. 21). In each case whether this condition is satisfied will be a question of fact. Section 1(2) provides that references to a 'tenant occupying a house as his residence' must be construed as applying where the tenant is, in right of the tenancy, occupying it as his only or main residence, whether or not he uses it also for other purposes. So a holiday home would not come within the Act. It is also provided by s. 1(2)(*a*) that references to 'a person occupying' apply where he occupies it in part only. So, where a tenant occupied a basement flat of a house and the upper floors were sub-let as separate flats, it was HELD by the Court of Appeal that the condition was satisfied: *Harris* v. *Swick Securities* (1969).

> NOTE: Section 37(1) provides that no reference to 'a person occupying property as his residence' is to be taken to extend to any occupation by a company or other artificial person. This means that a company or other artificial person cannot claim the benefit of the 1967 Act.

Procedure for enfranchisement

18. Exercise of the right: the tenant's notice. A tenant may exercise his rights under the Act by serving on the landlord notice of his desire to have the freehold or an extended lease of his house. The notice must be in the prescribed form and must contain particulars of his claim and the way in which he claims to satisfy the conditions.

19. Landlord's counter-notice. Where a tenant gives notice of his desire to have the freehold or an extended lease, the landlord must within two months give the tenant notice in reply in the prescribed form stating whether he admits the tenant's right and, if he does not, the grounds on which it is not admitted.

20. Enfranchisement. Where a tenant has a right to acquire the freehold and he gives to the landlord a written notice of his desire to have it, except as is provided by the Act, the landlord is bound to make to the tenant, and the tenant to accept, a grant of the house and premises in fee simple absolute: s. 8(1). Where notice is served, the rights and obligations of the landlord and tenant arising from the notice enure for the benefit of and are enforceable against them as rights and obligations arising under a contract for a sale freely entered into between the landlord and the tenant: s. 5(1). This means that if either party fails to perform his part of the bargain the other will have the ordinary contractual rights and remedies.

21. Purchase price. By virtue of s. 9(1) the price to be paid by the tenant for the freehold enfranchisement is the amount which at the date of the tenant's notice, the house and premises might be expected to realise if sold in the open market by a willing seller, with the tenant and members of his family who reside in the house not buying or seeking to buy, and on the following bases:

(a) that it is being sold subject to the tenancy but on the assumption that the Act confers no right to acquire the freehold but that the tenancy has been extended under the Act, unless it already has been extended: s. 9(1)(*a*);
(b) that it is being sold subject to the same rent charges as in the sale to the tenant: s. 9(1)(*b*);
(c) that it is being sold subject to the same rights and burdens as in the sale to the tenant: s. 9(1)(*c*).

The aim of these provisions is to produce a price that will reflect the value of the site or ground alone. This is in accordance with the general philosophy behind the Act (*see* 1). If the parties are unable to agree the price it will be determined by the Leasehold Valuation Tribunal.

In *Jones* v. *Wrotham Park Settled Estates* (1979), a landlord was able to obtain an artificially increased price by a complicated transaction involving the creation of an interest superior to the purchasing tenant's interest. The effect of the decision has been negated as regards such transactions made after 15th February 1979 by the terms of the Leasehold Reform Act 1979. Section 1(1) provides that as against a tenant in possession claiming under the Act of 1967, s. 8, the price payable on a conveyance for giving effect to that section may not be made less favourable by reference to any transaction since 15th February 1979 involving the creation or transfer of an interest superior to (whether or not preceding) his own, or any alteration since that date of the terms on which such an interest is held.

22. Purchase price; alternative method. By virtue of s. 9(1A), where the rateable value of the house and premises is above £1,000 in Greater London or £500 elsewhere on 31st March 1991 or, if it had no rateable value on that date, if the value by applying the formula in s. 1(1)(a) (see **14** above) exceeds £16,333, there is a different method of determining the price which is as follows. The price is to be the amount which at the relevant time the house and premises, if sold in the open market by a willing seller, might be expected to realise on the following bases:

(a) that the vendor is selling an estate in fee simple, subject to the tenancy, but on the assumption that the 1967 Act conferred no right to acquire the freehold;
(b) that at the end of the tenancy the tenant has the right to remain

in possession of the house and premises under the provisions of Part I of the Landlord and Tenant Act 1954;

(c) that the tenant has no liability to carry out any repairs, maintenance or redecorations under the terms of the tenancy or Part I of the Landlord and Tenant Act 1954;

(d) that the price be diminished by the extent to which the value of the house and premises has been increased by any improvement carried out by the tenant or his predecessors in title at their own expense;

(e) that (subject to **(a)** above) the vendor was selling subject, in respect of rentcharges, to the same annual charge as the conveyance to the tenant is to be subject to, but the purchaser would otherwise be effectively exonerated until the termination of the tenancy from any liability or charge in respect of tenant's incumbrances; and

(f) that (subject to **(a)** and **(b)** above) the vendor was selling with and subject to the rights and burdens with and subject to which the conveyance to the tenant is to be made.

23. Purchase price: further alternative method. In a case where the right to acquire the freehold arises by virtue of the provisions introduced by the 1993 Act the price shall be determined in accordance with s. 9(1A) but in addition under ss. 9(1C) and 9A respectively there is payable:

(a) not more than 50% of the 'marriage value', i.e. value arising by virtue of the coalescence of the freehold and leasehold interests; and

(b)(*i*) compensation for the diminution in value of any interest of the landlord in other property resulting from the acquisition of his interest in the house and

(*ii*) any other loss or damage which results therefrom to the extent that it is referable to his ownership of any interest in other property.

In **(b)**(*ii*) above the kinds of loss falling within that provision include loss of development value in relation to the house: s. 9A(3).

24. The tenant's right to withdraw. On ascertaining the amount payable as the price for the house, the tenant may give written notice to the landlord that he is unable or unwilling to acquire the house at the price he must pay: s. 9(3). The effect is that the notice of desire to have the freehold ceases to have effect and the tenant cannot give any further notice for the following three years: *ibid.*

25. Extended lease. Where a tenant of a house has a right to an extended lease and gives to the landlord written notice of his desire to have it, then except as is provided by the Act, the landlord is bound to grant to the tenant and the tenant to accept in substitution for the existing lease a new lease of the house and premises for a term expiring 50 years after the term date of the existing tenancy: s. 14(1). By s. 5(1), where a tenant has given notice, the rights of the landlord and tenant arising from the notice enure for the benefit of and are enforceable against them to the same extent as rights and obligations arising under a contract for a lease freely entered into between the landlord and the tenant.

26. The rent under the new tenancy. There are detailed provisions for determining the rent payable under the new tenancy from what would have been the expiry of the old tenancy. In summary, the rent is to be an up-to-date ground rent – that is the letting value of the site for the use to which the house is put but without the buildings there. It is calculated by reference to the values prevailing on the date it is first to be paid, i.e. the expiry date of the old tenancy. This means that the rent will have to be calculated in the year preceding the expiry date. There is also provision for re-assessment of the ground rent after 25 years to bring it up to date with market trends: Act of 1967, s. 15(2).

27. Exclusion of further rights. When a tenancy has been extended under s. 14, the right to acquire the freehold can still be exercised but only by notice given not later than the expiry date of the old tenancy. Also there is no right to a further extension. At the end of an extended term the protection of the Landlord and Tenant Act 1954 will not be available to the tenant under the extended lease.

28. Landlord's overriding rights. There are two main situations where a landlord may have rights which exclude the tenant's rights under the Act. They are as follows.

(a) Where a tenancy has been extended under s. 14, the landlord may at any time not earlier than a year before the original term date of the tenancy (i.e. the date at which the old tenancy would have expired), apply to the court for an order that he may resume possession of the property on the ground that for purposes of redevelopment he proposes to demolish or reconstruct the whole or a substantial part of the house and premises. If the court is satisfied that the landlord has established this ground it must make an order and the tenant will be entitled to compensation: s. 17.

(b) Where the tenant has a right to acquire the freehold or an extended lease and has given notice of his desire but no effect has been given to it and the landlord purchased his interest, or it was created, before 18th February 1966, the landlord may apply to the court for an order that he may resume possession on the ground that it is required by him for the only or main residence of himself or an adult member of his family: s. 18. If the court is satisfied that the landlord has established this ground it must make an order for possession but the tenant is entitled to compensation.

29. Exceptions to the right to enfranchise. There are various exceptions to the right to enfranchise. Not all are set out here but they include the following.

(a) Certain long tenancies held from public authorities complying with specified conditions: para. 2 of Sch. 4A to the 1967 Act added by the Housing and Planning Act 1986.

(b) Certain long tenancies granted by housing associations: para. 3 of Sch. 4A.

(c) Shared ownership leases granted under Part V of the Housing Act 1985: para. 1 of Sch. 4A.

(d) Certain leases for the elderly granted by a registered housing association: para. 4 of Sch. 4A.

(e) Leases granted under the 'right to buy'.

(f) National Trust Land.

(g) Crown land.

(h) Leases granted by charitable housing trusts after the commencement of the 1993 Act amendments: s. 1(3) of the 1967 Act.

(i) Leases granted by charitable housing trusts before the commencement of the 1993 Act amendments but otherwise enfranchisable due to the new ss. 1A and 1B: see s. 1(3A) of the 1967 Act.

Miscellaneous matters

30. Sub-tenants. There are special provisions in the 1967 Act, Sch. 1, which deal with the situation where the tenant entitled to enfranchise is a sub-tenant. The effect of these is that it is the person in possession who will be entitled to enfranchise, and the purchase money will be divided between the owners of intermediate tenancies and the freeholder.

The way the Act works is that one person, called the reversioner, acts for the owners of all interests above the tenant in possession. The owner of the first leasehold interest up the chain who has an expectation of possession of 30 years or more is the reversioner. If no leaseholder satisfies this test, it is the freeholder. The reversioner has the power to execute the conveyance of the freehold to the claimant.

31. Court proceedings. If any dispute arises between the parties there is provision for determination of such disputes by the courts. In summary, matters of valuation will generally be decided by a Leasehold Valuation Tribunal while matters of law will be decided by the county court.

The High Court (Chancery Division) has jurisdiction in relation to matters concerning schemes of management and the procedure where the landlord cannot be found. Thus disputed claims to an entitlement to acquire the freehold or an extended lease will be adjudicated on by the county court. Issues concerning the price will be decided by a Leasehold Valuation Tribunal (*see* the Act of 1967, ss. 20,21 and the Housing Act 1980, s. 142, Sch. 22).

The members of a Leasehold Valuation Tribunal are, in fact, the same persons as sit on the rent assessment committee, though their functions are different: *see* the Housing Act 1980, s. 142(2), and **29** below.

32. Schemes of management. Many large estates, such as the Grosvenor Estate in London, depend on leasehold covenants to maintain the high standard of the estate. These covenants give the landlord extensive control over the properties on the estate. The Act interferes with this by allowing enfranchisement which removes the control by covenants. Section 19 of the Act provides for a scheme of management which may enable the old landlord to retain some control over the properties formerly in the ownership of an estate. This applies to areas where all the houses are held under one head landlord. The Minister may certify that, in order to maintain adequate standards of appearance and amenity and regulate development in the area, in the event of tenants acquiring the landlord's interest in their houses, it is in the Minister's opinion likely to be in the general interest that the landlord should retain powers of management in respect of the houses. The next step is for the High Court, on an application made within one year of the giving of the certificate, to approve a scheme giving the landlord such powers and rights as are covered by s. 19 as the court thinks fair and practicable. The matters covered by s. 19 include:

(a) regulation of development, use or appearance of the properties;
(b) power to carry out repairs in or to any property;
(c) obligations on those interested in the properties to maintain them;
(d) inspection of the property.

If a scheme is approved its provisions are enforceable against persons who have acquired the freehold of their houses. By this means the general benefit of identical leasehold covenants – a sort of local law – can be preserved in the interests of all.

33. Enforcement of a scheme. A scheme when approved is to be registered under the Local Land Charges Act 1975 as a local land charge. It then binds those who later occupy or hold an interest in the property as if they had covenanted with the landlord to be bound by the scheme.

34. Estate management schemes. This is a scheme to enable a landlord or certain public bodies to retain powers of management in respect of, and rights against, houses and premises which the landlord may be required to sell as a result of the 1993 Act. It is a scheme approved by a Leasehold Valuation Tribunal for an area occupied directly or indirectly under leases held under one landlord: s. 69 of the 1993 Act. The scheme may make provision:

(a) regulating the redevelopment, use or appearance of property;
(b) empowering the landlord to maintain, repair or renew such property;
(c) imposing obligations to maintain, repair or renew on those occupying or interested in such property;
(d) permitting inspection of the property: s. 69(3).

Once approved the scheme is a local land charge and registrable as such. Any acquisition under the 1993 Act will take effect subject to its provisions: s. 70 of the 1993 Act.

35. Procedure for making scheme. Within specified time limits application must be made to a Leasehold Valuation Tribunal for approval of a scheme. The limit is generally within two years of the relevant provisions of the 1993 Act coming into force: s. 70(1). There are two exceptions, namely (1) where the Secretary of State consents to an out of time application and (2) applications within conservation areas. The tribunal must have regard primarily to the benefits likely to result from the scheme to the area as a whole and to the extent to which it is reasonable to impose obligations on those acquiring the landlord's interest: s. 70(3). But the tribunal must also have regard to the past development and present character of the area and to architectural or historical considerations, to neighbouring areas and to the circumstances generally: s. 70(3). In certain circumstances, particular public bodies may make an application: s. 73. There are complex provisions in s. 74 dealing with the interaction between pending applications to the tribunal and claims to enfranchise. These are outside the scope of this book.

36. Missing landlords. By virtue of the 1967 Act, s. 27, where a tenant of a house has a right to acquire the freehold but is prevented from giving notice because the person to be served cannot be found or his identity cannot be ascertained, on an application to the High Court, the court may make an order the effect of which will be to vest the freehold in the tenant as if he had given notice. The procedure is that the tenant must show that all reasonable efforts have been made to find the landlord or to ascertain his identity. The court then will cause a conveyance to be executed and the tenant must pay into court the sum a surveyor selected by the court certifies to be a fair price for the freehold calculated in accordance with s. 9. The money in court will be held to the account of the missing person in case he should be found.

37. Leasehold Valuation Tribunal. Prior to the Housing Act 1980, the Lands Tribunal had jurisdiction to deal with disputes relating to prices, rents, values, etc. arising out of the 1967 Act. The 1980 Act transferred that jurisdiction to Leasehold Valuation Tribunals. They are actually rent assessment committees undertaking different functions. An appeal lies against the decision of a Leasehold Valuation Tribunal to the Lands Tribunal: Housing Act 1980, s. 142, Sch. 22, para. 2.

Progress test 27

1. To what tenancies does the Leasehold Reform Act 1967 apply? **(4)**

2. What is a 'house' for the purposes of the 1967 Act? **(5)**

3. What policy underlies the 1967 Act? **(1)**

4. Can a tenant enfranchise when he has a lease of mixed premises? **(6)**

5. What is a long tenancy for the purposes of the 1967 Act? **(8)**

6. What is the effect of the proviso to s. 4(1)? How does it operate in favour of the landlord? **(10)**

7. What are the rateable value limits for the purposes of the 1967 Act? How may they take account of structural alterations? **(12 to 16)**

8. T has a house in the country where he spends his weekends and a flat in London where he spends his working week. Can T enfranchise either of his leases of these properties? **(17)**

9. How does a tenant exercise, and a landlord oppose, his right to enfranchise? **(18, 19)**

10. How is the purchase price for the freehold calculated under the 1967 Act? **(21 to 23)**

11. Is a tenant bound to purchase the freehold once he has given notice? **(24)**

12. When is a tenant entitled to an extended lease under the 1967 Act? **(25)**

13. What is the rent payable under an extended lease? **(26)**

14. What is the effect upon the tenant's rights of the court ordering an extended lease? **(27)**

15. When may a landlord resist a tenant's application to enfranchise? **(28)**

16. Which courts or tribunals are involved in the resolution of disputes under the 1967 Act? **(31)**

17. What is a scheme of management? How is it enforced? **(32, 33)**

18. T holds a long lease at a low rent of his house. He wishes to enfranchise but cannot locate his landlord. Advise T on what steps he may take to enfranchise. **(36)**

19. What are the effects of the amendments made by the 1993 Act?

Part five
Agricultural tenancies

28

Agricultural holdings

Introduction

1. Generally. Tenants of agricultural holdings have been the subject of a number of Acts since 1875. The earlier Acts were concerned with compensation. Now, tenants are given protection both as regards compensation and security of tenure. The principal Act today is the Agricultural Holdings Act 1986. In this and the following chapters these abbreviations are generally used:

(a) 'the 1986 Act': Agricultural Holdings Act 1986;
(b) 'the Minister': the Minister of Agriculture;
(c) 'the Tribunal': the Agricultural Land Tribunal.

Unless otherwise stated, all references are to the 1986 Act.

2. Outline. It is proposed to deal with this subject in the following way:

(a) definition of an agricultural holding (*see* **3–6**);
(b) the obligations and terms of tenancies of agricultural holdings (*see* **7–13**);
(c) compensation (*see* Chapter 29);
(d) security of tenure and contracting out (*see* Chapter 30).

Definitions

3. Agricultural holding. Section 1 defines an 'agricultural holding' as 'the aggregate of the land (whether agricultural land or not) comprised in a contract of tenancy which is a contract for an agricultural tenancy, not being a contract under which the said land is let to the tenant during his continuance in any official appointment or employment held under the landlord.' This definition comprises the following main elements:

(a) a contract of tenancy;
(b) which is a contract for an agricultural tenancy.

4. Contract of tenancy. The expression 'contract of tenancy' is defined as a letting of land, or agreement for letting land, for a term of years or from year to year: s. 1(5). This definition is extended by the operation of s. 2(2) which provides that where any land is let, or a licence is granted to occupy land, for use as agricultural land for an interest less than a tenancy from year to year, in circumstances which otherwise would make the land an agricultural holding, then the agreement takes effect as if it were a tenancy from year to year. The effect of this provision is that tenancies less than from year to year and licences to use land as agricultural land are converted into tenancies from year to year.

5. A contract for an agricultural tenancy. A contract of tenancy relating to any land is a contract for an agricultural tenancy if, having regard to (*a*) the terms of the tenancy, (*b*) the actual or contemplated use of the land at the time of the conclusion of the contract and subsequently, and (*c*) any other relevant circumstances, the whole of the land comprised in the contract, subject to such exceptions only as do not substantially affect the character of the tenancy, is let for use as agricultural land: s. 1(2). In considering whether a contract which was not originally one for an agricultural tenancy has subsequently become one, there must be disregarded any use in breach of the terms of the tenancy unless the landlord has permitted, consented or acquiesced in it: s. 1(3).

The expression 'agricultural land' means land used for agriculture and which is so used for the purposes of a trade or business: s. 1(4). The word 'agriculture' includes horticulture, fruit-growing, seed-growing, dairy farming and livestock breeding and keeping, the use of land as grazing land, meadow land, osier land, market gardens and nursery grounds, and the use of land for woodlands when that use is ancillary to the farming of land for other agricultural purposes: s. 96(1).

6. Grazing and mowing agreements. There are two exceptions to the sweeping effect of s. 2(1). First, by s. 2(3)(*a*) lettings of land or licences to occupy land made only for the purpose of grazing or mowing during a specified part of the year are not converted into tenancies from year to year. So, for example, a grazing or mowing agreement for 364 days out of a year, or a lesser period out of a year, will not be converted. This is important because it means that these agreements are outside the protection of the Act. Secondly, by s. 2(3)(*b*), an agreement for the letting of land, or the granting of a licence to occupy land, by a person whose interest in the land is less than a tenancy from year to year and cannot take effect as such a tenancy by virtue of s. 2(1), is exempt from the operation of s. 2(1).

The parties' obligations

7. At common law and by custom. By reason of the peculiar nature of agricultural lettings there have always been special rules concerning the parties' rights and obligations which do not apply to other lettings. In particular, at common law a tenant of a farm is under an implied obligation to use the farm in a husband-like manner in accordance with the 'custom of the country.' This means the customs which are prevalent throughout an area and which have existed for a reasonable period.

8. Provisions for security written tenancy agreements. The parties' obligations will normally be regulated by the terms of the tenancy agreement. Where there is no written agreement, the Act contains provisions which, if the parties take advantage of them, will secure a written agreement. In particular, s. 6(1) provides that where there is not in force in respect of an agricultural holding any written agreement embodying the terms of the tenancy, or there is such an agreement but it lacks any of the matters specified in Sch. 1 (*see* **9**), the landlord or the tenant may require the other party to enter into such an agreement, and in default of agreement he may refer the terms of the tenancy to arbitration.

9. Matters for which provision is to be made in a written tenancy agreement. Schedule 1 prescribes the matters for which provision is to be made in a written agreement. The matters include:

(a) the names of the parties;
(b) particulars of the holding;
(c) the term;
(d) the rent and when it is payable;
(e) liability for rates;
(f) a covenant by one party to maintain and repair fixed equipment.

10. Prescribed terms. By s. 7(3) there are incorporated into all contracts of tenancy of agricultural holdings (except in so far as liability for such matters is imposed by a written agreement on the other party) certain prescribed terms concerning the maintenance, repair and insurance of fixed equipment. The relevant regulations are the Agriculture (Maintenance, Repair and Insurance of Fixed Equipment) Regulations 1973 as amended. In summary, the effect of these regulations is to cast on the landlord the responsibility of repairing the structure of the various buildings, of insuring and reinstating them and of painting the exterior of the buildings every five years. Also, they cast on the tenant the responsibility of repairing the buildings in so far as the landlord is not bound to repair them, to paint the interior every seven years and to maintain the fences, hedges, walls stiles, gates and similar items. Finally, they provide for the other party to do repairs and recover their cost when the party who is bound to do them fails to execute them.

11. Rent. The parties are free to agree the rent payable. This is, however, subject to s. 12, which provides that either party may require the rent to be determined by arbitration. Sch. 2 provides that the arbitrator will determine the rent at which the holding might reasonably be expected to be let by a prudent and willing landlord to a prudent and willing tenant taking into account all relevant factors including the terms of the tenancy, the character and situation of the holding, the productive capacity of the holding and its related earning capacity and the current level of rents for comparable lettings, but disregarding any effect on rent of:

(a) tenant's improvements or fixed equipment other than those executed or provided under an obligation imposed on the tenant by the terms of his contract of tenancy,
(b) landlord's improvements in so far as the landlord has received grants in respect of the execution thereof,
(c) the fact that the tenant who is a party to the arbitration is in occupation of the holding,

(d) any dilapidations, damage or deterioration caused or permitted by the tenant.

If the arbitrator considers that the existing rent is the rent properly payable, he will direct that the rent should continue unchanged.

12. Effect of determination of rent. Where the arbitrator determines a rent, or directs that the rent shall stay unchanged or the parties agree a rent, the position is as follows.

Once a rent has been fixed, whether by agreement or by arbitration, then (except in the case of a tenancy for a fixed term) that rent will continue for the next three years and cannot be varied for three years from either the start of the tenancy or the date of the last variation or the date of the last direction by the arbitrator that the rent should continue unchanged: Sch 2. In the case of a fixed term tenancy, the rent will stay the same for the duration of the term unless there is provision for its review in the terms of the tenancy.

13. Increase of rent for certain landlord's improvements. Section 13(1) provides that where a landlord has carried out certain improvements to the holding, he is entitled to an increase in the rent. The relevant improvements include those carried out,

(a) at the request of, or in agreement with, the tenant; or
(b) in pursuance of directions given by the Tribunal under s. 11 (which deals with the provision of fixed equipment necessary to comply with statutory requirements);
(c) in compliance with a direction given by the Minister.

Progress test 28

1. What is meant by an agricultural holding? **(3)**

2. Which is the main Act governing the law relating to agricultural holdings? **(1)**

3. Which of the following constitutes 'agriculture': (*a*) a fishery; (*b*) a market garden; (*c*) a forest? **(5)**

4. What contracts come within the expression 'contract for an agricultural tenancy' as used in the Agricultural Holdings Act 1986? **(5)**

5. What are grazing and mowing agreements? **(6)**

6. How may a party to an oral tenancy of an agricultural holding secure a written agreement?   **(8)**

7. What matters may be dealt with in such a written agreement?   **(9)**

8. What are the 'prescribed terms'?   **(10)**

9. What rent is payable under a tenancy of an agricultural holding? **(11)**

Compensation on the termination of the tenancy

1. Generally. At the end of a tenancy when the tenant quits, both parties may be entitled to compensation in respect of certain matters. In this chapter first the landlord's rights are considered and then the tenant's rights.

The landlord's rights

2. Deterioration of a particular part of the holding. The landlord of an agricultural holding is entitled to recover compensation from a tenant of the holding, on the tenant's quitting the holding on the termination of the tenancy, in respect of the dilapidation or deterioration of, or damage to, any part of the holding or anything in or on the holding which is caused by non-fulfilment by the tenant of his responsibilities to farm in accordance with the rules of good husbandry: s. 71. The amount of compensation payable is the cost, as at the date of quitting, of making good the dilapidation, deterioration or damage: provided that in no case shall the compensation exceed the amount, if any, by which the landlord's reversion is diminished owing to the dilapidation, deterioration or damage: s. 71(2) and (5). In lieu of claiming compensation under s. 71(1), the landlord may claim compensation under the terms of the tenancy at the end of the tenancy: but again subject to the limitation that it shall not exceed the diminution in value of the landlord's reversion: s. 71(3) and (4). This provision therefore gives the landlord a choice between his ordinary remedies under the tenancy and a special statutory claim.

3. General deterioration of the holding. Where, on the quitting of the holding by the tenant, on the termination of the tenancy, the landlord shows that the value of the holding generally has been reduced by non-fulfilment by the tenant of his responsibilities to farm in accordance with the rules of good husbandry, he is entitled to recover from the tenant compensation equal to the decrease in value of the holding attributable to the dilapidation, deterioration or damage: s. 72.

The tenant's rights

4. Disturbance. Section 60 makes provision for the payment of disturbance compensation to a tenant. It is payable when either:

(a) the landlord gives notice to quit; or
(b) the tenant gives counter-notice to a notice to quit part given by the landlord;

and in consequence of the notice or counter-notice the tenant quits the holding.

Disturbance compensation is 'basic compensation' and 'additional compensation'. Neither compensation is, however, payable when the landlord serves notice to quit and relies successfully on Cases C to G: (*see* 30:**9** *et seq.*)

5. The amount of basic disturbance compensation. Section 60(3) provides that the amount of **basic** compensation payable is the amount of the loss or expense directly attributable to the quitting of the holding which is unavoidably incurred by the tenant upon or in connection with the sale or removal of his household goods, implements of husbandry, fixtures, farm produce or stock on or used in connection with the holding and any expenses reasonably incurred by him in the preparation of his claim. Alternatively, the tenant can claim as compensation an amount equal to one year's rent at the rate at which rent was payable immediately before the end of the tenancy without proof of loss or damage. If the tenant makes his claim under the first method, he is not entitled to compensation in excess of two years' rent of the holding. Where the tenant claims under the first method he must give the landlord (*a*) a reasonable opportunity of making a valuation of the sale of goods etc. and (*b*) written notice of his intention to make a claim at least one month before the end of the tenancy.

> NOTES:(1)   There are special provisions regarding sub-tenancies in s. 63(1) and (2).
>
> (2)   There are special provisions in s. 63(3) regarding a notice to quit part of a holding which is less than 1/4 of the original holding.

6. Additional compensation. Section 60 (4) provides that the amount of additional compensation is four times the annual rent of the holding at the rate which was payable immediately before the end of the tenancy. However, no additional compensation is payable where:

(a) Case A or H is successfully relied upon by the landlord, or
(b) the landlord successfully relies upon any of the matters in s. 27(3)(*a*), (*b*), (*c*) and (*e*),

unless either the Tribunal is satisfied as to the matter in s. 27(3)(*f*) or, in the case of reliance by the landlord on the matter in s. 27(3)(*b*), it would have been so satisfied if (*f*) had also been relied upon.

NOTE: Section 27 is considered in 30: **5**.

7. Compensation on early resumption. Where the tenancy terminates by reason of notice to quit pursuant to a provision authorising resumption of possession for some specified purpose other than use for agriculture, and the tenant quits in consequence, compensation is payable to the tenant, in addition to any other compensation: s. 62(1). The amount is equal to the value of the additional benefit, if any, which would have accrued to the tenant if the tenancy had been terminated on the expiration of 12 months from the end of the year current when the notice was given: s. 62(2).

8. Compensation for improvements. This is payable by the landlord to the tenant on his quitting the holding on the termination of the tenancy. It replaces the old customary right to compensation, and falls into two parts:

(a) compensation for improvements begun before 1st March 1948 (*see* **9**);
(b) compensation for relevant improvements (*see* **10**).

9. Improvements begun before 1st March 1948. Sections 64(4) and Sch. 9, Part I deal with this. The improvements are those specified in Sch. 9, Part II, provided the improvements were begun before 1st March 1948.

The amount of compensation is an amount equal to the increase attributable to the improvement in the value of the holding as a holding having regard to its character and situation and the average requirements of tenants reasonably skilled in husbandry: Sch. 9, Part I, para 2(1).

10. Relevant improvements. These are improvements begun on or after 1st March 1948, provided they appear in the lists in Sch. 7 or

Sch. 8, Part I. Consent is required to carry out the improvements in Sch. 7, otherwise compensation will not be payable. If the landlord refuses his consent to the improvements in Part II of Sch. 7, the Tribunal may approve the carrying out of the improvement on terms: s. 67.

SCHEDULE 7

Part I: Improvements to which consent of landlord required

1. Making or planting of osier beds.
2. Making of water meadows or works of irrigation.
3. Making of watercress beds.
4. Planting of hops.
5. Planting of orchards or fruit bushes.
6. Warping or weiring of land.
7. Making of gardens.
8. Provision of underground tanks.

Part II: Improvements to which consent of landlord or approval of the Tribunal required

9. Erection, alteration or enlargement of buildings, and making or improvement of permanent yards.
10. Carrying out of works in compliance with an improvement notice under the Housing Acts.
11. The erection or construction of loading platforms, ramps, hard standings for vehicles, or other similar facilities.
12. Construction of silos.
13. Claying of land.
14. Marling of land.
15. Making or improvement of roads or bridges.
16. Making or improvement of water courses, culverts ponds, wells or reservoirs, or of works for the application of water power for agricultural or domestic purposes or of works for the supply, distribution, or use of water for such purposes.
17. Making or removal of permanent fences.
18. Reclaiming of waste land.
19. Making or improvement of embankments or sluices.
20. Erection of wirework for hop gardens.
21. Provision of permanent sheep-dipping accommodation.
22. Removal of bracken, gorse, tree roots, boulders or other like obstructions to cultivation.
23. Land drainage (other than mole drainage and works carried out to secure the efficient functioning thereof).

24. Provision or laying-on of electric light or power.

25. Provision of facilities for the storage or disposal of sewage or farm waste.

26. Repairs to fixed equipment, being equipment reasonably required for the proper farming of the holding, other than repairs which the tenant is under an obligation to carry out.

27. The grubbing up of orchards or fruit bushes.

28. Planting trees otherwise than as an orchard and bushes other than fruit bushes.

The measure of compensation for relevant improvements in the above list is an amount equal to the increase attributable to the improvement in the value of the agricultural holding as a holding having regard to the character and situation of the holding and the average requirements of tenants reasonably skilled in husbandry.

SCHEDULE 8: PART I

1. Mole drainage and works carried out to secure its efficient functioning.

2. Protection of fruit trees against animals.

3. Clay burning.

4. Liming (including chalking) of land.

5. Application to land of purchased manure (including artificial manure), and fertiliser, whether organic or inorganic.

6. Consumption on the holding of corn (whether produced on the holding or not) or of cake or other feeding stuff not produced on the holding by horses, cattle, sheep, pigs or poultry.

The measure of compensation for a relevant improvement in this list is the value thereof to an incoming tenant, calculated in accordance with the method prescribed by regulations made under the Act: s. 66(2).

11. Tenant right. Part II of Sch. 8 specifies 'other matters' for which a tenant is entitled to compensation. These are 'tenant right' matters.

SCHEDULE 8: PART II

Tenant right matters

7. Growing crops and severed or harvested crops and produce, being in either case crops or produce grown on the holding in the last year of the tenancy, but not including crops or produce which the tenant has a right to sell or remove from the holding.

8. Seeds sown and cultivations, fallows and acts of husbandry performed on the holding at the expense of the tenant (including the growing of herbage crops for commercial seed production).

9. Pasture laid down with clover grass, lucerne, sainfoin or other seeds, being either:

(*a*) pasture laid down at the expense of the tenant otherwise than in compliance with an obligation imposed on him by an agreement in writing to lay it down to replace temporary pasture comprised in the holding when the tenant entered thereon which was not paid for by him; or

(*b*) pasture paid for by the tenant on entering the holding.

10. Acclimatisation, hefting or settlement of hill sheep on hill land.

11. In areas of the country where arable crops can be grown in an unbroken series of not less than six years and it is reasonable that they should be grown on the holding or part of it, the residual fertility value of the soil of the excess qualifying leys, if any.

The measure of compensation is as for Part I (*see* **10**).

12. Special system of farming. Where the tenant of a holding shows that by the continuous adoption of a system of farming which has been more beneficial to the holding,

(a) than the system of farming required by the contract of tenancy; or

(b) in so far as no system of farming is so required, than the system of farming normally practised on comparable holdings,

the value of the holding has been increased during the tenancy, he is entitled to compensation: s. 70. It is payable by the landlord on the tenant quitting the holding on the termination of the tenancy. The amount of compensation is the increase in value.

Compensation is not payable under this provision unless:

(a) the tenant has, not later than one month before the end of the tenancy, given the landlord notice of his intention to claim compensation; and

(b) a record has been made of the condition of the fixed equipment on the holding and of the general condition of the holding.

If no notice is given or no record is made, no compensation is payable. Compensation is not recoverable in respect of any matter arising before the date of making the record.

13. Compensation generally. It must be remembered that, save in the case of disturbance, compensation is only payable to the tenant on his quitting the holding on the termination of the tenancy. If these conditions are not both satisfied, no compensation will be payable. Any claim arising out of the Act, or any custom or agreement, or the terms of the tenancy shall be determined by arbitration in accordance with the provisions of Schedule 11.

14. Successive tenancies. Where a tenant has remained in a holding during two or more tenancies, that fact does not prejudice either landlord or tenant in any claim for compensation: *see* ss. 69 and 73.

Progress test 29

1. How do a landlord's statutory rights to compensation tie in with his contractual remedies under the tenancy? **(2)**

2. To what compensation is a landlord entitled at the end of a tenancy of an agricultural holding? **(3)**

3. What conditions must be satisfied if a tenant is to receive disturbance compensation? **(4, 5)**

4. How much basic compensation does a tenant get for disturbance? **(5)**

5. What additional payments may a tenant receive as disturbance compensation? **(6)**

6. What is compensation for: (*a*) tenant right; (*b*) special system of farming? **(11, 12)**

Security of tenure

Introduction

1. Generally. The security of tenure provisions operate in the following ways. First, as has already been seen, s. 2(2) converts interests less than a tenancy from year to year into tenancies from year to year. Secondly, s. 3(1) provides that tenancies for two years or more, instead of terminating on the expiration of the term for which they were granted, are to continue as tenancies from year to year. The effect of these two provisions is that almost all lettings or licences to use agricultural land will take effect as tenancies from year to year. The exceptions are:

(a) grazing and mowing agreements for a specified period of the year only (*see* 28: **6**);

(b) tenancies for a fixed term which is more than one but less than two years; such a term will be outside s. 2(1) because it is not for an interest less than a tenancy from year to year and will also be outside s. 3(1) because it is less than two years: *Gladstone* v. *Bower* (1960), *EWP Ltd* v. *Moore* (1992);

(c) Section 3(1) has been modified by s. 4 which applies only to tenancies granted after 12th September 1984 and where the original grantee, or the survivor of the original grantee dies during the term. If he dies one or more years before the expiry of the term, the tenancy does not continue by virtue of s. 3(1) but instead ends on the date of expiry. If he dies at any other time before the expiry of the term and no notice to quit has been given, the tenancy does not continue by virtue of s. 3(1) but instead continues for a further 12 months only from the expiry of the term;

(d) contracting out of s. 3(1) is now possible under s. 5 (*see* **35** post).

Thirdly, the common law rules (*see* 7: **13**) concerning the termination of tenancies from year to year are altered by Part III of the Act: *see* **2** to **29**.

Fourthly, Part IV of the Act contains provision for succession on the death or the retirement of a tenant of an agricultural holding: *see* **17** to **28**.

Notice to quit

2. Length of notice to quit. Section 25(1) provides that a notice to quit an agricultural holding, notwithstanding any provision to the contrary in the contract of tenancy, will be invalid if it purports to end the tenancy before the expiration of 12 months from the end of the then current year of the tenancy. This therefore alters the common law rule that only six months' notice is needed to determine a yearly tenancy. Section 25(2) makes certain exceptions which include the following:

(a) where the tenant is insolvent;
(b) where notice is given pursuant to a provision in the contract authorising the resumption of possession for some purpose other than the use of the land for agriculture;
(c) a notice given by a tenant to a sub-tenant.

In the case of these exceptions, the ordinary common law rules regarding the period of the notice apply. There are further exceptions where:

(a) in response to an award of an increased rent (*see* 28: **11**), the tenant can give at least six months notice to end on the anniversary of the tenancy (s. 25(3));
(b) where a certificate of bad husbandry (*see* **9**) has been given the Tribunal may specify a minimum period of not less than two months which need not expire on the anniversary.

3. Restrictions on the operation of notices to quit. Section 26 contains various restrictions on the operation of a notice to quit an agricultural holding given to the tenant. Where a notice is served on the tenant, he may within one month from the giving of it, serve on the landlord a written counter-notice requiring s. 26(2) to apply to the notice to quit. If the tenant does this, the notice to quit will not have any effect unless the Tribunal gives consent to its operation under s. 26(1).

4. Tribunal's consent under s. 26(1). Section 27(1) provides that the Tribunal shall consent under s. 26 to the operation of a notice to quit an agricultural holding if, but only if, it is satisfied as to one or more of the matters in s. 27(3). Even if the Tribunal is satisfied, however, s. 27(2) provides that the tribunal shall withhold consent if, in all the circumstances, it appears to it that a fair and reasonable landlord would not insist on possession. This gives the Tribunal an overriding discretion about whether the notice should take effect.

5. The grounds for consent. The grounds for consent are contained in s. 27(3) and are:

(a) that the carrying out of the purpose for which the landlord proposes to end the tenancy is desirable in the interests of good husbandry as respects the land to which the notice relates, treated as a separate unit;

(b) that the carrying out of the purpose is desirable in the interest of sound management of the estate of which the land to which the notice relates forms a part;

(c) that the carrying out of the purposes is desirable for the purposes of agricultural research, experiment or demonstration, or for the purposes of the enactments relating to smallholdings;

(d) that the carrying out of the purpose is desirable for the purposes of the enactments relating to allotments;

(e) that greater hardship would be caused by withholding than by giving consent; or

(f) that the landlord proposes to end the tenancy for the purpose of the land being used for a use other than agriculture and not falling within Case B.

6. Exclusion of the requirement of consent to certain notices. The requirement of consent to a notice to quit is now excluded in eight cases: s. 26(2) and Pt. I of Sch 3. If the landlord serves notice to quit relying on any of these cases, he does not need the consent of the Tribunal. When the landlord gives the notice to quit he must clearly state which of these cases, if any, he relies upon. Where a notice to quit relies on a case specified in Pt. I of Sch. 3 but is given by a landlord who has no honest belief in the matter asserted, the notice may be held to be fraudulent and void at common law: *Rous* v. *Mitchell* (1991). These cases are considered in the following paragraphs, from Sch 3, Pt. I.

7. Case A. Where the holding is let as a smallholding by a smallholdings authority or the Minister and was so let on or after 12th September 1984, and

(a) the tenant has attained the age of 65, and

(b) if the result of the notice to quit taking effect would be to deprive the tenant of living accommodation occupied by him under the tenancy, suitable alternative accommodation is, or will be, available for him, and

(c) the tenancy contained an acknowledgement signed by the tenant that the tenancy is subject to this case or its predecessor, and it is stated in the notice to quit that it is given by reason of the said matter.

8. Case B. The notice to quit is given on the ground that the land is required for a use, other than for agriculture:

(a) for which permission has been granted on an application made under the enactments relating to town and country planning,

(b) for which permission under those enactments is granted by a general development order by reason only of the fact that the use is authorised by

(*i*) a private or local Act,

(*ii*) an order approved by both Houses of Parliament, or

(*iii*) an order made under section 14 or 16 of the Harbours Act 1964,

(c) for which any provision that

(*i*) is contained in an Act, but

(*ii*) does not form part of the enactments relating to town and country planning, deems permission under those enactments to have been granted,

(d) which any such provision deems not to constitute development for the purposes of those enactments, or

(e) for which permission is not required under the enactments relating to town and country planning by reason only of Crown immunity,

and that fact is stated in the notice.

This case covers the situation where the landlord requires the land for a non-agricultural use. It does not apply to a permission granted to the National Coal Board relating to open-cast mining where there is a condition requiring restoration to agriculture or forestry. It was substituted by the Agricultural Holdings (Amendment) Act 1990.

9. Case C. Where not more than six months before the giving of the notice to quit, the Tribunal granted a certificate under para. 9 of Pt. II of Sch. 3 that the tenant was not fulfilling his responsibilities to farm in accordance with the rules of good husbandry and that fact is stated in the notice.

10. Case D. At the date of the giving of the notice to quit the tenant has failed to comply with a written notice served on him by the landlord requiring him, either

(a) within two months of the service of the notice to pay any rent due in respect of the agricultural holding to which the notice to quit relates; or

(b) within a reasonable period specified in the notice to remedy any breach by him that was capable of being remedied of any term or condition of the tenancy which was not inconsistent with the fulfilment of his responsibilities to farm in accordance with the rules of good husbandry,

and it is stated in the notice to quit that it is given in accordance with these matters.

11.   Case D: summary.   Case D has two limbs to it. The first limb concerns failure by the tenant to comply with a notice calling on him to pay arrears of rent (*see* **12**). The second limb is where the tenant is in breach of his obligations and he fails to comply with a notice calling on him to remedy the breach; this form of notice is surrounded with restrictions on its operation (*see* **13**).

12.   Case D: notice to pay rent.   There is a prescribed form for this notice: see the Agricultural Holdings (Forms of Notice to Pay Rent or Remedy) Regulations 1987. If the tenant fails to comply with the notice requiring him to pay the rent the landlord will be entitled to give notice to quit under Case D. The tenant cannot then give a counter-notice. By virtue of the Agricultural Holdings (Arbitration on Notices) Order 1987, art. 9, however, he can demand arbitration as to the reason stated in the notice to quit provided he does so within one month after service of the notice to quit.

13.   Case D: notice to remedy.   This part of Case D is subject to many restrictions which are only summarised here. Before looking at the restrictions it is first necessary to distinguish between two types of notice to remedy. First, there is a notice to do works of repair, maintenance or replacement ('a notice to do work'); secondly, there is a notice to remedy any other breach. It is now possible to summarise the procedure. There are the following stages:

(a) the landlord must first serve a valid notice to remedy and this must:

    (*i*)   be in the prescribed form *see* **12** *above;*

    (*ii*)   specify the period (not less than six months in any case) within which the breach is to be remedied and the period must be reasonable;

(b) if it is a notice to do work, the tenant must have the notice referred to arbitration at this stage if he wishes to dispute (*a*) his liability under the tenancy to do any of the work specified in the notice, (*b*) any item on the ground that it is unnecessary or unjustified, or (*c*) the substitution of a different method or material for that which the notice would otherwise require to be followed or used; if the tenant is raising any of the above issues, then any other question arising under the notice to do work must be raised at the same time;

(c) the arbitrator may then make an award which affects the operation of the notice and while the arbitration is going on the time for doing the work is suspended;

(d) if the tenant fails to comply with the notice, at the end of the period specified for compliance, the landlord may serve notice to quit relying on Case D;

(e) within one month of the service of the notice to quit, the tenant may demand arbitration as to the reason stated in the notice to quit; arbitration is available whether the notice is a notice to do work or a notice to remedy some other breach; the operation of the notice to quit is suspended until the end of the arbitration;

(f) if the tenant fails in his challenge to the reason stated in the notice to remedy or does not challenge it, in the case of a notice to do work, he may serve a counter-notice under s. 28(2) within one month of the giving of the notice to quit; or if there has been an unsuccessful arbitration, within one month of the delivery of the arbitrator's award to him;

(g) if the tenant does give such a counter-notice, the notice to quit will not operate unless the Tribunal consents to its operation; however, the Tribunal must consent unless it appears to them, having regard to (*i*) the extent to which the tenant has failed to comply with the notice to do work, (*ii*) the consequences of that failure and (*iii*) the circumstances surrounding such failure, that a fair and reasonable landlord would not insist on possession.

14. Case E. At the date of the giving of the notice to quit the interest of the landlord in the holding to which the notice to quit relates had been materially prejudiced by the commission by the tenant of a breach, which was not capable of being remedied, of any term or condition of the tenancy that was inconsistent with the fulfilment by the tenant of his responsibilities to farm in accordance with the rules of good husbandry, and it is stated in the notice that it is given by reason of the matters aforesaid.

15. Case F. At the date of the giving of the notice to quit the tenant was a person who had become insolvent, and the notice states that is given by reason of those matters.

16. Case G. The notice to quit is given **(a)** following the death of a person who immediately before his death was the sole (or sole surviving) tenant under the contract of tenancy and **(b)** not later than the end of the period of three months beginning with the date of any relevant notice, and it is stated that it is given by reason of that person's death.

For the purpose of this case it is provided that 'tenant' does not include an executor, administrator, trustee in bankruptcy or other person deriving title from a tenant by operation of law. The reference to the date of any relevant notice is a reference to the giving of notice by or on behalf of the executor or administrator of the tenant's estate informing the landlord of the tenant's death or the date on which the landlord was given notice of an application to the Tribunal for succession, whichever is the earlier.

17. Restrictions on the operation of Case G. Certain restrictions on Case G are contained in s. 43. In summary they are that the notice to quit will not have effect unless either:

(a) no application to become the tenant of the holding is made under s. 39 within three months after the death of the tenant; or
(b) an application or applications having been made, either:
  (*i*) none of the applicants is determined by the Tribunal to be in their opinion a suitable person to become tenant; or
  (*ii*) the Tribunal consents under s. 44.

18. Survivor's application for a tenancy. Section 39 provides that where the sole or sole surviving tenant of an agricultural holding dies and is survived by an eligible person (*see* **19**) or persons, then any eligible person may within the 'relevant period' apply to the Tribunal for a direction entitling him to a tenancy of the holding. The relevant period is the period of three months beginning with the death of the tenant. The procedure is governed by the Agricultural Land Tribunals (Succession to Agricultural Tenancies) Order 1984.

NOTES: (1) An application under s. 39 may be made whether or not a notice to quit relying on Case G has been served.
(2) There can be up to two successions but no more: s. 37(1).

19. Eligible person. An eligible person is defined by ss. 36(3) and 35(2) as:

(a) the wife or husband of the deceased;
(b) a brother or sister of the deceased;
(c) a child of the deceased;
(d) any person who in the case of any marriage to which the deceased

was a party, was treated by the deceased as a child of the family in relation to that marriage.

These persons are called 'close relatives.'

Further, in order to be an eligible person, a close relative must show that (*i*) in the seven years ending with the date of death, his only or principal source of livelihood throughout a continuous period of not less than five years, or two or more discontinuous periods amounting to not less than five years, derived from his (or in the case of a widow from her or the deceased's or both of their) agricultural work on the holding or on an agricultural unit of which the holding forms part and (*ii*) he is not an occupier of a commercial unit of agricultural land.

20. Not fully eligible person. Section 41 enables the Tribunal, where it considers it to be fair and reasonable, to treat as eligible a person who is not fully eligible. It only applies, however, where the condition relating to principal source of livelihood, though not satisfied fully, is satisfied to a material extent.

21. The application. The following points should be noted regarding an application by a person under s. 39.

(a) The applicant must satisfy the Tribunal that he is an eligible person; the Tribunal then determines whether he is in its opinion a suitable person to become the tenant: s. 39(2). In doing so it must give the landlord an opportunity to be heard.

(b) If the applicants include a person validly designated by the deceased in his will as the person he wished to succeed him as tenant of the holding, the Tribunal must first determine whether that person is suitable and then only if he is not may it consider other applicants: s. 39(4).

(c) If the Tribunal decides that only one applicant is a suitable person it must make a direction entitling him to a tenancy of the holding: s. 39(5). This is, however, subject to the opportunity of the landlord to obtain the Tribunal's consent to the operation of a notice to quit under s. 44 (*see* **22**).

(d) If the Tribunal considers two or more applicants to be suitable then it must determine which is the more or most suitable person to be tenant: s. 39(6).

(e) In making its decision the Tribunal must:

(*i*) give the landlord a chance to state his views on the suitability of the applicants;

(*ii*) take into account the practical experience possessed by each applicant;

(*iii*) take into account the age, health and financial standing of the applicants.

(f) When the Tribunal has to choose between applicants it may direct, with the landlord's consent, that two, three or four applicants are to have a joint tenancy.

22. Opportunity for landlord to obtain Tribunal's consent. Before giving a direction entitling an applicant to a tenancy and where a notice to quit has been served on death, the Tribunal must give the landlord an opportunity to apply for consent to the operation of the notice: s. 44. In effect this gives the landlord a last chance to stop the succession of a new tenant.

23. Effect of a Tribunal's s. 39 direction. A direction by the Tribunal entitling an applicant or applicants to a tenancy of the holding entitles him or them to a tenancy of the holding from the relevant time on the same terms as those on which the holding was let immediately before it ceased to be let under the contract of tenancy under which it was let at the date of death; such a tenancy is deemed at that time to be granted by the landlord to and accepted by the applicant.

The 'relevant time' here means the end of the 12 months immediately following the end of the year of the tenancy in which the deceased died. But if the application followed a notice to quit in reliance on Case G and the notice would have ended the tenancy at a time after the end of those 12 months, it means that time.

24. Arbitration on the successor's tenancy's terms. When a direction has been made under s. 30, the landlord or the tenant may, at any time within the 'prescribed period' (which is the period between the giving of the direction and the end of the three months immediately following the relevant time), by written notice served on the other party demand a reference to arbitration of one or both of the questions:

(a) what variations in the terms of the tenancy to which the tenant is entitled are justified having regard to the circumstances of the holding and the length of time since the holding was first let on those terms;
(b) what rent should be or should have been properly payable in respect of the holding at the relevant time.

25. Exceptions to Case G. The preceding seven paragraphs have been concerned with applications for a new tenancy under s. 39. It will be recalled (*see* **17**) that this consideration started from the consideration of Case G because applications under the section may restrict the operation of Case G (*see* **17**). These restrictions outlined in **17** do not apply, however, in certain situations which include the following:

(a) if at the date of death the tenancy is the subject of a valid notice to quit to which s. 26(1) applies, being a notice given before that date and which the Tribunal consented to or where a counter-notice was not served in the month following the notice;
(b) if on the date of death the tenancy is the subject of a valid notice to quit given before that date and falling within cases C or F;
(c) if on the date of death the tenancy is the subject of a valid notice to quit given before that date and falling within Cases B, D or E, and either (*i*) the relevant time limits for reference to arbitration or giving counter-notice have elapsed without the same occurring or (*ii*) the question referred to arbitration was determined before the date of death so as to uphold the notice and the time for counter-notice in respect of the notice to quit expired without such notice being served or (*iii*) the Tribunal consented before the date of death to the operation of the notice;
(d) if the holding consists of land held by a smallholding authority or the Minister for the purposes of smallholdings;
(e) if the tenancy was granted by trustees in whom the land is vested on charitable trusts the sole or principal object of which is the settlement or employment in agriculture of persons who have served in any of Her Majesty's naval, military or air forces;
(f) if on the date of death the holding was held by the deceased under a tenancy for a fixed term of years of which more than 27 months was unexpired or a tenancy for a fixed term of more than one but less than two years.

26. Tenancies granted after 12th July 1984. The succession provisions (*see* **17–25**) do not apply to tenancies granted after 12th July 1984 unless:

(a) the tenancy was granted pursuant to the succession provisions, or
(b) the parties agree in the written contract of tenancy that Part IV shall apply in relation to the tenancy, or
(c) the tenancy was granted to a person who immediately before 12th July 1984 was a tenant of the same, or substantially the same, agricultural holding.

27. Succession on retirement. There are two cases where succession may occur on retirement. First, there may be a succession where, by agreement between landlord and tenant, the tenant retires in favour of a close relative who is granted a new tenancy or takes an assignment of the retiring tenant's existing tenancy: s. 37(2). Secondly, ss. 49 to 58 contain a scheme of succession not dependent on the landlord's agreement. In summary, the principal conditions are:

(a) the tenancy was granted before 12th July 1984 or falls within the exceptions listed in **26**;
(b) the tenancy must be from year to year;
(c) the retiring tenant must at the retirement date be at least 65 years old or by reason of bodily or mental infirmity incapable of farming in accordance with the rules of good husbandry;
(d) the nominated successor must be a close relative of the retiring tenant, be eligible (*see* **19**) and be found suitable (*see* **21** (*a*));
(e) the retiring tenant must serve on the landlord a retirement notice indicating the person he wishes to succeed him as tenant from a specified date.

28. Succession on retirement; other provisions. There are consequential provisions modelled on the provisions relating to succession. They are contained in ss. 49 to 58 but are outside the scope of this book.

29. Case H. The notice to quit is given by the Minister and:

(a) the Minister certifies in writing that the notice to quit is given in order to enable him to use or to dispose of the land for the purposes of effecting any amalgamation or the re-shaping of any agricultural unit; and
(b) the instrument under which the tenancy was granted contains an acknowledgement signed by the tenant that the tenancy is subject to the provisions of this Case.

30. Miscellanea. This concludes the consideration of the Cases and notices to quit. There are miscellaneous matters to be considered which are dealt with in the following paragraphs. They are:

(a) notice to quit a part of the holding (**31–33**)
(b) contracting out (**34–35**).

Notice to quit part

31. Notice to quit a part of the holding. Section 31 provides that a notice to quit part of a holding held on a tenancy from year to year given by the landlord will not be invalid on the ground that it relates to part only if it is given:

(a) for the purpose of adjusting the boundaries between agricultural units or parts of them; or

(b) with a view to the use of the land to which the notice relates for any of the following:

    (*i*) erection of farm labourers' cottages;

    (*ii*) provision for gardens of the same;

    (*iii*) provision of allotments;

    (*iv*) planting of trees;

    (*v*) opening of a deposit of coal or other minerals;

    (*vi*) making of a reservoir or water-course;

    (*vii*) making of a road, railway, wharf or pier;

    (*viii*) the letting of land as a smallholding.

32. Tenant's right to treat notice to quit part as notice to quit the whole. Where a notice to quit part is given to the tenant of an agricultural holding and it is rendered valid by s. 31, it is provided by s. 32 that the tenant may within 28 days give notice to the landlord that he accepts it as a notice to quit the entire holding.

33. Reduction of rent. Where the landlord resumes possession of part of a holding, the tenant is entitled to a reduction of rent proportionate to that part of the holding.

Contracting out

34. Contracting out. Section 26(1), which provides that a notice to quit will not have effect unless the Tribunal consents to its operation, does not state whether the parties may contract out of it. If the parties could do so, the security of tenure provisions would be defeated and landlords granting new tenancies might insist that tenants contract out. It has been held in *Johnson* v. *Moreton* (1980) that parties cannot contract out of s. 26(1), because such a term would be contrary to public policy, being an attempt to oust the jurisdiction of the Tribunal.

Johnson v. *Moreton* (1980). L granted to T a lease for ten years from 1st January 1967. T covenanted not to serve a counter-notice under

s. 24(1) of the 1948 Act (the predecessor provision to s. 26(1)). In November 1975 L served a notice to quit on T who served a counter-notice. L treated the counter-notice as valid but served a second notice on T relying on Case E (i.e. claiming the landlord's interest was materially prejudiced by the breach of covenant). The breach of covenant relied upon was the service of the counter-notice. An arbitrator was appointed and a special case stated for the opinion of the court as to the validity of the notice relying on Case E. The House of Lords HELD: despite the absence of any words prohibiting contracting out, it was not possible to do so. The covenant was therefore void, being contrary to public policy and L could not rely on it to prevent the tenant serving a counter-notice.

35. Statutory intervention. Section 5 provides for contracting out where:

(a) the term is not less than two nor more than five years;
(b) before the grant the prospective landlord and tenant agreed that s. 3 should not apply;
(c) they jointly applied for and obtained the approval of the Minister; and
(d) the contract is in writing and contains a statement that s. 3 does not apply.

Progress test 30

1. What is the effect of the decision in *Johnson* v. *Moreton*? **(34)**

2. What agreements do not take effect as tenancies from year to year under the Act? **(1)**

3. How does the Act alter the common law rules relating to notices to quit? **(1)**

4. When must a counter-notice to a notice to quit be served? What is the effect of such a counter-notice? **(3)**

5. What is the role of the Agricultural Land Tribunal in relation to notices to quit? **(3)**

6. On what grounds may consent be given to the operation of a notice to quit? **(5)**

7. What is an 'eligible person'? How is a 'not fully eligible person' to be treated as eligible? **(19, 20)**

8. What is Case A? How does it operate? **(7)**

9. L gives notice to quit to T, tenant of an agricultural holding. The notice relies on Case C. Advise T. **(9)**

10. What is a 'notice to pay rent' and a notice to remedy a breach? How does the procedure relating to each notice differ? **(13)**

11. Summarise the procedure where a landlord relies on Case D. **(13)**

12. What requirements must a notice to remedy satisfy? **(13)**

13. What is Case E? **(14)**

14. What restrictions are placed on a landlord serving notice to quit under Case G? **(17)**

15. Who is the 'tenant' for the purposes of Case G? **(16)**

16. What exceptions apply to the restrictions on the operation of Case G? **(25)**

17. How may an eligible person apply for a tenancy under the Act? **(21)**

18. What is Case H? **(29)**

19. What is the effect of a notice to quit part of an agricultural holding? **(31)**

The Rent (Agriculture) Act 1976

The statutory scheme

1. Introduction. The Rent (Agriculture) Act 1976 (referred to in parts of this chapter as the 1976 Act) affords security of tenure to certain agricultural workers housed by their employers. Prior to 1976 such workers were often outside the protection of the Rent Act either because they were licensees or because they paid no rent. The 1976 Act gives them protection analogous to that given to other residential tenants by the Rent Act. It also imposes a duty on housing authorities to re-house certain workers. The intention behind this latter provision is that new workers may then move into houses occupied by old workers so that there may be some mobility of labour notwithstanding the security of tenure. The 1976 Act only applies to licences and tenancies granted before 15th January 1989. Thereafter, by virtue of the Housing Act 1988, ss. 24 and 34, protection is by way of assured agricultural occupancies under ss. 24 to 26 of the 1988 Act. This is a regime of protection based on the concept of assured tenancies: (*see* Chapter 21).

2. Summary of protection. The scheme of the 1976 Act is similar to that of the Rent Act 1977, and provides for a system of protected occupancies (the equivalent of protected tenancies) which on their termination become statutory tenancies which continue so long as the 'tenant' occupies the dwelling-house as his residence. Possession of a dwelling-house cannot be recovered unless the landlord makes out one of the Cases in Sch. 4 to the 1976 Act. These cases are similar to those in Sch. 15 to the 1977 Act (*see* Chapter 17). There is one major difference in that an occupier of agricultural land may apply to the relevant housing authority when he needs vacant possession of a house subject to a protected occupancy and he cannot provide alternative accommodation and the authority ought in the interests of efficient agriculture to provide the alternative accommodation. If those circumstances are satisfied the authority will come under a duty to re-house the protected occupier. This ties in with the grounds for possession because one of the grounds is that alternative accommodation is provided or arranged by the housing authority. There is also a system for regulating the rent payable under a protected occupancy or a statutory tenancy.

Scope of protection

3. Protected occupiers and protected occupancies. The 1976 Act gives protection to what is called a 'protected occupier'. This is defined in the following way. Section 2(1) provides that where a person has, in relation to a dwelling-house, a relevant licence or tenancy and the house is in qualifying ownership or has been in qualifying ownership at any time during the subsistence of the licence or tenancy (whether it was at the time a relevant licence or tenancy or not) he will be a protected occupier of the dwelling-house if:

(a) he is a qualifying worker; or
(b) he has been a qualifying worker at any time during the subsistence of the licence or tenancy.

4. Elements. It will be seen that this is a complicated definition which introduces a number of new concepts. The essential elements are:

(a) there must be a relevant licence or tenancy (*see* **5, 6**);
(b) the property must be a dwelling-house in qualifying ownership (or one which has been in qualifying ownership at some time during the licence or tenancy) (*see* **8**); and
(c) the occupier must be a qualifying worker or have been a qualifying worker at some time during the licence or tenancy (*see* **7**).

5. Relevant licence. The 1976 Act, Sch. 2, para. 1, defines 'relevant licence' as any licence under which a person has the exclusive occupation of a dwelling-house as a separate dwelling and which would be a protected tenancy,

(a) if it was a tenancy; and
(b) if certain of the provisions in the Rent Act 1977 were modified.

The provisions of the Rent Act 1977 which have to be modified concern the exceptions to that Act. The main modifications are that:

(a) the exclusion from protection of tenancies at a low rent under the Rent Act 1977, s. 5, does not apply;

(b) the exclusion from protection of tenancies comprised in an agricultural holding and occupied by the person responsible for the control of the farming under the Rent Act 1977, s. 10, does not apply;

(c) for the Rent Act 1977, s. 7 there is substituted the following:

'a tenancy is not a protected tenancy if it is a bona fide term of the tenancy that the landlord provides the tenant with board or attendance; but board does not include meals provided in the course of employment.'

The test for determining if an agreement gives rise to a relevant licence is therefore to ask if the agreement would give rise to a protected tenancy if the agreement was assumed to be a tenancy and the Rent Act 1977 was then applied with the above modifications.

6. Relevant tenancy. The 1976 Act, Sch. 2, para. 2 defines a 'relevant tenancy' as a tenancy under which a dwelling-house is let as a separate dwelling and which

(a) is not a protected tenancy under the Rent Act 1977, but
(b) would be such a tenancy if certain of the provisions of the 1977 Act were modified.

The provisions which have to be modified are those already set out in 5 above.

7. Qualifying worker. The 1976 Act, Sch. 3, para. 1 provides that a person is a qualifying worker for the purposes of the Act at any time if, at that time, he has worked whole-time in agriculture, or has worked in agriculture as a permit worker, for not less than 91 out of the last 104 weeks.

NOTE: The Act contains detailed provisions in Sch. 3 to determine what constitutes whole-time and permit work, but the provisions are outside the scope of this book.

8. Dwelling-house in qualifying ownership. The 1976 Act, Sch. 3, para. 3 provides that a dwelling-house, in relation to which a person ('the occupier') has a licence or tenancy is in qualifying ownership at any time if, at that time, the occupier is employed in agriculture and the occupier's employer either:

(a) is the owner of the dwelling-house; or
(b) has made arrangements with the owner of the dwelling-house for it to be used as housing accommodation for persons employed by him in agriculture.

In this context 'employer' means the person or one of the persons by whom the occupier is employed in agriculture, and 'owner' in relation to the dwelling-house means the occupier's immediate landlord or, where the occupier is a licensee, the person who would be the occupier's immediate landlord if the licence were a tenancy.

9. Protected occupiers. A protected occupier may be either:

(a) a protected occupier in his own right (*see* **10**); or
(b) a protected occupier by succession (*see* **11**).

10. Protected occupiers in their own right. It has already been seen that under s. 2(1) a protected occupancy arises when the conditions in **5–8** above are satisfied. An occupier under such an occupancy is called a protected occupier in his own right. Section 2 extends the meaning of this expression to cover the following situations:

(a) where a person has a relevant licence or tenancy and the dwelling-house is in qualifying ownership, or has been at any time during the licence or tenancy, he is a protected occupier if and so long as he is incapable of working in agriculture because of a qualifying injury or disease;
(b) where a person has a relevant licence or tenancy then he will be a protected occupier if his licence or tenancy was granted in consideration of his giving up possession of another dwelling-house of which he was a protected occupier or statutory tenant.

NOTE: Qualifying injuries are defined in Sch. 3, para. 2, but they are outside the scope of this book.

11. Protected occupiers by succession. After the death of a protected occupier of the dwelling-house ('the original occupier') it is possible for him to be succeeded as a protected occupier by a member of his family: s. 3. The succession provisions operate in the following way:

(a) where the original occupier was a man (or woman) who died leaving a widow (or widower) who was living in the dwelling-house immediately before the death, after the death, if the widow (widower) has a relevant licence or tenancy in relation to the dwelling-house, she (he) will be a protected occupier of the dwelling-house;
(b) where the original occupier did not have a surviving spouse who was living in the dwelling-house immediately before the death, but one or more persons who were members of his family were residing with him at the time of and for six months prior to the death, if that

person or any of them has a relevant licence or tenancy in relation to the dwelling-house, that person will be a protected occupier;

The expression 'protected occupier by succession' is used in the Act to refer to a person who is a protected occupier by virtue of these provisions.

12. Statutory tenancies and tenants. Section 4 of the 1976 Act provides that where a person ceases to be a protected occupier of a dwelling-house on the termination of his licence or tenancy, if and so long as he occupies the dwelling-house as his residence, he will be the statutory tenant of it. (This provision is parallel to that in the 1977 Act concerning statutory tenancies.) There is also a provision in terms similar to s. 3 (*see* **11**) for determining the statutory tenant by succession where the original occupier dies. This latter provision has been amended by the Housing Act 1988, s. 39 in relation to deaths after 15th January 1989, so that:

(a) a person who was living with the original occupier as his or her wife or husband is treated as the spouse of the original occupier;
(b) the residence condition for members of the family is now that they be 'residing with him in the dwelling-house for the period of two years prior to the death';
(c) the succession is to an assured tenancy of the dwelling-house.

13. Security of tenure. The 1976 Act operates in a way similar to the Rent Act 1977. Section 6(1) provides that a court may not make an order for possession of a dwelling-house subject to the protection of the 1976 Act except in the cases specified in Sch. 4 to the Act. Cases 1–X of Sch. 4 are discretionary grounds and are similar to the discretionary grounds in the Rent Act 1977, Sch. 15. Cases XI–XIII (in Sch. 4, Part II) are those where the court must make an order for possession. In the discretionary cases the court has wide powers in making an order for possession to defer its operation or to make it subject to conditions: s. 7.

In the following paragraphs the Cases are set out in a summary form; reference must be made to the Cases themselves for the detailed provisions.

Discretionary grounds for possession

14. Case I. Alternative accommodation provided other than by housing authority. This case applies where the court is satisfied that suitable alternative accommodation is available for the tenant or will be when the order for possession takes effect. The accommodation concerned here is accommodation provided otherwise than by the housing authority. There are detailed provisions as to when accommodation is suitable.

15. Case II. Alternative accommodation provided or arranged by the housing authority. This case applies where the housing authority has made a written offer to the tenant of alternative accommodation or given notice that another person has offered to re-house the tenant. The landlord must show that the tenant has accepted the offer or that he has not accepted it and the tenant does not satisfy the court that he acted reasonably in failing to accept the offer. The court must also be satisfied that the accommodation is suitable.

16. Cases III–X. These cases are the equivalent of some of the cases under the 1977 Act. In summary and with their Rent Act equivalent, they are as follows:

(a) *Case III*: Non-payment of rent or breach of obligation (Case 1);

(b) *Case IV*: Nuisance or annoyance, immoral or illegal use (Case 2);

(c) *Case V*: Deterioration in the condition of the dwelling-house (Case 3);

(d) *Case VI*: Deterioration in the condition of furniture (Case 4);

(e) *Case VII*: Notice to quit by the tenant (Case 5);

(f) *Case VIII*: Assigning, sub-letting or parting with possession of the dwelling-house or part of it without the consent of the landlord (Case 6 with certain differences);

(g) *Case IX*: Dwelling-house reasonably required by the landlord for occupation for himself, a son or daughter over the age of 18, or his father or mother, or the father or mother of his wife or her husband (Case 9);

(h) *Case X*: Excessive charge for sub-letting part of the dwelling-house (Case 10).

Cases where the court must order possession

17. Case XI. This applies where an owner-occupier who occupied the house, prior to the grant of a tenancy, as his residence requires the dwelling-house as a residence for himself or anyone who resided with him when he last occupied the dwelling-house as his residence. This is equivalent to Case 11 of, and para. 2(*a*) of Part V in, Sch. 15 to the Rent Act 1977.

18. Case XII. This applies where the person who granted the tenancy acquired the dwelling-house, or any interest in it with a view to occupying it as his residence at such time as he should retire from regular employment, and has retired, and requires it as his residence or has died and a member of his family residing with him at the time of his death, requires it as his residence. This is equivalent to Case 12 of, and para. 2(*b*) and (*c*) of Part V in, Sch. 15 to the Rent Act 1977.

19. Case XIII. This is where the dwelling-house is overcrowded within the meaning of Part X of the Housing Act 1985 so as to render the occupier guilty of an offence.

20. Effect of determination of superior tenancy. Section 9 provides for the protection of sub-tenants on the determination of a superior tenancy.

21. Terms and conditions of statutory tenancies. The Act of 1976, Sch. 5, contains provisions which regulate the terms and conditions under which a statutory tenant holds. The schedule refers to the licence or tenancy on the termination of which the statutory tenancy arises as the 'original contract'. In outline the provisions of Sch. 5 are:

(a) so long as he retains possession, the statutory tenant must observe and will be entitled to the benefit of all the terms of the original contract;
(b) if the original contract was a licence, the statutory tenancy will be a weekly tenancy;
(c) if the original contract was a licence, the statutory tenancy will include any term which would be implied if the contract had been a tenancy;
(d) the Landlord and Tenant Act 1985, s. 11 applies to the dwelling-house;
(e) the tenant must use the house only as a private dwelling-house, and must not assign, sub-let or part with possession of it;
(f) the tenant must give the landlord access for executing repairs;
(g) there is provision as to the payment of rates;
(h) there is provision as to the length of notice to quit to be served by the tenant on the landlord;
(i) there is provision for the variation of the terms of the statutory tenancy.

22. Agreed rents. The Act makes provision in s. 11 for agreed rents. There is no liability to pay rent under Sch. 5 (*see* **21**) until a rent is determined in accordance with the Act. Section 11(1) provides that the landlord and the statutory tenant may by agreement fix the rent payable under a statutory tenancy or may agree that no rent shall be payable. By s. 11(2) the rent so fixed must not exceed

(a) where a rent is registered, the amount so registered;
(b) where a rent is not so registered, the amount of rent based on rateable value as defined in s. 12 which is called a provisional rent (*see* **23**).

The amount of any excess over these limits cannot be recovered from the tenant: s. 11(5).

23. Provisional rents. Section 12 of the 1976 Act applies where a rent is not registered by providing for a provisional rent which is a 'rent based on rateable value'. Where the dwelling-house had a rateable value on 31st March 1990 this expression means the weekly or other periodical equivalent of an annual sum equal to the prescribed multiple of the rateable value of the dwelling-house.

Where the dwelling-house had no rateable value on 31st March 1990 this expression means the weekly or other periodic equivalent of an annual amount equal to the rent at which it is estimated the dwelling-house might reasonably be expected to let from year to year if the tenant undertook to pay all the usual tenant's rates and taxes and to bear the costs of rent, insurance and other expenses necessary to maintain the dwelling-house in a state to command that rent: s. 12 as amended by the References to Rating (Housing) Regulations 1990. Where a rent is not registered this is the lawfully recoverable rent. There is provision in s. 12 for increasing the rent up to the amount of the rent based on rateable value if the rent is currently less than that amount.

24. Registration of rent. Section 13 of the 1976 Act provides that there shall be a part of the register under Part IV of the 1977 Act in which rents may be registered for dwelling-houses which are subject to statutory tenancies. There are detailed provisions for increasing the rent up to the registered rent by notice of increase. There are also phasing provisions for increasing the rent in stages.

25. Protected occupancies and statutory tenancies: supplemental provisions. Part III of the 1976 Act contains various supplemental provisions. In summary they are as follows:

(a) s. 20 provides for the avoidance of any requirement that the rent be payable in advance or, if the rental period is more than six months, earlier than six months before the end of the rental period;

(b) s. 21 provides for the recovery of rent paid in excess of the recoverable rent;

(c) s. 22 provides for the rectification of rent in the light of the determination of the recoverable rent;

(d) s. 23 deals with the situation where the tenant shares accommodation with persons other than his landlord;

(e) s. 26 gives the county court jurisdiction to determine the question whether any person is a protected occupier or any question concerning the terms of a statutory tenancy.

26. Rehousing. It will be remembered that Case II (*see* **15**) provides that a landlord may recover possession when alternative accommodation is provided or arranged by the housing authority. Part IV of the Act provides a scheme whereby the housing authority may become under a duty to re-house. There are two stages to this process:

(a) the application to the housing authority concerned (*see* **27**);

(b) the creation of the duty of the housing authority (*see* **28**).

27. Application to the housing authority. Section 27 provides that an application may be made by the occupier of land used for agriculture to the housing authority concerned on the grounds that:

(a) vacant possession is or will be needed of a dwelling-house which is subject to a protected occupancy or a statutory tenancy, in order to house a person who is or is to be employed in agriculture by the applicant; and

(b) the applicant is unable to provide, by any reasonable means, suitable alternative accommodation for the occupier of the dwelling-house; and

(c) the authority ought, in the interests of efficient agriculture, to provide the suitable alternative accommodation.

28. The duty of the housing authority. On receipt of the application the authority must notify the occupier of the dwelling-house. Thereafter it may take the advice of an agricultural dwelling-house advisory committee (ADHAC) if it wishes. This will give advice on the case made by the applicant in the interests of efficient agriculture and regarding the urgency of the application. The authority must then notify its decision to the applicant and the occupier as to whether it is satisfied that the applicant's case is substantiated under s. 27. If it is so satisfied the notice must state the action it proposes to take; if not, it must give its reasons. If it is satisfied, the authority is under a duty to use its best endeavours to provide the suitable accommodation. The duty is enforceable at the suit of the applicant by an action against the authority for damages for breach of statutory duty. The duty does not, however, continue if, when the accommodation becomes available, the person for whom it is to be provided is employed by the applicant in the same capacity as that in which he was employed by the applicant when he made the application and will continue to be so employed if provided with the alternative accommodation. An authority's decision that the applicant's case is not substantiated will be susceptible to judicial review in accordance with the ordinary principles of administrative law.

Finally, there are detailed provisions in s. 28 for securing the notification to the authority of any material change of facts concerning the application. There are also criminal penalties for failure to comply with these provisions.

29. Effect of the Housing Act 1988. Section 34(4) of the Housing Act 1988 provides that a licence or tenancy which is entered into on or after 15th January 1989 cannot be a relevant licence or tenancy for the purposes of the 1976 Act except in certain limited and exceptional circumstances.

Section 24(1) of the 1988 Act provides that a licence or tenancy of a dwelling-house is an 'assured agricultural occupancy' either (*a*) it is an assured tenancy which is not an assured shorthold tenancy or, (*b*) a tenancy which is not an assured tenancy because it falls within para. 3 (tenancies at a low rent) and/or para. 7 (tenancies of agricultural holdings) of Sch. 1 to the 1988 Act or (*c*) a licence under which a person has exclusive occupation of a dwelling-house as a separate dwelling and (*ii*) the 'agricultural worker condition' is for the time being fulfilled with respect to the dwelling-house. The agricultural worker condition is dealt with in Sch. 3. In summary, it is an amalgam of the various conditions summarised in **4** to **8** above. Section 24(3) then provides that ss. 1 to 19 of the 1988 Act apply to every assured agricultural occupancy with certain amendments as set out in ss. 24 to 26. This means that the code relating to assured tenancies (*see* Chapter 21) applies to assured agricultural occupancies with suitable modifications.

The combined effect of the above two provisions of the 1988 Act is that (*i*) licences or tenancies granted to agricultural workers prior to 15th January 1989, and otherwise qualifying for protection, will be protected by the 1976 Act and (*ii*) licences or tenancies granted to agricultural workers after that date and otherwise qualifying for protection will be assured agricultural occupancies and subject to the regime under the 1988 Act (*see* Chapter 21) with certain modifications set out in ss. 24 to 26.

Progress test 31

1. What is the scope of the 1976 Act?   **(2)**

2. Explain the following terms:
   (a) protected occupier;
   (b) protected occupancy;
   (c) relevant licence;
   (d) qualifying worker.   **(3, 5, 7)**

3. What conditions must be satisfied for a house to be in qualifying ownership?   **(8)**

4. Distinguish between a protected occupier in his own right and one by succession.   **(10, 11)**

5. What are the similarities between the 1976 Act and the Rent Act 1977?   **(13)**

6. What are the discretionary grounds for recovering possession of a dwelling-house subject to the 1976 Act?   **(14)**

7. What are the mandatory grounds for recovering possession?   **(17)**

8. On what terms will a statutory tenant occupy his dwelling-house?   **(21)**

9. Who is responsible for repairs in a statutory tenancy under the 1976 Act?   **(21)**

10. How is a rent determined for a statutory tenancy under the 1976 Act?   **(22)**

11. What is a provisional rent?   **(23)**

12. Explain the provisions for registration of rents under the 1976 Act.   **(24)**

13. What is Case 11? How does it fit into the scheme of protection under the 1976 Act?   **(17)**

14. What is an ADHAC? What are its duties?   **(28)**

15. What is the effect of the Housing Act 1988 upon protection under the 1976 Act?   **(29)**

Part six
Public sector residential tenancies

32

Secure tenancies

1. Introduction. The Housing Act 1980 conferred security of tenure on public sector residential tenants and gave them the 'right to buy'. The operation of the 1980 Act was extended by the Housing and Building Control Act 1984. The Housing Act 1985 consolidated a mass of housing legislation including that relating to secure tenancies and the right to buy in Parts IV and V respectively. At the same time Housing Associations legislation was consolidated into the Housing Associations Act 1985. The Housing Act 1985 has since been amended by the Housing and Planning Act 1986, the Housing Act 1988, the Local Government and Housing Act 1989 and the Leasehold Reform, Housing and Urban Development Act 1993.

It can be seen from the above that in 13 years, there has been a flood of legislation dealing with public sector residential lettings. It is not possible in a handbook such as this to deal fully with all the different aspects of this legislation. It is therefore proposed to confine the consideration of public sector residential tenancies to the following:

(a) secure tenancies (*see* this chapter),

(b) the right to buy (*see* Chapter 33),

(c) a summary of the Housing Act 1988, (*see* Chapter 34).

Students must therefore treat this and the following chapters as an outline only of the relevant legislation and must refer to the more detailed textbooks, or to the relevant Acts, for a full study of the topic.

Unless otherwise stated, references in this chapter are to the Housing Act 1985.

2. Definition of a secure tenancy. A secure tenancy is one under which a dwelling-house is let as a separate dwelling and in relation to which both 'the landlord condition' and 'the tenant condition' are satisfied: s. 79(1). In summary there must be:

(a) a tenancy (*see* **3**);
(b) of a dwelling-house (*see* **4**);
(c) let as a separate dwelling (*see* **5**);
(d) satisfaction of the landlord condition (*see* **6**); and
(e) satisfaction of the tenant condition (*see* **7**).

Each of these requirements is considered in the following paragraphs. There are, of course, exceptions to the above which will be considered at **8–21** below.

3. There must be a tenancy. For the distinction between a tenancy and licence *see* 2:**15**. In certain circumstances a licence may be a secure tenancy. Section 79(3) provides that Part IV (which deals with secure tenancies) applies in relation to a licence to occupy a dwelling-house (whether or not granted for a consideration) as it applies in relation to a tenancy. Section 79(4), however, provides that s. 79(3) does not apply to a licence which was granted as a temporary expedient to a person who entered the dwelling-house or any other land as a trespasser.

4. A dwelling-house. Section 112(1) provides that in this context a dwelling-house may be a house or part of a house. Section 112(2) provides that land let together with a dwelling-house will be treated as part of the dwelling-house unless the land is agricultural land exceeding two acres.

5. Let as a separate dwelling. The law appears to be the same as for Rent Act 1977 cases: *see* 16: **7,8**.

6. The landlord condition. The landlord condition is that the interest of the landlord must belong to one of certain specified bodies which include the following:

(a) a local authority, defined as a county council, a district council, a London Borough Council, the Common Council of the City of London or the Council of the Isles of Scilly;

(b) a new town corporation,
(c) a housing action trust,
(d) an urban development corporation,
(e) the Development Board for Rural Wales,
(f) certain housing co-operatives.

7. The tenant condition. The tenant condition is that the tenant is an individual and occupies the dwelling-house as his only or principal home; or, where the tenancy is a joint one, that each of the joint tenants is an individual and at least one of them occupies the dwelling-house as his only or principal home: s. 81.

Exceptions

8. Introduction. Schedule 1 deals with tenancies which are not secure tenancies. The categories where a tenancy is not a secure one are set out below.

(1) long leases (*see* **9**);
(2) premises occupied in connection with employment (*see* **10**);
(3) land acquired for development (*see* **11**);
(4) accommodation for homeless persons (*see* **12**);
(5) temporary accommodation for persons taking up employment (*see* **13**);
(6) short term arrangements (*see* **14**);
(7) temporary accommodation during works (*see* **15**);
(8) agricultural holdings (*see* **16**);
(9) licensed premises (*see* **17**);
(10) student lettings (*see* **18**);
(11) 1954 Act tenancies (*see* **19**);
(12) almshouses (*see* **20**).

9. Long leases. A tenancy is not a secure one if it is a long tenancy. A long tenancy is one granted for a term certain exceeding 21 years, whether or not it is (or may become) terminable before the end of that term by notice given by the tenant or by re-entry or forfeiture.

10. Premises occupied in connection with employment. A tenancy is not a secure one if the tenant is an employee of the landlord or, if not such an employee, is an employee of anybody listed in para. 2(1) of Sch. 1, and his contract of employment requires him to occupy the dwelling-house for the better performance of his duties. This exception also covers lettings to a member of a police force where the dwelling-house is provided for him free of rent and rates in pursuance of regulations made under s. 33 of the Police Act 1964.

It also covers lettings where the tenant is an employee of a fire authority and (*a*) his contract of employment requires him to live in close proximity to a particular fire station and (*b*) the dwelling-house was let to him by the authority in consequence of that requirement.

> NOTE: After there has been a letting of a dwelling falling within **10**, the landlord may let the dwelling for periods in aggregate amounting to not more than three years without creating a secure tenancy provided (*i*) the letting takes place within three years of the grant of a tenancy to which **10** applies and (*ii*) the landlord gives notice that this exception is to apply.

11. Land acquired for development. A tenancy is not a secure one if the dwelling-house is on land which has been acquired for development and the dwelling-house is used by the landlord, pending development of the land, for temporary housing accommodation.

12. Accommodation for homeless persons. A tenancy granted under certain provisions relating to homelessness (*see* ss. 63(3), 65(3) and 68(1)) is not a secure one before the end of a period of 12 months after the authority notifies the tenant whether he is homeless.

13. Temporary accommodation for persons taking up employment. A tenancy of a dwelling-house in a district granted to someone who was not immediately before the grant resident in the district is not a secure one for a year if it was granted to meet the person's need for temporary accommodation within the district in order to work there and for enabling him to find permanent accommodation there. Also, before the grant of the tenancy, the tenant must have obtained employment in the district or its surrounding area and the landlord must have notified the tenant in writing that this exception applies. In relation to a district, the surrounding area means the area of each adjoining district. The exception ceases to apply if before the end of the year, the tenant has been notified by the landlord that the tenancy is to be regarded as a secure tenancy.

14. Short-term arrangements. A tenancy is not a secure one if:

(a) the dwelling-house has been leased to the landlord with vacant possession for use as temporary housing accommodation;
(b) the terms on which it has been leased include provision for the

lessor to obtain vacant possession from the landlord on the expiry of a specified period or when required by the lessor;

(c) the lessor is not a body which is capable of granting secure tenancies; and

(d) the landlord has no interest in the dwelling-house other than under the lease in question or as mortgagee.

15. Temporary accommodation during works. A tenancy is not a secure one if:

(a) the dwelling-house has been made available for occupation by the tenant or his predecessor in title while works are carried out on the dwelling-house which he previously occupied as his home; and

(b) the tenant (or his predecessor in title) was not a secure tenant of that other dwelling-house at the time when he ceased to occupy it as his home.

16. Agricultural holdings. A tenancy is not a secure one if the dwelling-house is comprised in an agricultural holding (within the meaning of the Agricultural Holdings Act 1986) and is occupied by the person responsible for the control (whether as tenant or as servant or agent of the tenant) of the farming of the holding.

17. Licensed premises. A tenancy is not a secure one if the dwelling-house consists of or comprises premises licensed for the sale of intoxicating liquor for consumption on the premises.

18. Student lettings. A tenancy of a dwelling-house is not a secure one before the expiry of the period of exemption if:

(a) it was granted for the purpose of enabling the tenant to attend a designated course at an educational establishment; and

(b) before the grant of the tenancy the landlord notified him in writing of the circumstances in which this exception applies and that in its opinion the proposed tenancy would fall within this exception;

unless the tenant has before the expiry of that period been notified by the landlord that the tenancy is to be regarded as a secure tenancy.

A landlord's notice under **(b)** must specify the educational establishment which the person concerned proposes to attend.

In this context:

(a) 'designated course' means any course of a kind designated in regulations made by the Secretary of State for the purposes of this paragraph;

(b) 'educational establishment' means a university or establishment of further education; and
(c) 'the period of exemption' means, in a case where the tenant attends a designated course at the educational establishment specified in the landlord's notice, the period ending six months after the tenant ceases to attend that (or any other) designated course at that educational establishment and, in any other case, the period ending six months after the grant of the tenancy.

19. Part II of the 1954 Act. A tenancy is not a secure one if it is one to which Part II of the Landlord and Tenant Act 1954 applies.

20. Almshouses. Certain licences to occupy an almshouse are not secure tenancies.

21. General. The provisions of some of the above categories are complex and are only summarised here. Where necessary students should refer to the detailed provisions of Sch. 1.

Security of tenure

22. Security of tenure for secure tenants. The Act gives security of tenure to secure tenants by:

(a) restricting the ways in which the tenancy can come to an end (*see* **23**);
(b) allowing for one succession on the death of a tenant (*see* **24, 25**); and
(c) providing that possession may only be recovered in certain limited cases (*see* **26** *et seq.*).

23. Restrictions on termination of a secure tenancy. The Act makes the following restrictions on the ways in which a tenancy may be determined:

(a) at the end of a tenancy for a term certain, there arises a periodic tenancy on the same terms as those of the first tenancy in so far as they are compatible with a periodic tenancy but not including any proviso for re-entry or forfeiture: s. 86(1), (2). The period of the tenancy will depend on the period for which rent was last payable under the first tenancy;
(b) a tenancy which is a weekly or other periodic one cannot be ended by the landlord except by obtaining a court order for possession of the dwelling-house: s. 82(1);

(c) where there is a tenancy for a term certain with a proviso for re-entry or forfeiture, the court cannot order possession in pursuance of that provision; the court may, however, make an order terminating the tenancy for a term certain (s. 82(3)) and there then arises a periodic tenancy under s. 86(1).

24. Succession on death of a tenant. Where a secure tenancy is a periodic one and, on the death of the tenant, there is a person qualified to succeed him, the tenancy vests in that person by virtue of s. 89(1). A person is qualified to succeed if:

(a) he occupied the dwelling-house as his only or principal home at the time of the tenant's death; and either
(b) he is the tenant's spouse; or
(c) he is another member of the tenant's family and has resided with the tenant throughout the period of 12 months ending with the tenant's death.

Where there is more than one person qualified to succeed the tenant:

(a) the tenant's spouse is to be preferred to another member of the tenant's family; and
(b) of two or more other members, such one of them is to be preferred as may be agreed between them or, in default of agreement, to be selected by the landlord: s. 89(2).

25. Exceptions to succession on death of tenant. The above provisions for succession do not apply where the tenant is a successor. A tenant is a successor if, inter alia:

(a) the tenancy was vested in him by virtue of s. 89;
(b) he was a joint tenant and has become the sole tenant;
(c) the tenancy is a periodic one which arose following the termination of a tenancy for a fixed term granted to another person or jointly to him and another person;
(d) he became the tenant on the tenancy being assigned to him or on its having vested in him on the death of the previous tenant; s. 88(1).

26. Recovery of possession in limited cases. There are two limitations on the landlord's right to possession. They are that the landlord:

(a) must first serve a notice on the tenant (s. 83)(*see* **27**); and
(b) then establish one of the specified grounds for possession (s. 84)(*see* **28–31**)

27. Notice requiring possession. A court cannot entertain proceedings for possession or for the termination of a secure tenancy against a secure tenant unless the landlord has served on the tenant a notice which complies with s. 83(2). The notice must:

(a) be in the form prescribed by the Secretary of State;
(b) specify the ground on which possession is sought;
(c) specify a date after which proceedings may be begun; in the case of a periodic tenancy the date must not be earlier than that on which the tenancy could have been brought to an end by notice to quit given on the same date as the notice under s. 83.

The notice remains in effect for only 12 months after the date specified in it and proceedings begun before the date or 12 months after the date are of no effect.

28. Grounds for possession. By virtue of s. 84(1), the court cannot make an order for possession of a dwelling-house let under a secure tenancy except on one or more of the grounds set out in Sch. 2. Further, the court cannot make an order unless the ground is specified in the notice given under s. 83(2).

29. Schedule 2. The specified grounds are as follows.

PART I

(a) *Ground 1.* Any rent lawfully due from the tenant has not been paid or any obligation of the tenancy has been broken or not performed.
(b) *Ground 2.* The tenant or any person residing in the dwelling-house has been guilty of conduct which is a nuisance or annoyance to neighbours, or has been convicted of using the dwelling-house or allowing it to be used for immoral or illegal purposes.
(c) *Ground 3.* The condition of the dwelling-house or of any of the common parts has deteriorated owing to acts of waste by, or the neglect or default of, the tenant or any person residing in the dwelling-house and, in the case of any act of waste by, or the neglect or default of, a person lodging with the tenant or a sub-tenant of his, the tenant has not taken such steps as he ought reasonably to have taken for the removal of the lodger or sub-tenant.
(d) *Ground 4.* The condition of any furniture provided by the landlord for use under the tenancy or for use in the common parts has deteriorated owing to ill-treatment by the tenant or any person residing in the dwelling-house and, in the case of any ill-treatment by a person lodging with the tenant or a sub-tenant of his, the tenant has

not taken such steps as he ought reasonably to have taken for the removal of the lodger or sub-tenant.

(e) *Ground 5.* The tenant is the person, or one of the persons, to whom the tenancy was granted and the landlord was induced to grant the tenancy by a false statement made knowingly or recklessly by the tenant.

(f) *Ground 6.* The tenancy was assigned to the tenant, or to a predecessor in title of his who is a member of his family and is residing in the dwelling, by an assignment made by virtue of s. 92 (assignments by way of exchange), and a premium was paid either in connection with that assignment or the assignment which the tenant or his predecessor himself made by virtue of that section. 'Premium' means a fine or other like sum and any other pecuniary consideration in addition to rent.

(g) *Ground 7.* The dwelling forms part of, or is within the curtilage of, a building which is held mainly for purposes other than housing purposes and consists mainly of accommodation other than housing accommodation and (*a*) the dwelling was let to the tenant or a predecessor in title in consequence of the tenant or his predecessor being in the employment of the landlord or certain specified bodies, and (*b*) the tenant or any person residing in the dwelling has been guilty of conduct such that, having regard to the purpose for which the building is used, it would not be right for him to continue in occupation of the dwelling.

(h) *Ground 8.* The dwelling-house was made available for occupation by the tenant or his predecessor in title while works were carried out on the dwelling-house which he previously occupied as his only or principal home and

(*i*) he (or his predecessor in title) was a secure tenant of that other dwelling-house at the time when he ceased to occupy it as his home;

(*ii*) he (or his predecessor in title) accepted the tenancy of the dwelling-house of which possession is sought on the understanding that he would give up occupation when, on completion of the works, the other dwelling-house was again available for occupation by him under a secure tenancy; and

(*iii*) the works have been completed and the other dwelling-house is so available.

PART II

(i) *Ground 9.* The dwelling-house is overcrowded, within the meaning of Part X in such circumstances as to render the occupier guilty of an offence.

(j) *Ground 10.* The landlord intends, within a reasonable time of obtaining possession of the dwelling-house:

(*i*) to demolish or reconstruct the building or part of the building comprising the dwelling-house; or

(*ii*) to carry out work on that building or on land let together with, and thus treated as part of, the dwelling-house; and cannot reasonably do so without obtaining possession of the dwelling-house.

(k) *Ground 10A.* The dwelling-house is in an area subject to a redevelopment scheme approved by the Secretary of State and the landlord intends within a reasonable time of obtaining possession to dispose of the dwelling-house in accordance with the scheme.

(l) *Ground 11.* The landlord is a charity and the tenant's continued occupation of the dwelling-house would conflict with the objects of the charity.

PART III

(m) *Ground 12.* The dwelling-house either forms part of a building, or is within the curtilage of, a building which is held mainly for purposes other than housing purposes and consists mainly of accommodation other than housing accommodation, or is situated in a cemetery and (*a*) the landlord reasonably requires the dwelling-house as a residence for some person engaged in the employment of the landlord or certain specified bodies or with whom, conditional on housing being provided, a contract for such employment has been entered into, and (*b*) the dwelling-house was let to the tenant or to a predecessor in title of his in consequence of the tenant or predecessor being in the employment of the landlord or of a body so specified and the tenant or predecessor has ceased to be in that employment.

(n) *Ground 13.* The dwelling-house has features which are substantially different from those of ordinary dwelling-houses and which are designed to make it suitable for occupation by a physically disabled person who requires accommodation of a kind provided by the dwelling-house and

(*i*) there is no longer such a person residing in the dwelling-house; and

(*ii*) the landlord requires it for occupation (whether alone or with other members of his family) by such a person.

(o) *Ground 14.* The landlord is a housing association or housing trust which lets dwelling-houses only for occupation (alone or with others) by persons whose circumstances (other than merely financial circumstances) make it especially difficult for them to satisfy their need for housing; and (*i*) either there is no longer such a person residing in the dwelling-house or the tenant has received from a local authority an offer of accommodation in premises which are to be let as a separate dwelling under a secure tenancy; and

(*ii*) the landlord requires the dwelling-house for occupation (whether alone or with other members of his family) by such a person.

(p) *Ground 15*. The dwelling-house is one of a group of dwelling-houses which it is the practice of the landlord to let for occupation by persons with special needs and

(*i*) a social service or special facility is provided in close proximity to the group of dwelling-houses in order to assist persons with those special needs;

(*ii*) there is no longer a person with those special needs resident in the dwelling-house; and

(*iii*) the landlord requires the dwelling-house for occupation (whether alone or with other members of his family) by a person who has those special needs.

(q) *Ground 16*. The accommodation afforded by the dwelling-house is more extensive than is reasonably required by the tenant and

(*i*) the tenancy vested in the tenant, by virtue of s. 89, on the death of the previous tenant;

(*ii*) the tenant was qualified to succeed by virtue of s. 87(6) (members of family other than spouse); and

(*iii*) notice of the proceedings for possession was served under s. 83, more than six months, but less than twelve months, after the date of the previous tenant's death.

30. Restrictions on court orders. By s. 84(2) the court is debarred from making an order under grounds 1–8 unless condition **(a)** below is satisfied. It cannot make an order under grounds 9–11 unless condition **(b)** is satisfied. It cannot make an order under grounds 12–16 unless both conditions are satisfied. The conditions are:

(a) that the court considers it reasonable to make an order;
(b) that the court is satisfied that suitable accommodation will be available for the tenant when the order takes effect.

The matters to be taken into account by the court in determining whether it is reasonable to make an order under ground 16 include:

(a) the age of the tenant;
(b) the period for which the tenant has occupied the dwelling-house; and

(c) any financial or other support given by the tenant to the previous tenant.

Sch. 2, Part IV contains detailed provisions for determining whether suitable accommodation will be available for a tenant.

31. Suspended orders. The county court has a wide power to adjourn the proceedings or to postpone the date for possession or stay or suspend the execution of the order, or impose conditions on making such orders: s. 85 of the 1985 Act and s. 89 of the Housing Act 1980.

Terms of a secure tenancy

32. Introduction. The terms of a secure tenancy will generally be those agreed between the parties. There are, however, some terms implied by statute. They relate to:

(a) sub-letting and lodgers (*see* **33**);
(b) assignment (*see* **34**);
(c) improvements (*see* **35**);
(d) variation of terms (*see* **36**);
(e) repairs (*see* **37**);
(f) heating charges (*see* **38**).

33. Sub-letting and lodgers. By virtue of s. 93(1)(a) it is a term of every secure tenancy that the tenant may allow any persons to reside as lodgers in the dwelling-house.

By virtue of s. 93(1)(b) it is a term of every secure tenancy that the tenant will not, without the written consent of the landlord, sub-let or part with the possession of part of the dwelling-house. Consent is not to be unreasonably withheld and, if unreasonably withheld, will be treated as given: s. 94(1) and (2).

34. Assignment. A secure tenancy which is either a periodic tenancy granted at any time or a tenancy for a fixed term granted after 5th November 1982 is not capable of being assigned unless (*a*) the assignment is made in pursuance of an order under the Matrimonial Causes Act 1973, s. 24, or (*b*) the assignment is made to a person who would be eligible for succession (*see* **24** above) if the tenant had died immediately before the assignment, or (*c*) the assignment is made by virtue of s. 92 (assignment by way of exchange): *see* s. 91(1) and (3). A secure tenancy which is for a fixed term and was granted before 5th

November 1982 ceases to be a secure tenancy if it is assigned unless the assignment falls within (*a*), (*b*) or (*c*) above: s. 91(2).

Section 92 provides that it is a term of every secure tenancy that the tenant may, with the written consent of the landlord, assign the tenancy to any person who is a secure tenant who has the written consent of his landlord to assign his tenancy to the other tenant or some other person who is a secure tenant who has the written consent of his landlord to assign. In other words this provision enables secure tenants to exchange their tenancies. The landlord may only refuse his consent on the grounds set out in Sch. 3 which are outside the scope of this book. The landlord may give his consent conditionally subject to a condition requiring the tenant to pay any outstanding rent or remedy any breach of covenant.

If the tenant under a secure tenancy parts with the possession of a dwelling-house or sub-lets the whole of it (or sub-lets first part of it and then the remainder) the tenancy ceases to be secure: s. 93(2). Where, on the death of the tenant, a secure tenancy is vested or otherwise disposed of in the course of the administration of his estate, the tenancy ceases to be a secure tenancy unless (*a*) the vesting is pursuant to the Matrimonial Causes Act 1973, s. 24, or (*b*) the vesting is to a person eligible for succession (*see* **24** above): s. 90.

35. Improvements. This is dealt with in 4:**18**. In addition, s. 100 provides that where a secure tenant has made certain improvements, the landlord has a power (not a duty) to make such payment to the tenant as the landlord considers to be appropriate at or after the end of the tenancy.

Sections 99A and B, added by section 122 of the 1993 Act, empower the Secretary of State to make regulations for entitling qualifying persons to be paid compensation at the time when the tenancy comes to an end. The compensation is for improvements begun not earlier than the commencement of section 122 of the 1993 Act, carried out with the written consent of the landlord and where at the end of the tenancy the landlord is a local authority and the tenancy is a secure tenancy.

36. Variation of terms. Section 102 provides that the terms of a secure tenancy may be varied in accordance with the provisions of the section but not otherwise; the variations may be effected by agreement or, in the case of rent or payments in respect of rates or services, by the landlord or the tenant in accordance with any provisions in the lease. If the tenancy is a periodic one, the variation may also be effected by the landlord by a notice of variation which must specify the variation effected by it and the date on which it takes effect and the period between the date of service and the date on which it takes effect must not be shorter than the rental period of the tenancy nor shorter than four weeks. Prior to serving a notice of variation the landlord must serve a preliminary notice on the tenant informing him of his intention to serve a notice of variation and must consider any comments made by the tenant in response to the preliminary notice: s. 103. In relation to rent or the payment of rates and services, however, there is no need to serve a preliminary notice.

37. Provision of information about tenancies. By s. 104 every body which lets dwelling-houses under secure tenancies must from time to time publish information about its secure tenancies to explain in simple terms the effect of, inter alia, the express terms of its secure tenancies and the effect of certain parts of the 1985 Act and the Landlord and Tenant Act 1985, ss. 11 to 16. A local authority which is a landlord under a secure tenancy must supply the tenant with the information relating to the right to buy – and the landlord's repairing obligations at least once in every year following its publication: s. 104(9).

38. Repairs. Section 96 as substituted by s. 121 of the 1993 Act provides that the Secretary of State may make regulations for entitling secure tenants whose landlords are local housing authorities to have qualifying repairs carried out, at their landlord's expense, to the dwelling-house of which they are tenants.

39. Heating charges. Under s. 108 the Secretary of State has power by regulations to require heating authorities (i.e. a landlord which operates its own generating station or other installation for producing heat and supplies heat produced by it to any premises) to adopt such methods of charging as ensure that the tenants pay no greater proportion of the cost of operating the installation and producing heat than is reasonable.

Progress test 32

1. What is a secure tenancy? **(2)**

2. What are the exceptions to secure tenancies? **(8)**

3. Explain how the 1985 Act gives security of tenure to secure tenants. **(22)**

4. How may a secure tenancy come to an end? **(23)**

5. What are the rules governing succession on the death of a secure tenant? **(24–25)**

6. How may the landlord of a secure tenant recover possession against the tenant? **(26)**

7. What is ground 8? Is there an equivalent ground in the Rent Act 1977? **(29)**

8. What terms are implied in a secure tenancy? **(32)**

9. Under what duty as regards information is a landlord of a secure tenant? **(37)**

Secure tenants: the right to buy

1. Introduction. The Housing Act 1980 gave to certain public sector tenants the right to buy their house or flat if they had lived there for at least two years. The price payable (*see* **10** *et seq.*) will be discounted so that the price payable by the tenant will be lower the longer he has lived in the house. A tenant who has a right to buy formerly had a right to a mortgage but now has a right to acquire on rent to mortgage terms (*see* **15** *et seq.*). The right to buy was extended by the Housing and Building Control Act 1984. The relevant provisions are now contained in Part V of the Housing Act 1985, as amended by the Housing and Planning Act 1986, the Housing Act 1988 and the Leasehold Reform, Housing and Urban Development Act 1993.

The right to buy

2. Introduction. A secure tenant of a house has the right to acquire the freehold of it if the landlord owns the freehold or, if the landlord does not own the freehold, to be granted a lease of it: s. 118(1). A secure tenant of a flat has the right to be granted a lease of it: s. 118(1). In addition, in either case the secure tenant has the right to leave the whole or part of the aggregate amount of the purchase price and certain costs outstanding on the security of a first mortgage of the dwelling-house or, if the landlord is a housing association, to have the whole or part of that amount advanced to him on security by the Housing Corporation. The right to buy only arises after the secure tenant has enjoyed that status for not less than two years or for periods amounting together to not less than two years: s. 119(1) and Schedule 4. There are two special cases:

(a) in the case of a joint tenancy the condition need only be satisfied with respect to one tenant;

(b) where the secure tenant becomes a secure tenant on the death of his spouse under s. 87, any period during which the deceased spouse was a secure tenant is to be counted for determining the two years.

3. Exceptions to the right to buy. There are several cases where the right to buy does not arise: *see* Sch. 5. The main ones are:

(a) if the landlord is a housing trust or a housing association which is a charity within the meaning of the Charities Act 1960: Sch. 5, para. 1;

(b) if the landlord is a co-operative housing association or a housing association which has never received a grant under certain specified enactments: *see* Sch. 5, paras. 2 and 3;

(c) where the landlord does not have, in the case of a house, a lease for a term exceeding 21 years commencing with the date when the tenant gave his notice claiming to exercise the right to buy, and, in the case of a flat, a lease for a term of not less than 50 years commencing with that date: Sch. 5, para. 4;

(d) if the landlord is a local authority, new town corporation, an urban development corporation, an aided school or the Development Board for Rural Wales, and the dwelling-house either is in a cemetery or in the curtilage of a building held mainly for purposes other than housing and consists mainly of accommodation other than housing accommodation and the dwelling-house is let to the tenant in consequence of his employment by the landlord: Sch. 5, para. 5;

(e) the dwelling-house has features which are substantially different from those of ordinary dwelling-houses and which are designed to make it suitable for occupation by physically disabled persons, and the dwelling-house is one of a group of dwelling-houses which it is the practice of the landlord to let for occupation by physically disabled persons, and a social service or special facilities are provided in close proximity to the group to assist those persons: Sch. 5, para. 7;

(f) the dwelling-house is one of a group of dwelling-houses which it is the practice of the landlord to let for occupation by persons who suffer, or have suffered, from a mental disorder and a social service or special facilities are provided for assisting those persons: Sch. 5, para. 9;

(g) the dwelling-house is one of a group of dwelling-houses which are particularly suitable, having regard to location, size, design, heating and other features, for occupation by elderly persons which it is the practice of the landlord to let for occupation by persons aged 60 or more or by them and physically disabled persons, and special facilities are provided to assist them: Sch. 5, para. 10;

(h) the Secretary of State has determined, on application by the landlord, that the right to buy is not to be capable of being exercised if the dwelling-house (*i*) is particularly suitable, having regard to its location, size, design and other features, for occupation by elderly persons

and (*ii*) it was let to the tenant for occupation by a person aged 60 or more provided that (*a*) the landlord must apply within 8 weeks of service of the notice exercising the right to buy and (*b*) the dwelling-house was first let before 1st January 1990: Sch. 5, para. 11;
(**i**) dwelling-houses held on certain Crown tenancies: Sch. 5, para. 12.

Further, the right to buy cannot be exercised by the tenant if he is obliged to give up possession of the dwelling-house pursuant to an order of the court, or if the person, or one of the persons to whom the right belongs, (*a*) has a bankruptcy petition pending against him, (*b*) has a receiving order in force against him, (*c*) is an undischarged bankrupt or (*d*) has made a composition or arrangement with his creditors the terms of which remain to be fulfilled: s. 121.

4. Dwelling-house, house and flat. Section 183 contains provisions dealing with the inter-relation of these words. The following rules emerge from s. 183:

(**a**) a dwelling-house is a house if it is a structure which can reasonably be called a house;
(**b**) where a building is divided horizontally, the units into which it is divided are *not* houses;
(**c**) where a building is divided vertically, the units into which it is divided *may* be houses;
(**d**) where a building is not structurally detached, it is not a house if a material part of it lies above or below the remainder of the structure.

Any dwelling-house which is not a house is a flat.
In most cases it will be easy to decide if a unit is a house or a flat. Where there is doubt, the proper approach is to apply rules (*a*)–(*d*) above. If the result of applying the rules is that the unit is not a house then it will be a flat. There is treated as included in the dwelling-house any land which is or has been used for the purposes of the dwelling-house if (*a*) the tenant serves written notice exercising the right to acquire the land at any time before exercising the right to buy and (*b*) it is reasonable to include the land: s. 184.

Procedural matters

5. Procedure for exercising right to buy. In order to exercise the right to buy, a secure tenant must serve a written notice claiming to exercise the right to buy: s. 122. The tenant may share the right with not more than three members of his family who occupy the dwelling-house as their only or principal home: s. 123. Within four weeks (eight weeks if the current landlord has not always been the tenant's landlord during the two years) of service the landlord must serve a written notice either admitting or denying the tenant's right and stating the reason why, in the opinion of the landlord, the tenant does not have the right to buy: s. 124. By section 125 where a secure tenant has claimed to exercise the right to buy and that right has been established, the landlord shall within eight weeks (twelve weeks in the case of acquisition of a lease) serve on the tenant a notice of the purchase price and other matters, including in the case of a lease information about estimated service charges and improvement contributions.

6. Purchase price. By s. 126(1) the price payable for a dwelling-house is the value of it at the date of service of the tenant's notice exercising the right to buy, less the discount.

7. The value of the dwelling-house. By s. 127 the value at the relevant time is taken to be the price which, at that time, the dwelling-house would realise if sold on the open market by a willing vendor on certain specified assumptions and disregarding:

(a) any improvements made by
    (*i*) the secure tenant;
    (*ii*) any person who under the same tenancy was a secure tenant before him; and
    (*iii*) any member of the secure tenant's family who, immediately before the secure tenancy was granted, was a secure tenant of the same dwelling-house under another tenancy; and
(b) any failure by any of the above persons to keep the dwelling-house in good internal repair.

8. Assumptions on sale of freehold. By s. 127(2) the assumptions are that:

(a) the sale is of an estate in fee simple with vacant possession;
(b) neither the tenant nor a member of his family residing with him wanted to buy;
(c) the dwelling-house was to be conveyed with the same rights and subject to the same burdens as it would be in pursuance of the 1985 Act.

9. Assumptions on grant of a lease. By s. 127(3) the assumptions are that:

(a) the vendor was granting a lease for 125 years or, if his interest is less than 125 years and 5 days, for 5 days before the term of the landlord's lease expires, with vacant possession;

(b) neither the tenant nor a member of his family residing with him wanted to take the lease;

(c) the ground rent would not exceed £10 per annum; and

(d) the grant was to be made with the same rights and subject to the same burdens as it would be in pursuance of the 1985 Act;

(e) any service charges or improvement contributions will not be less than those in the landlord's notice under s. 125 (*see* **5** above).

10. Discount. A discount is available to those who are exercising the right to buy. The starting point is to calculate, in accordance with Sch. 4, the period during which the secure tenant, the secure tenant's spouse or the secure tenant's deceased spouse, was a public sector tenant or the spouse of a public sector tenant. When that period has been calculated there are these basic rules to apply under s. 129(2):

(a) If the period is less than three years the discount is 32 per cent in the case of a house and 44 per cent in the case of a flat.

(b) If it is three years or more, in the case of a house the discount is 32 per cent plus 1 per cent for each complete year by which the period exceeds two years, but not exceeding 60 per cent and, in the case of a flat, it is 44 per cent plus 2 per cent for each complete year by which the period exceeds two years but not exceeding 70 per cent.

Under s. 129(2A) the Secretary of State has power by order to increase the minimum percentage discount, the annual percentage increase and the maximum percentage discount.

11. Limits on the discount. The discount cannot reduce the price below the amount which the Secretary of State determines to be the cost incurred in respect of the dwelling-house as is to be treated as incurred after 31st March 1974 or such later date as the Secretary of State may specify by order: s. 131(1). Further, the discount cannot in any case reduce the price by more than such sum as the Secretary of State may by order prescribe: s. 131(2).

12. Repayment of discount on early disposal of freehold or leasehold. Where a discount is granted and there is a relevant disposal of the freehold or leasehold within three years of the initial sale, a proportion of the discount must be repaid to the landlord: s. 155. The repayment is the amount of the discount less one-third thereof for each complete year after the initial sale: s. 155(2). There are exceptions to this rule requiring repayment where, inter alia, the disposal is to a 'qualifying person', i.e. one of the two joint owners, a spouse, or a member of the family residing in the house for twelve months ending with the disposal: s. 160.

13. Meaning of relevant disposal. A relevant disposal is (*a*) a further conveyance of the freehold or assignment of the lease or (*b*) a grant of a lease or sub-lease for more than 21 years otherwise than at a rack rent, whether the disposal is of the whole or part of the dwelling-house: s. 159(1). For the purposes of (*b*) above, it is assumed that any option to renew or extend a lease or sub-lease is exercised and that any option to terminate a lease or sub-lease is not exercised.

14. Enforcement of recovery of discount. Any liability to repay a discount that may arise by reason of an early disposal takes effect as a charge in favour of the landlord on the dwelling-house having priority immediately after any legal charge securing any amount left outstanding by the tenant in exercising the right to buy or advanced to him by, inter alia, the Housing Corporation or any building society, for the purpose of enabling him to exercise the right to buy and immediately after any charge securing redemption of the landlord's share under the right to acquire on rent to mortgage terms: s. 156.

15. Right to acquire on rent to mortgage terms. The Housing Act 1980 included the right to a mortgage. A tenant could also defer completion for up to two years. Alternatively, the tenant could claim a 'shared ownership' lease. These rights were intended to assist tenants with insufficient resources to exercise the right to buy. All three rights are abolished by the Leasehold Reform, Housing and Urban Development Act 1993. They are replaced by the right to acquire on rent to mortgage terms: see s. 108 of the 1993 Act amending the 1985 Act. In summary, this converts the tenant's rent payments into mortgage repayments. The difference between the amount of these payments and what the tenant would otherwise pay to buy under the right to buy is a charge on the property to be paid on disposal or on the death of the last member of the tenant's family to live there.

16. When the right arises. The right to acquire on rent to mortgage terms arises when a secure tenant's right to buy has been established and his notice claiming to exercise it remains in force: Housing Act 1985, s. 143(1). The right cannot be exercised if the tenant has claimed or been found entitled to claim housing benefit at any time from twelve months before claiming the right up to the date of the conveyance or grant: s. 143A. The right cannot be exercised if the tenant's financial resources are too high: s. 143B. The details of s. 143B are outside the scope of this book. However in essence underlying the calculations is the principle that if the tenant's rental payments could support a mortgage of 80% of the price payable for the dwelling-house under the right to buy then the tenant should not be able to exercise the rent to mortgage right.

17. Exercising the right. The right is exercised by the tenant giving written notice to the landlord: s. 144(1). The notice may be withdrawn at any time by notice served on the landlord and the tenant may then complete in the ordinary way: s. 144(2) and (4). Exercising the right ends any notice to complete served by the landlord: s. 144(3). Where a notice has been served under s. 144 the landlord must serve on the tenant as soon as practicable a written notice either admitting the right or denying it giving reasons: s. 146(1). Where the landlord admits the right he must also give the tenant certain specified information: s. 146(2). Within twelve weeks of the landlord's notice the tenant must serve a written notice on the landlord stating either (*a*) that he intends to pursue his claim to exercise the right to acquire on rent to mortgage terms and the amount of the initial payment he proposes to make or (*b*) that he withdraws that claim and intends to pursue his claim to exercise the right to buy or (*c*) that he withdraws both of those claims: s. 146A(1). If the tenant fails to serve notice under s. 146A the landlord can serve written notice requiring the tenant to do so within 28 days: s. 146B(1). If the tenant does not comply with that notice then the notice claiming to exercise the right to acquire on rent to mortgage terms is deemed to be withdrawn: s. 146B(4). Where the tenant has served notice of his intention to pursue his claim the landlord must as soon as practicable serve notice informing the tenant of the 'landlord's share' and the amount of the 'initial discount'. The 'landlord's share' is that part of the price payable under the right to buy less the tenant's initial payment: s. 148. The 'initial discount' is a proportion of the usual discount (see **10**): s. 148. When the tenant has established his right to rent to mortgage, the landlord is under a duty to complete the transaction: s. 150. The conveyance must deal with the redemption of the landlord's share: s. 151A.

18. Redemption of 'landlord's share'. In certain circumstances the 'landlord's share' must be repaid: Housing Act 1985, Sch. 6A. This is achieved by imposing on the tenant a covenant to make a final payment to redeem the landlord's share immediately after either (*a*) a relevant disposal or (*b*) the expiry of one year from a relevant death.

The value of the landlord's share is the percentage share which the landlord has before redemption, multiplied by the value of the property at the time of redemption: Sch. 6A, para. 3. A 'relevant disposal' is a further conveyance of the freehold or an assignment of the lease or the grant of a lease for more than 21 years unless at a rack rent (s. 159) but excluding (*a*) transfers between spouses, (*b*) transmission by will or on an intestacy or (*c*) disposal pursuant to a court order on divorce or family provision. A 'relevant death' is, in effect, the death of the last member of the tenant's family to live in the dwelling-house. There is also a power given to the tenant to redeem either wholly, or in part, subject to a minimum of 10% of the property's value: Sch. 6A, para. 10. The tenant's liability to redeem the landlord's share must be secured by a mortgage having priority immediately after the charge securing any loan advanced to the tenant by an approved lending institution for the purpose of enabling him to exercise the right to acquire on rent to mortgage terms: s. 151B(2).

19. Notices to complete in case of right to acquire on rent to mortgage terms. Sections 152 and 153 contain provisions regarding notices to complete where the matter is proceeding under the right to acquire on rent to mortgage terms. They correspond to those considered in **26** below except that the landlord's first notice to complete cannot be served earlier than twelve months from the landlord's notice under s. 146.

20. Notice of purchase price. Where a secure tenant has claimed to exercise the right to buy and that right has been established, under s. 125 the landlord must within eight weeks (in the case of the sale of a freehold) or 12 weeks (in the case of the sale of a lease) serve on the tenant a notice describing the dwelling-house and stating inter alia:

(a) the price, showing the value, the discount and improvements disregarded;
(b) the provisions of the conveyance or grant;
(c) that the tenant has the right to have the value determined by the District Valuer;
(d) that the tenant has the right to acquire on rent to mortgage terms;
(e) information regarding the right to acquire on rent to mortgage terms;
(f) where appropriate, estimates and information about service charges and improvement contributions;
(g) a description of any structural defect known to the landlord affecting the dwelling-house or the building in which it is situated;

(h) the effect of failure to complete;

(i) the effect of ss. 125D and E (see **21** and **22** below).

21. Tenant's notice of intention. Where a notice under s. 125 has been served on the tenant he must, within twelve weeks of the later of (*a*) the service of the notice under section 125 and (*b*) the notice of determination or re-determination of value by the district valuer, serve a written notice on the landlord stating either (*a*) that he intends to pursue his claim to exercise the right to buy or that he withdraws that claim or (*b*) that he claims to exercise the right to acquire on rent to mortgage terms: s. 125D(1).

22. Landlord's notice in default. At any time after the expiry of the period mentioned in **21** above, under s. 125E the landlord may serve on the tenant written notice requiring him, if he has failed to serve the notice required by s. 125D(1), to serve that notice within 28 days and informing him of the effect of s. 125E. If the tenant does not comply with the notice, the notice claiming to exercise the right to buy shall be deemed to be withdrawn at the end of that period: s. 125D(4).

23. Determination of value by District Valuer. Any question arising as to the value of a dwelling-house will be determined by the District Valuer: s. 128(1). A tenant can require the District Valuer to determine the value by written notice served on the landlord not later than three months after service of the notice under s. 125 (*see* **20**). The District Valuer must consider any representations made by the landlord or tenant. After the determination, the landlord must serve a notice on the tenant stating the effect of the determination: s. 128(5).

24. Change of parties. In ss. 136, 137 there are provisions dealing with change of tenant and landlord. The rules to be derived from these sections are:

(a) Where after a secure tenant has given notice claiming the right to buy, another person becomes the secure tenant either
(*i*) under the same secure tenancy; or
(*ii*) under a periodic tenancy arising by virtue of s. 86 (*see* **32:23**), on the coming to an end of the secure tenancy, the new tenant is in the same position as if he had given the notice: s. 136(1);
(b) where, after a secure tenant has given a notice claiming the right to buy, the freehold passes to another body, all parties are in the same position as if the other body had become the landlord before the notice was given: s. 137.

25. Children succeeding parents. Schedule 4, para. 4 contains provisions dealing with the case of children succeeding deceased parents as secure tenants of the dwelling-house. Certain periods count toward the periods required under s. 119 (the residential qualification: *see* 2) and s. 129 (the discount: *see* 10).

26. Completion. Section 140 contains provisions relating to the completion of the sale or lease. It enables the landlord to serve at least 56 days notice on the tenant requiring him, if all relevant matters have been agreed or determined, to complete the transaction within a specified period of not less than 56 days, or if any relevant matters are outstanding, to serve on the landlord within that period written notice specifying those matters, and, in any event, informing the tenant of the effect of the notice, (the 'landlord's first notice to complete'). The landlord may not serve this notice before the times specified in s. 134(3) have expired. Under section 141, if the tenant does not comply with the above notice, the landlord may serve on him a further written notice requiring him to complete within a specific period of not less than 56 days, which period may be extended by the landlord under s. 141(3). If the tenant does not comply with this notice, (the 'landlord's second notice to complete') then the notice claiming the right to buy is deemed to be withdrawn at the end of the period specified therein or any extended period: s. 141(4). Under s. 138(1) the landlord is under a duty to complete as soon as all matters relating to the grant of the freehold or the lease and the amount of the mortgage are agreed or determined; the duty is enforceable by the tenant by an injunction: s. 138(3).

27. Conveyance of freehold and grant of lease. There are detailed provisions in Sch. 6 to the Act dealing with the terms for conveyance of the freehold and the grant of the lease. The conveyance and grant must conform with Sch. 6; the detailed provisions are outside the scope of this book.

28. Terms of mortgage deed. The mortgage must, unless otherwise agreed, conform with the following:

(a) it must provide for repayment of the amount secured in equal instalments of principal and interest combined;
(b) the period over which repayment is to be made must be 25 years or, at the option of the mortgagor, a shorter period, but shall be capable of being extended by the mortgagee; and
(c) it may contain such other terms as may be agreed between the

mortgagor and the mortgagee, or as may be determined by the county court to be reasonably required by the mortgagor or the mortgagee.

29. Dwelling-houses in National Parks and areas of outstanding natural beauty. Section 157 contains special provisions dealing with dwelling-houses in these areas.

30. Costs. Where a tenant exercises his right to a mortgage, the landlord or the Housing Corporation may charge to him the costs incurred by it in connection with the tenant's exercise of the right to a mortgage, subject to limits prescribed by the Secretary of State: s. 178(2). Save as aforesaid the tenant is not obliged to pay any part of the landlord's costs and any agreement to that effect is void: s. 178(1).

31. Tenant's sanction for landlord's delay. Section 153A gives a tenant a remedy where the tenant has claimed the right to buy, has served an 'initial notice of delay', followed by an 'operative notice of delay' and the landlord has failed to complete. The remedy is that payment of rent after service of the 'operative notice of delay' can be attributed to the purchase price.

Powers of the Secretary of State

32. Secretary of State's power to intervene. Where it appears to the Secretary of State that tenants generally, or a tenant or tenants of a particular landlord, have or may have difficulty in exercising the right to buy effectively and expeditiously, he may, after giving the landlord notice of his intention to do so, use his powers under s. 164(1). Those powers are in wide terms and enable the Secretary of State to do all things as appear to him necessary or expedient to enable secure tenants to exercise the right to buy or the right to a mortgage. In summary the effect of ss. 164 and 165 (which enables the Secretary of State to vest dwelling-houses in tenants by means of a vesting order) is that if a landlord creates difficulties in performing his duties under this Part of the 1985 Act, the Secretary of State can step in and perform all the functions of the local authority already described.

33. Further powers. The Secretary of State has power under s. 167 to direct that covenants or conditions may be contained in the conveyance or grant, notwithstanding that they are not consistent with Sch. 6 (*see* **23** above). Section 168 deals with the effect of such directions on the old covenants. Section 169 gives to the Secretary of State power to obtain information or documents necessary for the purposes of deciding whether to exercise his powers above under ss. 164, 167 or 168.

34. Power to give assistance. Where, in relation to any proceedings or prospective proceedings, one party has claimed the right to buy, he may apply to the Secretary of State for assistance which includes giving advice, procuring or attempting to procure a settlement and arranging representation by a solicitor or counsel on the grounds that (*a*) the case raises a question of principle, or (*b*) it is unreasonable to expect the applicant to deal with the case without assistance, or (*c*) there are other special considerations: s. 170.

35. Power to extend right to buy. The Secretary of State may by order extend the right to buy to cases where the landlord has a lease-hold interest only but one or more of the superior interests is owned by a local authority, new town corporation, the Housing Corporation, a housing association, an urban development corporation or the Development Board for Rural Wales.

Defective houses

36. Defective houses. Where the right to buy has been exercised and the house proves to be defective in some way, the owner *may* be entitled to assistance whether by way of a reinstatement grant or re-purchase: *see* the Housing Act 1985, Part XVI. This only applies however to defects of design or construction by virtue of which the value of the dwelling has been substantially reduced. Further, it only applies to dwellings of a class (which may include only one dwelling) which the Secretary of State designates as defective.

Progress test 33

1. When does the right to buy arise?   **(1, 2)**

2. What are the exceptions to the right to buy?   **(3)**

3. How may the right to buy be exercised?   **(5)**

4. How is the purchase price calculated?   **(6, 7)**

5. What is the amount of the discount? **(10, 11)**

6. When is the discount repayable? **(12, 13)**

7. What are the tenant's rights as regards mortgages? **(15 *et seq.*)**

8. What limits are there to the right to acquire or rent to mortgage terms? **(15 *et seq.*)**

9. If the parties cannot agree on the purchase price, how is it determined? **(23)**

10. How can the sale or lease of the house be completed? **(26)**

The Housing Act 1988

1. Introduction. The Housing Act 1988 deals with various matters relating to public sector residential tenancies. It is outside the scope of this book to examine most of them. Instead, attention will be drawn, in outline, to the most significant changes as far as secure tenants are concerned. Students should refer to the Act itself for the others, and the more detailed provisions.

2. Change of landlord, secure tenants. Part IV of the 1988 Act has the effect of conferring on persons approved by the Housing Corporation the right to acquire from a public sector landlord (*a*) the fee simple estate in any buildings comprising or containing one or more dwelling-houses which, on the relevant date, are occupied by certain secure tenants ('qualifying tenants') of the public sector landlord and (*b*) the fee simple estate in any other property which is reasonably required for occupation with buildings falling within (*a*): *see* s. 93(1). The acquisition must be in accordance with Part IV.

3. The matters to be considered. The matters arising out of s. 93(1) are:

(a) approved person (*see* **4**),
(b) a public sector landlord (*see* **5**),
(c) the relevant date (*see* **6**),
(d) qualifying tenants (*see* **7**),
(e) the property to be acquired (*see* **8**),
(f) procedure for acquisition (*see* **9, 10**).

4. Approved person. The right conferred by Part IV is not exercisable except by a person for the time being approved by the Housing Corporation: s. 94. Neither a public sector landlord nor a county council, nor any other body which the Corporation has reason to believe might not be independent of such a landlord or council, may be approved: s. 94(1). A body shall not be regarded as independent of a public sector landlord or county council if the body is, or appears likely to be, under the control of, or subject to influence from, such a landlord or council or particular members or officers of such a landlord or council: s. 94(2).

5. Public sector landlord. These are defined by s. 93(2) as

(a) a local housing authority,
(b) a new town corporation,
(c) a housing action trust,
(d) the Development Board for Rural Wales.

6. The relevant date. In relation to an acquisition or proposed acquisition under Part IV, this means the date on which is made the application under s. 96 claiming to exercise the right conferred by Part IV: s. 93(5).

7. Qualifying tenants. A secure tenant of a public sector landlord is a qualifying tenant if, and only if, his secure tenancy is held directly from the landlord or owner of the fee simple estate: s. 93(3). A secure tenant is not a qualifying tenant if either (*a*) he is obliged to give possession by a possession order, or (*b*) the circumstances fall within certain exceptions to the right to buy.

8. Property to be acquired. (1) A building is excluded from acquisition under Part IV if, on the relevant date, (*a*) any part or parts of the building is or are occupied or intended to be occupied otherwise than for residential purposes and (*b*) the internal floor area of that part exceeds 50 per cent of the internal floor area of the building, taken as a whole but disregarding the internal floor area of any common parts or common facilities: s. 95(1).

(2) A building is also excluded from an acquisition under Part IV if (*a*) it contains two or more dwelling-houses which on the relevant date are occupied by secure tenants who are not qualifying tenants, and (*b*) the number of dwelling-houses which on that date are occupied by such tenants exceeds 50 per cent of the total number of dwelling-houses in the buildings: s. 95(3).

(3) A dwelling-house is excluded from acquisition under Part IV if it is occupied by (*a*) a secure tenant within certain exceptions to the right to buy, or (*b*) a tenant who is not a secure tenant: s. 95(4).

(4) A building is excluded from acquisition if it is the subject of another application under Part IV not yet disposed of: s. 95(5).

(5) Property is excluded from acquisition under Part IV if it is held (*a*) for pleasure grounds or (*b*) for open space and burial grounds.

Subject to the above exceptions, the property to be acquired is as set out in 2 (*a*) and (*b*) above.

9. Initial procedures. Under s. 96(1) application has to be made in the prescribed form to the public sector landlord concerned, accompanied by a plan showing (*i*) the buildings proposed to be acquired under s. 93(1) (*a*) and (*ii*) the property proposed to be acquired under s. 93(1) (*b*). Within four weeks of the relevant date, the landlord must serve on the applicant notice specifying (*a*) the name and address of every tenant or licensee of a dwelling-house within the buildings proposed to be acquired and (*b*) the general nature of his tenancy or licence: s. 97(1). Within twelve weeks of the relevant date the landlord must serve on the applicant a notice giving details of the property to be included in and excluded from the acquisition and other matters relevant to the acquisition: s. 98(1). There is a provision for resolving disputes. Within eight weeks of the notice under s. 98(1), or the determination of any dispute, the landlord must serve notice specifying the price in accordance with s. 99(2). Any dispute is to be determined by the District Valuer. The foregoing are described as the initial procedures.

10. Final procedures. Following the determination by the District Valuer of the price or, if there is no determination, service of the landlord's notice under s. 99, the applicant must consult the qualifying and certain other tenants: s. 102. The next stage is for the applicant to give notice of intention to proceed with the acquisition: s. 103. However, the applicant is not entitled to give that notice if, in response to consultation, less than 50 per cent of the tenants entitled to be consulted, have given notice of their wishes, or more than 50 per cent of the tenants entitled to be consulted have given notice of their wish to continue as tenants of the landlord: s. 103(2). When the landlord has served his notice of intention to proceed and any dispute on it has been determined, then the landlord must make to the applicant a grant of the property included in the acquisition for an estate in fee simple absolute, subject to any rights to be retained by the landlord: s. 104(1).

11. Subsequent disposals. A person who acquires any property under Part IV shall not dispose of it except with the consent of the Secretary of State (s. 105(1)) or in the case of exempt disposals under s. 105(7).

Part seven
Part 1 of the Leasehold Reform, Housing and Urban Development Act 1993

35

The right to collective enfranchisement (Chapter I, Part I of the 1993 Act)

1. General introduction. The introduction to Chapter 23 considered some of the complaints made by tenants of residential flats in multi-occupied buildings, such as blocks of flats. These complaints were addressed by Parts II and III of the Landlord and Tenant Act 1987 as regards the repair, maintenance and insurance of the building and common parts, plant and machinery.

Another significant complaint made by tenants was that with the passage of time the value of their interests was diminishing so that their leases were wasting assets. Where the tenant's lease had, say, less than forty years to run, lenders were reluctant to make mortgage advances on the security of such a wasting asset, which in turn affected the marketability and hence the value of the lease yet further.

This complaint was addressed to a certain extent by Part 1 of the Landlord and Tenant Act 1987, which conferred on certain tenants 'the right of first refusal', i.e. the right to acquire their landlord's interest before the landlord could dispose of the same to a third party (see Chapter 23).

Part 1 of the Landlord and Tenant Act 1987 has not been an unqualified success however. Legitimate avoidance techniques have been devised by some landlords and their advisers and because of this or simply because the landlord does not wish to sell his interest, the right of first refusal might never arise.

Tenants holding long leases of flats were particularly aggrieved by this as, by contrast, tenants holding long leases of houses were able to acquire compulsorily the freehold (enfranchise) or an extended lease under the Leasehold Reform Act 1967 (see Chapter 27).

2. The Leasehold Reform, Housing and Urban Development Act 1993. Tenants holding long leases of residential flats have now been given rights of collective enfranchisement and a similar right to acquire an extended lease to that enjoyed by tenants holding long leases of houses, by Part I of the Leasehold Reform, Housing and Urban Development Act 1993 ('the Act').

3. Scope of this Chapter. This Chapter is concerned with the right to collective enfranchisement conferred by Chapter I of Part I of the Act (ss. 1–38) which came into force on 1st November 1993: SI 1993 No 2134. The right to acquire a new lease is dealt with in Chapter 36 of this book.

The provisions of Part I of the Act have been variously described as 'complex' and 'comprehensive'. Indeed some commentators have asserted that the complexity and cost of implementing those provisions (in particular, the provisions of Chapter I) are so great that many of the tenants for whose benefit the Act was passed will be deterred from pursuing their new rights.

This Chapter examines the provisions of Chapter I of Part I of the Act in some detail but before doing so, an outline of the main provisions may be helpful. References in the Outline to paragraph numbers, e.g. (**4**), are to the numbered paragraphs of this Chapter.

Outline

(**a**) Chapter I applies to premises consisting of a self-contained building or part of a building, containing two or more flats held by qualifying tenants. The total number of flats held by qualifying tenants must be not less than two-thirds of the total number of flats contained in the premises (**4**). Chapter I does not apply to small premises with a resident landlord (**5**) and there are additional, miscellaneous exceptions (**6**).

(**b**) Chapter I confers on qualifying tenants the right to have the freehold acquired on their behalf by a person or persons appointed by them. This is known as 'the right to collective enfranchisement' (**7**).

(c) The qualifying tenants can acquire, in addition to the freehold of the building containing their flats, the freehold of other property which is demised to a qualifying tenant or over which any qualifying tenant may have rights **(8)**.

(d) The qualifying tenants are also entitled to acquire superior leasehold interests **(9)** but may be required to lease back certain property to the freeholder **(10)**.

(e) A 'qualifying tenant' is one who holds a long lease of a flat at a low rent **(11** and **12)**.

(f) The qualifying tenants will require detailed information concerning superior interests to enable them to make a claim to exercise the right to collective enfranchisement. They are able to obtain this information by serving 'discovery notices' on the holders of superior interests **(13)**.

(g) The qualifying tenants make their claim to exercise the right to collective enfranchisement by serving a notice ('the initial notice') upon 'the reversioner'. The reversioner will usually be the freeholder and will generally conduct all aspects of the transaction on behalf of all relevant landlords **(14)**.

(h) The 'initial notice' must be given by not less than two-thirds of the qualifying tenants, who hold not less than one-half of the total number of flats contained in the premises. Furthermore, not less than one-half of the qualifying tenants by whom the initial notice is given must satisfy 'the residence condition' **(15)**.

(i) The initial notice must contain detailed information as to such matters as the property and interests to be acquired and the proposed purchase price. Valuations of all interests to be acquired must have been obtained before the initial notice is served **(15** and **16)**.

(j) The qualifying tenants giving the initial notice are referred to as 'the participating tenants' **(18)**. All proceedings subsequent to the giving of the initial notice are conducted on behalf of the participating tenants by their 'nominee purchaser' **(19)**.

(k) The reversioner and other relevant landlords have rights of access to the specified premises for valuation and other purposes **(20)**. The reversioner can also require the nominee purchaser to provide evidence of any tenant's right to participate **(21)**.

(l) The reversioner must respond to the initial notice by serving a counternotice either admitting or disputing the participating tenants' right to exercise the right to collective enfranchisement. The counternotice may also state that the right to collective enfranchisement will be resisted on the ground that an appropriate landlord intends to redevelop the whole or part of the specified premises **(22)**.

(m) If the reversioner does not admit the claim to exercise the right to collective enfranchisement, the nominee purchaser must apply to the Court for a declaration within two months (23).

(n) If the reversioner's counternotice has stated that an appropriate landlord intends to redevelop, that appropriate landlord must apply to the Court for a declaration within two months. He must satisfy the Court that not less than two-thirds of all long leases of the flats contained in the specified premises will expire within five years and that he intends to redevelop the premises when those leases have terminated (24).

(o) If the reversioner admits the participating tenants' entitlement to exercise the right to collective enfranchisement his counternotice must state which (if any) of the proposals contained in the initial notice are accepted and (if appropriate) his counterproposals (26).

There are special provisions dealing with cases where the reversioner fails to give a counternotice (44) or if he or other relevant landlords cannot be found (46).

(p) The price payable by the nominee purchaser for the freehold is comprised of three elements:

   (*i*)　the value of the freeholder's interest (29);

   (*ii*)　the freeholder's share of the marriage value – at least 50% (30);

   (*iii*)　compensation for loss resulting from enfranchisement (31).

(q) The price payable for intermediate leasehold interests is the aggregate of

   (*i*)　the value of the interest in question (33); and

   (*ii*)　compensation for loss resulting from acquisition of the interest (34).

The freeholder's share of the marriage value may be divided between the freeholder and other relevant landlords (35).

(r) Following agreement or determination of the terms of acquisition, a contract must be prepared by the reversioner for exchange (38) together with the conveyance (39). If a binding contract is not entered into within the 'appropriate period' the Court can make an Order vesting the interests to be acquired in the nominee purchaser (43).

(s) Payment of the price agreed or determined enables the nominee purchaser to acquire the freehold and the intermediate leasehold interests free of any mortgages (40).

(t) The nominee purchaser is responsible for the reversioner's and other relevant landlords' costs of enfranchisement (41).

(u) If the terms of acquisition cannot be agreed, they can be determined by a 'leasehold valuation tribunal' (42).

(v) The initial notice can be withdrawn before a binding contract is entered into or can be deemed to be withdrawn in a variety of circumstances.

If the initial notice is withdrawn or deemed to have been withdrawn no subsequent initial notice can be given claiming to exercise the right to collective enfranchisement for at least 12 months (**47**).

4. Premises to which Chapter I applies. Sections 3 and 4 of the Act define the premises to which Chapter I applies.

The following conditions must be satisfied:

(a) the premises must consist of a self-contained building or part of a building, the freehold of which is owned by the same person; and
(b) the premises must contain two or more flats held by qualifying tenants; and
(c) the total number of flats held by qualifying tenants must not be less than two-thirds of the total number of flats contained in the premises: s. 3(1).

A building is self-contained if it is structurally detached.

A part of a building is self-contained if

(a) it constitutes a vertical division of the building and the structure of the building is such that the part in question could be redeveloped independently; and
(b) the 'relevant services' (being those provided by means of pipes, cables or other fixed installations) provided for occupiers of that part are either provided independently of the relevant services provided for other occupiers of the building, or could be so provided without carrying out works likely to result in a significant interruption in the provision of any of those services for occupiers of the remainder of the building: s. 3(2).

Chapter I does not apply if any part or parts of the premises are neither

(a) occupied, or intended to be occupied, for residential purposes; nor
(b) comprised in any common parts of the premises

and the internal floor area of that part or parts exceeds 10 per cent of the internal floor area of the premises as a whole: s. 4(1).

NOTES: (1) Any part of the premises referred to in s. 4(1) (e.g. a garage, parking space or storage area) which is used or intended for use in conjunction with a particular dwelling contained in the premises to which Chapter I applies is assumed to be occupied or intended to be occupied for residential purposes: s. 4(2).

(2) The internal floor area of a building or part of a building is the floor area of the whole of the interior of that building or part, without interruption

(ie. so as to include the areas occupied by internal walls, baths, kitchen units and the like) but excluding common parts ('common parts' being defined in s. 101 (1)): s. 4(3).

The broad effect of s. 4 is that Chapter I will not apply to, for example, a self-contained building which contains shops or offices as well as flats, if the internal floor area of those shops or offices exceeds 10% of the internal floor area of the building (excluding common parts) as a whole.

5. Exception: premises with a resident landlord. Section 4(4) provides that Chapter I does not apply to premises with a resident landlord and which do not contain more than four units. A 'unit' is a flat or any other separate set of premises either

(a) adapted or constructed for use as a dwelling; or
(b) let, or intended for letting, on a business lease (e.g. a shop or office): s. 38(1).

Premises are premises with a resident landlord if

(a) they are not and do not form part of a purpose-built block of flats (as to which see s. 10(6)); and
(b) the freeholder, or an adult member of the freeholder's family
(*i*) occupies a flat contained in the premises as his only or principal home; and
(*ii*) has so occupied such a flat for not less than the last twelve months: s. 10(1).

6. Miscellaneous exceptions. Chapter I does not apply
(a) to premises which are presently held on lease from the Crown: s. 94(1);
(b) to any property which is inalienably vested in the National Trust for Places of Historic Interest or Natural Beauty: s. 95;
(c) to any property within the precinct of a cathedral church: s. 96.

7. The right conferred by Chapter I, Part I of the Act. Section 1 of the Act confers upon 'qualifying tenants' (see **11** below) of flats contained in premises to which Chapter I applies (see **4**, **5**, and **6** above) on the 'relevant date', the right to have the freehold of those premises acquired on their behalf by a person or persons appointed by them and at a price determined in accordance with Chapter I (see **27** to **37** below).

This right is referred to as 'the right to collective enfranchisement'.

NOTES: (1) The 'relevant date' is the date on which notice of the qualifying tenants' claim to exercise the right to collective enfranchisement is given under s. 13: s. 1(8).

(2) 'Flat' is defined in s. 101(1).

(3) Any attempt to contract out of Chapter I, Part I is void: s. 93(1).

8. The freehold property which can be acquired. In addition to the freehold of the building which contains their flats (see **4** above) and which is referred to in s. 1 as 'the relevant premises', the qualifying tenants are entitled to acquire the freehold of any other property owned by the freeholder of the relevant premises which is

(a) 'appurtenant property' demised by a lease held by a qualifying tenant of a flat contained in the relevant premises, i.e. any garage, outhouse, garden, yard or appurtenances belonging to, or usually enjoyed with the flat: s. 1(7); and

(b) property which any qualifying tenant is entitled to use in common with the occupiers of other premises, whether or not those premises are contained in the relevant premises. This would include common entrance halls, private roads serving the relevant premises, etc: s. 1(2) and (3).

> NOTES: (1) As regards the property in common use referred to at **(b)** above, the qualifying tenants can, as an alternative, be granted permanent rights over that property or any other property so that, thereafter, the occupier of the flat in question has, as nearly as may be, the same rights as were enjoyed by the qualifying tenant under the terms of his lease. As a further alternative, there may be acquired from the freeholder the freehold of any other property over which any such permanent rights may be granted: s. 1(4).
>
> (2) The qualifying tenants are entitled to make a claim to exercise the right to collective enfranchisement in relation to premises which are less extensive than the entirety of the premises to which their right extends: s. 1(5).

9. Acquisition of superior leasehold interests. The qualifying tenants' immediate landlord may not be the freeholder but may be a tenant himself. Indeed there may be a chain of superior leasehold interests interposed between the qualifying tenants and the freeholder.

In order to give effect to the underlying purpose of Chapter I, i.e. to enable qualifying tenants to acquire collectively the freehold, s. 2 entitles the qualifying tenants to acquire

(a) any leasehold interest in the 'relevant premises' which is superior to their own; and

(b) any leasehold interest in property which consists of, or includes
  (*i*) any common parts of the relevant premises; or
  (*ii*) any appurtenant property which is demised by the lease held
by a qualifying tenant (e.g. a garage) or property which a qualifying
tenant is entitled, under his lease of the flat, to use in common with
the occupiers of other premises: ss. 2(1) to (3).

NOTES: (1) Where the superior lease of any property referred to in **(a)** or
(b) above also demises other property, s. 2(1) does not oblige or give any
right to the qualifying tenants to acquire the leasehold interest in that other
property: s. 2(4).
  (2) Special provisions apply where the qualifying tenant of a flat is a
public sector landlord, the flat is let under a secure tenancy (under the
Housing Act 1985) and superior leasehold interests are held by public
sector landlords: ss. 2(5) and (6).

10. Lease back to the freeholder. Section 36 and Schedule 9 of the
Act contain detailed provisions requiring the qualifying tenants'
nominee purchaser to grant back to the freeholder leases of certain
property. In summary:

(a) if any flat is let on a secure tenancy and the freeholder is the secure
tenant's immediate landlord, or the secure tenant's landlord, as well
as all intermediate landlords and the freeholder, is a public sector
landlord, the nominee purchaser must grant the freeholder a lease-
back of the flat or unit (used as a dwelling) in question;
(b) if
  (*i*) any flat is let by a housing association under a tenancy which
is not a secure tenancy; and
  (*ii*) the tenant of the flat is not a qualifying tenant; and
  (*iii*) the housing association is the freeholder;
the nominee purchaser must grant the housing association a lease-
back of the flat or unit (used as a dwelling) in question;
(c) if any unit is not a flat let to a qualifying tenant, e.g. vacant flats,
or shops and offices comprised in the premises acquired on behalf of
the qualifying tenants, the freeholder may give the nominee purchaser
notice that he requires the nominee purchaser to grant him a lease-
back of the unit(s) in question;
(d) if the premises acquired on behalf of the qualifying tenants are
premises with a resident landlord (see **5**) by virtue of the fact that the
freeholder occupies a flat or other unit contained in those premises
and the freeholder is himself a qualifying tenant of that flat or other
unit, the freeholder may give the nominee purchaser notice that he
requires the nominee purchaser to grant him a lease back of the flat
or unit in question.

Any lease back granted in accordance with these provisions will be for a term of 999 years at a peppercorn rent.

11. Qualifying tenants. By s. 5 a person is a qualifying tenant of a flat if he is the tenant of the flat under a long lease at a low rent and

(a) the lease is not a business lease;
(b) the flat does not form part of housing accommodation provided by a charitable housing trust in pursuit of its charitable purposes and the charitable housing trust is the tenant's immediate landlord;
(c) the lease is not a sublease granted out of a superior lease which is not itself a long lease at a low rent, in breach of the terms of that superior lease, and the breach has not been waived.

There can only be one qualifying tenant of a flat at any one time and accordingly where e.g. the landlord, A, of a tenant, B, who holds a long lease at a low rent, is himself a tenant under such a lease then B alone is the qualifying tenant.

If joint tenants hold a long lease of a flat at a low rent, they jointly constitute the qualifying tenant of the flat in question: ss. 5(3) and (4).

NOTES: (1) If there is a tenant or joint tenant of three or more flats, whether under a single lease or otherwise, there can be no qualifying tenant of any of those flats: s. 5(5).

(2) If a body corporate is a tenant of a flat then for the purpose of establishing if it is a tenant of three or more flats (and hence is not a qualifying tenant), any flat let to an associated company is treated as being let to that body corporate: s. 5(6).

12. 'Long lease' and 'low rent'. It is sufficient for most purposes to note that a 'long lease' is one granted for a term of years certain exceeding 21 years. Section 7 deals with 'long leases' in detail.

In summary a lease of a flat is a lease at a 'low rent' if

(a) no rent was payable during the 'initial year', i.e. the period of one year beginning with the date of commencement of the lease; or
(b) the aggregate amount of rent payable during the initial year did not exceed

(*i*) two-thirds of the letting value of the flat on the date of commencement of the lease – in cases where the lease was entered into before 1st April 1963;

(*ii*) two-thirds of the rateable value on the date of the commencement of the lease (or if later, the date on which a rateable value was first ascribed to the flat) – in cases where the lease was granted on or after 1st April 1963 but before 1st April 1990, or on or after 1st April 1990 in pursuance of a contract made before that date;

(*iii*) £1000 if the flat is in Greater London, or £250 if elsewhere – in any other case: s. 8.

NOTE: The 'date of commencement of a lease' means the date of commencement of the term of the lease: s. 101(5).

13. Preliminary enquiries by tenants. Section 11 entitles a qualifying tenant to serve notices (which are sometimes, although not in the Act itself, referred to as 'discovery notices') upon

(a) his immediate landlord or any person receiving rent on behalf of his immediate landlord; and

(b) the freeholder of the 'relevant premises' (being, essentially, the whole or part of the building in which the flat is contained: s. 11(9));

(c) any tenant of the whole of the relevant premises;

(d) any tenant or licensee of any separate set or sets of premises contained in the relevant premises;

(e) any tenant or licensee of the whole or any part of any common parts contained in the relevant premises; or

(f) any tenant or licensee of the whole or part of any property not contained in the relevant premises

(*i*) which is demised by a lease to a qualifying tenant; or

(*ii*) which any qualifying tenant is entitled to use under the terms of his lease, in common with other persons.

The purpose of such notices is to enable the qualifying tenant to obtain information as to the identity of the holder of the freehold interest and any person holding a leasehold or other inferior interest, details of those interests and such other information as the qualifying tenant may reasonably require in connection with the making of a claim to exercise the right to collective enfranchisement: ss. 11(1) to (4).

A qualifying tenant may also require any of the persons mentioned at paragraphs **(b)** to **(f)** above (who presumably include his immediate landlord) to provide a list of relevant documents, to permit him to inspect those documents and (on payment of a reasonable fee) to provide copies of those documents: ss. 11(5) and (6).

Any person upon whom such a notice is served or who is required to provide a list of relevant documents, permit inspection of or to provide copies of relevant documents, must provide the information or otherwise comply with the qualifying tenant's request as appropriate, within 28 days: s. 11(7).

NOTES: (1) Section 11(8) obliges any person who has received a notice from a qualifying tenant under s. 11(4) to notify the qualifying tenant of any disposal of his interest in the relevant premises, or the acquisition by him of any further interest, which occurs within 6 months of his receipt of the qualifying tenant's notice. The notification must be made within 28 days of the disposal or acquisition in question.

(2) Section 12 obliges a recipient of a s. 11(4) notice to notify the qualifying tenant if he has received a notice under s. 13 claiming to exercise the right to collective enfranchisement, or a copy of such a notice, provided that the claim is still current (as to which see s. 12(6)). Furthermore he must so notify the tenant who served the s. 11(4) notice if he receives a notice under s. 13 or a copy of any such notice within 6 months of receipt of the s. 11(4) notice (and the tenant is not one of the qualifying tenants by whom that notice is given): s. 12(4).

14. 'The reversioner'. Section 13 requires the qualifying tenants to serve their notice claiming to exercise the right to collective enfranchisement upon 'the reversioner'.

Where the claim to exercise the right to collective enfranchisement does not involve the acquisition of any interests other than the freehold or other interests held by the freeholder, the freeholder is 'the reversioner': s. 9(1).

In all other cases, the identity of the reversioner is ascertained in accordance with the provisions of Part 1 of Schedule 1 to the Act: s. 9(2). Unless the Court otherwise directs 'the reversioner' will be the freeholder.

The freeholder and the holders of all other interests in the premises to which the qualifying tenants' claim relates are referred to as 'relevant landlords': s. 9(2).

The reversioner conducts, on behalf of all relevant landlords, all proceedings arising out of any notice under s. 13 claiming to exercise the right to collective enfranchisement: s. 9(3). Part II of Schedule 1 contains detailed provisions concerning the conduct of proceedings by the reversioner on behalf of other relevant landlords and the circumstances in which any of the other relevant landlords can act independently.

15. Claiming the right to enfranchise – 'the initial notice'. A claim to exercise the right to collective enfranchisement is made by the giving of a notice ('the initial notice') under s. 13.

Valuations of the freehold and leasehold interests must be obtained from a qualified surveyor by the qualifying tenants who propose to serve an initial notice, before an initial notice is served: s. 13(6).

The initial notice must be given by a number of qualifying tenants of flats contained in the premises at the relevant date (i.e. the date the initial notice is given: s. 1(8)) which (*i*) is not less than two-thirds of the total number of qualifying tenants; and

(*ii*) is not less than one-half of the flats contained in the premises.

Furthermore, not less than one-half of the qualifying tenants by whom the initial notice is given must satisfy the 'residence condition': s. 13(2).

The 'residence condition' is that the qualifying tenant has occupied the flat as his only or principal home

(a) for the last twelve months; or

(b) for periods amounting to three years in the last ten years: s. 6(2).

A company or other artificial person cannot satisfy the residence condition: s. 6(3).

Example

(*i*) A self-contained building contains 80 flats;

(*ii*) 60 of the flats (i.e. more than half) are let on long leases at a low rent i.e. to qualifying tenants;

(*iii*) 45 of the qualifying tenants (i.e. more than two-thirds) give an initial notice;

(*iv*) 25 of the tenants by whom the initial notice is given (i.e. more than half) satisfy the residence condition.

Conclusion: the initial notice is valid.

---

16. The initial notice: contents. The requirements of a valid initial notice are as follows:

(a) it must be in writing: s. 99(1);

(b) it must be given to the reversioner: s. 13(2)(a) and see **14** above;

(c) it must be given by an appropriate number of qualifying tenants, not less than half of whom satisfy the residence condition: s. 13(2)(b) and see **15** above;

(d) it must specify and be accompanied by a plan showing

(*i*) the relevant premises of which the freehold is proposed to be acquired (see ss. 1(1) and (2), ss. 3 and 4 and **4** above) which are referred to as 'the specified premises';

(*ii*) the appurtenant property and the common property of which the freehold is proposed to be acquired (see ss. 1(2)(a) and (3) and **8** above);

(*iii*) any property of the person who holds the freehold of the specified premises over which it is proposed that rights (which must be specified in the notice) should be granted;

(e) it must contain a statement of the grounds on which it is claimed that the specified premises are, on the relevant date (i.e. the date the initial notice is given: s. 1(8)), premises to which Chapter I applies;

(f) it must specify

(*i*) any leasehold interests proposed to be acquired under or by virtue of s. 2(1)(a) or (b) (see **9** above); and

(*ii*) any flats or other units which it is considered must be leased back (see Part II of Schedule 9 and **10** above);

(g) it must specify the proposed purchase price for each of

(*i*) the freehold interest in the specified premises;

(*ii*) the freehold interest in any appurtenant property and any property which a qualifying tenant is entitled to use in common with others proposed to be acquired;

(*iii*) any leasehold interest proposed to be acquired.

(h) it must state the full names of all the qualifying tenants of flats contained in the specified premises and the addresses of their flats and contain the following particulars in relation to each of those tenants, namely

(*i*) sufficient particulars to identify the lease, including the date of the lease, the term granted and the date of commencement of the term;

(*ii*) such further particulars as are necessary to show that the lease is a lease at a low rent; and

(*iii*) if it is claimed that he satisfies the residence condition, particulars of the period or periods falling within the preceding ten years for which he has occupied the whole or part of his flat as his only or principal home;

(i) it must state the full name or names of the person(s) appointed as the nominee purchaser for the purposes of s. 15 (see **19** below) and an address in England and Wales at which notices may be given to that person or those persons under Chapter I;

(j) it must specify the date by which the reversioner must respond to the notice by giving a counter-notice under s. 21 (which date must not be less than two months after the date the initial notice is given: s. 13(5));

(k) it must contain a statement confirming that the qualifying tenants by whom it is given have obtained the valuations required by s. 13(6) (see **15** above) and state the name of the qualified surveyor in question: s. 13(6);

(l) it must state whether copies of the initial notice are being given to anyone other than the recipient and if so, whom: para 12(2), Part II, Schedule 3;

(m) it must be signed by each of the tenants by whom it is given: s. 99(5)(a).

NOTES: (1) Schedule 3 applies by virtue of s. 13(13). Part 1 of Schedule 3 deals with restrictions on participation by individual tenants, the effect of initial notices on other notices, forfeiture, etc. These provisions are detailed and important; for example, during the currency of a claim to exercise the right to collective enfranchisement, a landlord cannot take proceedings to enforce any right of re-entry or forfeiture terminating the lease of a flat held by a participating tenant, without leave of the Court. If the Court grants leave, the tenant in question ceases to be entitled to participate in the claim to exercise the right to collective enfranchisement.

(2) Part II of Schedule 3 sets out procedures for giving copies of the initial notice to relevant landlords. The qualifying tenants must give copies of the initial notice to all persons known or believed by them to be relevant land-lords. Where the recipient of the initial notice, or a copy, is the reversioner or another relevant landlord, the recipient must give a copy of the initial notice to any person known or believed by him to be a relevant landlord who is not stated in the copy of the initial notice received by the recipient as being a person who has received a copy of the initial notice, or who the recipient knows has not received a copy of the initial notice.

(3) Failure to comply with Part II of Schedule 3 can result in the initial notice ceasing to have effect or in defaulting persons incurring liability to the qualifying tenants by whom the initial notice was given, the reversioner or any other relevant landlord.

(4) Part III of Schedule 3 deals with the consequences of inaccuracy or misdescription in the initial notice and the effect on the initial notice of any tenant's lack of qualification to participate.

(5) The initial notice can (and should) be registered under the Land Charges Act 1972 or made the subject of a notice or caution under the Land Registration Act 1925: s. 97(1).

17. Effect of initial notice on subsequent transactions. Provided that the initial notice has been registered under the Land Charges Act 1972 or made the subject of a caution or notice under the Land Registration Act 1925 (as appropriate) and so long as the initial notice continues in force

(a) the freeholder of the specified premises and of any other freehold property proposed to be acquired by the initial notice cannot
    (*i*) make any disposal severing his interest in the same; or
    (*ii*) grant any lease which, had it been granted prior to the date of the giving of the initial notice, would have been liable to acquisition on behalf of the participating tenants; and
(b) no other relevant landlord can grant any such lease as is mentioned in **(a)**(*ii*) above.

Any purported disposal, or grant of any such lease, will be void: s. 19(1).
    Furthermore, provided that the initial notice has been registered or

made the subject of a notice or caution as mentioned above, and continues in force,

(a) if the freeholder disposes of his interest in the specified premises or any other freehold property proposed to be acquired by the initial notice; or
(b) any other relevant landlord disposes of his leasehold interest,

the person who acquires any such interest is placed in the same position as the reversioner or other relevant landlord from whom that person has acquired his interest: ss. 19(2) and (3).

If a binding contract for any disposal has been entered into by the freehold owner of the specified premises or any other relevant landlord before the date the initial notice is given and is still in force at that date, the operation of that contract is suspended: s. 19(4). Furthermore, if a binding contract is entered into in pursuance of the initial notice, the obligation of the parties to the 'suspended contract' are discharged unless the suspended contract makes provision for the eventuality of the giving of an initial notice: ss. 19(5) and (6).

18. The participating tenants. The qualifying tenants who participate in any claim to exercise the right to collective enfranchisement are, prima facie, those who gave the initial notice and known as 'the participating tenants': s. 14(1).

The number and identities of the participating tenants can change as a result of a variety of matters including:

(a) a participating tenant ceasing to be such a tenant e.g. by his landlord obtaining leave to bring proceedings for forfeiture of the tenant's lease: paragraph 7 of Schedule 3;
(b) assignment of the participating tenant's lease: s. 14(2);
(c) a qualifying tenant who was not one of the participating tenants who gave the initial notice subsequently electing to participate (which he can only do with the agreement of all present participating tenants): s. 14(3);
(d) the death of a participating tenant: s. 14(5).

Section 14 deals with these situations and, in cases (b), (c) and (d) above,

(*i*) provides for appropriate notifications to be given to the nominee purchaser; and
(*ii*) requires the nominee purchaser to advise the reversioner of the change in circumstances by notice pursuant to s. 14(8) and provides for copies of that notice to be given to all relevant landlords.

19. The nominee purchaser. The nominee purchaser has the conduct, on behalf of the participating tenants, of all proceedings arising out of the initial notice, with a view to the eventual acquisition by him, on behalf of the participating tenants, of such freehold and other interests as fall to be so acquired under a contract entered into in pursuance of the initial notice: s. 15(1).

The Act does not expressly provide that the nominee purchaser must be any particular person(s), have any particular qualifications or be a single or any greater number of persons. As a general proposition therefore it can be assumed that the nominee purchaser must be one or more persons or artificial persons (e.g. companies), having full legal capacity, or any combinations of such persons, up to a maximum of four such persons.

In the first instance the nominee purchaser is to be the person(s) specified as such in the initial notice: s. 15(2).

Sections 15 and 16 deal with the appointment, replacement, retirement or death of any nominee purchaser and provide for the service of certain notices upon the participating tenants, the reversioner and the relevant landlords if, and depending on which of, those events occur.

The provisions of s. 15(10) and s. 16(8) are particularly important as they provide that if the participating tenants fail to give certain notices to the reversioner as to the identity of the nominee purchaser within certain time limits, the initial notice is deemed to be withdrawn (as to the consequences of which, see **47** below).

NOTE: If at any time between the date the initial notice is given and 'the valuation date' (namely, the date on which the price to be paid for the specified premises is determined by agreement or a leasehold valuation tribunal: paragraph 1, Part 1, Schedule 6)

(a) there subsists any agreement between the nominee purchaser and any other person (other than a participating tenant) for the disposal to that other person of any 'relevant interest' (i.e. any interest in the specified premises or any other freehold property proposed to be acquired in the initial notice: s. 18(3)), or

(b) where the nominee purchaser is a company, any person other than a participating tenant holds any share by virtue of which a relevant interest may be acquired,

the nominee purchaser must notify the reversioner as soon as possible: s. 18(1).

If the nominee purchaser fails to do so and it may be reasonably assumed that the existence of that agreement or shareholding would have resulted in an increase in the price payable to the reversioner or any other relevant landlord, the nominee purchaser and the participating tenants will be jointly and severally liable to pay the amount of that increase to the reversioner or the relevant landlord affected (as the case may be): s. 18(2).

20. Access for valuation and other purposes. Following the giving of an initial notice the reversioner and any other relevant landlord (and any person acting on their behalf) are entitled to have access to any part of the specified premises (i.e. of which the freehold is proposed to be acquired) and any part of any property over which it is proposed the nominee purchaser should have rights. This right of access is for the purpose of obtaining valuations: s. 17(1).

Furthermore, the nominee purchaser (and any person acting on his behalf) has a similar right of access where access is reasonably required by him in connection with any matter arising out of the initial notice: s. 17(2).

These rights of access are exercisable at any reasonable time on not less than 10 days notice to the occupier of, or person entitled to occupy, the premises in question: s. 17(3).

21. Reversioner's right to require evidence of tenant's right to participate. Within the period of 21 days beginning with the relevant date (i.e. the date on which the initial notice is given), the reversioner may give a notice to the nominee purchaser requiring him to deduce the title of any person by whom the initial notice was given to the lease of a flat contained in the specified premises: s. 20(1).

The nominee purchaser must comply with any such notice within 21 days: s. 20(2).

The purpose of this procedure is to enable the reversioner to obtain proof that the persons who gave the initial notice are in fact qualifying tenants and that the initial notice is valid.

If the nominee purchaser fails to comply within 21 days and the effect of excluding any such person or persons from

(a) the calculation of the number of qualifying tenants; or
(b) the persons by whom the initial notice was given,

would be to render the initial notice invalid (see s. 13(2)(b) and **15** above), the initial notice is deemed to have been withdrawn (as to which see **47** below): s. 20(3).

NOTE: The reversioner may also serve notice on the nominee purchaser requiring him to provide evidence of the period(s) of occupation by any qualifying tenant who is claimed in the initial notice to satisfy the residence condition. That notice must be given within 21 days of the relevant date and the nominee purchaser must comply by giving the reversioner a statutory declaration by the qualifying tenant in question within the period of

21 days beginning with the date the reversioner's notice is given: paragraph 2 of Schedule 1 to The Leasehold Reform (Collective Enfranchisement and Lease Renewal) Regulations 1993, SI 1993 No 2407.

22. Reversioner's counternotice. It will be recalled that the initial notice must specify a date by which the reversioner must respond by giving a counternotice and that such date must not be less than two months after the date the initial notice is given (ss. 13(3)(g) and (5) and see **16** above).

The reversioner must give a counternotice by the date so specified: s. 21(1).

That counternotice must be in writing (s. 99(1)) and specify an address in England and Wales at which notices may be given to the reversioner: s. 21(6).

The counternotice must

(a) state that the reversioner does not admit the participating tenants' entitlement to exercise the right to collective enfranchisement and specify the reasons why this is so: s. 21(2)(b) (and see **23** below); or
(b) admit the participating tenants' entitlement to exercise the right to collective enfranchisement: s. 21(2)(a) (and see **26** below); or
(c) (*i*) contain an admission or non-admission of the participating tenants' entitlement to exercise the right to collective enfranchisement in accordance with paragraphs (a) or (b) above; and

(*ii*) state that an application for an Order under s. 23(1) is to be made by a specified 'appropriate landlord' on the grounds that he intends to redevelop the whole or a substantial part of the specified premises: s. 21(2)(c) (and see **24** and **25** below).

NOTE: Section 21(8) and Schedule 4 to the Act contain provisions requiring the reversioner to provide the nominee purchaser with copies of any notices and counternotices received by the reversioner, or any other relevant landlord, in connection with any claim by any tenant to a new lease of his flat in accordance with Chapter II of the Act (see Chapter 36).

Generally, the nominee purchaser must be provided with copies of any such notices or counternotices when the reversioner's counternotice under s. 21(1) is given or as soon as possible thereafter.

23. The reversioner does not admit the validity of the initial notice. If the reversioner states in his s. 21 counternotice that he does not admit that the participating tenants are entitled to exercise the right to collective enfranchisement, the nominee purchaser must apply to the Court within two months of the date on which the reversioner's counternotice is given: s. 22(2).

That application is for a declaration that the participating tenants were, on the relevant date, entitled to exercise the right to collective enfranchisement in relation to the specified premises: s. 22(1).

If the nominee purchaser's application is dismissed, the initial notice ceases to have any effect: s. 22(6).

However, if the Court makes an Order declaring that the participating tenants were entitled to exercise the right to collective enfranchisement, the Court will also make an Order declaring the reversioner's counternotice to be of no effect and requiring the reversioner to give a further counternotice to the nominee purchaser by a date to be specified in the Order: s. 22(3).

NOTES: (1) The Court will not make an Order declaring the reversioner's counternotice to be of no effect and requiring the reversioner to serve a further counternotice if the counternotice also states that an application for an Order under s. 23(1) is to be made by a specified 'appropriate landlord' and either that application is pending or the time for making that application has not expired: s. 22(4) and see **24** and **25** below.

(2) If no application under s. 22(1) is made by the nominee purchaser, or that application is subsequently withdrawn, the initial notice is deemed to have been withdrawn (as to which see **47** below): s. 29(1)

24. Proposed redevelopment by an 'appropriate landlord'. Section 23(1) empowers the Court to make an Order declaring that the right to collective enfranchisement shall not be exercisable on the grounds that an 'appropriate landlord' intends to redevelop the whole or a substantial part of the specified premises.

The application for an Order under s. 23(1) must be made within two months of the date upon which the reversioner's s. 21 counternotice is given to the nominee purchaser (s. 23(3)) and can only be made if the reversioner's counternotice has stated that an application for an Order under s. 23(1) is to be made.

The application must be made by an 'appropriate landlord', namely the reversioner or any other relevant landlord or any two or more relevant landlords who are acting together (whether or not they include the reversioner): s. 23(10).

On the hearing of the application, the appropriate landlord must satisfy the Court

(a) that not less than two-thirds of all the long leases on which flats contained in the specified premises are held are due to terminate within five years of the relevant date (i.e. the date upon which the initial notice was given); and

(b) that for the purposes of redevelopment the appropriate landlord intends, once the leases in question have so terminated (*i*) to demolish or reconstruct, or

(*ii*) to carry out substantial works of construction

on the whole or a substantial part of the specified premises; and
(c) that the appropriate landlord could not reasonably do so without obtaining possession of the flats demised by those leases s. 23(2).

NOTE: The case law concerning s. 30(1)(f) of the Landlord and Tenant Act 1954 (relating to business tenancies) considered in Chapter 14 and the inclusion of redevelopment break clauses in renewal leases of business premises (see *National Car Parks Limited* v. *Paternoster Consortium Limited* (1989) in particular) is likely to be of assistance in ascertaining if the land-lord can satisfy the Court on points (b) and (c) above.

If an Order under s. 23(1) is made by the Court, the initial notice ceases to have effect (s. 23(4)) and no subsequent initial notice can be given within 12 months of the date on which the Order becomes final: s. 13(9).

If, however, the application under s. 23(1) is dismissed, the Court must make an Order

(a) declaring the reversioner's counternotice to be of no effect; and
(b) requiring the reversioner to give a further s. 21 counternotice to the nominee purchaser by a date specified in the Order: s. 23(5).

In cases where the reversioner has given a s. 21 counternotice to the nominee purchaser stating that an application is to be made by an appropriate landlord for an Order under s. 23(1), but no such application is made, or an application is made but subsequently withdrawn, the reversioner must give a further s. 21 counternotice to the nominee purchaser. That further counternotice must be given within two months of

(a) the date following the expiry of the appropriate landlord's time for applying for an Order under s. 23(1) (which, as mentioned above, is two months from the date of the reversioner's 'original' counter-notice under s. 21); or
(b) the date of withdrawal of the s. 23(1) application,

as appropriate: s. 23(6) and (7).

25. Interaction of s. 22 with s. 23. If the reversioner's counternotice has stated

(a) that the reversioner does not admit the participating tenants' entitlement to exercise the right to collective enfranchisement; and
(b) that an application for an Order under s. 23(1) is to be made by an appropriate landlord,

two applications to the Court are likely to be made at or about the same time, namely

(*i*) the nominee purchaser's application under s. 22(1) for an Order declaring that the participating tenants are entitled to exercise the right to collective enfranchisement (see **23** above); and

(*ii*) the appropriate landlord's application under s. 23(1) for an Order declaring that the right to collective enfranchisement shall not be exercisable on the grounds of proposed redevelopment of the specified premises (see **24** above).

Logically, the nominee purchaser's application under s. 22(1) should be dealt with first, as if it is unsuccessful there is no need for the appropriate landlord to proceed with the application under s. 23(1). Section 23(4) therefore provides that although in these circumstances the appropriate landlord's s. 23(1) application must be made (i.e. the proceedings issued and served) in good time, the application cannot be proceeded with until the nominee purchaser's application under s. 22(1) has been disposed of. In other words, the s. 23(1) application is stayed until the s. 22(1) application is disposed of.

Furthermore, if the reversioner has given a s. 21(1) counternotice stating that an application for an Order under s. 23(1) is to be made by an appropriate landlord but either no such application is made, or the application is withdrawn, the requirement for the reversioner to give a further counternotice imposed by s. 23(6) does not apply. The reversioner's further counternotice must instead be given by the date specified in the Court's Order under s. 22(3) in the nominee purchaser's proceedings under s. 22(1): s. 23(8). Once again this is logical as unless and until the nominee purchaser's application under s. 22(1) succeeds, i.e. the validity of the initial notice has been established, no purpose would be served by requiring the reversioner to give a further counternotice.

26. The reversioner admits the participating tenants' entitlement to exercise the right to collective enfranchisement. In these circumstances, the following additional requirements apply to the reversioner's counternotice under s. 21(1):

(a) it must state which (if any) of the proposals contained in the initial notice are accepted by the reversioner and specify

(*i*) in relation to any proposal which is not so accepted, the reversioner's counter-proposal; and

(*ii*) any additional lease back proposals by the reversioner: s. 21(3)(a).

NOTE: The reversioner may wish to make additional lease back proposals if the initial notice did not specify all flats or units to which the mandatory lease back provisions of Part II of Schedule 9 apply, or if the freeholder wishes to take advantage of the 'optional' lease back provisions of Part III of Schedule 9 (see **10** above).

(b) If the initial notice proposes that the nominee purchaser should acquire the freehold of any property which any qualifying tenant is entitled, under the terms of the lease of his flat, to use in common with the occupiers of other premises (e.g. communal gardens or estate roads), and the reversioner counter-proposes (in accordance with s. 1(4) – see **8** above) that in lieu thereof

(*i*) the nominee purchaser should be granted permanent rights over that property or any other property; or

(*ii*) the nominee purchaser should acquire the freehold of any other property over which such permanent rights may be granted, the counter-proposal must be set out in the reversioner's counter-notice and specify

(A) the nature of those rights and the property over which it is proposed the same should be granted; or

(B) the alternative freehold property which the reversioner pro-poses should be transferred to the nominee purchaser, as appropriate: s. 21(3)(b).

(c) It must state which interests (if any) the nominee purchaser is to be required to acquire in accordance with s. 21(4): s. 21(3)(c).

NOTE: Section 21(4) deals with cases where the interest in any property which would remain in the hands of the freeholder of the specified premises, or any other relevant landlord, after the nominee purchaser's acquisition of the specified premises

(*i*) would for all practical purposes cease to be of use and benefit to him; or

(*ii*) would cease to be capable of being reasonably managed or maintained by him.

In such cases the nominee purchaser may be required to acquire that interest also.

Example

The freeholder owns a building containing flats held by qualifying tenants and an administrative office used by caretakers and other staff employed by the freeholder for the purposes of management of the building.

The freeholder also owns two garages nearby which are used by the freeholder's caretakers and other staff.

If the nominee purchaser acquires the freehold to the building, it will no longer be necessary for the freeholder to employ caretakers and other staff for the management of the building and thus, it will be unnecessary for him to maintain the two garages for use by his staff.

In these circumstances the two garages may, for all practical purposes, cease to be of use and benefit to the freeholder. Section 21(4) entitles the freeholder to require the nominee purchaser to acquire his interest in the two garages in addition to the specified premises.

(d) If the freeholder of the specified premises or any other relevant landlord wishes to retain rights over

(*i*) any property in which he has an interest which is included in the proposed acquisition by the nominee purchaser; or

(*ii*) any property in which he has an interest which the nominee purchaser is to be required to acquire in accordance with s. 21(4),

on the grounds that such rights are necessary for the proper management or maintenance of property in which he is to retain a freehold or leasehold interest, those rights must be stated in the reversioner's counternotice: s. 21(3)(d).

(e) The reversioner's counternotice must include a description of any provisions which the reversioner or any other relevant landlord considers should be included in any conveyance to the nominee purchaser in accordance with s. 34 and Schedule 7: s. 21(3)(e).

> NOTE: Section 34 and Schedule 7 contain detailed provisions dealing with such matters as
> rights of support
> rights of passage of water, etc.
> rights of way
> and restrictive covenants
> to which the property to be acquired by the nominee purchaser, is to be subject or to have the benefit.

Price payable by the nominee purchaser

27. General. The price payable by the nominee purchaser for the freehold and other interests to be acquired by him on behalf of the participating tenants, is determined in accordance with Schedule 6 to the Act: s. 32(1).

The provisions of Schedule 6 are detailed and are examined here in outline only. References hereafter to paragraph numbers are to the numbered paragraphs of Schedule 6.

'The valuation date' in respect of freehold and intermediate leasehold interests to be acquired by the nominee purchaser means the date on which the interest in the specified premises which is to be acquired from the freeholder, is determined either by agreement or by a leasehold valuation tribunal: paragraph 1(1) (and see **42** below).

28. Price payable for freehold of specified premises: paragraph 2. This is the aggregate of

(a) the value of the freeholder's interest determined in accordance with paragraph 3;

(b) the freeholder's share of the marriage value determined in accordance with paragraph 4; and

(c) any compensation payable to the freeholder for loss arising from enfranchisement, determined in accordance with paragraph 5.

29. The value of the freeholder's interest in the specified premises: paragraph 3. This is the amount that interest might be expected to realise if sold on the open market by a willing seller (with neither the nominee purchaser nor any participating tenant buying or seeking to buy) on the assumptions

(a) that the vendor is selling for an estate in fee simple

   (*i*) subject to any leases subject to which the freeholder's interest is to be acquired by the nominee purchaser (including therefore any lease of any unit, e.g. a vacant flat, which the nominee purchaser is required to lease back to the freeholder), but

   (*ii*) subject also to any intermediate or other leasehold interests which are to be acquired by the nominee purchaser;

(b) that the qualifying tenants have no right under the Act to acquire any interest in the specified premises or any new lease of an individual flat (although the effect of any notice given by a tenant, other than a participating tenant, claiming a new lease of his flat in accordance with Chapter II of the Act can be taken into account);

(c) that any increase in the value of any flat held by a participating tenant attributable to an improvement carried out at his own expense by the tenant or by any predecessor in title, is to be disregarded; and

(d) that the vendor is selling with and subject to the rights and burdens, to which the conveyance of the freeholder's interest to the nominee purchaser is to be made, including in particular such permanent or extended rights and burdens which are to be created in order to give effect to Schedule 7 (see **26**(e) above).

   NOTES: (1) Further assumptions can be made if those assumptions would be made in determining the value of the freeholder's interest if sold on the open market by a willing seller: paragraph 3(2).

(2) Any deduction on account of any defect in the freeholder's title, which would be allowed between a willing seller and a willing buyer on a sale of the freeholder's interest on the open market, must likewise be made when valuing the freeholder's interest for the purposes of the Act: paragraph 3(3).

(3) The value of the freeholder's interest in any flat or other unit which is to be leased back to him is taken to be the difference between

(a) the value of his freehold interest in it, and

(b) the value of his interest in it under the lease back on the assumption that the lease back was granted to the freeholder on the valuation date: paragraph 3(4).

30. The freeholder's share of the marriage value: paragraph 4. The marriage value of any property is the amount by which the value of two (or more) interests in that property (e.g. the freehold and a leasehold interest), when transferred into the ownership of one person, exceeds the combined value of those interests when they are held by different persons. In short, 1+1 may equal 3 when both interests are held by one person. This may be so because e.g. ownership of both interests by one person provides a redevelopment opportunity which would not be available if those interests were in different ownerships.

Paragraph 4(2) provides that the marriage value is any increase in the aggregate value of the freehold and every intermediate interest in the specified premises when regarded as interests in the control of the participating tenants, as compared with the aggregate value of those interests when held by the persons from whom they are to be acquired, which is an increase in value

(a) attributable to the potential ability of the participating tenants, once those interests have been so acquired, to have new leases granted to them without payment of any premium and without restriction as to length of term, and

(b) which if those interests (i.e. the freehold and any intermediate leasehold interests) were being sold to the nominee purchaser on the open market by willing sellers, the nominee purchaser would have to agree to share with the sellers in order to reach agreement as to price.

The freeholder's share of the marriage value is the greater of

(*i*) such proportion of the same as is determined by agreement between the reversioner and the nominee purchaser or, in default of agreement, as is determined by a leasehold valuation tribunal, as the proportion which would have been determined by an agreement between the parties on a sale on the open market by a willing seller, or (*ii*) 50%: paragraph 4(1).

31. Compensation for loss resulting from enfranchisement: paragraph 5. If in consequence of the acquisition of his interest in the specified premises the freeholder suffers

(a) any diminution in the value of his interest in other property;
(b) any other loss or damage resulting from the acquisition of his interest in the specified premises that is referable to his ownership of any interest in other property,

he is entitled to such amount as is reasonable to compensate him for the loss or damage so suffered: paragraph 5(1) and (2).

It is expressly provided that the kind of loss for which the freeholder is entitled to be compensated includes loss of development value in relation to the specified premises to the extent that such loss is referable to his ownership of any interest in other property: paragraph 5(3) and (4).

> NOTE: The fact that any loss or damage the freeholder will suffer could have been avoided or reduced if he had taken advantage of the 'optional' lease back provisions of s. 36 and Part III of Schedule 9 (see **10** above), does not affect the amount of the compensation payable: paragraph 5(5).

32. Price payable for intermediate leasehold interests: paragraph 6. A separate price is payable for each intermediate leasehold interest which is to be acquired. That price is the aggregate of

(a) the value of the interest as determined in accordance with paragraph 7; and
(b) any compensation payable to the owner of that interest in accordance with paragraph 8.

> NOTE: If an intermediate leasehold interest has a negative value (e.g. because the rents receivable by the owner of that interest from his tenants are less than the rent payable by him to his own landlord), the price payable by the nominee purchaser is nil: paragraph 6(2).

33. Value of intermediate leasehold interests: paragraph 7. Unless the intermediate leasehold interest is a 'minor intermediate lease' (as to which see the notes below) the value of that interest is ascertained in a similar way to the valuation of the freehold of the specified premises: paragraph 7(1) and see paragraph 3 and **29** above.

Accordingly, the value of an intermediate leasehold interest is the amount that interest might be expected to realise if sold on the open market by a willing seller (with neither the nominee purchaser nor any participating tenant buying or seeking to buy) on the assumptions:

(a) that (where applicable) the intermediate leasehold interest is being sold subject to any leases intermediate between that interest and any lease held by a qualifying tenant of a flat contained in the specified premises;

(b) that the qualifying tenants have no right under the Act to acquire any interest in the specified premises or any new lease of an individual flat (although the effect of any notice given by a tenant, other than a participating tenant, claiming a new lease of his flat in accordance with Chapter II of the Act can be taken into account); and

(c) that any increase in the value of any flat held by a participating tenant attributable to an improvement carried out at his own expense by the tenant or by an predecessor in title is to be disregarded.

NOTES: (1) Notes 1 and 2 to **29** above are equally applicable with appropriate modifications to make them referable to a sale of the intermediate leasehold interests.

(2) A 'minor intermediate lease' is a lease which

(a) has an expectation of possession (in broad terms meaning a reversion) of not more than one month; and

(b) produces a profit rent of not more than £5 per year.

Paragraph 7(2)–(10) contains detailed provisions relating to (*inter alia*) the nature and valuation of minor intermediate leases.

34. Compensation for loss resulting from acquisition of intermediate leasehold interests: paragraph 8. Paragraph 5(1)–(4) applies for the purpose of calculating the compensation payable to the owner of an intermediate leasehold interest. See **31** above (with the exception of the note thereto which has no application to the holders of intermediate leasehold interests).

35. Share of the marriage value payable to the owners of intermediate leasehold interests: paragraph 9. If the price payable for the freehold of the specified premises includes an amount in respect of the freeholder's share of the marriage value (see **30** above) and the nominee purchaser is to acquire any intermediate leasehold interests, the freeholder's share of the marriage value is divided between the freeholder and the owners of the intermediate leasehold interests in proportion to the value of their respective interests in the specified premises: paragraphs 9(1) and (2).

The full amount of the freeholder's share of the marriage value is payable by the nominee purchaser to the reversioner. The reversioner must then account to the freeholder (if the freeholder is not also the reversioner) who must in turn account to the owners of the intermediate leasehold interests for their share of the marriage value: paragraph 9(3).

36. Price payable for other interests: paragraphs 10–13. As has been seen, the qualifying tenants are also entitled to acquire (via the nominee purchaser) the freehold to

(a) any appurtenant property demised by a lease held by a qualifying tenant of a flat contained in the relevant premises; and
(b) any property which any qualifying tenant is entitled to use in common with the occupiers of other premises (see **8** above).

It has also been seen that the nominee purchaser may be required to acquire the interest of any relevant landlord (which could be a freehold or leasehold interest) in any other property which will cease for all practical purposes to be of use and benefit to that relevant landlord or which will cease to be capable of being reasonably managed or maintained by him (see s. 21(4) and **26** above).

Additionally it has been seen that the qualifying tenants may be entitled to acquire any leasehold interests in property which consists of or includes

(a) any common parts of the relevant premises; or
(b) any appurtenant property which is demised by the lease held by a qualifying tenant, or property which a qualifying tenant is entitled, under his lease of the flat, to use in common with the occupiers of other premises (see s. 2(3) and **9** above).

Paragraphs 10 to 13 contain provisions for ascertainment of the price payable for those interests and (where appropriate) for apportionment of the freeholder's share of the marriage value between the freeholder and the owners of any such leasehold interests.

Broadly speaking, the price payable for those interests is ascertained, with appropriate modifications, in a similar way to that in which the prices for the freehold and intermediate leasehold interests in the specified premises are ascertained (see **28** to **35** above).

37. Valuation of interests with negative values: paragraphs 14 to 21. The detailed provisions of paragraphs 14 to 21 will not be considered here save to note that notwithstanding the fact that the value of any interest to be acquired may be a negative amount, the value of the same is taken to be nil: paragraphs 14(1) and 18(1).

Procedure following agreement or determination of the terms of acquisition

38. Exchange of contracts. The Secretary of State may prescribe regulations as to the procedure for giving effect to the initial notice and similar matters by virtue of s. 98(1).

Reference has already been made to The Leasehold Reform (Collective Enfranchisement and Lease Renewal) Regulations 1993, SI 1993 No 2407 (see the note to **21** above). The detailed provisions of those Regulations will not be considered here but paragraphs 6 and 7 of Schedule 1 to those Regulations should be noted.

Paragraph 6 requires the reversioner to prepare the draft contract and give it to the nominee purchaser within the period of 21 days beginning with the date on which the terms of acquisition are agreed or determined.

The nominee purchaser must give the reversioner a statement of any proposals for amending the draft contract within the period of 14 days beginning with the date the draft contract is given to him by the reversioner. If he fails to do so, the nominee purchaser is deemed to have approved the draft contract.

The reversioner must provide an answer to the nominee purchaser's statement, within the period of 14 days beginning with the date the statement is given, giving any objections to or comments on the proposals in the statement. If he fails to do so, he is deemed to have agreed the nominee purchaser's proposals for amendment of the draft contract.

Paragraph 7 entitles the reversioner to require the nominee purchaser to pay a deposit on exchange of contracts. The amount of the deposit will be £500 or 10% of the price, whichever is the greater.

NOTE: Section 98(1) provides that subject to or in the absence of any regulations made by the Secretary of State, the procedure for giving effect to the initial notice and the rights and obligations of all parties in relation to the investigation of title and other matters arising in giving effect to the initial notice, shall be, as nearly as may be, the same as in the case of a contract of sale freely negotiated between the parties.

39. The Conveyance. Section 34 and Schedule 7 contain detailed provisions dealing with such matters as covenants to which the property to be acquired by the nominee purchaser is to be subject or to have the benefit.

Section 34(1) and (2) envisages the completion of a single conveyance to the nominee purchaser of the freehold of the specified premises. That conveyance will grant the nominee purchaser an estate in fee simple absolute in the specified premises and provide for the disposal to the nominee purchaser of any leasehold interests in the specified premises which he is to acquire.

By virtue of paragraph 6(1)(b)(iv) of Schedule 1 to the Act (and subject to paragraph 7 of that Schedule), the reversioner is to receive the price payable for the acquisition of any interest by the nominee purchaser (but see **40** below).

> NOTES: (1) The same provisions apply to any separate conveyance of any other freehold property to be acquired by the nominee purchaser which may be required.
>
> (2) The conveyance must contain a statement in the following form: 'This conveyance [or transfer] is executed for the purposes of Chapter I of Part I of the Leasehold Reform, Housing and Urban Development Act 1993': s. 34(10) and SI 1993 No 3045.

40. Discharge of existing mortgages. If any interest to be acquired by the nominee purchaser is subject to a mortgage, the general rule is that the nominee purchaser must, in the first instance, apply the consideration payable for that interest in or towards the redemption of the mortgage. If an interest to be acquired by the nominee purchaser is subject to more than one mortgage, the consideration payable for that interest must be applied in or towards redemption of those mortgages according to their priorities.

Provided that the nominee purchaser complies with these requirements, the conveyance to the nominee purchaser operates to discharge the relevant interest from the mortgage and from the operation of any order made by a Court for the enforcement of the mortgage. Furthermore, any term of years created for the purposes of the mortgage is extinguished: s. 35(1) and paragraph 2 of Schedule 8 to the Act.

This is the case whether or not the consideration payable for the relevant interest is sufficient to satisfy the mortgage. If the consideration payable is insufficient, the mortgagee's rights or remedies against any other property comprised in the same or any other security are preserved as are the personal liabilities of the relevant landlord and any other person (e.g. a guarantor) to the mortgagee.

> NOTE: Section 35 and Schedule 8 contain detailed provisions relating to the discharge of mortgages including provisions enabling the nominee purchaser to acquire the relevant interest free of any mortgage by making an appropriate payment into Court in cases of difficulty (e.g. if the mortgagee cannot be identified or traced).

41. Costs of enfranchisement. Section 33(1) imposes a liability on the nominee purchaser to pay the reasonable costs incurred by the reversioner and any other relevant landlord in pursuance of the initial notice, of and incidental to various matters, including

(a) any investigation reasonably undertaken as to whether or not any interest in the specified premises or any other property is liable to be acquired or as to any other matter arising out of the initial notice;
(b) deducing title;
(c) providing abstracts of title;
(d) any valuation; and
(e) any conveyance.

However if on any voluntary sale a stipulation for payment of any costs by the purchaser would be void, the nominee purchaser is not liable for those costs.

Costs incurred by the reversioner or any other relevant landlord in respect of professional services rendered by any person (e.g. a Valuer or Solicitor) will only be regarded as reasonable if and to the extent that costs in respect of those services could reasonably have been expected to be incurred by the reversioner or that relevant landlord if he was to be personally liable for those costs: s. 33(2).

Miscellaneous matters

42. Failure to agree the terms of acquisition – the role of leasehold valuation tribunals. If the nominee purchaser and the reversioner have been unable to agree any of the terms of acquisition (e.g. the interests to be acquired, the amounts payable as the purchase price for those interests or the provisions to be contained in any conveyance – see s. 24(8)) within the period of two months beginning with the date on which the reversioner's counternotice was given, a leasehold valuation tribunal may determine any matters in dispute on the application of the nominee purchaser or the reversioner: s. 24(1).

The application must be made within the period of 6 months beginning with the date on which the reversioner's counternotice was given to the nominee purchaser: s. 24(2).

If no such application is made, the initial notice is deemed to have been withdrawn (as to which see **47** below): s. 29(2).

NOTE: A leasehold valuation tribunal has jurisdiction to determine a number of matters under the Act. Those matters are set out in s. 91(2).

That jurisdiction is exercised by a rent assessment committee which is known as a 'leasehold valuation tribunal' when constituted for the purposes of exercising that jurisdiction: s. 91(1) and (3). For procedure, see SI 1993 No 2408.

43. Failure of parties to enter into a binding contract. If the parties have not entered into a binding contract by the expiry of the 'appropriate period', i.e.

(a) within the period of two months beginning with the date on which the terms of acquisition were agreed (any such agreement being an agreement subject to contract: s. 38(4)); or
(b) within the period of two months beginning with the date on which any decision by a leasehold valuation tribunal determining all or any of the terms of acquisition becomes final; or
(c) within such other period as may have been fixed by a leasehold valuation tribunal in making its determination,

the nominee purchaser or the reversioner can apply to the Court for an Order under s. 24(4): see s. 24(3) and (6).

That application must be made within the period of 2 months immediately following the expiry of the appropriate period: s. 24(5).

If no such application is made the initial notice is deemed to have been withdrawn (as to which see **47** below): s. 29(2).

Under s. 24(4) the Court has power to make an Order

(a) providing for the interests to be acquired by the nominee purchaser to be vested in him on the terms agreed or on the terms which were determined by a leasehold valuation tribunal; or
(b) providing for those interests to be vested in the nominee purchaser on those terms, but subject to such modifications specified in the Court's Order as may have been determined by a leasehold valuation tribunal, on the application of the nominee purchaser or the reversioner, to be required by reason of any change in circumstances since the terms of the acquisition were agreed or determined; or
(c) providing for the initial notice to be deemed to have been withdrawn (as to which see **47** below).

NOTE: Schedule 5 to the Act contains supplemental provisions relating to vesting orders including provisions for the nominee purchaser to pay monies into Court and the execution of conveyances by a person designated by the Court.

44. Failure of reversioner to give counternotice. If the reversioner fails to give a counternotice in response to the initial notice, as required by s. 21(1) (see **22** above) or any further counternotice required by virtue of s. 22(3) or s. 23(5) or (6) (see **23** and **24** above) the nominee purchaser can apply to the Court for an Order determining the terms on which he is to acquire the interests and rights specified in the initial notice in accordance with the proposals contained in the initial notice: s. 25(1).

That application must be made within the period of 6 months beginning with the date by which the reversioner's counternotice or further counternotice should have been given: s. 25(4).

If no such application is made the initial notice is deemed to have been withdrawn (as to which see **47** below): s. 29(4).

The Court will not make an Order under s. 25(1) unless it is satisfied as to the participating tenants' entitlement to exercise the right to collective enfranchisement and that copies of the initial notice were given to every relevant landlord in accordance with Part II of Schedule 3 (see the notes to **16** above): s. 25(3).

The Court's Order under s. 25(1) will, if appropriate, make provision for any mandatory lease-back to the freeholder in accordance with s. 36 and Part II of Schedule 9 (see **10** above): s. 25(2).

45. Failure to enter into a binding contract following Order under s. 25(1). If the Court has made an Order determining the terms of acquisition under s. 25(1) and the parties have not entered into a binding contract by the expiry of the 'appropriate period', i.e.

(a) the period of two months beginning with the date on which the Order under s. 25(1) becomes final; or

(b) such other period as may have been fixed by the Court,

the nominee purchaser can apply to the Court for an Order under s. 25(6): s. 25(5) and (8).

That application must be made within the period of two months beginning immediately after the end of the appropriate period: s. 25(7). If no such application is made, the initial notice is deemed to have been withdrawn (as to which see **47** below): s. 29(4).

Under s. 25(6) the Court has power to make an Order

(a) providing for the interests to be acquired by the nominee purchaser to be vested in him

  (*i*) on the terms determined by the Court's Order under s. 25(1); or

  (*ii*) on those terms, but subject to any modifications specified in the Order which have been determined by a leasehold valuation tribunal, on the application of the nominee purchaser or the reversioner, as being required to reflect any change in circumstances since the s. 25(1) Order was made; or

(b) providing for the initial notice to be deemed to have been with-drawn at the end of the 'appropriate period' (as to which see **47** below).

46. Procedure if the freeholder or the other relevant landlords cannot be found. (A) If the freeholder or the other relevant land-lords cannot be identified or found it will not be possible to give an initial notice and comply with the provisions of Part II of Schedule 3 (see the notes to **16** above) regarding the giving of copies of the initial notice.

In these cases, provided that not less than two-thirds of the quali-fying tenants wish to make a claim to exercise the right to collective enfranchisement, those tenants (as opposed to any nominee purchaser) can apply to the Court for a Vesting Order under s. 26(1).

That Order will provide for the vesting of the interests in question, in a person appointed by the qualifying tenants making the applica-tion, on such terms as may be determined by a leasehold valuation tribunal: s. 27(1).

The terms so determined by a leasehold valuation tribunal will include

(a) 'the appropriate sum' to be paid into Court by the qualifying tenants' appointee (which will be determined in accordance with s. 27(5) – equivalent in effect to the price which would be payable if the interest in question were being acquired in accordance with an initial notice, plus any actual or estimated amounts the leasehold valuation tribunal determines as being due from any tenant(s) of the owner of the interest in question); and

(b) the form of the conveyance to the qualifying tenants' appointee: s. 27(3)(a).

Upon the qualifying tenants' appointee paying 'the appropriate sum' into Court, a conveyance of the interests in question will be ex-ecuted in his favour by a person designated by the Court: s. 27(3).

NOTES: (1) Section 26(5) makes provision for cases where the relevant landlord is traced after the application for a vesting order has been made but before any interest has vested in the qualifying tenants' appointee.

(2) The application for a vesting order can be withdrawn at any time before the conveyance to the qualifying tenants' appointee is executed but (inter alia) leave of the Court may be required if the 'missing' freeholder or any of the 'missing' relevant landlords is traced after the application has been made: s. 26(6).

(B) If

(a) some relevant landlords can be identified and traced but one or more relevant landlord cannot be identified or traced; and

(b) not less than two-thirds of the qualifying tenants wish to make a claim to exercise the right to collective enfranchisement

those tenants can apply to the Court for an Order dispensing with the requirement to give the initial notice or (as the case may be) a copy of it, to the relevant landlord who cannot be identified or traced: s. 26(2).

If such an order is made any initial notice, or copy of it, subsequently given (i.e. to the relevant landlords who can be identified and traced) must contain a statement as to the effect of the Order: s. 26(7).

If the relevant landlord who cannot be identified or traced is the freeholder, the Court can make an Order appointing any other relevant landlord to be the reversioner: s. 26(3).

NOTE: Before making any Order under s. 26(1) or (2) the Court may require the qualifying tenants to take further steps, by advertisement or otherwise, to trace the 'missing' person: s. 26(5).

47. Withdrawal from acquisition by participating tenants and deemed withdrawal of initial notice. (A) At any time before a binding contract has been entered into, the participating tenants may withdraw the initial notice by giving a 'notice of withdrawal' under s. 28(1).

The notice of withdrawal must be given to the nominee purchaser, the reversioner in respect of the specified premises and to every relevant landlord known or believed by the participating tenants to be acting independently: s. 28(2).

The nominee purchaser must give a copy of the notice of withdrawal to any relevant landlord acting independently who is not named in the notice of withdrawal as a recipient of that notice: s. 28(3).

If the participating tenants give a notice of withdrawal, they are jointly and severally liable for all 'relevant costs' incurred by the reversioner and every other relevant landlord down to the time when the notice of withdrawal is given. The nominee purchaser is not liable for any such costs in these circumstances: s. 28(4), (5) and (6).

NOTE: 'Relevant costs' means costs for which the nominee purchaser would otherwise have been liable under s. 33 (see **41**): s. 28(7)

(B) As has been seen, there are a variety of circumstances in which the initial notice will be deemed to have been withdrawn (see **19, 21, 23, 42, 43, 44** and **45**).

In these circumstances, the participating tenants are liable for the reversioner's and other relevant landlords' costs in the same way as if a notice of withdrawal had been given (see **(A)**) but the nominee purchaser is also jointly and severally liable for those costs: s. 29(6) and s. 33(7).

If the initial notice is deemed to have been withdrawn in accordance with s. 15(10) or s. 16(8) (failure by the participating tenants to give notice of the appointment of a new nominee purchaser following the death, retirement or termination of the appointment of the original nominee purchaser), the nominee purchaser is not liable for any such costs: s. 29(7).

> NOTE: If the initial notice is withdrawn, or deemed to have been withdrawn, no subsequent initial notice can be given until the expiry of the period of 12 months beginning with the date the notice of withdrawal is given, or the date of deemed withdrawal, as the case may be: s. 13(9).
>
> In other words, the qualifying tenants are debarred from making a claim to exercise the right to collective enfranchisement for 12 months.

48. The Court and enforcement of obligations under Chapter I. Where references are made in Chapter I to 'the Court', the Court in question is the county court: s. 90(1). The county court also has jurisdiction to determine any question arising under or by virtue of Chapter I which is not specifically identified in Chapter I (except questions which fall to be determined by a leasehold valuation tribunal): s. 90(2).

If any person fails to comply with any requirement imposed on him by Chapter I, any person interested can

(a) give notice to the person in question requiring him to make good his default; and

(b) apply to the Court for an order requiring that person to make good his default if he fails to comply with that notice within 14 days: s. 92.

> NOTE: The Rules of the Court dealing specifically with Chapter I are contained in CCR Order 49, rule 9.

Progress test 35

1. To what premises does Chapter I apply? **(4)**

2. What is 'the right to collective enfranchisement'? **(7)**

3. What property and interests in the same can be the subject of a claim to exercise the right to collective enfranchisement? **(8 and 9)**

4. The building in question contains 2 shops and a number of vacant flats. Advise the freeholder of his rights in the event that a claim to exercise the right to collective enfranchisement is made.   **(10)**

5. Who are the 'qualifying tenants'?   **(11 and 12)**

6. How is a claim to exercise the right to collective enfranchisement initiated?   **(15 and 16)**

7. What action must the reversioner take on receipt of an 'initial notice'?   **(22)**

8. What is the position if a landlord has plans to redevelop the building?   **(24)**

9. How is the price payable for the freehold made up and what is the freeholder's share of 'the marriage value'?   **(28 and 30)**

10. The reversioner and the nominee purchaser are unable to agree the price. Advise the nominee purchaser.   **(42)**

11. An initial notice has been served but the reversioner has not served a counternotice. Advise the nominee purchaser.   **(44)**

12. The terms of acquisition were agreed more than two months ago but the nominee purchaser has failed to exchange contracts. Advise the reversioner.   **(45 and 47)**

Individual right of tenant to acquire a new lease (Chapter II, Part I of the 1993 Act)

1. General introduction. As was noted in the introduction to Chapter 35, a significant complaint made by tenants of residential flats in multi-occupied buildings, such as blocks of flats, was that, with the passage of time, the value of their interests was diminishing. Their leases were, in effect, wasting assets.

A conventional long lease is often for a term of 99 years or more. If the tenant's lease had only, say, 40 years to run, it was less attractive to prospective purchasers and its value was affected accordingly. Additionally, lenders were reluctant to make mortgage advances on the security of such a wasting asset, which in turn affected the marketability and hence the value of the lease yet further.

By contrast, tenants holding long leases of houses were able to compulsorily acquire the freehold (enfranchise) or an extended lease under the Leasehold Reform Act 1967 (see Chapter 22).

2. The Leasehold Reform, Housing and Urban Development Act 1993. Tenants holding long leases of residential flats have now been given rights of collective enfranchisement, and a similar right to acquire an extended lease to that enjoyed by tenants holding long leases of houses, by Part I of the Leasehold Reform, Housing and Urban Development Act 1993 ('the Act').

3. Scope of this chapter. This Chapter is concerned with the right of an individual tenant to acquire a new lease of his flat, conferred by Chapter II of Part I of the Act (ss. 39–62), which came into force on 1st November 1993: SI 1993 No 2134. The right to collective enfranchisement is dealt with in Chapter 35 of this book.

The provisions relating to the exercise of the right to collective enfranchisement are detailed and require co-ordinated action by a number of tenants. It is anticipated therefore that many tenants will instead exercise the individual right to acquire a new lease.

This Chapter examines the provisions of Chapter II of Part I of the Act in some detail but before doing so, an outline of the main provisions may be helpful. References in the Outline to paragraph numbers, e.g. **(4)**, are to the numbered paragraphs of this Chapter.

Outline

(a) Chapter II confers upon qualifying tenants of flats, who have occupied their flats for at least 3 years in the last 10 years, the right to acquire a new lease on payment of a premium. The new lease is granted in substitution for the existing lease and is for a term expiring 90 years after the expiry of the existing lease, at a peppercorn rent**(4)**.

(b) Generally, a tenant of a flat under a long lease, at a low rent, is a 'qualifying tenant' **(5)** and **(6)**.

(c) 'The landlord' or 'competent landlord', for the purposes of Chapter II, is the holder of a superior interest in the flat (freehold or leasehold) which is sufficient to enable him to grant the new lease. If there is a chain of superior tenancies, the holder of the interest lowest down the chain which is sufficient to enable him to grant the new lease is the competent landlord **(7)**. The tenant can give notices to his immediate landlord and superior landlords requiring them to provide details of their respective interests **(8)**.

(d) A claim to exercise the right to acquire a new lease is made by the giving of a 'tenant's notice' under s. 42 **(9)** and **(10)**. The tenant's notice must contain certain information, including particulars of the flat, the tenant's existing lease and the tenant's occupation of the flat, and set out the tenant's proposals as to the premium payable for, and the terms of, the new lease. The tenant's notice must also specify a date, not less than 2 months hence, by which the landlord should serve counter-notice **(11)**.

(e) The landlord is entitled to require the tenant to provide evidence of the period(s) of occupation of the flat relied on by the tenant **(13)** and all landlords are entitled to have access to the flat to obtain valuations **(14)**.

(f) The landlord must give a counter-notice under s. 45 by the date specified in the tenant's notice. The counter-notice must admit or dispute the tenant's right to acquire a new lease. In either case the counter-notice may also state that a landlord intends to apply to the Court for an Order declaring that the tenant's right to acquire a new lease should not be exerciseable in view of intended redevelopment **(15)**. If no counter-notice is given, the tenant can ask the Court to determine the terms on which he is to acquire a new lease **(44)**. If the landlord cannot be traced, the tenant can apply to the Court for a vesting order, which will result in a new lease, on terms determined by a leasehold valuation tribunal, being executed by a person designated by the Court **(46)**.

(g) If the landlord's counter-notice does not admit the tenant's claim to acquire a new lease and/or states that an application to the Court will be made for an Order that the tenant's right to acquire a new lease should not be exerciseable on the grounds of intended redevelopment, the landlord (or a landlord in the latter case) must make the appropriate application to the Court within 2 months of the giving of the counter-notice **(16)** and **(17)**.

(h) Any new lease granted will be for a term expiring 90 years after the expiry of the tenant's existing lease, at a peppercorn rent **(20)** and (prima facie) be of the premises demised by the tenant's existing lease **(21)**. Generally, the new lease will be on similar terms to the terms of the existing lease **(22)** but provision for payment of a service charge during the extra 90 years will be made in most cases **(23)**. Certain terms of the existing lease may have to be excluded **(24)** and other terms must be included **(26)**.

(i) If the competent landlord is not the tenant's immediate landlord, all intermediate leasehold interests are deemed to be surrendered and regranted, subject to the new lease to the tenant, when the new lease is granted **(28)**.

(j) In order to secure the grant of the new lease the tenant must pay a premium and certain amounts due to the holders of the intermediate leasehold interests (if any), and tender payment of any outstanding rent and other sums due under his existing lease together with landlords' costs **(29)** and **(41)**.

(k) The premium payable to the landlord **(30)** is the aggregate of the diminution in value of the landlord's interest in the flat **(31)**, the landlord's share of the marriage value **(32)** and any compensation payable to the landlord for loss arising out of the grant of the new lease **(33)**.

(l) The amount payable by the tenant to the owner of an intermediate leasehold interest **(34)** is the aggregate of the diminution in value of that interest **(35)** and any compensation payable to the owner of that interest **(36)**. The owner of an intermediate leasehold interest may also be entitled to part of the landlord's share of the marriage value **(37)**.

(m) Regulations dealing with conveyancing procedure and similar matters have been made **(38)**.

(n) Alienation provisions contained in any superior lease of the tenant's flat are of no effect in relation to the grant of the new lease **(28)** and, generally, the new lease is binding on all mortgagees of superior interests **(39)**. If the tenant's existing lease is mortgaged, the new lease is substituted as the mortgagee's security **(40)**.

(o) If any of the terms on which the tenant is to acquire the new lease cannot be agreed, the matters in dispute can be determined by a leasehold valuation tribunal **(42)**.

(p) The tenant's notice can be withdrawn at any time before the new lease is granted, and can be deemed to have been withdrawn, or cease to have effect, in a variety of circumstances. Generally, the tenant will then be liable for all landlords' costs. If the tenant's notice is withdrawn, or deemed to have been withdrawn, no further claim to exercise the right to acquire a new lease can be made for 12 months **(47)** and **(48)**.

(q) There is no limitation upon the number of new leases the tenant can acquire pursuant to Chapter II but having acquired a new lease, the tenant does not have any security of tenure conferred on tenants by other legislation **(50)**. Likewise, any sub-tenant whose sub-lease derives out of the tenant's new lease does not benefit from any of the statutory provisions which would otherwise confer security of tenure **(51)**.

(s) The landlord may be able to determine the new lease for redevelopment purposes during the 12 months preceding the date on which the tenant's existing lease would have expired, or during the last 5 years of the term of the new lease. The tenant is then entitled to compensation equivalent to the open market value of the determined new lease **(52)**.

(t) Contracting out of Chapter II is generally not permissible **(53)**.

(u) In certain circumstances the Court can set aside an agreement for surrender of a qualifying tenant's lease or for the grant of a new lease **(54)**.

4. The right conferred by Chapter II, Part 1 of the Act. A qualifying tenant of a flat (see below) who has, on 'the relevant date', occupied the flat as his only or principal home

(*i*) for the last 3 years, or

(*ii*) for periods amounting to 3 years in the last 10 years,

has the right to acquire a new lease of the flat on payment of a premium: s. 39(1) and (2). The new lease is granted in substitution for the tenant's existing lease and is for a term expiring 90 years after the expiry of the term created by the tenant's existing lease, at a peppercorn rent: s. 56(1).

NOTES: (1) 'Flat' is defined in s. 101(1) but see also s. 62(2) to (4).

(2) 'The relevant date' is the date upon which notice of the claim to

exercise the right to acquire a new lease is given under s. 42; s. 39(8).

(3) Occupation by the tenant of any part of the flat in question is sufficient, whether or not that occupation was under the lease by virtue of which the tenant is a qualifying tenant: s. 39(5).

(4) Occupation by a company or other artificial person does not constitute occupation for the purposes of s. 39(2): s. 39(5).

(5) Where two or more persons together constitute the qualifying tenant of a flat, it is sufficient if one of those joint tenants has occupied the flat for the requisite period: s. 39(6).

5. Qualifying tenants. Section 39(3) applies s. 5 (except sub-sections (5) and (6)) and ss. 7 and 8 of the Act for the purpose of establishing whether or not any person is 'a qualifying tenant'. Accordingly, a person is a qualifying tenant of a flat if he is the tenant of the flat under a long lease at a low rent and

(a) the lease is not a business lease;

(b) the flat does not form part of housing accommodation provided by a charitable housing trust in pursuit of its charitable purposes and the charitable housing trust is the tenant's immediate landlord;

(c) the lease is not a sub-lease granted out of a superior lease which is not itself a long lease at a low rent, in breach of the terms of that superior lease, and the breach has not been waived: s. 5(2).

There can only be one qualifying tenant of a flat at any one time and if joint tenants hold a long lease of a flat at a low rent, they jointly constitute the qualifying tenant of the flat in question: ss. 5(3) and (4).

NOTE: A person can be (or be amongst those constituting) the qualifying tenant of two or more flats, whether he is the tenant of those flats under one lease or under two or more separate leases: s. 39(4).

Example
_____

(1) T holds a single lease of flats 1, 2 and 3 in a block of flats. T occupies flat 1 as his only home and sublets flats 2 and 3.

Conclusion: T is a qualifying tenant of flat 1.

(2) T holds a lease of flat 1 which he occupies as his only home. T is also the joint tenant with his son, B, of flat 2 under a separate lease. B occupies flat 2 as his only home.

Conclusion: (i) T is a qualifying tenant of flat 1; and (ii) T and B together constitute the qualifying tenant of flat 2.

_____

6. 'Long lease' and 'low rent'. It is sufficient for most purposes to note that a 'long lease' is one granted for a term of years certain exceeding 21 years. Section 7 deals with 'long leases' in detail (see 35:**12**).

In summary, a lease of a flat is a lease at a 'low rent' if

(a) no rent was payable during the 'initial year', i.e. the period of one year beginning with the date of commencement of the lease; or

(b) the aggregate amount of rent payable during the initial year did not exceed

(*i*) two-thirds of the letting value of the flat on the date of commencement of the lease – in cases where the lease was entered into before 1st April 1963;

(*ii*) two-thirds of the rateable value on the date of the commencement of the lease (or if later, the date on which a rateable value was first ascribed to the flat) – in cases where the lease was granted on or after 1st April 1963 but before 1st April 1990, or on or after 1st April 1990 in pursuance of a contract made before that date;

(*iii*) £1,000 if the flat is in Greater London, or £250 if elsewhere – in any other case: s. 8.

NOTE: The 'date of commencement of a lease' means the date of commencement of the term of the lease: s. 101(5).

7. The landlord for the purposes of Chapter II. 'The landlord' for the purposes of Chapter II is referred to in s. 40 and Schedule 11 to the Act (see below) as 'the competent landlord' and may, or may not, be the tenant's immediate landlord.

The competent landlord is the owner of an interest in the flat in question which

(a) is an interest in reversion expectant (whether immediately or not) on the termination of the tenant's lease; and

(b) is either a freehold interest or a leasehold interest of sufficient duration to enable its owner to grant the tenant a lease for a term expiring 90 years after the 'term date' of the tenant's existing lease; 'the term date' of the tenant's existing lease being (in most cases) the date of expiry of the term created by the tenant's existing lease: s. 101(1).

If there is a chain of tenancies between the tenant's existing lease and the freehold, the competent landlord (and thus 'the landlord' for the purposes of Chapter II) is the owner of that interest lowest down the chain which satisfies conditions (a) and (b) above: s. 40(1).

In all the examples below it is assumed that the qualifying tenant, T, holds a long lease of his flat, at a low rent, for a term expiring on 25th December 2000.

(1) T's immediate landlord, IL, is the freeholder – IL is the competent landlord;

(2) T's immediate landlord, IL, holds a lease which expires on 25th

December 2010. IL's immediate landlord, F, is the freeholder – F is the competent landlord;

(3) T's immediate landlord, IL, holds a lease which expires on 25th December 2010. IL's immediate landlord, CL, holds a lease for a term expiring on 25th December 2100 – CL is the competent landlord.

Where, as in examples (2) and (3) above, the immediate landlord is not the competent landlord, the competent landlord conducts on behalf of all 'other landlords' (i.e. those landlords whose interests are intermediate between the interests of the tenant and the competent landlord) all proceedings arising out of any notice given by the tenant under s. 42 claiming to exercise the right to acquire a new lease of the flat in question. This is the case whether those proceedings are for resisting or giving effect to the tenant's claim: s. 40(2).

> NOTES: (1) Schedule 11 to the Act contains detailed provisions dealing with the procedure in cases where the competent landlord is not the tenant's immediate landlord. References to the relevant provisions of Schedule 11 will be made below when appropriate.
>
> (2) Schedule 2 to the Act makes special provision for cases where the competent landlord or any of the 'other landlords' falls into one of the special categories of landlord dealt with in that Schedule, e.g. mortgagees in possession, landlords under a disability, university or college landlords or ecclesiastical landlords.

8. Preliminary enquiries by the tenant. Section 41 entitles a qualifying tenant of a flat to give notices to

(*i*) his immediate landlord or anyone receiving rent on behalf of the immediate landlord;

(*ii*) the freeholder;

(*iii*) the holders of superior leasehold interests in the flat;

requiring the recipient to provide information as to

(a) whether or not the qualifying tenant's immediate landlord owns the freehold interest in the flat;

(b) the name and address of the person who owns the freehold interest in the flat;

(c) the name and address of the owners of all leasehold interests in the flat which are superior to the qualifying tenant's interest;

(d) the duration of and the extent of the premises demised by each such superior lease;

(e) whether or not the recipient has received a notice (or a copy of a notice) under s. 13 of the Act claiming to exercise the right to collective enfranchisement, which is still current (see 35:**16**);

(f) the date on which any s. 13 notice was given and the name and address of the 'nominee purchaser' (see 35:**19**).

The precise information to be provided by the recipient of the notice depends upon the identity of the recipient.

The recipient of any notice given by the qualifying tenant under s. 41 must provide the requisite information within the period of 28 days beginning with the date of the giving of the notice: s. 41(6).

> NOTE: A claim to exercise the right to collective enfranchisement under Chapter 1 of the Act prevails over an individual tenant's claim to exercise the right to acquire a new lease of his flat. Accordingly, while a qualifying tenant can give a notice under s. 42 claiming to exercise the right to acquire a new lease of his flat, that claim will be suspended if a notice claiming to exercise the right to collective enfranchisement has been given under s. 13 and the claim to exercise the right to collective enfranchisement is still current. Reference should be made to the detailed provisions of s. 54.

9. Claiming the right to acquire a new lease – 'the tenant's notice'. A claim to exercise the right to acquire a new lease is made by the giving of a notice ('the tenant's notice') under s. 42: s. 42(1).

The tenant's notice must be given to the landlord (namely, the competent landlord – see **7** above) and to any 'third party' to the tenant's lease: s. 42(2).

A 'third party' to the tenant's lease means any person who is a party to the lease apart from the tenant and his immediate landlord. In many cases therefore, the third party (if any) will be any surety for the tenant or any management company which is a party to the lease.

While s. 42(2)(a) requires the tenant's notice to be given to the competent landlord, the tenant's notice is regarded as having been given to the competent landlord if it is given to any of the other landlords instead: para 1, Schedule 11.

If the tenant's notice is given instead to one of the other landlords, the tenant must give a copy of the notice to every person known or believed by him to be either the competent landlord or one of the other landlords: para 2(2), Schedule 11.

If the tenant's notice is given to the competent landlord, the tenant must also give a copy to all other landlords of whom he is aware: para 2(1), Schedule 11.

In all cases, the tenant's notice must state if copies are being given to other persons in accordance with paragraph 2 of Schedule 11, and if so, to whom: para 2(3), Schedule 11.

> NOTES: (1) If
> (a) the tenant fails to give copies of the tenant's notice in accordance with paragraph 2 of Schedule 11 with the result that either the competent land-

lord or one of the other landlords does not receive a copy before the end of the period by which the landlord is to respond (i.e. not less than 2 months after the date of the giving of the tenant's notice: s. 42(3)(f) – see **15** below); and

(b) the competent landlord or other landlord in question has previously notified the tenant of his interest in the flat in response to a notice given by the tenant under s. 41 (see **8** above),

the tenant's notice ceases to have effect: para 4(1), Schedule 11.

(2) See also the note to **10** below.

10. Provision of further copies of the tenant's notice by landlords. The competent landlord and any other landlord who receives the tenant's notice, or a copy of it (referred to here as 'the Recipient' for convenience) must forthwith give a copy of the tenant's notice to anyone known or believed by him to be the competent landlord or one of the other landlords if

(a) the competent landlord or any other landlord is not stated to be a recipient of a copy of the tenant's notice in the copy of the tenant's notice received by the Recipient; or

(b) the Recipient knows that the competent landlord or any of the other landlords has not received a copy of the tenant's notice: para 3(1)(a), Schedule 11.

In so doing, the Recipient must

(a) supplement the statement in the tenant's notice pursuant to paragraph 2(3) of Schedule 11, as to the identities of the persons who are being given copies of the tenant's notice, by adding any further persons to whom he (the Recipient) is giving copies or who are known by him to have received a copy; and

(b) notify the tenant of the persons so added by him: para 3(3), Schedule 11.

Furthermore, if the Recipient knows who is, or believes himself to be, the competent landlord, he must forthwith give a notice to the tenant advising the tenant of the identity of the competent landlord and give a copy of that notice to all other persons known or believed by him to be one of the other landlords and to the competent landlord (if the Recipient does not believe himself to be the competent landlord): para 3(1)(b), Schedule 11.

NOTE: If

(a) the tenant fails to give copies of the notice in accordance with paragraph 2 of Schedule 11 (see **9** above) or unreasonably delays doing so; or

(b) the competent landlord or any other landlord fails to comply with the

requirements of paragraph 3 of Schedule 11, or unreasonably delays doing so, then
the tenant or the landlord guilty of the non-compliance or unreasonable delay is liable for any loss thereby suffered by the tenant, the competent landlord or any other landlord, as the case may be.

11. The tenant's notice – contents. The requirements of a valid tenant's notice are as follows:

(a) it must be in writing: s. 99(1);

(b) it must state the full name of the tenant and the address of the flat in respect of which he claims a new lease: s. 42(3)(a);

(c) it must contain sufficient particulars of the flat to identify the property to which the claim extends: s. 42(3)(b)(i);

(d) it must give sufficient particulars of the tenant's lease to identify it, including (i) the date of the lease; (ii) the term for which it was granted; and (iii) the date of the commencement of the term: s. 42(3)(b)(ii);

(e) it must give such particulars as are necessary to show that the tenant's lease is a lease at a low rent: s. 42(3)(b)(iii) (and see **6** above);

(f) it must contain particulars of the period or periods, falling within the preceding 10 years, for which the tenant has occupied the whole or part of the flat as his only or principal home: s. 42(3)(b)(iv) (and see s. 42(4) and **4** above);

(g) it must specify the premium the tenant proposes to pay for the new lease and any other amounts payable to owners of intermediate leasehold interests in accordance with Schedule 13 (see **29** et seq. below) which the tenant proposes to pay: s. 42(3)(c);

(h) it must specify the terms which the tenant proposes should be contained in the new lease: s. 42(3)(d);

(i) it must state the name of the person (if any) appointed by the tenant to act for him in connection with his claim and an address in England and Wales at which notices may be given to any such person: s. 42(3)(e);

(j) it must specify the date by which the landlord must respond to the tenant's notice by giving a counter-notice under s. 45 (which date must be not less than 2 months after the date of the giving of the tenant's notice: s. 42(5)): s. 42(3)(f);

(k) it must be signed by the tenant(s) by whom it is given: s. 99(5)(a);

(l) it must state if copies are being given to other persons in accordance with para 2 of Schedule 11, and if so, to whom: para 2(3), Schedule 11 and see **9** above.

NOTES (1) Schedule 12 applies by virtue of s. 42(9). Some of the more important provisions of Schedule 12 are briefly referred to at **12** below as regards the effects of the tenant's notice. It should be noted here however that

(a) a tenant's notice is of no effect if it is given after the tenant has given notice terminating his lease of the flat (unless that notice is superseded by the grant of a new tenancy): para 1, Part I, Schedule 12;

(b) a tenant's notice is generally of no effect if given more than 2 months after a landlord's notice terminating the lease has been given under s. 4 of the Landlord and Tenant Act 1954 or served under paragraph (1) of Schedule 10 to the Local Government and Housing Act 1989: para 2, Part I, Schedule 12;

(c) a tenant's notice is of no effect if given after an Order for possession has been made against him in any proceedings: para 3(1), Part 1, Schedule 12;

(d) a qualifying tenant cannot give a tenant's notice while any proceedings are pending against him to enforce a right of re-entry or forfeiture, except with leave of the Court: para 3(2), Part 1, Schedule 12.

(2) The tenant's notice is not invalidated by any inaccuracy in any of the particulars required by s. 42(3) or by any misdescription of any of the property to which the claim relates: para 9(1), Part II, Schedule 12.

(3) The Court can grant leave to amend the tenant's notice on such terms as the Court may think fit, if the tenant's notice specifies any property which he is not entitled to have demised to him under a new lease granted in pursuance of Chapter II, or if the tenant's notice fails to specify any property which he is entitled to have demised to him: para 9(2), Part II, Schedule 12.

12. Effects of tenant's notice. A tenant's notice continues in force until

(a) a new lease is granted in accordance with the notice; or

(b) until the date upon which it is withdrawn, or deemed to be withdrawn in accordance with Chapter II; or

(c) until such other time as the notice ceases to have effect by virtue of any provision of Chapter II: s. 42(8).

As previously mentioned, Schedule 12 applies by virtue of s. 42(9) and contains detailed and important supplementary provisions as to the effects of a tenant's notice. In particular

(a) any notice to terminate the tenant's lease given by the tenant or given by the landlord under s. 4 of the Landlord and Tenant Act 1954 or served under paragraph 4(1) of Schedule 10 to the Local Government and Housing Act 1989 is of no effect if given or served during the currency of the tenant's claim to exercise the right to acquire a new lease: para 4, Part 1, Schedule 12;

(b) during the currency of the tenant's claim and for 3 months thereafter, the lease of the flat will not terminate by effluxion of time, notice to quit given by the tenant's immediate landlord or the termination (e.g. by forfeiture) of a superior lease: para 5(1), Part 1, Schedule 12;

(c) no proceedings to enforce a right of re-entry or forfeiture may be brought without leave of the Court during the currency of the tenant's claim: para 6, Part 1, Schedule 12;

(d) if a tenant is granted relief under s. 16 of the Landlord and Tenant Act 1954 and his tenancy is cut short, any tenant's notice given by him under s. 42 is of no effect or, if already given, ceases to have effect: para 7, Part 1, Schedule 12.

> NOTE: For the purposes of certain provisions of Part 1 of Schedule 12 (e.g. suspension of the date on which the tenant's lease will come to an end by effluxion of time or notice to quit, or suspension of the immediate landlord's right to bring any proceedings for forfeiture – see (a), (b) and (c) above) a tenant's notice under s. 42 can have the effects set out in Schedule 12 even if the notice is not valid. For those purposes, a claim to exercise the right to acquire a new lease made by an invalid tenant's notice remains 'current' until the notice is set aside by the Court or withdrawn, or until the notice would cease to have effect or be deemed to have been withdrawn if it were a valid notice: para 8(1)(c)(ii), Part 1, Schedule 12.

Section 43 sets out further general provisions as to the effects of a tenant's notice. In broad terms, s. 43 provides that the benefits and obligations arising from a tenant's notice are enforceable as between the landlord and the tenant to the same extent as if those benefits and obligations had arisen from a contract for leasing freely entered into between the landlord and the tenant. Those benefits and obligations are assignable and can devolve upon the landlord's or the tenant's personal representatives. However, the tenant's rights and obligations are not capable of subsisting apart from the lease of the entire flat. Accordingly unless those rights and obligations are assigned to any assignee of the lease of the flat, the tenant's notice is deemed to have been withdrawn at the date of the assignment of the lease (as to which see **47** below).

> NOTE: The tenant's notice can (and should) be registered under the Land Charges Act 1972 or made the subject of a notice or caution under the Land Registration Act 1925: s. 97(1).

13. Landlord's right to require evidence of the tenant's right to acquire a new lease. Within 21 days of the relevant date (i.e. the date upon which the tenant's notice is given) the landlord is entitled to give notice to the tenant requiring the tenant to deduce title to the tenancy and give evidence by statutory declaration of the occupation on which he relies.

The tenant must comply with any such notice within 21 days beginning with the date the landlord's notice was given: paragraph 4 of Schedule 2 to the Leasehold Reform (Collective Enfranchisement and Lease Renewal) Regulations 1993; SI 1993 No 2407.

14. Access by landlords for valuation purposes. Following the giving of the tenant's notice the landlord and any other landlord (and any person acting on their behalf) are entitled to have access to the flat for the purpose of obtaining a valuation of their respective interests in the flat: s. 44(1).

This right is exerciseable at any reasonable time on giving not less than 3 days' notice to the tenant: s. 44(2).

15. Landlord's counter-notice. It will be recalled that the tenant's notice must specify a date by which the landlord must respond by giving a counter-notice and that such date must not be less than 2 months after the date the tenant's notice is given (ss. 42(3)(f) and (5) and see **11** above).

The landlord must give a counter-notice by the date so specified: s. 45(1).

The counter-notice must be in writing (s. 99(1)) and specify an address in England and Wales at which notices may be given to the landlord: s. 45(4).

The counter-notice must

(a) state that, for reasons specified in the counter-notice, the landlord does not admit the tenant's right to acquire a new lease: s. 45(2)(b); or
(b) state that the landlord admits the tenant's right to acquire a new lease of his flat: s. 45(2)(a); or
(c) (*i*) contain an admission or non-admission of the tenant's right to acquire a new lease in accordance with paragraphs **(a)** or **(b)** above; and
(*ii*) state that the landlord intends to make an application for an order under s. 47(1) on the grounds that he intends to redevelop any premises in which the flat is contained: s. 45(2)(c).

NOTES: (1) Where the tenant's immediate landlord is not the competent landlord, the counter-notice given by the competent landlord must specify the other landlords on whose behalf he is acting: paragraph 5, Part II, Schedule 11 (and see again s. 40(2) and **7** above).

(2) If the counter-notice admits the tenant's right to acquire a new lease the landlord cannot subsequently dispute that the tenant is a qualifying tenant or that he has occupied the flat as his only or principal home for the period(s) specified in the tenant's notice (unless there has been misrepresentation or concealment of material facts): s. 45(5).

(3) A counter-notice given by the competent landlord, any agreement entered into by the competent landlord with the tenant and any determination in proceedings between the competent landlord and the tenant is binding on the other landlords. Provided that the competent landlord acts in good faith and with reasonable care and diligence, he has no liability for any loss which might be suffered by any of the other landlords: para 6(1) and (4), Part II, Schedule 11.

(4) The other landlords must give the competent landlord all information and assistance he may reasonably require: para 8, Part II, Schedule 11.

(5) Any of the other landlords may be separately represented in any legal proceedings in which their title to any property comes into question or relating to the determination of any amount payable to them in pursuance of the tenant's exercise of the right to acquire a new lease. Furthermore, any such landlord may also require any such amount to be paid direct to him instead of to the competent landlord. In each case, an appropriate notice must be given to the tenant and to the competent landlord: para 7, Part II, Schedule 11.

(6) The competent landlord's authority to act on behalf of the other landlords does not extend to bringing any proceedings for an Order under s. 47(1) (whereby the tenant's claim to acquire a new lease can be defeated if a landlord intends to redevelop the premises in which the tenant's flat is contained).

If any of the landlords intend to apply for such an Order (and the landlord's counter-notice is thus in the form described at (c) above), the counter-notice must identify the landlord(s) who intend(s) to make that application: para 9, Part II, Schedule 11.

16. The landlord does not admit the tenant's right to acquire a new lease. If the landlord states in his s. 45 counter-notice that he does not admit the tenant's right to acquire a new lease, he must apply to the Court within 2 months of the date on which his counter-notice is given: s. 46(2).

That application is for an Order declaring that, on the relevant date, the tenant had no right to acquire a new lease: s. 46(1).

If the application is successful, the tenant's notice ceases to have effect: s. 46(3).

However, if the landlord's application is dismissed the Court will make an Order declaring the landlord's counter-notice to be of no effect and requiring the landlord to give a further counter-notice by a date to be specified in the Order: s. 46(4).

NOTE: The Court will not make an Order declaring the landlord's counter-notice to be of no effect and requiring the landlord to give a further counter-notice if the counter-notice also states that the landlord intends to apply for an Order under s. 47(1) (to defeat the tenant's claim to a new lease on the ground of intended redevelopment) and the s. 47(1) application is pending or the time for making that application has not expired: s. 46(5).

17. Proposed redevelopment by a landlord. Section 47(1) empowers the Court to make an Order declaring that the right to acquire a new lease should not be exerciseable by the tenant by reason of the landlord's intention to redevelop any premises in which the tenant's flat is contained.

The application must be made within 2 months of the date upon which the landlord's counter-notice is given (s. 47(3)) and can only be made if the landlord's counter-notice has stated that an application for an Order under s. 47(1) is to be made.

The application can be made by the competent landlord, or any other landlord, or by any two or more of the landlords acting together: para 9, Part II, Schedule 11.

On the hearing of the application, the landlord must satisfy the Court

(a) that the tenant's lease is due to terminate within 5 years of the relevant date (i.e. the date on which the tenant's notice was given); and
(b) that for the purposes of redevelopment, the landlord intends, once the lease has so terminated
  (*i*) to demolish or reconstruct, or
  (*ii*) to carry out substantial works of construction
  on the whole or a substantial part of any premises in which the flat is contained; and
(c) that he could not reasonably do so without obtaining possession of the flat: s. 47(2).

NOTE: The case law concerning s. 30(1)(f) of the Landlord and Tenant Act 1954 (relating to business tenancies) considered in Chapter 13 and the inclusion of redevelopment break clauses in renewal leases of business premises (see *National Car Parks Limited* v. *Paternoster Consortium Limited* (1989) in particular) is likely to be of assistance in ascertaining if the landlord can satisfy the Court on points **(b)** and **(c)** above.

If an Order under s. 47(1) is made by the Court, the tenant's notice ceases to have effect and no subsequent tenant's notice can be given within 12 months of the date on which the Order becomes final: s. 42(7).

If however, the application under s. 47(1) is dismissed, the Court will make an Order

(a) declaring the landlord's counter-notice to be of no effect; and
(b) requiring the landlord to give a further counter-notice by a date specified in the Order: s. 47(4).

In cases where the landlord has given a counter-notice stating that an application is to be made for an Order under s. 47(1), but no such application is made, or an application is made but subsequently withdrawn, the landlord must give a further counter-notice within 2 months of

(a) the date following the expiry of the landlord's time for applying for an Order under s. 47(1) (which, as mentioned above, is 2 months from the date of the landlord's 'original' counter-notice under s. 45); or
(b) the date of withdrawal of the s. 47(1) application,

as appropriate: s. 47(5) and (6).

18. Interaction of s. 46 with s. 47. If the landlord's counter-notice has stated

(a) that the landlord does not admit the tenant's right to acquire a new lease, and
(b) that an application for an Order under s. 47(1) is to be made,

two applications to the Court are likely to be made at or about the same time, namely
(*i*) the landlord's application under s. 46(1) for an Order declaring that the tenant has no right to acquire a new lease (see 16 above); and
(*ii*) the landlord's application for an Order under s. 47(1) declaring that the tenant's right to acquire a new lease shall not be exerciseable by reason of proposed redevelopment of premises containing the tenant's flat (see 17 above).

Logically, the landlord's application under s. 46(1) should be dealt with first, as if it is successful, there is no need for the landlord to proceed with the application under s. 47(1). Section 47(3) therefore provides that although in these circumstances the landlord's s. 47(1) application must be made (i.e. the proceedings issued and served) in good time, the application cannot be proceeded with until such time as any Order dismissing the s. 46(1) application becomes final.

Furthermore, if the landlord has given a counter-notice stating that an application for an Order under s. 47(1) is to be made, but either no such application is made, or the application is withdrawn, the requirement for the landlord to give a further counter-notice imposed by s. 47(5) does not apply: s. 47(7). The landlord's further counter-notice must instead be given by the date specified in the Court's Order under s. 46(4) in the landlord's proceedings under s. 46(1). Once again this is logical as unless and until the landlord's application under s. 46(1) is dismissed, i.e. the validity of the tenant's notice has been established, no purpose would be served by requiring the landlord to give a further counter-notice.

19. The landlord admits the tenant's right to acquire a new lease. In these circumstances, the following additional requirements apply to the landlord's counter-notice under s. 45:

(a) it must state which (if any) of the proposals contained in the tenant's notice are accepted by the landlord and which of those proposals (if any) is not accepted; and

(b) in relation to any proposal which is not accepted, it must specify the landlord's counter-proposal: s. 45(3).

20. The new lease – duration and rent. Subject to the provisions of Chapter II, upon the tenant giving a tenant's notice, pursuant to s. 42, to exercise the right to acquire a new lease, the landlord is bound to grant and the tenant is bound to accept a new lease of the flat, at a peppercorn rent, for a term expiring 90 years after the term date of the existing lease: s. 56(1).

> NOTES: (1) The 'term date' of the existing lease is (in most cases) the date of expiry of the term created by the tenant's existing lease: s. 101(1).
>
> (2) The new lease is granted in substitution for the tenant's existing lease: s. 56(1)(a).
>
> (3) The payments required to be made by the tenant on the grant of the new lease are considered at 29 et seq. below.

21. Property to be comprised in the new lease. The new lease will prima facie be a lease of the flat demised by the tenant's existing lease, including any garage, outhouse, garden, yard and appurtenances belonging to, or usually enjoyed with, the flat and let to the tenant on the relevant date: s. 62(2).

> NOTE: The property demised by the new lease will not include underlying minerals comprised in the tenant's existing lease if the landlord requires the minerals to be excepted and proper provision is made for the support of the premises demised by the existing lease as they are enjoyed on the relevant date: s. 39(7).

22. Other terms of the new lease – general. The general rule laid down by s. 57(1) is that the new lease will be a lease on the same terms as those of the existing lease, as they apply on the relevant date, with any modifications required or appropriate to take account of

(a) the omission from the new lease of property comprised in the existing lease but not comprised in the flat (e.g. underlying minerals – see s. 39(7) and 21 above);

(b) any alterations made to the property demised since the grant of the existing lease;

(c) (in an appropriate case) the combined effect of and any differences between the terms of the two or more leases which are treated as the tenant's existing lease for the purposes of Chapter II (see s. 7(6) and s. 39(3)).

> NOTE: If there is any agreement collateral to the existing lease, e.g. for use of a parking space not demised by the existing lease, for so long as the tenant is the tenant of the flat, that agreement will be continued by the new lease or an agreement collateral thereto: s. 57(3).

23. Other terms of the new lease – service charges. If the landlord will be responsible for the provision of services or for repairs, maintenance or insurance during the continuance of the new lease, the new lease may provide for payments to be made by the tenant (whether as rent or otherwise) in respect of those matters: s. 57(2)(a).

Furthermore, if the existing lease does not require the tenant to make any payment in respect of those matters, or only requires the tenant to pay a fixed amount in respect of the same, that arrangement cannot be continued beyond the term date of the existing lease. The new lease must (in the absence of agreement to the contrary) provide that, as from the term date of the existing lease, the tenant will pay a variable service charge in respect of those matters and that the tenant's liability to make the service charge payments will be enforceable by distress, re-entry, or otherwise as if it were a liability for payment of rent: s. 57(2)(b).

The general rule therefore appears to be that the status quo under the existing lease should be preserved until the term of the existing lease would have expired by effluxion of time. However s. 57(6) provides that any term of the existing lease may be excluded or modified

(a) if necessary to remedy a defect in the existing lease; or

(b) it would be unreasonable to include that term (or include it without modification) in view of changes occurring since the date of commencement of the existing lease which affect the suitability, on the relevant date, of the provisions of the existing lease.

It might therefore be argued that it would be unreasonable to include in the new lease a term of the existing lease providing for payment of a fixed amount by the tenant in respect of the provision of services until the term date of the existing lease (the situation thereafter being covered by s. 57(2)(b)), if the existing lease was granted at a time when a substantial increase in the cost of providing services, due to inflation, was not reasonably forseeable. It should be noted however that in the context of renewal of business leases, a similar argument was rejected by the House of Lords (see *O'May* v. *The City of London Real Property Company Limited* (1983) and 13:**6**).

> NOTE: If the new lease is granted after the term date of the existing lease, the tenant must (on the grant of the new lease) pay the service charges, or the balance thereof, for the period from the term date (or if later, the relevant date) which would have been payable had the new lease been granted on the term date (or if later, the relevant date): s. 57(5).

24.   Other terms of the new lease – terms of the existing lease which must be excluded.   In the absence of agreement to the contrary any term of the existing lease or any agreement collateral thereto which

(a)   provides for or relates to renewal of the lease,
(b)   confers any option to purchase or right of pre-emption in relation to the flat demised by the existing lease, or
(c)   provides for the termination of the existing lease before its term date otherwise than for any breach of its terms (e.g. a landlord's option to determine),

must be excluded from the new lease: s. 57(4).

25.   Other terms of the new lease – permitted departures from terms of existing lease and variation of 'prescribed' terms by agreement.   Reference has already been made (see **23** above) to s. 57(6) which provides that terms of the existing lease may be excluded from the new lease, or only included subject to modification, if it is necessary to do so to remedy a defect in the existing lease, or it would be unreasonable to include the term in question in the new lease (or to include that term without modification) in view of changes occurring since the date of commencement of the existing lease (i.e. the date of the commencement of the term of the existing lease: s. 101(5)).

Section 57(6) also enables the landlord and the tenant to agree that the terms required to be included in or excluded from the new lease, or any agreement collateral thereto, or otherwise having effect by virtue of s. 57(1) to (5) (see **22** to **24** above) shall in fact be excluded from, or included in the new lease, or shall not have effect (as the case may be).

26.   Other terms of the new lease – terms which must be included.   The new lease must

(a)   contain a statement that it is granted under s. 56, which complies with any requirements prescribed by rules made under s. 144 of the Land Registration Act 1925: s. 57(11) – and see SI 1993 No 3405 which prescribes a statement in the following form: 'This lease is granted under Section 56 of the Leasehold Reform, Housing and Urban Development Act 1993'; and

(b) provide, in accordance with s. 59(3), that no long lease which is a sub-lease created out of the new lease, shall confer on the subtenant any right to acquire a new lease under Chapter II as against the tenant's landlord (whether the tenant's immediate landlord, the competent landlord or any superior landlord, including any landlord superior to the competent landlord – paragraph 10(2), Part II, Schedule 11): s. 57(7)(a);

(c) reserve to the tenant's immediate landlord for the time being, the right to obtain possession of the flat for redevelopment in accordance with s. 61 (see 52 below): s. 57(7)(b).

27. Other terms of the new lease – third parties. If there is a third party to the existing lease or any agreement collateral thereto (e.g. a guarantor or a management company), that third party must (in the absence of agreement to the contrary with the landlord and tenant) be a party to the new lease or (as may be appropriate) any agreement collateral thereto, and execute the same accordingly: s. 57(9).

Accordingly, if for example, a management company is a party to the existing lease and responsible for the provision of services for the benefit of the tenant and the occupiers of other flats within the same block, the existing regime for the provision of services and for payment of service charges (if appropriate) is preserved.

The third party to the existing lease cannot however be required to assume any obligations in respect of any period after the term date of the existing lease: s. 57(9).

If, by virtue of s. 57(9), the third party is required to discharge any function down to the term date of the existing lease, and it is necessary or expedient for the tenant's proper enjoyment of the property demised by the new lease for provision to be made for the continued discharge of that function after the term date (e.g. for the continued provision of services from which the tenant benefits), provision will be made in the new lease, or an agreement collateral thereto, for the discharge of that function to be continued after the term date by the third party or some other person: s. 57(10). As mentioned above, a third party to the existing lease cannot be compelled to assume obligations in respect of any period after the term date of the existing lease. It might nonetheless be desirable, in the interests of all occupiers of the block, for the existing management structure to be preserved and thus a management company (particularly perhaps a management company of which all tenants of flats within the block are members) might well be willing to continue to provide services to the tenant (and be paid an appropriate service charge by the tenant in return) after the term date of the existing lease. In other cases however, the landlord may himself be compelled to assume responsibility for the provision of services from which the tenant benefits.

28. Effect of new lease on intermediate leasehold interests. As has been seen (see 7 above) the competent landlord may not be the tenant's immediate landlord, and there may be a number of intermediate leasehold interests in the flat (or the flat and other premises) between the tenant's existing lease of the flat and the competent landlord's interest.

In order to enable the competent landlord to grant the new lease to the tenant, there is a deemed surrender and re-grant of those intermediate leasehold interests: para 10(1), Part II, Schedule 11. The competent landlord would otherwise be unable to grant the tenant the right to occupy the flat after the term date.

The 're-granted' intermediate leasehold interests therefore take effect subject to the new lease granted to the tenant pursuant to Chapter II, and the covenants and other provisions of the new lease must be framed and take effect accordingly. In particular, in determining any service charge provisions to be included in the new lease in accordance with s. 57(2) (see 23 above) account is to be taken of obligations imposed on any of the other (i.e. immediate or intermediate) landlords by virtue of the new lease or any superior lease: para 10(2), Part II, Schedule 11.

NOTES: (1) The landlord is not bound to enter into any covenant for title beyond that implied from the grant. Furthermore, a person entering into any covenant required of him as landlord is entitled to expressly limit his personal liability for any breach of that covenant to breaches for which he is responsible: s. 57(8). The competent landlord may be required, for example, to enter into covenants with the tenant to provide services to the tenant during periods when the competent landlord will not be the tenant's immediate landlord. The 'primary' obligation to provide services in accordance with those covenants will be that of the tenant's immediate landlord from time to time. The competent landlord is therefore able to escape personal liability for any breaches of those covenants by the immediate landlord which he (the competent landlord) would otherwise have to the tenant by reason of privity of contract or otherwise.

(2) Any alienation provisions contained in any superior lease of the flat are of no effect in relation to the grant of the new lease to the tenant pursuant to Chapter II. Accordingly, if the competent landlord is himself a lease-holder he is entitled to grant the new lease to the tenant without the consent of his own landlord even if his own lease provides that he must obtain his own landlord's consent before granting any sub-lease: s. 56(5).

Payments to be made by the tenant on the grant of the new lease

29. General. The tenant's right to the grant of a new lease is conditional upon

(a) his payment of the premium payable under Schedule 13 (see **30** below): s. 56(1)(b); and

(b) his payment of any amounts payable to the holders of any intermediate leasehold interests in accordance with Schedule 13 (see **34** below): s. 56(2); and

(c) his tendering to the landlord the amount, so far as ascertained, of
(*i*) any sums payable by him or recoverable from him as rent in respect of the flat, up to the date of tender;
(*ii*) any costs for which he is liable under s. 60 (see **41** below); and
(*iii*) any other sums due and payable by him under or in respect of the existing lease: s. 57(3).

The provisions of Schedule 13 are detailed and examined here in outline only. References hereafter to paragraph numbers are to the numbered paragraphs of Schedule 13.

NOTES: (1) If the amount for which the tenant is liable in respect of any of the matters referred to in **(c)** above is not ascertained or fully ascertained the tenant must instead offer reasonable security for payment of the amount in question when it has been ascertained.

(2) The landlord must account to any other person to whom any amount referred to in **(c)** above is due, for the amount so tendered (e.g. if rent and other sums due under the existing lease are tendered by the tenant and the competent landlord is not the immediate landlord): s. 56(4).

30. The premium payable by the tenant in respect of the grant of the new lease: paragraph 2. The premium payable by the tenant is determined in accordance with Schedule 13 and is the aggregate of

(a) the diminution in value of the landlord's interest in the flat as determined in accordance with paragraph 3;

(b) the landlord's share of the marriage value as determined in accordance with paragraph 4; and

(c) any compensation payable to the landlord under paragraph 5.

31. Diminution in value of landlord's interest: paragraph 3. This is the difference between

(*i*) the value of the landlord's interest in the flat prior to the grant of the new lease; and (*ii*) the value of his interest in the flat once the new lease is granted.

In each case that value is the amount which, at 'the valuation date' (see the notes below), the interest might be expected to realise if sold on the open market by a willing seller (with the tenant not buying or seeking to buy) on the assumptions

(a) that the vendor is selling for an estate in fee simple (or such other interest as is held by the landlord) subject to the relevant lease (i.e. the existing lease or the new lease as the case may be) and any intermediate leasehold interests;

(b) that no premises containing the tenant's flat can be collectively enfranchised in accordance with Chapter 1 of the Act and that there is no right to require any new lease in accordance with Chapter II;

(c) that any increase in the value of the flat attributable to an improvement carried out by the tenant at his own expense, or any predecessor in title, is to be disregarded;

(d) that (subject to **(b)** above) the vendor is selling with and subject to the rights and burdens with and subject to which the relevant lease (i.e. the existing lease or the new lease as the case may be) has effect.

NOTES: (1) 'The valuation date' means the date when all of the terms of acquisition (apart from those relating to the premium and any other amounts payable by virtue of Schedule 13) have been determined either by agreement or by a leasehold valuation tribunal (see 42 below); para 1.

(2) Further assumptions can be made if those assumptions would be made in determining the value of the landlord's interest if sold on the open market by a willing seller: para 3(4).

(3) Any deduction on account of any defect in the landlord's title which would be allowed between a willing seller and a willing buyer on a sale of the landlord's interest on the open market must likewise be made when valuing the landlord's interest for the purposes of the Act: para 3(5).

(4) Paragraph 3(6) contains provisions which result in the disregard of any increase in the value of the landlord's interest arising from transactions occurring after 1st November 1993 (when Chapter II came into force) involving the creation or transfer of an interest superior to the interest held by the tenant, or the alteration of the terms on which any such superior interest is held.

32. The landlord's share of the marriage value: paragraph 4. The marriage value of any property is the amount by which the value of two (or more) interests in that property (e.g. the freehold and a leasehold interest), when transferred into the ownership of one person, exceeds the combined value of those interests when they are held by different persons.

Paragraph 4(2) of Schedule 13 provides that the marriage value is the difference between the aggregate of the values of

(a) the interest of the tenant under his existing lease,
(b) the landlord's interest in the flat prior to the grant of the new lease, and
(c) all intermediate leasehold interests in the tenant's flat (if any) prior to the grant of the new lease;

and the aggregate of the values of

(a) the interest to be held by the tenant under the new lease,
(b) the landlord's interest in the tenant's flat once the new lease is granted, and
(c) all intermediate leasehold interests in the tenant's flat (if any) once the new lease is granted.

The landlord's share of the marriage value is the greater of
(*i*) such proportion of the same as is determined by agreement between the landlord and the tenant or, in default of agreement, as is determined by a leasehold valuation tribunal as the proportion which would have been determined by an agreement between the parties, on the valuation date, on a sale on the open market by a willing seller, or
(*ii*) 50%.

NOTE: The value of all such interests mentioned above is the value on 'the valuation date' (see Note (1) to **31** above) and is determined, in accordance with paragraph 3 (see **32** above) in the case of the landlord's interest, and in accordance with paragraph 8 (see **35** below) in the case of intermediate leasehold interests: para 4(3).

33. Compensation for loss arising out of grant of new lease: paragraph 5. If, in consequence of the grant of the new lease, the landlord suffers

(a) any diminution in the value of his interest in any other property;
(b) any other loss or damage that is referable to his ownership of any interest in other property,

he is entitled to such amount as is reasonable to compensate him for the loss or damage so suffered: para 5(1) and (2).

It is expressly provided that the kind of loss for which the landlord is entitled to be compensated includes loss of development value in relation to the tenant's flat, i.e. any increase in the value of the landlord's interest in the flat which is attributable to the possibility of demolishing, reconstructing, or carrying out substantial works of construction affecting the flat (whether together with any other premises or otherwise): para 5(3) and (4).

34. Amounts payable to owners of intermediate leasehold interests: paragraph 6. A separate amount is payable by the tenant to the owner of each intermediate leasehold interest. That amount is the aggregate of

(a) the diminution in value of that interest as determined in accordance with paragraph 7; and
(b) any compensation payable to the owner of that interest under paragraph 9: para 6.

35. Diminution in value of intermediate leasehold interests: paragraphs 7 and 8. This is the difference between
   (*i*) the value of the intermediate leasehold interest prior to the grant of the new lease; and
   (*ii*) the value of that interest once the new lease is granted,
in each case determined at 'the valuation date' (see Note (1) to **31** above) in accordance with paragraph 8: para 7.

Unless the intermediate leasehold interest is an interest under 'a minor intermediate lease' (as to which see the notes below) its value is ascertained in a similar way to the valuation of the landlord's interest in accordance with paragraph 3 (see **31** above), with appropriate modifications.

Accordingly, the value of an intermediate leasehold interest is the amount which, at the valuation date, that interest might be expected to realise if sold on the open market by a willing seller (with the tenant not buying or seeking to buy) on the assumptions

(a) that the vendor is selling subject to the relevant lease (i.e. the existing lease or the new lease as the case may be) and to any leases intermediate between the interest being valued and the relevant lease;
(b) that no premises containing the tenant's flat can be collectively enfranchised in accordance with Chapter 1 of the Act and that there is no right to acquire any new lease in accordance with Chapter II;
(c) that any increase in the value of the flat attributable to an improvement carried out by the tenant at his own expense, or any predecessor in title, is to be disregarded;
(d) that (subject to **(b)** above) the vendor is selling with and subject to the rights and burdens with and subject to which the relevant lease (ie the existing lease or the new lease as the case may be) has effect: para 8(1).

NOTES: (1) The notes to **31** above apply, with appropriate modification, to the valuation of any intermediate leasehold interest.

(2) A 'minor intermediate lease' is a lease which

(*i*) has an expectation of possession (in broad terms meaning a reversion) of not more than one month; and

(*ii*) produces a profit rent of not more than £5 per year.

Paragraph 8(3)–(9) contains detailed provisions relating to (inter alia) the nature and valuation of minor intermediate leases.

36. Compensation payable to owners of intermediate leasehold interests: paragraph 9. The compensation to which the owners of intermediate leasehold interests are entitled is in respect of the same type of loss or damage arising out of the grant of the new lease, and ascertained in the same way, as compensation payable to the landlord (see **33** above).

37. Share of the marriage value payable to the owners of intermediate leasehold interests: paragraph 10. If the premium payable by the tenant to the landlord includes an amount in respect of the landlord's share of the marriage value (see **32** above) and there are any intermediate leasehold interests, the landlord's share of the marriage value is divided between the landlord and the owners of the intermediate leasehold interests in proportion to the amount by which the value of their respective interests in the flat will be diminished in consequence of the grant of the new lease: para 10(1) and (2). The amount of that diminution in value is the amount determined

(a) in accordance with paragraph 3 (see **31** above) in the case of the landlord's interest; and

(b) in accordance with paragraphs 7 and 8 (see **35** above) in the case of the interests of the owners of intermediate leasehold interests: para 10(3).

The full amount of the landlord's share of the marriage value is payable, as part of the premium, to the landlord. The landlord must then account to the owners of the intermediate leasehold interests for their respective shares of the marriage value: para 10(4).

Other procedural matters, mortgages and costs

38. General. The Secretary of State may prescribe regulations as to the procedure for giving effect to the tenant's notice and similar matters by virtue of s. 98(1).

Reference has already been made to The Leasehold Reform (Collective Enfranchisement and Lease Renewal) Regulations 1993, SI 1993 No 2407 (see **13** above). Reference should be made to the detailed provisions of those Regulations but certain provisions of Schedule 2 to those Regulations should be noted here:

Paragraph 2 entitles the landlord to give the tenant a notice, at any time while the tenant's notice is in force, requiring the tenant to pay a deposit. The amount of the deposit will be £250 or 10% of the amount proposed in the tenant's notice as payable on the grant of the new lease in accordance with Schedule 13, whichever is the greater.

Paragraph 3 provides for return of the deposit if the tenant's notice is withdrawn, or deemed to be withdrawn, or ceases to have effect.

Paragraph 4 deals with the landlord's right to require the tenant to provide evidence of his right to acquire a new lease and was dealt with at **13** above.

Paragraph 5 entitles the tenant to give notice to the landlord requiring the landlord to deduce title. The landlord must comply within 28 days.

Paragraph 6 requires the tenant to give the landlord a statement of any objections to, or requisitions on, the landlord's proof of title within 14 days of that proof being given. The landlord must give an answer to that statement within 14 days, whereupon the tenant must give the landlord a further statement of any objection to or comments on the answer within 7 days.

Any objection or requisition not included in the tenant's statement, or (in the case of any objection) the tenant's further statement, is deemed waived and any matter which could have been so raised, but is not, is deemed not to be or form a defect in title for the purposes of paragraphs 3(5) and 8(1) of Schedule 13 (see Note (3) to **31** above and Note (1) to **35** above).

Paragraph 7 requires the landlord to prepare a draft lease and give it to the tenant within 14 days of the date of agreement or determination of the terms of acquisition. The tenant must give the landlord a statement of his proposed amendments within 14 days failing which he is deemed to have approved the draft lease.

If the tenant gives the landlord a statement of his proposed amendments within the time prescribed, the landlord must give the tenant an answer within 14 days. If he fails to do so he is deemed to have approved the amendments to the draft lease proposed by the tenant.

The landlord must prepare the engrossment of the new lease and any counterparts required and give the counterpart(s) to the tenant for execution a reasonable time before the completion date. The tenant must give the executed counterpart(s) to the landlord, and the landlord must give the duly executed lease to the tenant, on completion or as soon as possible thereafter.

Paragraph 8 provides that following approval or deemed approval of the draft lease the landlord or the tenant can give notice to the other requiring completion on the first working day after 21 days.

Paragraph 9 provides that the tenant must, on request by the landlord, cancel any land charge, notice, or caution registered in respect of the tenant's notice, if the tenant's notice is withdrawn, deemed to have been withdrawn, or otherwise ceases to have effect.

NOTE: Section 98(1) provides that subject to or in the absence of any regulations made by the Secretary of State, the procedure for giving effect to the tenant's notice and the rights and obligations of all parties in relation to the investigation of title and other matters arising in giving effect to the tenant's notice, shall be, as nearly as may be, the same as in the case of a contract of leasing freely negotiated between the parties.

39. Effect on mortgages of landlords' interests. The new lease granted to the tenant pursuant to Chapter II is deemed to be authorised as against, and binding upon, any persons interested in any mortgage on the landlord's interest (referred to hereafter as 'the mortgagees'). This is the case even if the existing lease was granted subsequent to the creation of the mortgage and is not authorised as against the mortgagees (e.g. because any necessary consent has not been obtained from the mortgagees): s. 58(1).

However, the new lease will not be binding on the mortgagees if the existing lease was granted

(a) after 1st November 1993 (when Chapter II came into force); and
(b) after the creation of the mortgage in question,

and would not, apart from s. 58(1), be binding on the mortgagees: s. 58(2).

Section 58(7) requires the landlord to take such steps as may be necessary to secure that the new lease is not liable to be defeated by virtue of s. 58(2). Presumably this requires the landlord, for example, to apply for all necessary consents from mortgagees. Furthermore, paragraph 11 of Schedule 11 provides that where, by reason of s. 58(2), it is necessary to make any payment to discharge the tenant's flat from a mortgage affecting any landlord's interest (i.e. the interests of the competent landlord and/or the owners of any intermediate leasehold interests), and the competent landlord is not the landlord liable, or primarily liable, under the mortgage in question, the competent landlord is not required to make any such payment otherwise than out of money made available for that purpose by the landlord who is so liable. However the landlord who is so liable is obliged to provide for the discharge of the mortgage in question.

These provisions suggest that the landlord whose interest is subject to the mortgage in question (including the competent landlord if the mortgage is on his interest) may have to redeem the mortgage if the new lease would otherwise be defeated by reason of s. 58(2).

If mortgagees hold the title deeds relating to the landlord's interest, the landlord must deliver an executed counterpart of the new lease to the mortgagees within one month of execution of the new lease: s. 58(3). If the landlord fails to do so, the obligation to deliver the counterpart to the mortgagees effectively becomes one of the terms of the mortgage: s. 58(6).

40. Effect on mortgages of tenant's existing lease. The tenant's existing lease is necessarily surrendered on the grant of the new lease. If the existing lease was subject to a mortgage, the new lease is substituted as the mortgagees' security: s. 58(4).

If the mortgagees were entitled to possession of the title deeds relating to the existing lease, they are likewise entitled to possession of the title deeds relating to the new lease, and the tenant must deliver the same to the mortgagees within one month of the date on which the new lease is received from the Land Registry following its registration: s. 58(5). If the tenant fails to deliver the title deeds relating to the new lease to the mortgagees, the obligation to do so effectively becomes one of the terms of the mortgage: s. 58(6).

41. Costs of new lease. Section 60(1) imposes a liability on the tenant to pay the reasonable costs incurred by the landlord, any other landlord (see s. 40(4) and **7** above) and any third party to the tenant's lease (see **27** above) in pursuance of the tenant's notice, of and incidental to

(a) any investigation reasonably undertaken of the tenant's right to a new lease;
(b) any valuation of the tenant's flat obtained;
(c) the grant of the new lease.

However, if on any voluntary sale a stipulation for payment of any costs by the purchaser would be void, the tenant is not liable for those costs.

Any costs so payable by the tenant in respect of professional services rendered by any person (e.g. a valuer or Solicitor) will only be regarded as reasonable if and to the extent that costs in respect of those services could reasonably have been expected to be incurred by the landlord (or as the case may be) if he was to be personally liable for those costs: s. 60(2).

NOTE: Section 60(1) does not oblige the tenant to pay any other party's costs of any proceedings before a leasehold valuation tribunal: s. 60(5).

Miscellaneous Matters

42. Failure to agree the terms of acquisition – the role of leasehold valuation tribunals. If any of the terms on which the tenant is to acquire a new lease ('the terms of acquisition' – see s. 48(7)) have not been agreed within 2 months of the date the landlord's counter-notice was given, the landlord or the tenant can apply to a leasehold valuation tribunal to determine the matters in dispute: s. 48(1).

Any application to a leasehold valuation tribunal must be made within the period of 6 months beginning with the date on which the landlord's counter-notice was given: s. 48(2).

If no such application is made the tenant's notice is deemed to have been withdrawn (as to which see **47** below): s. 53(1).

NOTE: See s. 91(1) to (3) as to the constitution and jurisdiction of leasehold valuation tribunals. For procedure, see SI 1993 No 2408.

43. Failure of parties to enter into new lease. If the new lease has not been entered into by the expiry of 'the appropriate period', i.e.

(a) within the period of 2 months beginning with the date when the terms of acquisition were agreed; or
(b) within the period of 2 months beginning with the date on which any decision by a leasehold valuation tribunal determining all or any of the terms of acquisition became final; or
(c) within such other period as may have been fixed by a leasehold valuation tribunal in making its determination,

the landlord or the tenant can apply to the Court for an Order under s. 48(3): see also s. 48(6).

That application must be made within the period of 2 months immediately following the expiry of the appropriate period: s. 48(5).

If no such application is made the tenant's notice is deemed to have been withdrawn (as to which see **47** below): s. 53(1).

Under s. 48(3) the Court has power to make such Order as it thinks fit with respect to the performance or discharge of any obligations arising out of the tenant's notice. In particular, the Court's Order may provide for the tenant's notice to be deemed to have been withdrawn at the end of the appropriate period (as to which see **47** below): s. 48(4).

44. Failure of landlord to give counter-notice. If the landlord fails to give a counter-notice in response to the tenant's notice, as required by s. 45(1) (see **15** above) or any further counter-notice required by s. 46(4) or s. 47(4) or (5) (see **16** and **17** above), the tenant can apply to the Court for an Order determining, in accordance with the proposals contained in the tenant's notice, the terms of acquisition: s. 49(1)

That application must be made within the period of 6 months beginning with the date by which the landlord's counter-notice or further counter-notice should have been given: s. 49(3). If no such application is made the tenant's notice is deemed to have been withdrawn (as to which see **47** below): s. 53(2).

The Court will not make an Order under s. 49(1) unless it is satisfied as to the tenant's right to acquire a new lease and that, if applicable, Part 1 of Schedule 11 has been complied with as respects the giving of copies of the tenant's notice (see **9** and **10** above): s. 49(2).

45. Failure to enter into lease following Order under s. 49(1). If the Court has made an Order determining the terms of acquisition under s. 49(1) and the new lease has not been entered into by the expiry of the 'appropriate period', i.e.

(a) the period of 2 months beginning with the date when the s. 49(1) Order became final; or
(b) such other period as may have been fixed by the Court (see s. 49(7)),

the landlord or the tenant can apply to the Court for an Order under s. 49(4).

That application must be made within the period of 2 months beginning immediately after the end of the appropriate period: s. 49(6). If no such application is made the tenant's notice is deemed to have been withdrawn (as to which see **47** below): s. 53(3).

Under s. 49(4) the Court can make such Order as it thinks fit with regard to the performance or discharge of any obligation arising out of the tenant's notice. In particular, the Order may provide for the tenant's notice to be deemed to have been withdrawn (as to which see **47** below): s. 49(5).

46. Procedure if the landlord or the owner of any intermediate leasehold interest cannot be found. (A) If a tenant wishes to exercise the right to claim a new lease but the landlord cannot be found or identified, he can apply to the Court for a Vesting Order under s. 50(1).

That Order will provide for the surrender of the tenant's existing lease and for the grant of a new lease on such terms as may be determined by a leasehold valuation tribunal: s. 51(1).

When a Vesting Order is made, the Court will designate a person by whom the new lease is to be executed (i.e. in place of the untraceable or unidentified landlord). The new lease will be in a form, and contain provisions, approved by a leasehold valuation tribunal. The tenant is entitled to be granted the new lease pursuant to the Vesting Order on paying 'the appropriate sum' into Court: s. 51(3).

'The appropriate sum' is the aggregate of the amounts determined by a leasehold valuation tribunal in respect of

(a) the premium payable (see **30** to **33** above);

(b) any other amounts payable pursuant to Schedule 13 (ie to owners of intermediate leasehold interests – see **34** to **36** above); and

(c) any amounts or estimated amounts due to the landlord from the tenant (whether due under or in respect of the tenant's lease of his flat or an agreement collateral thereto): s. 51(5).

> NOTES: (1) A leasehold valuation tribunal has power to determine that the Vesting Order shall have effect in relation to property which is less extensive than the property specified in the tenant's application under s. 50(1): s. 51(2).
>
> (2) In making its determination of the property to be demised or as to the rights with or subject to which the property is to be demised, a leasehold valuation tribunal will assume that the landlord has no interest in property other than that to be demised and any minerals underlying the same, unless the contrary is shown: s. 51(4).
>
> (3) See ss. 51(7) and (8) as to the applicability of Sections 57 to 59 and Section 61 and Schedule 14, to a new lease granted in accordance with a Vesting Order.
>
> (4) Section 50(4) makes provision for (inter alia) cases where the landlord is traced after an application for a Vesting Order has been made but before the new lease has been granted pursuant to the Vesting Order. In particular, s. 50(4)(a) provides, in terms, that all parties are then to be treated as if a tenant's notice had been given at the date of the application for a Vesting Order.
>
> (5) The application for a Vesting Order can be withdrawn at any time before execution of the new lease but the landlord's consent or leave of the Court may be required if the 'missing' landlord is traced after the application is made: s. 50(5).

(B) In cases where the competent landlord can be traced but it is not possible to give a copy of the tenant's notice to any 'other landlord' (see s. 40(4) and **7** above – essentially, the owners of the intermediate leasehold interests), because that other landlord cannot be found or identified, the tenant can apply to the Court under s. 50(2) for an Order dispensing with the need to give a copy of the tenant's notice to the 'missing' landlord: s. 50(2).

Any tenant's notice subsequently given must contain a statement of the effect of the s. 50(2) Order: s. 50(6).

NOTES: (1) The Court will not make an Order under s. 50(1) or s. 50(2) unless it is satisfied as to the tenant's right to acquire a new lease and that the tenant is not precluded from giving a valid tenant's notice by any provision of Chapter II (e.g. because the tenant has previously served a tenant's notice and recently withdrawn the same – see s. 42(7) and **47** below): s. 50(3).

(2) Before making any Order under s. 50(1) or (2) the Court may require the tenant to take further steps, by advertisement or otherwise, to trace the 'missing' person: s. 50(4).

47. Withdrawal and deemed withdrawal of tenant's notice. (A) At any time before a new lease is entered into the tenant can withdraw the tenant's notice by giving a notice of withdrawal under s. 52(1) to the landlord, every 'other landlord' (see s. 40(4) and **7** above) and any third party to the tenant's lease: ss. 52(1) and (2).

The tenant is then liable to those persons under s. 60 (see **41** above) for costs incurred by them down to the time when the notice of withdrawal is given: s. 52(3).

(B) As we have seen, there are a variety of circumstances in which the tenant's notice will be deemed to have been withdrawn (see **12, 42, 43, 44** and **45,** above).

In these circumstances the tenant is liable to the landlord, every 'other landlord' (see s. 40(4) and **7** above) and any third party to the tenant's lease for costs incurred by them down to the time of the deemed withdrawal of the tenant's notice: s. 60(3).

NOTE: If the tenant's notice is withdrawn or deemed to be withdrawn, no subsequent tenant's notice can be given until after the expiry of the period of 12 months beginning with the date the tenant's notice is withdrawn or deemed to be withdrawn: s. 42(7).

48. Costs where tenant's notice ceases to have effect. If the tenant's notice ceases to have effect by virtue of s. 47(1) (landlord intending to redevelop – see **47** above) or s. 55(2) (compulsory acquisition procedures), the tenant is not liable for any other party's costs under s. 60: s. 60(4).

However as we have seen (see Note (1) to **9** above) a tenant's notice can also cease to have effect by virtue of paragraph 4(1) of Schedule

11. In such a case, the tenant will be liable for costs under s. 60 by virtue of s. 60(3).

49. Cancellation of Land Charges, etc. following withdrawal, etc. of tenant's notice. If a tenant's notice is withdrawn, deemed to be withdrawn or otherwise ceases to have effect, the tenant must, on the landlord's request, cancel any registration of the tenant's notice as a land charge, or any notice or caution registered in respect of the tenant's notice: para 9, Schedule 2, of The Leasehold Reform (Collective Enfranchisement and Lease Renewal) Regulations 1993.

50. Renewal of and security of tenure under new lease. A new lease granted pursuant to Chapter II is itself a long lease at a low rent and a qualifying tenant is therefore entitled to acquire a further new lease pursuant to Chapter II in reliance on the same: s. 59(1).

There is no limitation upon the number of times a new lease may be acquired but as a form of quid pro quo s. 59(2)(a) provides that none of the statutory provisions relating to security of tenure for tenants shall apply to the new lease. Having once exercised the right to acquire a new lease therefore, the tenant's right to remain in possession depends solely upon the new lease and any further new lease he (or his successors) may acquire pursuant to Chapter II.

51. Position of sub-tenants. Where a new lease has been granted pursuant to Chapter II, the security of tenure afforded to tenants by

(a) Section 1 of the Landlord and Tenant Act 1954 or Schedule 10 to the Local Government and Housing Act 1989;
(b) Part II of the Landlord and Tenant Act 1954 (business tenancies):
(c) Part VII of the Rent Act 1977;
(d) The Rent (Agriculture) Act 1976; or
(e) Part I of the Housing Act 1988 (assured tenancies),

is not available to any sub-tenant whose sub-lease derives directly or indirectly out of the new lease and whose sub-tenancy was granted after the term date of the tenant's existing lease: s. 59(2)(b) and (c).

Furthermore, a sub-tenant who holds a long lease created immediately or derivatively out of a new lease acquired by a qualifying tenant pursuant to Chapter II, does not himself have any right to acquire a new lease pursuant to Chapter II as against the tenant's landlord: s. 59(3). The sub-tenant may be able to exercise the right to acquire a new lease as against his immediate landlord however. If, for example,

(a) a qualifying tenant's existing lease is for a term expiring on 25th December 2050; and

(b) he acquires a new lease pursuant to Chapter II, for a term expiring on 25th December 2140; and

(c) the tenant subsequently grants a long sub-lease at a low rent for a term expiring on, say, 25th December 2020,

the sub-tenant would be able to acquire a new lease for a term expiring on 25th December 2110 from the tenant.

> NOTE: In view of the fact that a sub-tenant of a tenant who has acquired a new lease pursuant to Chapter II will not have the same statutory protection as regards security of tenure, etc. as a sub-tenant from a tenant who does not have the right to acquire a new lease (or who has that right but does not exercise the same), s. 59(4) requires that in cases where a new lease has been granted, any person
>
> > *(i)* who grants a sub-lease; or
> >
> > *(ii)* negotiates (either as principal or agent) with a view to the grant of a sub-lease,
>
> must inform the prospective sub-tenant that the sub-lease is to be derived out of a new lease granted pursuant to Chapter II. This provision does not apply if that person knows that the prospective sub-tenant is already aware of that fact or if that person is himself unaware of the position.

52. Landlord's right to terminate new lease for development. The landlord has two opportunities to apply to the Court to terminate the new lease during its term, and to obtain possession of the flat, if he intends to redevelop premises containing the flat.

The landlord can apply to the Court for an Order pursuant to s. 61(1)

(a) at any time during the period of 12 months ending with the term date of the existing lease (i.e. the lease of the flat held by the tenant prior to the grant of the new lease pursuant to Chapter II); and

(b) at any time during the period of 5 years ending with the term date of the new lease: s. 61(2).

The landlord's application is for an Order declaring that the landlord is entitled, as against the tenant, to obtain possession of the flat and the tenant is entitled to be paid compensation by the landlord for the loss of the flat.

No such Order will be made unless the Court is satisfied

(a) that for the purposes of redevelopment the landlord intends to demolish or reconstruct, or to carry out substantial works of construction on the whole or a substantial part of any premises in which the flat is contained; and

(b) that he could not reasonably do so without obtaining possession of the flat: s. 61(1).

Schedule 14 applies by virtue of s. 61(4) and contains detailed provisions as to the date upon which the new lease will determine, the effect on sub-tenancies and the amount of compensation payable to the tenant by the landlord (and in certain cases by the tenant to a business sub-tenant). In summary:

(1) The new lease will determine on such date as is fixed by the Court having regard to the conduct of the parties and the preparations made by the landlord to carry out the redevelopment in question.

(2) The Court will not require the tenant to give up possession prior to the term date of the existing lease (i.e. the lease held by the tenant before he acquired any new lease pursuant to Chapter II).

(3) The amount of compensation payable to the tenant is determined by a leasehold valuation tribunal, in the absence of agreement, and equates to the value of the new lease if sold on the open market by a willing seller subject to certain assumptions (including an assumption that no premises containing the flat can be collectively enfranchised under Chapter 1 of the Act and that there is no right to acquire a new lease of the flat under Chapter II).

(4) On termination of the lease all immediate and derivative subleases also terminate.

(5) A business sub-tenant cannot make or pursue a request for a new tenancy under Part II of the Landlord and Tenant Act 1954 if the landlord makes an application for an Order under s. 61(1), and the compensation payable to the tenant may have to be shared with the sub-tenant.

> NOTE: If the tenant has been granted a further new lease pursuant to Chapter II, the landlord can also apply to the Court for an Order under s. 61(1) during the 5-year period ending with the term date of any previous lease granted to the tenant under Chapter II: s. 61(3).

53. Contracting out. Generally, any agreement which purports to exclude or modify a qualifying tenant's right to acquire a new lease, or provides for the termination or surrender of his lease, or the imposition of any penalty or disability on the tenant, if he gives a tenant's notice, is void: s. 93(1).

Likewise any agreement purporting to exclude or modify any right to compensation under s. 61 is void.

Section 93(2) preserves the tenant's ability to surrender his lease and sanctions agreements made after a tenant's notice is given which exclude or restrict the tenant's right to acquire a new lease for a period not exceeding 3 years.

Contracting out is however permissible with the approval of the Court under s. 93(4) but not, it would seem, in cases where a landlord is proposing to grant a lease to a prospective tenant who has no pre-existing interest in the flat, or to an existing tenant of the flat who is not a qualifying tenant (e.g. a tenant under a Housing Act 1988 assured tenancy).

54.   Court's power to set aside or vary agreements entered into by a qualifying tenant.   In two cases, the Court has power to set aside, or vary, an agreement entered into by a tenant who has the right to acquire a new lease under Chapter II, i.e. if the tenant has entered into an agreement

(i) for the surrender of his lease, without the prior approval of the Court (presumably any such approval could be sought under s. 90(2) – see **55** below); or
(ii) for the grant of a new lease, without any of the terms of acquisition having been determined by a leasehold valuation tribunal: s. 93(3).

It seems to be arguable that s. 93(3) only empowers the Court to set aside or vary 'an agreement for the grant of a new lease' as opposed to the new lease itself or any of its terms.

Section 93(3) also empowers the Court to set aside or vary any agreement for surrender of the tenant's new lease entered into when the landlord is claiming possession under s. 61 (see **52** above) and without the prior approval of the Court.

NOTES: (1)   The Court's powers under s. 93(3) include power to give such other relief (in addition to, or instead of, setting aside or varying the agreement) as appears to be just, having regard to the situation and the conduct of the parties.

(2)   The Court will exercise its powers under s. 93(3) if it does not consider that the agreement in question adequately recompenses the tenant for his rights under Chapter II.

(3)   The Court's powers under s. 93(3) can be exercised on application by the tenant to a County Court, or by any Court in which any proceedings brought on the agreement in question are pending.

55.   The Court and enforcement of obligations under Chapter II.
Where references are made in Chapter II to 'the Court', the Court in question is the County Court: s. 90(1). The County Court also has jurisdiction to determine any question arising under or by virtue of Chapter II which is not specifically identified in Chapter II (except questions which fall to be determined by a leasehold valuation tribunal): s. 90(2).

If any person fails to comply with any requirement imposed on him by Chapter II any person interested can

(a) give notice to the person in question requiring him to make good his default; and
(b) apply to the Court for an Order requiring that person to make good his default if he fails to comply with that notice within 14 days: s. 92.

> NOTE: The Rules of Court dealing specifically with Chapter II are contained in County Court Order 49, Rule 9.

Progress test 36

1. What right is conferred upon qualifying tenants by Chapter II?   **(4)**

2. Who is 'the competent landlord' and what steps can the tenant take if the competent landlord cannot be traced?   **(7, 8 and 46)**

3. What is 'a tenant's notice' and what information must it contain? **(9 and 11)**

4. After a tenant's notice has been given, the tenant who gave that notice fails to pay rent. The landlord wishes to sue for possession. Advise the landlord.   **(12)**

5. What form may the landlord's counter-notice take?   **(15 and 19)**

6. A landlord of a block of flats plans to redevelop the block. He receives a tenant's notice from one of the tenants. Advise the landlord.   **(15 and 17)**

7. What effect does the grant of the new lease have upon intermediate leasehold interests?   **(28)**

8. What premium is payable on the grant of the new lease and what is the landlord's share of the marriage value?   **(30 and 32)**

9. What amounts are payable to owners of intermediate leasehold interests?   **(34)**

10. A tenant has given a tenant's notice. His landlord has asked him to pay a deposit. Advise the tenant.   **(38)**

11. The landlord and the tenant are unable to agree the amount of the premium. The landlord's counter-notice was given 5 months ago. Advise the tenant. **(42 and 47)**

12. In what circumstances can the landlord terminate the new lease for redevelopment? **(52)**

Appendix 1

Specimen lease

This LEASE made the. . . . day of. . . . One Thousand Nine Hundred and. . . . BETWEEN . . . .
. . . . (hereinafter called 'the Lessor' which expression where the context admits includes the persons deriving title under the Lessor) of the one part and . . . .
. . . . (hereinafter called 'the Lessee' which expression where the context admits includes the persons deriving title under the Lessee) of the other part WITNESSETH and IT IS HEREBY DECLARED as follows:

1. IN consideration of the rent hereinafter reserved and of the covenants by the Lessee hereinafter contained the Lessor HEREBY DEMISES unto the Lessee ALL THAT building known as . . . .
. . . .
EXCEPTED AND RESERVED unto the Lessor full right of passage and running of water and soil from all neighbouring lands and houses of the Lessor through all drains channels and sewers in and under the premises and the right to build on any neighbouring land of the Lessor notwithstanding that the erection of the buildings may interfere with the access of light or air to the property hereby demised TO HOLD (except and reserved as aforesaid) unto the Lessee from 1st July 1988 for a term of years expiring on 1st July 1993 (determinable nevertheless as hereinafter mentioned) YIELDING AND PAYING therefor during the said term unto the Lessor the yearly rent of TWELVE THOUSAND FIVE HUNDRED POUNDS (£12,500) clear of all deductions (except as hereinafter mentioned) by equal quarterly payments on the usual quarter days in every year the first of such payments to be made in advance on the signing hereof for the rent to 29th September 1988 ALSO YEILDING AND PAYING (by way of further rent) the amount from time to time expended by the Lessor in effecting and maintaining the insurance of the premises against loss or damage by fire and other risks usually covered by a householder's comprehensive policy in a sum not exceeding the full value thereof such further rent to be paid by the Lessee without any deduction on the quarter day for payment of rent which occurs next after the expenditure by the Lessor and for the hiring costs of the door telephone.

2. THE Lessee hereby covenants with the Lessor as follows;

(1) During the said term to pay the said yearly rents at the times and in manner aforesaid;

(2) To pay all rates taxes charges assessments and outgoings whether parliamentary parochial or otherwise of an annual or recurring nature which now are or which at any time hereafter shall be assessed or imposed upon the premises or any part thereof;

(3) At all times during the said term at the Lessee's own cost when and as often as need or occasion shall require well and substantially to repair amend renew uphold support maintain paint grain varnish paper whitewash and cleanse the interior of the premises and the fixtures and fittings and appurtenances belonging thereto save for the reinstatement caused by accidental fire or any other risk insured against by the Lessor;

(4) At the end or other sooner determination of the said term peaceably to surrender and yield up the premises the interior being so well and substantially maintained painted and cleansed as aforesaid unto the Lessor together with all fixtures which at any time during the said term shall have been affixed or shall belong to the premises (tenant's fixtures only excepted);

(5) That the Lessor or any persons authorised by the Lessor may twice in every year during the said term upon appointment previously made at all reasonable times in the daytime enter into and upon the premises to view and examine the state and condition thereof and of all defects decays or wants of reparation or amendment (which upon such view shall be found) give or leave notice in writing at or upon the premises for the Lessee to repair and amend the same;

(6) At the Lessee's own expense within three months from the giving or leaving of such notice well and sufficiently to repair and amend the same accordingly;

(7) That the Lessee will permit the Lessor and persons authorised by the Lessor at all reasonable hours in the daytime to enter into and upon the premises for the purpose of executing alterations or repairs to the adjoining premises or for carrying out upon the premises such repairs (if any) as either the Lessor or the Lessee may be liable to effect hereunder or for complying with any statutory obligation imposed on the owner or occupier of the demised premises Provided That where the Lessee is liable to effect the repairs this power shall not be exercised until the Lessee has made default for 30 days after being required in writing to do the work and in that case shall be liable on demand to make good to the Lessor the costs of effecting the repairs with interest at £15 per cent p.a. from the date of the demand;

(8) Not during the said term to use exercise or carry on or permit

or suffer to be used exercised or carried on in or upon the premises or any part thereof any noisy or offensive trade or business whatsoever but will use the premises only as and for a private dwelling-house;

(9) Not without the consent in writing of the Lessor to make any structural alteration in or addition to the premises or erect any new building thereon or carry out any operation or institute or continue any use of the premises for which planning permission is required without the consent of the Lessor such consent not to be unreasonably withheld;

(10) Not to assign charge underlet or part with the possession of the premises or any part thereof but in the event of an assignment or underletting being required by the Lessee the Lessor shall grant consent to any assignment or underletting of the whole in the case of a responsible and desirable person with proper references being put forward to the reasonable satisfaction of the Lessor;

(11) Within one month after any assignment charge or underlease of the premises or any part thereof shall have been executed or after the devolution of the said term or any derivative term to produce the disposition or evidence of the devolution to the Lessor's Solicitors for registration to whom a fee of £25 shall be paid for each registration;

(12) Not to do or permit to be done upon the demised premises or any part thereof any act or thing which may invalidate or render voidable any policies of insurance from time to time effected against loss or damage by fire and other risks of the premises or of any fixtures and chattels therein belonging to the Lessor or which may operate to increase the premiums payable in respect of any such policy;

(13) Not to do or permit to be done on the demised premises or any part thereof anything which may be or grow to be a nuisance damage inconvenience or annoyance to the Lessor or to the owners or occupiers of any adjacent premises;

(14) Not to allow any public meeting or sale by auction to be held on the premises or permit to be placed on the premises any bill signboard placard hoarding or other outward mark;

(15) Within seven days of the receipt by the Lessee of any notice order or proposal made given or issued to the Lessee by a planning authority under or by virtue of any enactment relating to town and country planning to give full particulars thereof to the Lessor and without delay to take all reasonable or necessary steps to comply with any such notice or order so far as such compliance is the responsibility of the Lessee under the other covenants of this Lease;

(16) To permit the Lessor or the Lessor's agents from time to time during the last three months before the expiration or sooner

determination of the said term to affix notices upon the premises advertising that they are to be sold, let or to be otherwise disposed of and also at all convenient times in the daytime (by agents or otherwise) to enter into with and show the premises to any person;

3. PROVIDED THAT if any part of the said rents shall be in arrear for twenty-one days (whether or not lawfully demanded) or if there shall be a breach of any of the covenants by the Lessee herein contained the Lessor may re-enter upon the premises and immediately thereupon the said term shall absolutely determine.

4. THE Lessor hereby covenants with the Lessee as follows:

(1) That the Lessee paying the rent hereby reserved and performing and observing all the covenants by the Lessee herein contained shall and may quietly hold and enjoy the premises during the said term without any lawful interruption by the Lessor or any person rightfully claiming through under or in trust for that party;

(2) That the Lessor will during the subsistence of the term hereby granted insure and keep insured against loss or damage by fire and all other risks usually covered by a householder's comprehensive policy the premises hereby demised and the building of which they form part to the full value thereof and will apply all insurance money in or towards reinstating or making good any of the said buildings which may be destroyed or damaged by fire and make up any deficiency out of his own money and during such time as the premises shall be rendered uninhabitable due to fire no rental shall be payable hereunder or if partially rendered uninhabitable a proportion of rental only shall be payable such proportion to be decided by the Landlord's Surveyor;

IN WITNESS whereof the parties hereto have hereunto set their hands and seals the day and year first before written

Signed sealed and delivered.   Signature . . . .
by . . . .

in the presence of . . . .

L. S.

Appendix 2

Examination technique

Examination questions in landlord and tenant tend to be problems based on a combination of the facts of different reported cases and involving a consideration of the relevant statutory code of protection. They aim to test the candidate's knowledge and application of principles of both the common law and statute.

A useful general approach to a landlord and tenant question is as follows. First, the matter should be considered by reference to basic common law principles (Chapters 1–9). Secondly, it must be considered whether any of the basic common law principles have been altered by statute. If so the modification must be applied to the problem.

The candidate may be assisted by the following general points on technique:

1. It need hardly be said that prior to the examination some work should be done. In particular, the candidate should familiarise himself with the contents of those books which appear on his syllabus. If it is not possible to remember the names of cases or provisions of each Act, the general principle to be derived from each case and provision must be understood and remembered.

2. Prior to the examination, the candidate should rough out some sort of timetable. This involves deciding how much time to set aside for (a) a first reading of the paper, (b) the answering of each question, (c) the re-reading of each answer, and (d) final checking.

3. Once in the examination room it should be checked how many questions have to be answered. The style of papers changes from year to year and the number of questions can be altered.

4. The entire paper should be carefully read and a decision made about which questions, if any, can be answered. The candidate should select whatever number is required. The first answer should be sketched out in skeleton form so as to set a logical framework to the answer. It should then be written out.

5. The candidate should then proceed from question to question in accordance with 4 above and trying to keep to the timetable worked out beforehand.

6. In so far as it is possible, the answer should

(a) be written legibly;
(b) show a good command of grammar;
(c) be relevant to the question;
(d) follow in a logical order.

7. In relation to each case, the most important thing to remember is the principle to be derived from the case. Then there follow the facts, the case name, the court and the date, in that order. Case names should never be invented.

8. Time should be left at the end to read through and check the answers.

9. It is normally preferable to attempt problem questions before discussion questions.

Index